ISLAM AND THE MALAY-
INDONESIAN WORLD

For Anna, Rachel and James

PETER G. RIDDELL

Islam and the Malay-Indonesian World

Transmission and Responses

UNIVERSITY OF HAWAI'I PRESS

HONOLULU

Published in the U.S.A. in 2001 by
University of Hawai'i Press
2840 Kolowalu Street
Honalulu, Hawai'i 96822

First published in Great Britain by
C. Hurst & Co. (Publishers) Ltd., London

Printed in Malaysia

Library of Congress Cataloging-in-Publication Data
Riddell, Peter G.
    Islam and the Malay-Indonesian world: transmission and
    responses / Peter G. Riddell.
        p. cm.
    Includes bibliographical references and index.
    ISBN 0-8248-2473-3 (alk. paper)
        1. Islam–Malaysia–History. 2. Islam–Indonesia–History.
    3. Sufism–Malaysia–History. 4. Sufism–Indonesia–History.
    I. Title.

BP63.M27 R54 2001
297'.09598–dc21   2001023503

PREFACE AND ACKNOWLEDGEMENTS

The primary goal of this study is to open various windows into Islamic religious thought in the Malay–Indonesian world over a period of around seven centuries, commencing with the establishment of Islam in the region during the latter part of the 13th century, and continuing on until the present day.

It is anticipated that the readership of this study will be quite varied. This work may arouse interest in Muslim Southeast Asia in both academic and general circles. Similarly, it is hoped that the present study will be applicable in western academic contexts where studies of Southeast Asia are being conducted; this work should prove to be a useful reference for undergraduate studies focusing upon Indonesia, Malaysia, Thailand and the Philippines. It may also be of interest to Islamic and Middle East studies programmes because of its use of Middle Eastern theological developments as a control in examining Southeast Asian Islam.

The book is designed to appeal to non-specialist readers as well as specialists, and it has been written with a style to maximise the accessibility to a potential non-specialist audience.

For the transliteration of Arabic words, I have largely followed the Library of Congress system detailed in Bulletin 91 of the Cataloging Service [September 1970]. I have adhered to this same system of transliteration for the names of pre-20th-century Malay writers. The names of later Malay/Indonesian writers have reflected the writers' own method of rendering their names.

This work has further developed some of my previously published research as listed in the bibliography. I am indebted to publishers who provided a platform for this earlier research, especially the following: Centers for South and Southeast Asian Studies, University of California at Berkeley (Riddell 1990a); Centre of Southeast Asian Studies, Monash University (Riddell 1993); Archipelago Press (Riddell 1996); Brill Academic Publishers (Riddell 1997a); Fitzroy Dearborn Publishers (Riddell 1999).

I am most grateful to St Mark's National Theological Centre, Charles Sturt University, for having provided me with an office and library facilities for conducting the important phase of fine-tuning and editing the manuscript in July 1999. Similar thanks are due to Alison Le Cornu for lending me her house in Watford between 21 December 1999 and 7 January 2000 (while others were celebrating the new millennium!) to undertake preparation of the final draft for distribution to readers.

I wish to express my appreciation to the following for having read and provided valuable comments on drafts of the manuscript: Miss Ailish Eves, Dr Robert Hunt, Professor Anthony Johns and Dr Tony Street.

I also wish to express my heartfelt thanks to LBC for its support in preparing this volume in various ways: a sabbatical break in early 2000 which allowed me to finalise the manuscript; computer and office facilities; and general encouragement from my colleagues to press on when my author's energy flagged.

Special thanks are due to my family for having so readily allowed me to retreat to secluded places at regular intervals to work on this manuscript.

Finally I wish to give my thanks to all those Muslim authors, past and present, whose works I enjoyed reading in preparing this volume. Their desire to know and please God comes through clearly in their writings. May He fully reveal Himself to us all.

London, June 2001   PETER G. RIDDELL

CONTENTS

Contents

TABLES

FIGURE

ABBREVIATIONS

ABIM   Angkatan Belia Islam Malaysia (Malaysian Islamic Youth Movement)

ABRI   Angkatan Bersenjata Republik Indonesia (Armed Forces of Indonesia)

IAIN   Institut Agama Islam Negeri (State Institute of Islamic Studies)

ICMI   Ikatan Cendekiawan Muslim Se-Indonesia (Indonesian Association of Muslim Intellectuals)

IIFSO   International Islamic Federation of Students Organizations

IIU   International Islamic University (Malaysia)

IPB   Institut Pertanian Bogor (Bogor Agricultural University)

IPHI   Ikatan Persaudaraan Haji Indonesia (Association of Indonesian Hajis)

JAKIM   Jabatan Kemajuan Islam Malaysia (Malaysian Department of Islamic Development)

MUI   Majelis Ulama Indonesia

NGOs   Non-Government Organisations

NU   Nahdatul Ulama (The Awakening of the Religious Scholars)

PAS   Parti Islam SeMalaysia (The Islamic Party of Malaysia)

RCTI   Rajawali Citra Televisi Indonesia (an Indonesian television channel)

SAW   'May peace and blessings of Allah be upon him'

UMNO   United Malays National Organisation

VOC   Vereenigde Oost-Indische Compagnie (Dutch East India Company)

MAPS

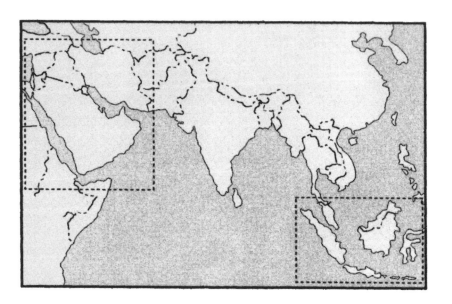

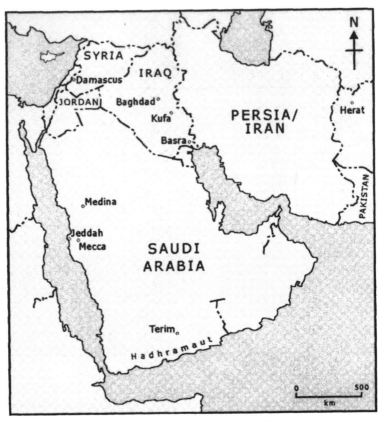

Arabia and surrounding lands.

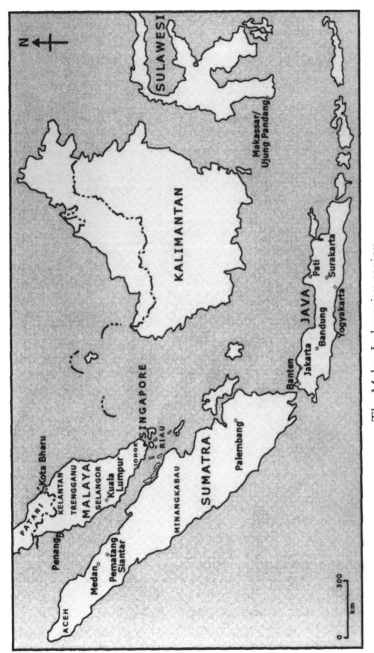

The Malay-Indonesian region.

1

INTRODUCTION

A considerable amount of research into the early Malay Islamic world has been carried out by both western and Southeast Asian scholars. The focus of the research which has dealt with the 13th to 15th centuries has been primarily historical, drawing on evidence available from inscriptions, historical sources originating in Southeast Asia, and European and Chinese court records. This focus has been of necessity more historical than religious, due to the paucity of records which attest to the theological development of Malay Muslim communities during the early centuries of Islamisation.

However, researchers are on much more solid ground in evaluating the religious development of Malay Muslim communities from the 16th century onwards. The principal Muslim port states were centres of flourishing trade activity, and Muslim scholars visited these centres from overseas, in addition to which local Muslim scholars visited India and the Arabian peninsula to undertake theological training. Much of the literary output of these early Malay Muslim scholars survives. Some has been edited, studied in detail and published, but there are still considerable numbers of Javanese Pegon, Malay and Arabic language manuscripts on various subjects from the early Islamic period in the region which are as yet unpublished.

During the colonial period, a considerable body of important research was undertaken by colonial scholars. Prominent names in this respect were the Dutchman Snouck Hurgronje and the Englishman Sir Richard Winstedt. Both were prolific writers and scholars, and their works continue to play a significant role in terms of our knowledge about Southeast Asian Islam during the colonial period. However, their research was primarily philological, sociological and historical, rather than being focused on matters of theological detail. More recent scholarship has provided significant advances in our knowledge of the religious life of the region during this period. However, as with the earlier period, much research needs to be undertaken to track the theological development of Muslim communities in the Malay region during the colonial period.

As for the development of Southeast Asian Islam since independence, this currently represents a popular focus of study for specialists in Asian Studies, both within Southeast Asia and in other countries. Many contemporary researchers have tracked the rise and fall of Islamic political parties since independence, such as the United Malays National Organisation (UMNO) and Parti Islam SeMalaysia (PAS) in Malaysia, as well as the changing face of Islamic movements such as the Nahdatul Ulama and the Muhammadiyah in Indonesia. Much work has been devoted to the study of opposition political movements whose aim was the establishment of an Islamic state, such as the Darul Islam movement in Indonesia in the 1950s. In addition, an increasing degree of attention has been devoted in recent years to the Southeast Asian response to the Islamic resurgence throughout the Muslim world in the 1970s and 1980s.

Nevertheless, further attention needs to be devoted to the religious dimension of Islam in modern Southeast Asia, especially in terms of English-language scholarship. It is striking that, while studies of resurgent Islam elsewhere in the Muslim world have often underlined scriptural and theological issues, the study of Islam in modern Southeast Asian politics and society has more often been characterised by an assumption of 'Islamicness', as it were, without sufficient regard being given to theological issues. This probably derives from decreasing interest among western scholars in theological matters, with a corresponding increase in interest in politics and society. While such approaches are crucial in developing new perspectives in the study of Southeast Asian Islam, they do reflect a western assumption that the sacred and the secular can be separated. This is an assumption which Southeast Asian Muslims do not necessarily share.

METHODOLOGY

The first key decision to be made in a study of this kind concerns the system of periodisation to be followed. A traditional western approach might focus on three periods, namely pre-colonial, colonial and post-colonial. However, to take such an approach would run the risk of being Euro-centric, of forcing Southeast Asia into a European mould, as it were. Voices from Southeast Asia can assist us in this regard:

Di Indonesia, yang termasuk dalam kawasan kebudayaan Melayu, berkembang tradisi pemikiran Islam yang dapat dibagi dalam dua periode: Periode pertama adalah tradisi intelektual yang berkembang sebelum bersentuhan dengan paham-paham pembaruan Jamal al-Din al-Afghani, Muhammad Abduh, Muhammad Iqbal dan sebagainya. Sedang periode kedua adalah pemikiran yang berkembang setelah terkena sentuhan modernisme tersebut.

In Indonesia, which belongs within the Malay cultural world, there emerged a tradition of Islamic thinking which can be divided into two periods. The first period reflects the intellectual tradition which developed prior to contact with the reformist thinking of Jamal al-Din al-Afghani, Muhammad Abduh, Muhammad Iqbal and others. The second period reflects the thinking which developed after contact with modernism.[1]

In terms of actual years, such a system of periodisation produces a considerable degree of imbalance, as it results in two periods which are approximately as follows: firstly 1300–1900, secondly 1900–2000. However, if one focuses not on years but on theological thought, such a periodic break-up lends itself well to analysis. We will accordingly affirm Hasan's comment presented above and use it as the basis for this present study, dividing it broadly into Islamic thought in the Malay–Indonesian world in the pre-modern and modern periods.

Part I of our study, consisting of chapters 2–7, will be contextual in focus. These chapters will address a range of theological issues relevant to the wider Islamic world beyond the specific Southeast Asian region. This will serve as a control which will anchor our primary Malay–Indonesian study within its worldwide Islamic context and enable us to identify the nature of

---

[1] Hasan 1987:12.

transmission of Islamic religious thought in various directions, both west to east and east to west.

Part II points us to our main goal with an examination of Malay–Indonesian Islamic thought in the pre-20th-century period.

In terms of Malay Islamic theology during the 13th to 15th centuries, the absence of Malay language manuscripts surviving from this period prevents us from drawing on local sources directly. However, Malay sources from later periods provide indications as to the identity of Arabic language theological works referred to in these earlier centuries by Malay Islamic scholars. Chapter 9 of this study therefore includes an examination of Arabic works which served to shape the theological orientations of early Malay theologians; these early works were often commentaries upon the Qur'an, and their selection and use by Malay scholars provides us with some important clues as to the focuses of interest of Malay Muslims in the 13th to 15th centuries.

With regard to the 16th and 17th centuries, we are able to benefit from the existence of local sources which have survived to this day. In this context, chapter 8 will examine the lives and selected writings of a number of Islamic theologians who played crucial roles in defining the Islamic profile of the Malay world in the early period of Islam in the region.

Chapter 10 examines a number of writers who lived during the 18th and 19th centuries. This chapter also includes reference to the role of both Malays based in Arabia and Arab immigrants to the Malay world as vehicles in the introduction of new ideas and issues to the Southeast Asian region.

Part III of this study concentrates upon Islamic religious thought in Southeast Asia in the 20th century. Essential source material for this stage of research is provided by examining selected writings of both famous and less well-known Islamic thinkers, as well as Islamic programming in the mass media, in both print and electronic forms.

THEMES AND WRITERS SELECTED

Given the vast time period being examined, it is not possible to focus upon all theological writings produced by Malay–Indonesian scholars in a study of this scope. We have therefore drawn up a selection of writings, produced by both famous and less well-known theologians, which provide comment upon a number of key themes. We have sought to identify themes which can be linked with the contextual studies presented in the chapters of Part I.

Table 1.1 shows the themes selected, and lists the principal writers addressing them.

Table 1.1. KEY THEMES ADDRESSED BY THE PRINCIPAL AUTHORS

Themes	Pre-modern authors/writings	C20 authors/writings
Variant readings of the Qur'an	Al-Baghawi; Cambridge Commentary on Q18; 'Abd al-Ra'uf	K. Shalihah; *Al Quraan Dan Terjemahnya*
Hadith as exegesis	Al-Baghawi; Cambridge Commentary on Q18	Shaleh, Dahlan and Dahlan
Angels/The Spiritual Realm		Hamka
Prophethood	Al-Baghawi; Cambridge Commentary on Q18; 'Abd al-Ra'uf	Nik Abdul Aziz Nik Mat; Hamka
Messiahship/Jesus	Al-Raniri	Hamka; Hasbullah Bakry
Eschatology	Cambridge Commentary on Q18; 'Abd al-Ra'uf; Nawawi al-Banteni	Hamka
Sin, divine punishment and forgiveness		Hamka
Doctrines and debates	Al-Raniri; 'Abd al-Ra'uf	Hamka; H. A. Mustofa; Nurcholish Madjid; Hadikusuma; Harun Nasution
People of the Book/Pluralism	Al-Raniri; 'Abd al-Ra'uf	Hamka; Ash-Shiddieqy; Anwar Ibrahim
Pantheism/Monism debate	Hamzah Fansuri; Shams al-Din al-Sumatrani; al-Raniri; 'Abd al-Ra'uf; Tuhfa; Yasadipura I; Yasadipura II; Ranggawarsita	
Saints and Sufis	Al-Raniri	Muhammad Zuhri

In discussing samples of the writing of these scholars, an attempt has been made to select works which have not been a major focus of English-language scholarship or into which much more research needs to be carried out. Thus works discussed include the following:

- Cambridge MS Or. Ii.6.45
- Hamzah Fansuri, Poem XXXI
- Shams al-Din al-Sumatrani, commentary on Poem XXXI by Hamzah Fansuri
  'Abd al-Ra'uf al-Singkili, *Lubb al-kashf*
- Yasadipura II, *Serat Sasanasunu*
- Ranggawarsita, *Wirid Hidayat Jati*
- Leiden Cod. Or. 2222
- Muhammad al-Nawawi al-Jawi, *Marah Labid*
- Hamka, *Pelajaran Agama Islam*; *Tafsir al Azhar*
- Muhammad Zuhri, 'Nobility of Character'
- Nik Abdul Aziz Nik Mat, *Tazkirah*
- Abdul Hadi Awang, *Tafsir al-Qur'an*
- Nurcholish Madjid, *Dar al-Islam dan Dar al-Harb*
- Anwar Ibrahim, 'Islam and Pluralism' (interview); speech to the Third International Convention of the Islamic Medical Association of North America
- Hasbullah Bakry, *Nabi Isa dalam al-Qur'an dan Nabi Muhammad dalam Bijbel*
- Hashbi Ash-Shiddieqy, *Tafsir al-Nur*
- Shaleh, Dahlan and Dahlan, *Asbabun Nuzul*
- *Al Quraan dan Terjemahnya*
- Shalihah, *Perkembangan Seni Baca AlQur'an dan Qiraat Tujuh di Indonesia*

In addition to the above writers and works, this study has drawn upon newspaper columns addressing theological themes, television programmes, and other relevant comment in a range of periodicals.

TERMINOLOGY

In choosing a title for this current study, the terms 'Malay' and 'Indonesian' have been intentionally co-located in the expression 'Malay–Indonesian'. The term 'Malay' has been used in two ways. First, it acts as a generic term of reference for the various communities throughout the Malay peninsula and archipelago commencing with the early Muslim sultanates of the 13th century and continuing on until the rise of nationalist movements from the turn of the 20th century onwards. Second, it maintains its relevance as a term of reference for developments pertaining among the Malays in modern Malaysia, Southern Thailand and the Southern Philippines. The term 'Indonesian' was popularised at the Indonesian Youth Congress of 1928 which identified the important national goals of the newly emerging successor to the Dutch colony throughout the archipelago. Thus, 'Indonesian' has been used as a term to refer to any part of the Indonesian archipelago during the 20th century. Hence the term 'Malay–Indonesian' is a convenient reference point for the full time period under examination.

On another issue of terminology, one is faced by an important decision in using terms such as 'orthodoxy' and 'heterodoxy'. Recent approaches to scholarship have tended to blur the lines between them, especially in the context of post-modernist thinking which tends to retreat from assigning labels of right, wrong; good, bad; mainstream or fringe.

Many writers, both non-Muslim and Muslim, often evince concern at what seems to many to be post-modernist anarchy. Bruce Kaye writes:

The great danger in postmodernism is that sovereignty will be reconstructed in terms of its caricature tyranny, while on the other hand in the secular mind difference will be so construed that religion has no place at all.[2]

In elaborating on his notion of 'perennial truth', Seyyed Hossein Nasr writes:

Tradition implies truths of a supraindividual character rooted in the nature of reality ... Tradition, like religion, is at once truth and presence ... It comes from the Source from which everything originates and to which everything returns ... Tradition is inextricably related to revelation and religion, to the sacred, to the notion of orthodoxy, to authority, to the continuity and regularity of transmission of the truth ... the meaning of tradition has become related more than anything else to that

[2] Kaye 1997:5.

perennial wisdom which lies at the heart of every religion.[3]

Abu Ameenah Bilal Philips states in forthright terms what he sees as orthodoxy and authenticity as follows:

When the term 'Islamic' is used [in his study], it refers to orthodox Islaam, that which is in accordance with the Qur'aan and the Sunna (authentic traditions of Prophet Muhammad [SAW]) as understood by the early generations of righteous, Muslim scholars.[4]

So, rather than acceding to post-modernist 'ideological correctness', I have deliberately used terms such as orthodoxy, heterodoxy, and associated terms, where I considered it necessary in order to understand the dynamics of the issue being examined. However, these terms are in no way meant to signify my own ideological biases; rather they are designed to help the reader identify where particular theologies and religious inclinations and practices fit in terms of mainstream Islamic theological thinking in the various periods under examination. Furthermore, the use of such terms needs to be seen within the boundaries of the Islamic faith tradition; for example, 'heterodox' is nowhere used in this study *vis-à-vis* other faith traditions.

THE MUSLIM SOUTHEAST ASIAN CONTEXT

Processes involved in the transmission of Islam to the Malay–Indonesian world during the past seven centuries have produced a theology which is in certain ways distinctive within the diversity of realisations of Islam throughout the world.

Traditionally scholars have tended to see Malay–Indonesian Islam as essentially derivative, inasmuch as Islamic thought in the region has characteristically responded to pulses emanating from other parts of the Muslim world, principally the Middle East and South Asia. At one level there is some truth in this claim. Individual scholars from Southeast Asia who stamped their identity on the theological developments of their era, such as al-Nawawi, needed to uproot themselves from Southeast Asia and settle in the Middle East in order to make their mark beyond the region of their birth. Moreover, Malay scholars who have established

---

[3] Nasr 1981b: 68.
[4] Philips 1997:1, note 2.

themselves as religious leaders within their own communities have often done so after spending lengthy periods studying in the Arab world. Examples from the pre-colonial era were Hamzah Fansuri and 'Abd al-Ra'uf al-Singkili, and Tok Kenali from more recent times. Their credibility as Islamic authorities was greatly enhanced in the eyes of their Southeast Asian disciples by having spent time studying with various masters in the Middle East.

Several explanations can be offered for the westward-facing orientation of Malay–Indonesian Muslims throughout history. Having acted as the original location of Islam, it is natural that the Middle East should continue to be seen as the 'centre' of the Islamic world. Moreover, the presence of the most holy sites of the faith in the Arabian peninsula means that the Muslim faithful turn to face Mecca in prayer on a daily basis. Furthermore, the absence of long-established centres of Islamic learning in Southeast Asia, playing the type of world-wide role enjoyed by al-Azhar University in Cairo, has ensured that Malay–Indonesian students have continued to 'head westward' for advanced study in the Islamic sciences down the centuries.[5]

Thus terms such as 'centre', 'heartland', and 'periphery' will be used at various points of this study.[6] Indeed, such terms are appropriate in that they imply horizontal difference rather than vertical superiority or inferiority. Our study will demonstrate that many Malay–Indonesian Muslim scholars can stake powerful claims to membership of the Islamic scholarly elite down through the ages. Malay–Indonesian Islam represents an essential element in the world mosaic of Islam.

This study will devote considerable attention to the process of transmission of Islamic thinking, from outside the Southeast Asian region to within. The study will also highlight the adaptations to the local religious environment, as the Islamic theology which was transmitted through the centuries from the Middle East and South Asia underwent varying degrees of change in Southeast Asia. Sometimes the changes produced local adaptations which came to be seen as heterodox. When this occurred, an inevitable process of renewal and reform was ultimately to follow.

---

5 Bluhm-Warn 1997:298.

6 Many other scholars of Islam likewise speak of the Muslim world in terms of its heartland and its periphery. See, for instance, Dobbin 1997:277.

These twin themes of *adaptation* and *reform* recur regularly throughout our study.[7]

Thus, given the multiple geographical and theological focuses outlined above, it would be of benefit to ground our study in basic Islamic theological principles as they evolved outside Southeast Asia before embarking on a journey through the development of Islamic religious thought in the Malay–Indonesian world during a seven-hundred-year period. A procedure of initially examining Islamic thought emanating from the Middle East before analysing the situation in Southeast Asia is consistent with earlier studies of Islamic thought in Southeast Asia[8] as well as contemporary pronouncements on theological issues made in popular sermons by Southeast Asian Muslim scholars.[9]

---

[7] An examination of occurrence of the term 'reformism' in this volume (cf. index) points to the cyclical nature of Islamic developments throughout history.

[8] Cf. Zoetmulder 1995.

[9] Refer chapter 13 of this present study.

PART I

SCRIPTURAL AND INTELLECTUAL FOUNDATIONS

2

ISLAMIC SCRIPTURE AND
TEXTUAL MATERIALS

The period of Muhammad's life from around 570 to 632, is considered by Muslims the gestation period of Islam. It is believed that during his life the system of Islam was conceived, the Qur'anic records took shape, and the ingredients were prepared for the emergence of the new faith. Over the next 250–300 years, successive layers of scripture were canonised and built upon to form the religion of Islam as we know it today.

The revelations previous to Islam, principally the Torah, Psalms and Gospel, came to be considered by Muslims to have been supplanted by the last revelation, namely the Qur'an. Once the Qur'anic text was compiled, successive layers of textual materials were drawn up to elucidate the text of the Qur'an: the Hadith; Islamic legal texts; commentaries on the Qur'an; and collections of prophetic stories which were crucial in transmitting the message of the new faith at the popular level throughout the world. Figure 2.1 demonstrates the successive layers of Islamic scripture and scholarly wisdom which, step by step, helped to crystallise the identity of Islam.

THE QUR'ANIC TEXT AND ITS VARIANT READINGS

The section which follows devotes attention to the Qur'anic text and its variant readings (qira'at). There is considerable evidence from the earliest period of Islam in the Malay–Indonesian world that Malay Muslim scholars were interested in the variant readings. For example, the Cambridge Malay Commentary on Chapter 18 of the Qur'an, one of the oldest surviving Islamic texts from the Malay world, includes information on the variant readings for the benefit of its audience. This interest was also reflected in the

13

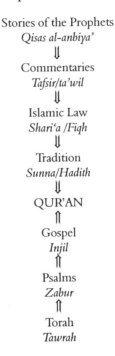

Figure 2.1.   SUCCESSIVE LAYERS OF SCRIPTURE AND
TEXTUAL MATERIALS

much more copious presentations of variant readings included in
Tarjuman al-Mustafid, the earliest Malay commentary on the
whole Qur'an, which is also examined later.

Furthermore, the interest of Indonesian and Malay Muslims in
this topic has evidently continued up to the present day, though the
field has increasingly come to be seen as the domain of specialists in
the Islamic sciences. Several studies of the variant readings have been
made in Indonesian and Malaysian, and either embedded within
publications on broader issues or published in their own right.

The canonisation process followed by Muslims which has
produced the Qur'anic text which we know today is an issue
attracting considerable scholarly attention and some debate.[1] Our

---

[1] The revisionist school of scholarship, of which John Wansbrough was one of the
pioneers, has been reassessing the source history of Islam and posing important
challenges about a range of subjects, including the dating of the Qur'anic text, both

purpose in this study is not to engage with this debate, and thus we will not address questions of historicity regarding the canonisation of the Qur'anic text. Our interest rather falls upon perceptions and beliefs held by Malay exegetes and Muslim scholars concerning this issue, which informed their own engagement with the Qur'anic text as they knew it. In the following paragraphs we will thus put ourselves in the shoes of early Malay scholars in examining the issue of scriptural canonisation.

Its compilation

The Islamic Hadith, or prophetic Traditions, offer quite detailed accounts of the early collecting of Qur'anic records. According to the Traditions, the first official collection of the Qur'an took place under the first Caliph, Abu Bakr (632–4), and was prompted by a fear that parts of the revelations would be lost forever, as the Companions who had learned the Qur'an directly from the prophet were being killed in increasing numbers in the early battles between the Muslims and their adversaries.[2]

However, if this first collection did occur, it did not lead to absolute uniformity in recording and use of the Qur'anic text across the Muslim world. By the middle of the 7th century several early collections of the revelations had been made by various Companions, each had gained popularity in a different district, and there were some variations among them in terms of the language and content of particular segments of the revelations. The number of these early codices is impossible to determine,[3] but the more prominent ones could be listed as follows:

- The codex of 'Abd Allah b. Mas'ud (d. *c.* 653) who had been a personal servant of the prophet. His codex was followed by the people of Kufa.[4]
- That of Ubayy b. Ka'b (d. 649 or 654) who served as the secretary to Muhammad in Medina after the *Hijrah*. His codex was

---

oral and written. This group does not accept that the Qur'anic record took shape entirely during the life of Muhammad, but rather that it represents composite materials which emerged over several generations.

[2] Denffer 1994:44.

[3] Blachère 1977:35.

[4] Welch 1986:407; Denffer 1994:52–3.

followed by Syrian Muslims.[5]

- The codex of 'Ali b. Abi Talib (d. 660) who became the fourth Caliph and whose assassination consolidated the emergence of the *Shi'a* sect.[6]
- That of Abu Musa 'Abd Allah b. Qays al-Ash'ari (d. 662) who was appointed by Umar as Governor of Basra. During his tenure of this position, his codex became the accepted standard among the population of Basra.[7]

The 'Uthmanic recension and post-'Uthmanic textual variation

This local variation in the text of the Qur'an was to lead to dissension, and to an early push for reform and standardisation – a theme which was to recur at intervals thrughout Islamic history. According to the Hadith, disagreement amongst Muslim troops from various parts of the early Empire as to the correct form of certain revelations led the Caliph 'Uthman (d. 655) to have an official collection made during his reign.[8] This became known as the 'Uthmanic recension. Upon completion of this authoritative recension, copies were sent to the various centres of Islam, namely Mecca, Basra, Kufa and Damascus, with strict instructions that previously-existing codices were to be destroyed.

The different copies of the 'Uthmanic text which were sent to the various metropolitan centres were not completely uniform and exhibited certain textual inconsistencies.[9] These could have been due in part to scribal error, but were more particularly the result of the inadequacies of the Arabic script used at the time. Due to these orthographic inadequacies, oral traditions continued to circulate and diversify after the 'Uthmanic recension was made.[10] New readings developed which combined the 'Uthmanic and Companion oral and textual traditions, with the Ibn Mas'ud and Ubayy codices particularly playing an active part in the emergence of new readings.[11]

---

5 Jeffery 1937:114.
6 Jeffery 1937:182.
7 Jeffery 1937:209.
8 For a full account of the method of compiling this collection, refer Blachère 1977:52ff and Welch 1986:405.
9 Gatje 1996:28.
10 Denffer 1994:58.

It is difficult to identify the exact date of the improvements to the Arabic script using vowels and diacritical points. Orthographic reforms were carried out under the fifth Umayyad Caliph, 'Abd al-Malik b. Marwan (ruled 685–705) and continued through several generations, only finishing towards the end of the 9th century.[12] This, of course, had allowed sufficient time for large numbers of readers (*qari* – *qurra'*) to emerge. They had become professionals in their activities and Blachère records that 'by the beginning of the 3rd/9th century their reputation had become extremely controversial'.[13] Such was their degree of organisation that the *qurra'* of Baghdad had formed a 'union', led by an elected head, the *shaykh al-qurra'*.

The fixing of canonical readings

Reform of the Arabic script had of course tended to highlight textual variations. The Qur'anic text was once again at the point where reform and standardisation were considered necessary. The figure credited with reform in this instance is Abu Bakr b. Mujahid (d. 936), the *shaykh al-qurra'* at Baghdad in the early 10th century. Ibn Mujahid made reference to several Hadith accounts which recorded Muhammad as saying that the Qur'an had been revealed to him in seven *ahruf* (now generally interpreted by Muslims as 'readings'). With reference to Hadith accounts, Ibn Mujahid wrote a work entitled *al-Qira'at al-sab'a* ('The Seven Readings')[14] which was soon adopted by the authorities as definitive regarding acceptable readings of the Qur'an.

Ibn Mujahid's choice of readers to form a canonical group of seven appears to have been based on two prime considerations:

- The ability to identify clear chains of transmission for each of the readers going back to the prophet.
- Fair representation from each of the great metropolitan centres of Qur'anic studies, i.e. Kufa, Basra, Medina, Damascus and Mecca.

Due to Ibn Mujahid's efforts, the authorities once again proscribed the pre-Uthmanic Companion codices of Ibn Mas'ud,

---

[11] Welch 1986:408.

[12] Blachère 1977:90.

[13] Blachère 1977:106.

[14] For a modern publication of this work, cf. Dif 1988.

Ubayy b. Ka'b and 'Ali b. Abi Talib which continued to circulate.[15] The seven readers whose systems were accepted as canonical as a result of Ibn Mujahid's writings were as follows:[16]

1. Nafi' b. Abd al-Rahman b. Abi Nu'aym al-Madani, whose system was popular in Medina.
2. 'Abd Allah b. Kathir (d. 737), who was followed by the population of Mecca.
3. 'Abd Allah b. Amir al-Yahsubi (d. 736), whose system was followed in Damascus.
4. Abu 'Amr b. al-Ala', who attained popularity in Basra.
5. 'Asim b. Bahdalah (d.724), whose system was followed in Kufa.
6. Hamzah b. Habib al-Zayyat (d. 772), whose system was also popular in Kufa.
7. 'Ali b. Hamzah al-Kisa'i (d. 804), another reader whose system was followed in the great centre of Kufa.

Some Muslim authorities in certain locations continued to advocate for alternative readings beyond the group of seven identified by Ibn Mujahid. This led to alternative systems of ten and fourteen readers,[17] though the core group of seven came to be seen as more authoritative.[18] The ten readings include the seven core plus those of:

* Abu Ja'far (d. 747) of Medina
* Ya'qub al-Hadhrami (d. 820) of Basra
* Khalaf (d. 843) of Kufa

After the identification of canonical readings by Ibn Mujahid, the popularity of some grew at the expense of others. With time, the reading of Abu 'Amr became widely accepted not only in Iraq but also in Egypt, Syria, the Hijaz, Yemen and Basra. That of Nafi' grew in a similar manner in Medina, spread into Egypt and eventually gained acceptance in Kairouan in Tunisia, as well as in Spain and the Maghreb in the Middle Ages. However, it was itself later displaced in popularity in Egypt by the system of Asim, transmitted by Hafs, which was adopted in Cairo in 1923 under the auspices of

---

15 Robson 1971:880; Denffer 1994:117.
16 *Al Quraan Dan Terjemahnya*, 130–1; Shalihah 1983:67.
17 Welch 1986:409; *Al Quraan Dan Terjemahnya*, 130–1. For a detailed discussion of the ten and fourteen readers, cf. Blachère 1977:121ff.
18 Peters 1990: vol. 2, 57, citing Ibn Khaldun.

King Fu'ad as the basis of the Egyptian standard edition of the Qur'an.[19] The result is that at the present day, only two systems of reading the Qur'an are in print among *Sunni* Muslims. The Kufan system of 'Asim, via Hafs, has become the standard throughout all the *Sunni* communities, except for those in west and north-west Africa, where the Medinan system of Nafi', via his transmitter Warsh, continues to be printed.[20]

Thus the interest of Muslim scholars both within and beyond the Middle East was not devoted in equal proportion to each of canonical readers. In Southeast Asia, some clearly had greater appeal than others, and this issue will be developed further in later discussion.

---

[19] Blachère 1977:131; Denffer 1994:117.

[20] Brockett 1988:31. Brockett also notes that 'Outside West and North-West Africa, the Medinan reading system has been maintained by the Zaydiya of the Yemen'.

3

DOCTRINES AND DEBATES

THE PLACE OF REVELATION

Having briefly explored the issue of the heart of Islamic revelation, the Qur'an, plus its variant readings which were to attract interest from early Malay Islamic scholars, we will now turn our attention to specific areas of doctrinal rivalry and conflict which related to the use of Islamic scripture. Again primary emphasis will be given to those issues which were later to cause conflict in the Malay world.

REASON VERSUS REVELATION

The rapid expansion of the Muslim Empire in the 7th century resulted in the Arab conquerors gaining control over many different nationalities, religious groups and social systems. From the earliest period of Islam, the Arabs gained access to wide-ranging fields of learning from the conquered peoples, and these were subsequently disseminated throughout the broader Islamic community. From the 8th to the 10th centuries, there was an intensive process of translating Hellenistic works into Arabic, which had the direct support of some of the 'Abbassid caliphs. Such efforts served to satisfy the great intellectual curiosity in the Islamic world, and met with the support of many leading figures such as Abu Yusuf Ya'qub b. Ishaq al-Kindi (d. 866) who wrote:

We should not be ashamed to acknowledge truth from whatever source it comes to us, even if it is brought to us by former generations and foreign peoples.

The influences from foreign sources upon Islam in these early centuries were many and varied, but none is more significant than the influence of Hellenistic thought. This made itself felt in many spheres of human knowledge, but it is the field of Greek philosophy and the influence it exerted upon Islamic theology which is particularly relevant for the purposes of this present study.

Greek philosophy was to play an important role in the emerging Islamic theology, but was also to provide a basis for ongoing conflict between various schools of thought within Islam. Greek philosophy, which proposed that human reason provided mankind with a means of learning certain eternal truths, was adopted by some Muslim scholars from the early period of Islam as a basis for formulating Islamic philosophy. This school of thought, while recognising the overall sovereignty of God in the world and the universe, nevertheless acknowledged that through reason mankind could gain important insights into a number of basic theological notions: creation, the world, and indeed, the nature of God. The Mu'tazila were leading exponents of such an approach to theology, as is succinctly described by Rippin and Knappert:

The Mu'tazilite position is that revelation is to be understood in the light of reason. God's actions which can be observed – that is, in the way in which the world operates – can be seen as rational; for God to be consistent, all His actions must be rational. Thus reason/rationality must interpret revelation.[1]

In opposition to this group were the more literalist conservatives, the *ahl al-hadith*, termed the Hadith-minded by Lapidus,[2] who saw the rationalists as drifting away from divine command. This group insisted that divinely sourced Islamic scripture, in the shape of the Qur'an and the Hadith, provided the answers for mankind's questions and represented the only legitimate source of law and morals. They prioritised the role of the Hadith as a source of guidance for the detailed minutiae of human actions. They demoted the importance of personal discretion, or individual personal opinion based on rational thinking (*ra'y*), as a guide in human belief and behaviour.

---

[1] Rippin and Knappert 1986:19.
[2] Lapidus 1988:103.

The issue was partly resolved by the great Muslim thinker al-Ash'ari (d. 935) who played a crucial role in 10th-century reform. He rejected rational metaphysics as a key to the nature of God and the universe, but accepted that reason could spell out certain meanings of revelation and could defend religious truth. Though criticised by the literalist conservative Ibn Hanbal on the latter count,[3] al-Ash'ari's view won wide support, and in a sense, al-Ash'ari achieved a satisfactory compromise between the conflicting theological viewpoints. He affirmed the overwhelming centrality of the divine revelation, the ultimate yardstick against which reform could be measured, but allocated a significant place to reason.

The priority of revelation is encapsulated by many orthodox creeds, such as that of al-Iji (d. 1355), who has the following to say:

There is no judge over [God] ... There is no judge except Him. Reason has no [power of] judging what things are good and what bad, and whether an action is an occasion for reward or for punishment. The good is what revelation declares good; the bad is what revelation declares bad.[4]

The scripture-minded literalists clashed with the more rationalist-minded theologians in the area of Qur'anic exegesis. Hadith-based exegesis was to assert itself during the formative years following the death of Muhammad as the only acceptable mechanism for commenting on the Qur'an. Though the predominance of this approach was to be challenged at various points of Islamic history, revelation-based exegesis was to reassert itself at regular intervals.

For example, such an approach was affirmed by the 14th-century scholar Ibn Taymiyya, who Watt describes as the 'most important representative' of the medieval Hanbalite school.[5] He continues to this day to exert a significant influence on contemporary developments in Islamic politics and theology.[6]

---

3 'Abduh 1966:36–7.

4 Al-Iji, 'Creed', cited in Watt 1994:87.

5 Watt 1994:11.

6 Ayubi 1991:65–6. For an excellent analysis of Ibn Taymiyya's influence upon radical Islamic groups in Egypt in the 1970s and 1980s, refer Sivan 1983.

In his multi-volume commentary,[7] he developed an approach to Qur'anic commentary writing which clearly gives priority to revelation over reason, as follows:

1. Preference should be given to explaining the content of a Qur'anic verse through reference to another Qur'anic verse.
2. If no relevant Qur'anic verses are available, then the commentator should refer to the Hadith reports.
3. If neither relevant Qur'anic verses nor Hadith reports are available to elucidate the Qur'anic verse in question, then the commentator should refer to writings by the Companions of the Prophet.
4. If none of the above-mentioned sources are available, then the commentator should refer to the writings of the generation which succeeded the Companions of the Prophet, known as the *Tabi'un* (the Followers). However, in this instance Ibn Taymiyya closely scrutinised the information at this level and sought a consensus among members of the Followers on a particular point before reporting it.[8]

Ibn Taymiyya's methodology contrasted starkly with the approach of many other exegetes who wrote their commentaries using a technique of deductive reasoning. Earlier Mu'tazilite writers had attached far more importance to the individual commentator's perceptions, individual intuitions and deductive reasoning. For example, al-Zamakhshari (d. 1144) considered that intensive contemplation over verses would inevitably lead to new ideas and fresh perspectives, rather than merely reporting the teachings of one's predecessors. In his schema, the dynamic element of exegesis was considered paramount. The demise of the Mu'tazila was largely due to their endorsement of deductive reasoning (*ra'y*) at the expense of the Hadith element in their writings.[9]

The debate concerning the respective priority of reason and revelation continues on to this day. For example, the modern exegete Azad distinguishes four stages of guidance for humanity: first

---

[7] Reference to this work is made by the great medieval scholar Ibn Battutah, but only fragments have survived.
[8] Hamka 1967:31.
[9] Speight 1988:65.

by instinct; second by the senses; third by reason; and finally by revelation and the prophets – 'revelation "perfects" the guidance, offered by reason'.[10] The dynamic of this modern debate has not only been evident in the Middle East. Reference to and the influences of this debate will be examined in a Southeast Asian context in subsequent chapters.

Predestination versus free will

An offshoot of the above tension between reason and revelation was the debate which erupted regarding free will and predestination.

The context for this debate in Islamic history has often been political. The first centuries of Islam witnessed the emergence of a group called the Qadariyya,[11] with which many associate the prominent theologian of the period, al-Hasan al-Basri (d. 728). The Qadariyya maintained that man was essentially a free agent who could choose between faith, piety and obedience to God, on the one hand, and rebellion and infidelity to God on the other. Their views were clearly in harmony with the pro-reason side of the above-mentioned debate.

Their opponents, who stressed that man lay under the authority and control of God, and as such was subject to God's predetermined order, were generally aligned with the political authorities of the day, the Umayyad caliphs. The latter had a vested interest in stressing obedience to higher authority and, indeed, they laid claim to a certain degree of divinely sanctioned authority themselves.[12]

Both sides sought scriptural support for their respective points of view. The Qadariyya pointed to Qur'anic statements such as the following:

… but Allah will leave, to stray, those who do wrong[13]

Q14:27

---

[10]   Baljon 1968:62.

[11]   Their name was derived from the term *qadar*, referring to the preordination of events in the world by God.

[12]   Watt 1948:165; Watt 1974:72; Ayubi 1991:14. Rippin and Knappert (1986:17) raise questions about whether there was as much of a political dimension to this debate as some scholars have made out.

[13]   i.e. individuals choose of their own accord to do wrong before God sends them astray.

They argued that this reference implied that individuals can exercise their own free will in selecting from the many life paths God offers them.[14]

In response, the opponents of the Qadariyya referred to references from the Qur'an which suggested that God, not man, is in control of the direction which an individual takes, such as the following:

Truly Allah leaveth, to stray, whom He will

Q13:27

Thus man should submit to the will and authority of God and, by extension, should also submit to the will and authority of temporal rulers enjoying divine sanction.

Thus the ambiguity of the revealed text compounded the problem. Moreover, the situation was exacerbated by the fact that in this early period the Hadith collections had not been properly canonised. Reports of Muhammad's sayings were used, and indeed sometimes invented, to suit the requirements of particular parties in the debate.

This debate was the subject of a significant volume of literary activity. One of the most compelling works is a treatise written by al-Hasan al-Basri to the Caliph 'Abd al-Malik.[15] In this work he employed reason to demonstrate that *qadar* (preordination) did not extend beyond the metaphysical realm, thus claiming that man could exercise moral and religious free will. He wrote:

Know, O Commander of the Faithful, that God is more just than to blindfold His servant and then to say to him: 'Look! I will not punish you!' or to make him deaf and then to say to him 'Listen! I will not punish you!' or to make him mute and then say to him 'Speak! I will not punish you!' This, O Commander of the Faithful, is plainer than that which is hidden from an intelligent person.[16]

This was a direct challenge to certain oppressive rulers who had justified their actions by appealing to *qadar*.[17] The challenge posed

---

[14] Rippin 1990:64–5. Cf. the Ash'arite doctrine of *kasb*, 'the human "acquisition" from God of the power to perform each act' (Martin *et al.* 1997:155).

[15] Rippin and Knappert 1986:115–21. Rippin and Knappert raise doubts about whether al-Hasan was in fact the author of this work.

[16] Al-Hasan al-Basri, *Risala*, cited in Rippin and Knappert 1986:120.

[17] Lambton 1979:407.

by the Qadariyya was in turn affirmed by the Mu'tazila, the group of speculative theologians who came to be seen as the champions of reason. Their concerns were five-fold: God's overarching unity; God's need to be just (which prevented Him from destining some people for punishment); the createdness of the Qur'an; the perpetual punishment of sinners; and a commitment to championing the right and forbidding the wrong.[18]

The compilation and canonisation of the authoritative Hadith collections in the 9th century, thus expanding the corpus of recognised revelatory material, aided a resolution of the ongoing debate. The relevant Hadith seemed to point believers in the direction of an overarching belief in divine control over all aspects of the individual's life.

Watt refers to 'the contradiction between the fatalistic teaching of many Traditions and the anti-fatalistic teaching of the Qur'an'.[19] The overarching deterministic tone of the Hadith accounts is evident in the following:

Narrated Anas bin Malik: The Prophet said, 'Allah puts an angel in charge of the uterus and the angel says, "O Lord, (it is) semen! O Lord, (it is now) a clot! O Lord, (it is now) a piece of flesh." And then, if Allah wishes to complete its creation, the angel asks, "O Lord, (will it be) a male or a female? A wretched (an evil doer) or a blessed (doer of good)? How much will his provisions be? What will his age be?" So all that is written while the creature is still in the mother's womb.'[20]

Narrated Imran bin Husain: A man said, 'O Allah's Apostle! Can the people of Paradise be known (differentiated) from the people of the Fire.' The Prophet replied, 'Yes.' The man said, 'Why do people (try to) do (good) deeds?' The Prophet said, 'Everyone will do the deeds for which he has been created to do or he will do those deeds which will be made easy for him to do.'[21]

It is related from 'Abd Allah ibn 'Umar that, 'The Apostle of God said, "The hearts of the sons of Adam are all between two fingers of the Merciful, like one heart. He turneth them as He wills." Then the Apostle of God said, "O God, turn our hearts to obey thee."'[22]

It is related from 'Aisha that, 'The Apostle of God was called to the funeral of a young child of one of the Helpers; and I said, "O Apostle of

---

18 Rippin and Knappert 1986:18–19.

19 Watt 1948:170.

20 al-Bukhari, *Sahih*, vol. 8, no. 594.

21 al-Bukhari, *Sahih*, vol. 8, no. 595.

22 Goldsack 1923:8, citing the Traditionist Muslim.

God, this one is blessed. He is one of the birds of paradise, for he has neither done evil nor thought it." He replied, "O 'Aisha, it may be otherwise, for verily God created a people for paradise when they were yet in their fathers' loins, and He created a people for the fire when they were yet in their fathers' loins."[23]

The overarching inclination of the Hadith reports towards a predestinarian view was reinforced by the main legal texts, which drew extensively on Hadith materials. An example is the Malikite manual *al-Risala*, written by Ibn Abi Zayd al-Qayrawani, which states:

Surely He who creates knows, besides He is the Gentle and Knowing one. He leads astray whom He likes to, and then He forsakes him out of His Justice. He also guides to the right path whom He wishes to and grants him success out of His grace.[24]

Again the approach of the 10th-century reforming thinker al-Ash'ari to this issue, which asserted itself over that of the Mu'tazila,[25] represented something of a middle course, by providing man with a measure of freedom to choose between options determined by God, with God knowing what options would be chosen before the event. Mankind was seen as being equipped to make proper choices by the provision of guidance from God in the form of scripture, as is indicated by this Hadith report:

… [Ali] replied, 'Verily I heard the Apostle of God say, "Beware! For there will be strife." I said, "O Apostle of God, what is the way out of such strife?" He replied, "The Word of God in which is the history of what happened before you, and information of what will come after you, and a command concerning the things which are amongst you. It is a separator between (true and false). It is not a vain utterance. He who is proud and abandons it, God will break him in pieces, and he who desires guidance from it, God will lead him astray. And it is the strong rope of God, and it is a wise admonition, and it is a straight road, and it is that by which men do not go astray. … It is a Book which, when the genii heard it, they said, 'Verily we have heard a wonderful Qur'an …'"[26]

---

23 Goldsack 1923:9, citing the Traditionist Muslim.

24 Ibn Abi Zayd al-Qayrawani, *al-Risala*, 1.03 Determination.

25 Though Mu'tazilite thinking lived on throughout the centuries through various writings, and underwent something of a renaissance in the 20th century, especially in Southeast Asia. This will be examined in later chapters.

26 Goldsack 1923:100, citing the Traditionist al-Tirmidhi.

Al-Ash'ari's significance in this regard is well summarised by the great late-19th-century reformist thinker and writer, Muhammad 'Abduh, in saying '... al-Ash'ari ... plotted a middle course, as is well known, between the early "orthodox" and the subsequent tendencies towards extremes.'[27] Some later thinkers, such as Ibn Qudama (d. 1223) seemed to emphasise a more hardline determinist approach to this issue within orthodox thought, which reflects his Hanbalite position which attached priority to *Sunna* over rational thought. This can be seen when he writes, 'The decree, of both good and evil, sweet and bitter, little and big, loved and detested, is from God.'[28] However, this represented in part a response to tendencies within Sufism considered as more heterodox, and did not significantly compromise the fine balance between free will and God's preordained plan achieved by al-Ash'ari.

This fine balance is well expressed in the following quote from al-Ghazali's *Ihya' 'Ulum al-Din*:

Question – Has man got freedom of action?
Answer – Man has got freedom of action but it is not opposed to our opinion that everything is the creation of God and man's freedom of will is also the creation of God. When man wishes, his wish has been created for him.[29]

Al-Ash'ari's pronouncements did not succeed in stifling what was a passionate and ongoing debate; the issue of predestination versus free will has remained live throughout Islamic history. Hadith references such as those presented above, supported by the contents of *Fiqh* manuals, have often served to generate a predestinarian sense of fatalism among the masses throughout the Muslim world. In response, Muslim scholars have endeavoured to educate the masses along the lines of the finely balanced Ash'arite framework described above. As Watt aptly observes:

... despite the widespread conception of Islam in the West, which appears to be supported by popular Muslim views, the great orthodox

27 Abduh 1966:36.
28 Ibn Qudama, 'Creed', cited in Rippin and Knappert 1986:121.
29 al-Ghazali, *Ihya' 'Ulum al-din*, cited in Karim 1982: vol. 4, 5.

theologians of Islam were never sheerly deterministic. On the contrary, they were trying to hold the balance between the two sides ...[30]

A practical example of this will be seen in the discussion of the Malay–Indonesian world in later chapters.

ESCHATOLOGY IN ISLAM

Islamic sacred scripture has much to say about *al-akhira* – the end of times. In fact, a concern with eschatological themes is primary to Islamic doctrine. If Christian doctrine points towards the death and resurrection of Christ as the watershed event in human salvation history, Islam points towards the Day of Judgement as the principal motivating factor for human belief and behaviour in the temporal world.

A survey of the Qur'anic text reveals a huge number of verses which remind both the believer and the unbeliever of impending judgement, reward and punishment.[31] However, as is so often the case, the Qur'an serves to provide a framework which is expanded in great detail by the prophetic Traditions, supplemented by legendary materials such as are contained in the Stories of the Prophets. The Qur'an sounds the warning of punishment for unbelievers and the promise of reward for the believers, but the Hadith accounts explain in detail the form that this punishment and reward will take.

The relatively late canonisation of the prophetic Traditions *vis-à-vis* the compilation of the Qur'anic text has caused many non-Muslim scholars to conclude that the Traditions were developed in large part as a response to a perceived lack in Qur'anic detail. Emerging Islamic theology required a detailed doctrine of the Hereafter, so Traditions were invented, and in order to increase their authority, they were associated with Muhammad. It is in this context that Seale writes that 'as Islamic *Sunna* (tradition) grew and expanded in the centuries that followed Muhammad's death, new horrors were added which the Prophet never conceived ... [such as] the interrogation in the grave and the torments that follow.'[32] The following Hadith account attributed to Ibn 'Abbas presents this graphically:

[30] Watt 1948:167.
[31] Cf. Sura 90.

Once the Prophet while passing through one of the grave-yards of Medina or Mecca heard the voices of two persons who were being tortured in their graves. The Prophet said, 'These two persons are being tortured not for a major sin (to avoid).' The Prophet then added, 'Yes (they are being tortured for a major sin). Indeed, one of them never saved himself from being soiled with his urine while the other used to go about with calumnies (to make enmity between friends).' The Prophet then asked for a green leaf of a date-palm tree, broke it into two pieces and put one on each grave. On being asked why he had done so, he replied, 'I hope that their torture might be lessened, till these get dried.'[33]

The wealth of detail presented in the Hadith accounts about the Judgement leads to a number of areas of inconsistency. The duration of Jesus' return is unclear. Similarly, the role of Jesus as *al-Masih*, *vis-à-vis* the Mahdi is confusing, with varying accounts presented. These Hadith details, and inconsistencies, are transferred to the classical writings which attempt to paint a portrait of the Judgement, and which often attempt to reconcile the scriptural inconsistencies by developing systematic doctrine.

Such an attempt occurs in the *Testament of Abu Hanifa*, where the great jurist maps out what he sees as an orthodox doctrine of the Hereafter.

Article 18: We confess that the punishment in the tomb shall without fail take place.
Article 19: We confess that, in view of the Traditions on the subject, the interrogation by Munkar and Nakir is a reality.[34]

His need to affirm that the punishment in the tomb and the interrogation occur points to a debate among classical Islamic theologians surrounding these events. The late-11th-century theologian al-Nasafi (d. 1114) reported that the Mu'tazila did not accept that these events took place, though he is in accord with Abu Hanifa in accepting their veracity.[35] Ibn Qudama (d. 1223) similarly took an anti-Mu'tazila line on these issues. In the following passage he affirms the priority of faith in revelation over reason, in a way which points to his Hanbalite allegiances, and underlines a literalist

32 Seale 1978:93.
33 *Sahih al-Bukhari*, vol. 1, no. 215.
34 Abu Hanifa, *Testament*, cited in Peters 1994:402.
35 Peters 1994:405.

interpretation of Qur'an and Hadith references to the punishment in the tomb:

Faith also requires belief in the reality of punishment in the tomb and the squeezing which will really take place and that Munkar and Nakir, the two angels, will come to the people in the grave asking about their Lord and their helper and prophet.[36]

Another matter of disagreement relates to whether punishment in Hell is eternal for the unbelievers, or whether those guilty of grave sin will be brought out of Hell after a time through intercession. The classical exegete Baydawi reports some scholars as suggesting that 'the good deed of the unbeliever … will bring about some lessening of punishment …'.[37] However, his exegetical predecessor Zamakhshari is not inclined to such a view.[38] In this he shows his undoubted sympathies for the views of the Mu'tazila, for whom the eternal punishment of sinners was a key plank in their belief.[39] Such disagreement among the classical scholars reflects the diverse viewpoints presented in the Hadith accounts regarding the events associated with the final Judgement.

One of the key classical texts dealing with the Hereafter and the Judgement is the *Tanbih al-ghafilin* (The Arousement of the Heedless) by al-Samarqandi (d. 983). This work has as its core a conjoining of Hadith accounts on various themes connected with the Hereafter, and as a result it presents the most graphic, gruesome portrayal of the terrors of Hell, as well as the physical delights of Paradise. God is portrayed as a calculating, vengeful God, who goes to considerable lengths to impose the most painful punishment on the unbelievers in Hell.

The Fire was stoked for a thousand years till it became red. Then it was stoked for a thousand years till it became white. Then it was stoked for a thousand more years till it became black, so that it is black as the darkest night.[40]

Such is the fate awaiting those in the Hereafter who do not make the right choices in the temporal world. However, al-Samarqandi

---

36 Ibn Qudama, 'Creed', cited in Rippin and Knappert 1986:123.
37 Gatje 1996:178. Cf. al-Baydawi 1996: vol. 5, 519.
38 Gatje 1996:182. Cf. al-Zamakhshari n.d.: vol. 2, 293.
39 Rippin and Knappert 1986:18.
40 Jeffery 1962:230.

not only paints a portrait of the punishments awaiting the doomed, but also provides the ingredients for living a life pleasing to God in this world, in giving reports such as the following:

It has been said that the most excellent of men is he who is found in possession of five good qualities, the first being that he abounds in worship of his Lord, the second is that it be evident that he is serviceable to people, the third is that folk have no fear of being harmed by him, the fourth is that he does not put his hope on what is in men's hands, and the fifth is that he makes preparation for death.[41]

Al-Samarqandi's work is interspersed with Qur'anic verses in places, but the small Qur'anic input is far outweighed in influence by Hadith accounts. The overriding tone of the work is therefore graphic in ugliness or opulence, respectively, depending on whether Hell or Paradise is being portrayed.

Thus the Hadith accounts were crucial in terms of Islamic eschatology, as they served to fill out the Qur'anic framework of warning and promise with vivid detail spelling out the result if Qur'anic injunctions were not heeded. However, the degree of detail in the Hadith accounts on the Judgement, compounded by the possible dubious veracity of some of these accounts, meant that they were somewhat contradictory in content, leading to disagreement and debate among Islamic scholars over details of the Judgement. This eschatological debate was picked up by Southeast Asian Islamic writers as will be seen later.

[41] Jeffery 1962:207.

4

EXEGESIS OF THE QUR'AN

In his study of the Abraham–Ishmael stories, Firestone[1] identifies four categories of Islamic interpretative literature used by Muslim scholars and communities to elucidate the Qur'anic references to these stories. These four categories were:

- *Hadith* or Prophetic Tradition
- *Tafsir*, or formal exegesis of the Qur'an
- *Qisas al-anbiya'*, or popular hagiographic literature
- *Ta'rikh*, or Islamic historiographical works.

The discussion which follows will elaborate on the first three of these categories, as they were to have a particularly powerful influence on Muslim Southeast Asia.

THE ROLE OF THE HADITH

Qur'anic exegesis, or *tafsir*, did not consolidate itself as a separate science until very early in the 3rd/9th century.[2] Rather, the centuries immediately following the death of Muhammad were characterised by the collection and recording of the revelations, the clarification of textual forms, and the compiling of the Hadith, or Tradition literature.

The Hadith consisted of various compilations of stories concerned with the life and teachings of the prophet. These were collected from accounts traced back to the Companions of the prophet. The Tradition literature included a wide range of subject matter, including theology, ethics, and exegesis; one of the

---

[1] Firestone 1990:11–12.
[2] Abdul 1976:142.

most authoritative of the Tradition collections, the *Jami' al-sahih* of al-Bukhari, contains a chapter on exegesis among sections relating to a range of other Islamic sciences. Thus the Tradition collections were eclectic; great importance was attached to a verifiable line of transmission in citing a particular textual interpretation, and schools emerged around certain leaders in particular cities.

The issue of interpreting the Qur'anic text was a matter of some considerable debate within the early Muslim community, with the key issues of disagreement revolving around the reason versus revelation debate described previously. Many scholars felt that it was inappropriate for human interpreters to base themselves on reason in interpreting the meaning of what was seen as God's word, and this attitude contributed to the relatively slow development of Qur'anic exegesis as a separate field.

Anecdotes from the classical writers provide testimony to the tensions existing among the early scholars. For example, al-Tabari relates the account of how a pious man, observing a teacher explaining the Qur'an, called out 'Better would it be for thee to have the tambourine playing at thy back than to sit here.' Similarly, Abu'l-Layth al-Samarqandi (d. 983/4) related that the caliph 'Umar, seeing a portion of Qur'anic text with an accompanying explanation of every verse, took a pair of scissors and cut it into pieces.[3] While many may challenge the historical accuracy of a report suggesting that the caliph destroyed a fragment of Qur'anic text, these accounts nevertheless provide reliable evidence of a lively debate in early Islam, and they also provide a plausible explanation for the absence of detailed works of exegesis in the first two centuries of Islam.

The authority accorded to the Hadith reports ensured that during the formative century and a half after the death of Muhammad, these reports constituted the only widely accepted form of commentary on the Qur'an. As the Hadith reports supposedly recorded the statements and actions of Muhammad, the use of these reports to explain particular verses of the Qur'an effectively represented, to early Muslims, a posthumous recourse to Muhammad to explain these troublesome verses. In this way,

---

[3] Mez 1996:196.

Muhammad could be seen as the first, and for some time the only, exegete of the Qur'an. Such a technique of exegesis, with Muhammad being made central to the exercise, was entirely consistent with the elevated view of the Hadith reports among Muslims, as is well articulated in the following words of the great 11th-century scholar al-Ghazali:

God has but one word which differs only in the mode of its expression. On occasions God indicates His word by the Quran; on others, by words in another style, not publicly recited, and called the Prophetic tradition. Both are mediated by the Prophet.[4]

Indeed, there was a sub-group of Hadith reports which could be clearly linked with the text of the Qur'an. These were those reports which provided the circumstances of revelation (*asbab al-nuzul*) of particular Qur'anic verses, and thus had an overt exegetical function. An example is the following:

The messenger of God was not feeling well, and for two or three nights he did not get up. A woman came to him and said, 'O Muhammad, I am afraid that your familiar spirit ... has abandoned you. I have not seen it near you for two or three nights.' Then God revealed. 'By the morning light and by the night when it is calm, your Lord has not left you, nor has He despised you.'[5]

The Hadith reports providing the *asbab al-nuzul* became increasingly important as instruments of Qur'anic exegesis, and this function has continued down to the present day throughout the Muslim world. Collections entitled *asbab al-nuzul* can be found across the Muslim world, including the Malay–Indonesian region, to this day.

According to classical sources, the debate about undertaking exegesis of the Qur'an beyond the Hadith texts was only resolved by the identification of a Hadith which stated that 'Whoever interprets the Qur'an according to his own light will go to Hell.'[6] This meant that every interpretation had to be traceable to Muhammad, it reinforced the importance of making extensive use of Hadith reports in subsequent exegetical

---

[4] Cited in Peters 1990: vol. 2, 192.
[5] Speight 1988:68, citing al-Bukhari. The Qur'anic reference is Q93:1–3
[6] Wensinck 1971:131, citing al-Tirmidhi.

writings, and it had the effect of making early commentators cautious and conservative in their approach to exegesis.

The subsequent development of individual works of Qur'anic exegesis added a dimension to the study of the Islamic sacred text, but the exegetical role played from the beginning by the Hadith was to continue unabated throughout the various periods of Islamic history. Some of the most widely used works of Hadith were the summary compilations based on a selection of all the authoritative collections. Examples were *Mishkat al-masabih* and the *Forty Hadith* of al-Nawawi (d. 1277),[7] which was translated into Malay during the 17th century.

THE EARLY EXEGETES

The earliest Qur'anic commentaries were largely compilatory, and were based on particular regional schools;[8] it is reported, for example, that Ibn Jurayj produced a commentary based on collections of the renowned Meccan Companion, Ibn 'Abbas, in the 2nd/8th century, though again only fragments remain.[9] The breadth of subject matter covered by these early commentaries widened, to cover such matters as philology and lexicography in addition to matters of theological doctrine.

Wansbrough's detailed examination of Qur'anic exegetical materials over a period of several centuries led him to apply a five-fold typology; namely narrative, legal, textual, rhetorical and allegorical exegesis. He concluded that the first four of this group represent the chronological order of evolution of Qur'anic exegetical styles. He states that 'Quranic exegesis would seem to have found its earliest expression within a basically narrative framework which may conveniently be described as haggadic',[10] and goes on to say that 'increasing sophistication discernible in the treatment of scripture corresponded to a demand, at least among the exegetes themselves, for finer and subtler terms of clarification and of dispute.'[11] Wansbrough's claim that narrative exegesis was the earliest of styles is a matter

---

7 Ibrahim and Johnson-Davies 1977.
8 Hermansen 1998:145.
9 Abbott 1967:95.
10 Wansbrough 1977:121.
11 Wansbrough 1977:119.

of debate. However, evidence from the Malay–Indonesian world presented later will suggest that narrative exegesis was to become the most popular of styles in terms of making scriptural exegesis accessible to a wide audience.

The earliest substantial commentary of the Qur'an which survives to the present day is the work attributed to Muqatil b. Sulayman, who died in Basra in 767. Details of his life are uncertain as are details of his theological position, owing to the fact that his commentary as it exists today appears to have gone through substantial editing processes.[12]

AL-TABARI'S JAMI' AL-BAYAN

The compilation of the commentary by al-Tabari (839–923), entitled *Jami' al-bayan fi tafsir al-Qur'an*, represents something of a watershed in the history of *tafsir*. It brought together the entire breadth of the material of tradition-based exegesis extant in his time,[13] and it thus serves as a crucial key to an understanding of exegetical activity in the first 250 years of Islam. It is an immense work; the first edition published in 1903 filled thirty volumes. It is most comprehensive in terms of the variety of fields it deals with, meticulously reproducing chains of transmission (*isnad*), paraphrasing the entire Qur'anic text, presenting grammatical discussion in great detail, relating widely varying interpretations drawn from his predecessors (though always indicating his preferred interpretation among these options), and much more.

Al-Tabari was writing at the time of the great ideological dispute discussed previously between the reason-based Mu'tazila and the conservative scripturalist *ahl al-hadith*. The eventual victory of the latter was due in large part to the influence of the staunchly conservative Ahmad ibn Hanbal. Al-Tabari's sympathies lay clearly with the *ahl al-hadith* in this dispute. He included a vast number of exegetical accounts from the Tradition materials in his commentary, and clearly prioritised the surface meaning of the Qur'anic text, rather than seeking to identify intricate inner meanings, or indeed seeking to engage in extensive

---

12 Rippin and Knappert 1986:3.
13 Gatje 1996:34.

allegorisation of the Qur'anic text as was the case with the Mu'tazila.[14]

Al-Tabari regularly made this point in his commentary. In commenting on Q5:114ff he stated 'the meaning of God's speech is always to be interpreted as lying closer to the ordinary manner of speaking of the one who makes the request than to some significance inaccessible or unknown to the speaker …'[15] A little later in his commentary on the same verse, al-Tabari adds, 'As to what was on the table … there is no advantage in knowing exactly what it was, nor is there any harm in not knowing, as long as the conclusions drawn from the verse correspond with *the external wording* of the revelation.'[16] In even clearer terms, al-Tabari comments as follows on Q12:20: 'Man's duty … is to believe in the external wording … of the revelation; he is not required to know anything which goes beyond this.'[17]

POST-TABARI DEVELOPMENTS

Al-Tabari's commentary cemented the field of *tafsir* once and for all as a fully fledged, independent Islamic science. This monumental work made a major contribution to exegesis in a wide variety of fields. After al-Tabari, there was a gradual streaming of commentaries, with works compiled often giving a particular emphasis to a specific field, such as philology, jurisprudence, scholasticism, and doctrinal and sectarian schools. This is not to say that the commentaries only focused on one central issue. Rather, many commentaries based themselves in a particular field, with additional sections interpolated which were connected with secondary fields.

Abdul provides a categorisation of these groupings which can be usefully compared to the previously mentioned typology of Wansbrough:

1. Philological commentaries, e.g. *Ma'ani al-Qur'an* by Abu 'Ubayda.
2. Philosophical commentaries, e.g. *Mafatih al-ghayb* by al-Razi.

---

[14] McAuliffe 1991:44.
[15] Peters 1994:29.
[16] Peters 1994:30. My emphasis. Cf. also Cooper 1987:224.
[17] Gatje 1996:65.

3. Juridic commentaries, e.g. *Madarik al-tanzil wa haqa'iq al-ta'wil* by al-Nasafi.
4. Narrative-based commentaries, e.g. those by al-Tha'labi, al-Baghawi and al-Khazin.
5. Commentaries by various streams and sects:
   a. Sufi, e.g. Sahl al-Tustari (d. 896), Ibn al-'Arabi (d. 1240). These commentaries tended to interpret Qur'anic verses on different levels, variously seen as literal, allegorical and mystical.
   b. Mu'tazilite, e.g. *al-Kashshaf* by al-Zamakhshari.
   c. Shi'ite, e.g. that by al-Tabarsi.

The above skeletal representation points to the breadth of exegetical activity in the Arab world in the first millennium after the death of Muhammad. The divisions presented above are by no means clear-cut; there was considerable overlap, and the appropriateness of these divisions is arguable. But it is agreed that there was grouping into schools, and there is overwhelming evidence that Qur'anic commentaries began to appear in significant numbers within 250 years of the death of the prophet. These commentaries were very much interdependent, but each preserved its own originality. Often, commentaries were written to explain other commentaries, such as al-Khafaji's *Inayat al-qadi wa kifayat al-radi fi sharh al-Baydawi,* which commented upon the famous linguistic/philological commentary of al-Baydawi.

The discussion that follows will not attempt to look in detail at all categories of exegesis. Rather, we will focus upon those commentaries which were to play a significant and direct role in the emergence of the science of exegesis as practised in the Malay world.

Wansbrough's conclusion that narrative commentaries represented the earliest style of exegesis bears closer examination. Some of the very earliest commentaries, written within a century or two of al-Tabari, depended essentially on narrative as the core feature of their approach to exegesis. Indeed, al-Tabari's commentary also includes many lengthy and colourful narrative pericopes. But narrative as an exegetical style was to reach its apogee in the writing of al-Tha'labi and his exegetical descendants.

Al-Tha'labi's al-Kashf wa al-bayan

Abu Ishaq Ahmad b. Ibrahim al-Tha'labi al-Nisaburi (d. 427/1035) was one of the earliest of the post-Tabari exegetes. He was famous in his lifetime as a reader, exegete, and preacher, and was described by Ibn Khallikan as follows: 'He was unique in his era in the field of exegesis, and he composed a great commentary which surpassed other commentaries.'[18]

Al-Tha'labi's most famous works were as follows:

* His Qur'anic commentary, entitled *al-Kashf wa al-bayan 'an tafsir al-Qur'an*
* A collection of Stories of the Prophets, entitled *Qisas al-anbiya' al-musamma 'ara'is al-majalis*

Al-Tha'labi's approach to exegesis was narrative-based, in which he drew upon a copious collection of Traditions and stories to illustrate the particular theological issues or lessons which he wished to address. In fact his own collection of Stories of the Prophets developed from his commentary, which provides an indication of the extent of narrative in *al-Kashf wa al-bayan*.

However, there is a degree of controversy which surrounds al-Tha'labi's commentary in Muslim circles, particularly surrounding his use of Traditions which were weak. Al-Dhahabi reports Abu al-Ghafar b. Isma'il al-Farisi as writing that '[al-Tha'labi's commentary] contained many traditions and many shaykh's names. But there are some scholars who considered that it could not be trusted and its reporting was not reliable.'[19]

His commentary has never been published, probably because of its ambiguous reputation.[20] In terms of al-Tha'labi's place within his own context, his approach to exegesis was consistent with a tradition-based methodology which pertained in his era. However, he lay outside the circle of the conservative *ahl al-hadith*, not because of any Mu'tazilite embracing of speculative methods, which he in fact shunned, but rather because he was considered as casting his net too widely among the less authoritative Hadith

---

18 Al-Dhahabi 1985: vol. 1, 221ff. Also al-Dawudi vol. 1, 66–67; al-Suyuti 1976: 28.

19 Al-Dhahabi 1985: vol. 1, 221.

20 Nevertheless, its content is still accessible via various manuscripts held by a number of libraries around the world.

records, as well as extra-scriptural sources, in order to find attractive ingredients for a narrative-based approach to exegesis.

In terms of Southeast Asian Islam, al-Tha'labi has not left a direct legacy. However, his influence was considerable, via later exegetes who chose to emulate his methodology.

Al-Baghawi's Ma'alim al-tanzil

An important commentary in the development of Islamic thought in the Malay world is *Ma'alim al-tanzil* by al-Baghawi (d. 1122). Al-Baghawi is another significant name in the emergence of a narrative-based stream of exegesis which became particularly popular in Islamic Southeast Asia. An examination of al-Baghawi and his writings would therefore be useful in providing an insight into the theological orientations and influences which provided a focus for studies of Islam in the early Malay world.

Al-Baghawi, also known as al-Farra', originated from the vicinity of Herat, located in present-day Afghanistan. The great medieval scholar al-Suyuti describes him as a Shafi'ite authority in exegesis, traditions and jurisprudence. He died sometime between 510/1117 and 516/1122.[21]

Al-Baghawi's great mentor in the field of Qur'anic exegesis was al-Tha'labi, arguably the great pioneer in developing narrative exegesis. Al-Baghawi's literary output covered a range of fields: *al-Masabih al-sunna* and *Sharh al-sunna* represent studies of the Traditions; *al-Tahdhib* was a study of jurisprudence; *Ma'alim al-tanzil* addressed exegesis of the Qur'an and was to influence studies in this field in the early Malay–Indonesian world. Al-Baghawi's varied writings demonstrate both a concern with using Tradition materials, and a commitment to drawing upon narrative as a major device for the illustration of doctrine and for interpretation of scripture. In these two elements he was clearly influenced by al-Tha'labi.

One of al-Baghawi's most famous works was *Masabih al-sunna*, a comprehensive collection of Tradition accounts, which clearly demonstrates al-Baghawi's general approach to presenting exegesis and Tradition. This work presents Tradition accounts in a set order and hierarchy, according to authority:

---

[21] Robson 1979a:919.

1. Reliable Traditions (*sahih*).
2. Good Traditions (*hasan*).
3. Traditions from a single authority considered unusual (*gharib*).
4. Traditions considered weak (*da'if*); i.e. of questionable authenticity because of content or origin.

It is important to note here that al-Baghawi carried out the practice which had caused the commentary by al-Tha'labi to become a cause of controversy; i.e. he included weak Traditions. This was to attract criticism from a number of leading, conservative Traditionists.

An examination of al-Baghawi's Qur'anic commentary *Ma'alim al-tanzil* ('The Signs of the Revelation') quickly reveals his substantial dependence upon the commentary of al-Tha'labi. However, he also drew on a range of other sources, which are identified in the preface to the *Ma'alim al-tanzil*.

Al-Baghawi's methodology is based on a verse-by-verse treatment of the Qur'anic text, with a presentation of a range of opinions drawn from his source materials. It should be noted, however, that al-Baghawi does not necessarily provide an indication of his preferred interpretation, when giving a range of interpretations by other scholars. Consider his commentary on Q18:77:

The words of the Almighty: (Then the two of them went until they came to people of a town). Ibn 'Abbas said [the town] was Antioch. Ibn Sirin said it was Eilat, which was the furthermost point of the earth from the Heavens. It was also said that it was Cyrenaica. Abu Hurayrah said it was a town in Andalus.

This contrasts with the practice of al-Tabari, who usually indicated which opinion he considered most valid in presenting alternatives. It is for this reason that al-Baghawi and the other narrative exegetes have been accused, at times, of presenting information for information's sake, without subjecting their data to critical scrutiny.

The rationale for al-Baghawi's decision not to mention lengthy chains of authority within the exegetical text was that he had already made a comprehensive listing of his sources in the preface to his work. The only exception to this is where he cites from a source not mentioned in his preface. For example in his comment on Q18:76, which includes the following *isnad*:

We are told by Isma'il b. 'Abd al-Qahir who reports from 'Abd al-Ghafar b. Muhammad who reports from Muhammad b. 'Isa who repeats from Ibrahim b. Muhammad b. Sufyan who repeats from Muslim b. al-Hajaj who repeats from Muhammad b. 'Abd 'Ala al-Qaysi who repeats from al-Mu'tamar b. Sulayman who draws on his father who draws on Ruqbah who draws on Abu Ishaq who draws on Sa'id b. Jubayr who draws on Ibn 'Abbas who draws on Abu b. Ka'b who said: the Prophet SAW said ...

The absence of lengthy chains of authority ensures that the text of his commentary contains a relatively fluid prose style which lends itself well to both skimming and detailed reading; also, as can be seen from the above example, the presence of such *isnad* chains would severely disrupt the flow of a narrative text, and one can readily grasp why al-Baghawi chose to exclude them on a regular basis. But not only does the relegation of source references to the preface prove beneficial to the style of the text, it also points to the author's overriding concern with the text itself, rather than with a meticulous and scholarly listing of his sources. The author has chosen to focus on the text – and in most instances that means to focus on the stories within his text – rather than sacrificing some of the fluid narrative for philological detail.

Ma'alim al-tanzil not only concerns itself with theological exposition, but addresses a range of other issues as well. There are regular discussions of variant readings on the Qur'anic text, and occasional references to grammatical detail, though this is infrequent. An example of discussion of the variant readings is provided in al-Baghawi's comment on Q18:77.

Ibn Kathir and Abu 'Amr and Ya'qub read it as *latakhidhta* with a single *ta'* and a *kasrah* on the *kha'*, and the others read it as *la-ttakhadhta* with doubling of the *ta'* and a *fatha* on the *kha'*, and [the difference between] these two words is like *atba'a* and *tabi'a 'alayhi* ...

But it is in presentation of story that al-Baghawi comes into his own. His commentary is memorable for its rich narrative content throughout. A cursory glance at the work quickly reveals the large proportion which is devoted to narrative commentary on Qur'anic verses, and a more detailed examination of the text reveals that al-Baghawi was eclectic not only in terms of the exegetical sources he drew upon, but also in terms of the religious traditions which he consulted in collecting the narratives contained in his commentary.

Al-Baghawi's work includes lengthy stories drawn from Jewish, Christian and Islamic traditions, and nowhere does the commentator identify a story as deriving from non-Islamic sources and therefore being less worthy of attention than stories drawn from the Islamic tradition. An example of such stories is the account of David and Bathsheba presented in *Sura Sad*, derived from Jewish tradition. A lengthy story drawn from Christian tradition which is included in his commentary is the account of the Seven Sleepers of Ephesus presented in al-Baghawi's treatment of the 18th Chapter of the Qur'an, *Sura al-Kahf*.

Though al-Baghawi's stories are lengthy, they are not the account of someone who merely wished to pad out his text. On the contrary, the style is that of someone who enjoyed story-telling and wished to address those who shared this pleasure. This is why al-Baghawi seems at times to be drawn into minute detail in his narratives, far more than is actually required for the purposes of his theological exposition. An example can be seen in his commentary on Q18:77, where he presents a range of related accounts of the meeting between Khidr and Moses, on the one hand, and the inhabitants of the town who refused to give them hospitality, on the other.

Abu b. Ka'b reported as follows from the Prophet SAW: until when the pair came upon some lowly inhabitants of a town, they circulated among their groupings and asked these people for food, but they refused to show the pair hospitality. It is also related that they circulated in the town and asked the inhabitants for food, but they refused to show the pair hospitality. It is also related that they circulated among the people and asked them for food, but they did not feed the pair nor invite them as guests nor show them hospitality.

The length of this passage seems to be out of proportion to the small point requiring amplification. Nevertheless, it serves several functions. It provides a clear example of a reduced chain of authority, thus signalling that the commentator wished to focus on the story. Second, it points to the commentator's interest in events, providing his readers with several (almost identical) accounts. Third, it demonstrated a concern with giving his readers variety, rather than merely selecting his preferred interpretation and presenting it as undisputed fact.

Al-Baghawi's commentary acts as the primary source of the Cambridge Malay commentary of which a detailed examination occurs later in this present study. It is likely that the rich narrative which underlies the exegetical style of this commentary served as a major point of attraction for authors of Malay exegetical works and their readers. The choice of al-Baghawi's commentary as a major source by the author of the Cambridge Malay commentary in the late 16th century probably reflected a degree of popularity which the *Ma'alim al-Tanzil* had enjoyed in the Malay world in earlier periods.

Al-Khazin's Lubab al-ta'wil

Just as the commentary by al-Tha'labi provided the core of al-Baghawi's *Ma'alim al-tanzil*, this latter work was itself to act as an exegetical ancestor for subsequent Arabic language commentaries. The third generation in an Arabic trilogy of narrative commentaries is represented by the work by al-Khazin (d. 1340), *Lubab al-ta'wil fi ma'ani al-tanzil*. This writer gained a significant following beyond the Arab world because of the widespread appeal of the stories contained in his commentary. Ironically, al-Khazin in a sense hijacked a significant part of al-Baghawi's popularity, for he reported the latter's stories generally verbatim, but his popular appeal appears to have surpassed that of al-Baghawi.

Details about the life of al-Khazin are sketchy. He was born in Baghdad in 678/1279,[22] but spent the bulk of his life in Syria, eventually dying at Aleppo in 741/1340. He is described by his contemporaries as very learned. His two principal writings were as follows:

- The Qur'anic commentary entitled *Lubab al-ta'wil fi ma'ani al-tanzil*
- *Maqbul al-manqul* in ten volumes

Al-Khazin depended very heavily for his commentary writing on al-Baghawi's *Ma'alim al-tanzil* as his principal source. This degree of dependence is clearly indicated by the alternative title of *al-Ta'wil li-ma'alim al-tanzil* for al-Khazin's commentary.[23] In his introduction, al-Khazin describes al-Baghawi's work as one of the

---

[22] Al-Dawudi n.d., vol. 1, 427.
[23] Al-Dawudi n.d., vol. 1, 427.

great commentaries, and explains his choice of it as a base for his own work by referring to it as 'a collection of the most reliable of the prophet's sayings, free from specious entries, distortion, and alteration ...'[24]

Given his dependence upon al-Baghawi, it is not surprising that al-Khazin's exegetical style is narrative-based and draws heavily on the Tradition collections of Bukhari, Muslim, Abu Da'ud, al-Tirmidhi, al-Kisa'i, and others. As a result of this eclecticism, the *Lubab al-ta'wil fi ma'ani al-tanzil* contains a wide variety of accounts based in history, as well as many elements drawn from Judeo–Islamic traditions, termed the *Isra'iliyyat*[25] in Muslim circles.

Al-Khazin's *Lubab al-ta'wil* has a mixed reputation in the Arab world, as many consider that it draws too heavily upon these stories brought into Islam by converts from Judaism. Such stories contribute to a narrative-based style of exegesis somewhat reminiscent of the Jewish *Aggadah*. However, this story-based style has a strong appeal to certain readers, including many in the Islamic states of Southeast Asia, where in contrast to its reception in the Arab world, the narrative style of exegesis of al-Baghawi and al-Khazin achieved a considerable degree of popularity, because of the important role of story-telling in local folklore and religious practice.

Al-Baydawi's Anwar al-tanzil wa asrar al-ta'wil

Another important commentator from the classical period whose work became popular in Muslim Southeast Asia was 'Abd Allah ibn 'Umar al-Baydawi (d. 1286). Like so many of the classical exegetes, al-Baydawi was of Persian ancestry. He produced a Qur'anic commentary, entitled *Anwar al-tanzil wa asrar al-ta'wil* (The Lights of Revelation and the Secrets of Interpretation), which employs a technique of phrase-by-phrase exegesis. This commentary was notable for a number of reasons.

First, he was writing within two hundred years of the great debate between the rationalist Mu'tazila and their more literalist, scripturalist adversaries, the *ahl al-hadith*. One of al-Baydawi's

---

24 Al-Khazin n.d.: vol. 1, 3. Arabic text: *jami'an li al-sahih min al-aqawil, 'ariyan 'an al-shabah wa al-tashif wa al-tabdil.*
25 Refer to the detailed discussion of the *Isra'iliyyat* in chapter 5.

great successes was in finding a formula for drawing upon some of the great Mu'tazilite writers while still being considered to remain within the boundaries of what had become orthodox thought. Indeed, his commentary is widely regarded as an abridgement of the Mu'tazilite commentary by al-Zamakhshari,[26] in much the same way that al-Khazin's work was closely based on the commentary of al-Baghawi.

Second, his commentary serves as a valuable compendium comprising wide ranging elements of the Islamic sciences. It presents linguistic information, including details on the variant readings of the Qur'anic text, narrative accounts, philosophical speculations and other key features, yet it manages to present this information in a compact study. Consider the following eclectic commentary on part of Q3:120:

(their guile has not hurt you at all); by the mercy of God, and His performance of His promise to those who persist and fear; and because whoever is zealous in the matter and accustoms himself to caution and persistence will suffer little and be bold against the enemy. The second *u* in *yadurrukum* (shall hurt you) is due to the attraction of the previous *u* like that in *muddu* (stretch out). Ibn Kathir, Nafi', Abu 'Amr and Ya'qub read *yadirkum* from *dara* with the same meaning.[27]

Third, *Anwar al-tanzil wa asrar al-ta'wil* is also useful in presenting a range of opinions drawn from his exegetical predecessors, as seen in the following translation of al-Baydawi's commentary on another part of Q3:120:

(Verily God comprehends what ye do); what ye do in the way of patience, fear, etc. Literally, 'causes His knowledge to surround', so that He will recompense you according to what you deserve. Others read 'what *they* do', i.e. in their enmity against you; so that He will punish them therefor.[28]

It should be noted in this excerpt, and elsewhere, that al-Baydawi does not always bother to provide a meticulous list of the sources of his varying accounts, nor does he indicate his own preferred option among these varied accounts, as al-Tabari tended to do.

---

[26] Robson 1979b:1129; Gatje 1996:36.
[27] Margoliouth 1894:84.
[28] Margoliouth 1894:84–5.

The principal reason for the widespread popularity of this commentary throughout the Muslim world, including Southeast Asia, is that it serves as a ready reference on a host of significant topics, and it presents its information in a manner which is both scholarly and accessible.

The Jalalayn

The commentary known as *Tafsir al-Jalalayn* (The Commentary of the Two Jalals) was written by Jalal al-Din al Mahalli (d. 1459) and Jalal al-Din al-Suyuti (d. 1505). The former was the teacher of the latter, and commenced the writing of the commentary, but the completion of the work was undertaken by al-Suyuti.

The Jalalayn commentary includes an ongoing paraphrase of the Qur'anic text, though in less detail than al-Baydawi's commentary. The following example represents Jalalayn comment upon Q2:8–9:

> (Among men are those who say, we believe in God and in the Last Day) – that is the Day of Resurrection, because it is the last of days: (but they are not believers. They endeavour to deceive God and those who have believed,) by making a show of the reverse of the infidelity that they conceal; (but they deceive not any except themselves;) for the punishment of their deceit shall come upon them, and they shall be disgraced in this world, in consequence of God's acquainting His Prophet with that which they conceal, and shall be punished in the world to come; (and they know not) that they deceive themselves.[29]

The textual paraphrase provided in the Jalalayn is supplemented by linguistic explanations, including information on the variant readings, and material from the Hadith and narrative elements. Thus, like the commentary by al-Baydawi, the Jalalayn provides its readers with a taste of wide-ranging Islamic sciences.

However, as can be seen from the above excerpt, it is relevant for a much more broad-based and less specialised audience than al-Baydawi's work. It is a very clearly arranged compendium, with exegetical comment provided in a quantity sufficient to elucidate the Qur'anic text, but not so voluminous that it drowns the scriptural core of the work. It generally avoids identifying sources of its various comments, and is clearly dedicated to imparting a didactic message without getting bogged down in scholarly detail. In

---

[29] Denffer 1994:137–8.

short, it is 'an ideal pedagogical tool for introductory studies into Qur'anic exegesis'.[30]

The Jalalayn commentary has played a major role in the education of countless millions of Muslims throughout the world, including Southeast Asia, during a period spanning five centuries. Though it has sometimes been regarded with a degree of disdain by specialists because of its relative accessibility to non-specialist readers, its importance as a work lies in the very fact that it was accessible to ordinary Muslims who could not engage with more specialised commentaries such as those by al-Tabari, al-Baydawi or al-Razi. The Jalalayn commentary has been translated into many non-Arabic Muslim languages, including Malay, where it served as the core for 'Abd al-Ra'uf al-Singkili's commentary in Malay written around 1675. 'Abd al-Ra'uf's work will be examined in more detail in chapter 8.

---

[30] Riddell 1990a:64.

5

LAW AND STORIES

ISLAMIC LAW

The life of a Muslim is traditionally governed by the twin science of Theology and Law. Theology provides a framework for religious belief, while Law provides a framework for actions.

Law plays the primary role,[1] and the Islamic sacred law, the *shari'a*, differs greatly from western ideas of law. First and primarily, it is much wider in its application, for it includes all human action in its scope: public and private actions, national and international situations, as well as the details of religious ritual and the ethics of social conduct. Second, the *shari'a* differs fundamentally from western law in that it is not man-made, according to Muslim belief, but is considered by Muslims to be grounded on divine revelation as revealed to the prophet Muhammad. The term *shari'a* occurs in the Qur'an – it is translated as '(right) Way' by Yusuf Ali in the following excerpt from Q45:18 – and its mention in the scriptures is considered as affirming its divine origins:

Then We put thee on the (right) Way of Religion: so follow thou that (Way) ...[2]

Q45:18

In addition to differences between Islamic law and Western law, which are to be expected, there exists a degree of variety within Islamic law as practised across the Muslim world. This relates to two principal areas: various schools of law have

---

1 Rippin 1990:74; Esposito 1991:75; Watt 1994:3.
2 Ali 1989:1297. The Arabic text is as follows: *thumma ja'alnaka 'ala shari'a min al-amr fa-ttabi'ha ...*

50

developed within Islamic orthodoxy, in addition to which various applications of these schools have emerged according to geographical location. Moreover, there are fundamental differences in approaching the law between Sunnis and Shi'ites from the standpoint of who has the authority to interpret it. This latter distinction will not be addressed here, given the overriding predominance of Sunni Islam in the Malay world.

Muslims in the Malay–Indonesian world since the earliest period of Islam have had two principal points of reference with regard to regulating their daily lives: their local customary law, or *adat*, and the detailed rules and regulations of the *shari'a*, known as *fiqh*. These have at times been supplemented by various civil-law codes which further complicate the picture. The net result has been that in some instances there has occurred a local 'fine-tuning' of Islamic law since the earliest period. This process has produced certain idiosyncratic features of Islamic law as practised in Southeast Asia. This issue will be explored further in subsequent chapters.

The emergence of the four schools of law

In significant recent research, Dutton has engaged with the long-running debate between Muslim scholars and Western revisionists concerning the emergence of Islamic jurisprudence.[3] Dutton articulates a ground-breaking third line of argument, based on his study of Imam Malik's *Muwatta'*. Enticing as this subject is, we will nevertheless not engage with the details of the debate, but will rather present the viewpoint most likely held by the vast majority of Islamic scholars in the Malay world concerning the origins of Islamic jurisprudence.

In the decades following the death of Muhammad in 632 CE, the Muslim authorities were too absorbed by the problems of administration arising from extensive military conquests to give priority to the elaboration of law. During the period of the Rightly Guided Caliphs (632–61 CE), it was the Caliphs themselves who served as principal and supreme legal authorities.[4] As Schacht comments, 'During the greater part of the first century Islamic Law, in the technical meaning of the term, did not

---

[3] Dutton 1999.
[4] Schacht 1964:14; Esposito 1991:76.

as yet exist.'[5] However, during the Umayyad caliphate a class of scholars (*'ulama'*) began to develop; moreover, the Umayyads established the office of *qadi* (judge), leading to the emergence of a nascent Islamic legal system. These *qadis* were drawn from a class of pious specialists who were concerned with reviewing wide-ranging matters of a legal and ethical nature, including the customary law adhered to by the prophet's Muslim community in Medina, with a view to systematisation.[6] From their efforts the earliest collections of *fiqh* began to emerge around the end of the first century of the Muslim era. However, the development of a fully-fledged and standardised Islamic legal system had to wait until the 'Abbasids wrested control of the Muslim empire from the Umayyads.

The early jurists came to be influenced by Roman, Byzantine, Rabbinic and Sassanian law, since during the first century with the territorial expansion of the Muslim realm, the Arabs came into contact with the customary law of the conquered territories. Moreover, influences from other legal, religious and social systems were brought into Islam by converts. Through these processes a number of specific rules of law of alien origin became incorporated in the nascent *shari'a*.[7] The result was considerable diversity in legal standards from one part of the Islamic empire to the other. The Qur'an was not a sufficient instrument in itself for establishing standard laws throughout the Islamic empire, as it was not intensively devoted to legal situations or judgements; only around 600 of its approximately 6,000 verses were concerned with matters of law.[8] Hence in the many legal circumstances where the Qur'an was not prescriptive, jurists and judges formed their own guidelines according to local context. Diversity resulted.

Criticism of this empire-wide legal eclecticism resulted in attempts to reform and standardise the Islamic legal systems which were emerging. A potential method of standardisation which could effectively supplement Qur'anic pronouncements was found in the *sunna*, or established Islamic practice. However,

---

[5] Schacht 1964:19.

[6] Schacht 1964:26–7.

[7] In a way reminiscent of the *Isra'iliyyat* described later. Rippin (1990:75) argues that Jewish and Roman Law came to represent the two principal ingredients of the emerging Islamic Law.

[8] Esposito 1991:77.

the *sunna* was not interpreted uniformly and it took some time for it to signify universally the practice of Muhammad; as Guillaume says, '*sunna* was first ancient custom, then contemporary, immediate past practice, and finally the ideal behaviour of the prophet as enshrined in tradition'.[9]

Because of the above situation, the early scholars came into conflict regarding the mechanism for establishing standardised legal systems. While there was general agreement on the need for establishment of standard legal procedures and judgements, there was disagreement on the question of how to achieve this. Some firmly advocated that the Hadith materials should be the principal focus to augment Qur'anic pronouncements, and this same group opposed a primary role for human powers of reason in determining legal formulae. In opposition to this group were those who wished to place a heavy emphasis on reason as the principal mechanism to augment the Qur'an in determining the eventual shape of a standard Islamic legal system.[10]

Different schools of law emerged, depending on both geographic location – Basra, Kufa, Medina and Damascus – and opinion regarding the respective roles of Hadith and reason. Under the influence of the great Islamic jurist al-Shafi'i (d. 819) these schools accepted the thesis that any authentic tradition of Muhammad's actions must be accepted as authoritative in terms of formulation of the law. Thus the *sunna*, now clarified as signifying the proven practices of the prophet,[11] came to represent one of the four valid sources of *fiqh*. The other three were the Qur'an itself, the consensus (*ijma'*) of the scholars, and analogical reasoning (*qiyas* or *ijtihad*)[12]; together these four sources constituted the *usul al-fiqh*, or rules of jurisprudential theory. Al-Shafi'i had made a major contribution to reconciling what had hitherto appeared to be unbridgeable gulfs between competing legal authorities.

The agreement that the practice of Muhammad should constitute one of the essential sources of law increased the need for authoritative collections of Hadith to be assembled – collections which supposedly only included Traditions which could be

---

9 Guillaume 1956:92.
10 Esposito 1991:77.
11 Schacht 1964:47.
12 Rippin 1990:80; Esposito 1991:83.

attested to have come from Muhammad himself.[13] A lengthy process ensued whereby the vast numbers of Traditions circulating were culled to form six collections regarded as authoritative by Sunni orthodoxy: those of al-Bukhari, Muslim, Abu Dawud, al-Nisa'i, al-Tirmidhi and Ibn Maja.

There was a certain amount of ongoing division of opinion among the schools on methods. Hallaq demonstrates that it took almost a century before al-Shafi'i's *usul al-fiqh* was to assert itself in the ongoing struggle between rationalists and traditionalists.[14] Nevertheless, by the end of the 10th century the consolidation of the four large schools of law was complete, and this situation has survived until now in Sunni Islam.

- The Hanafi school originated from the school of law in Iraq and was named after its leading scholar Abu Hanifah (d. 150/767)
- The Maliki school developed from the school in Medina and was similarly named after its leading scholar Malik b. Anas (d. 179/796)
- The Shafi'i school derived from the followers of al-Shafi'i
- The Hanbali school developed from the teachings and writings of Ibn Hanbal (d. 241/855)

The Hanbalite school was notable in prioritising Tradition over analogical reasoning, whereas the Malikites allocated no overriding authority to the Hadith accounts.[15] The Hanafites were the strongest advocates of the use of *qiyas*,[16] a position strongly opposed by the Hanbalites. Over the centuries, the Hanbalite school came to represent one of the most conservative, scripture-based forces within the diverse faces of Sunni Islam.

Although these four schools of law differ from each other in a number of particulars,[17] each nevertheless acknowledges the orthodoxy of its fellows. The Hanafites are the most numerous and widespread, largely because they were the only group afforded

---

13 Guillaume 1956:89.
14 Hallaq 1993:601.
15 Guillaume 1956:99.
16 Watt 1994:8.
17 E.g. Hanafites only allow for the eating of fish among the aquatic species, whereas the Malikites accept the eating of all aquatic species (Rippin 1990:82).

official recognition during the Ottoman period.[18] Their respective centres of strength are as follows: [19]

- Hanafites – Iraq, Syria, Afghanistan, India, Turkish Central Asia.
- Malakites – North and West Africa, Upper Egypt.
- Shafi'ites – Lower Egypt, Hijaz, South Arabia, East Africa, coastal parts of India, Malaysia and Indonesia. This is the school which is of primary relevance for the purposes of this present study.
- Hanbalites – Saudi Arabia.

In addition to these orthodox schools, various heterodox schools of law have also survived, but none possesses the significance of the above-mentioned four groups.

In the earliest days, every adequately qualified jurist had the right to go back to the original sources and apply them to each problem which arose, but from about the end of the third century of the Muslim era, all subsequent generations of Sunni jurists were bound to accept the decisions of their great predecessors as authoritative. As a result, after a period of great legal activity and development, the law became increasingly fixed,[20] for as the years passed a dominant opinion asserted itself. Many scholars argued forcefully that the *shari'a* was permanent and needed no revisions to keep pace with social developments; in this they cited Qur'anic verses such as the following:

It is not fitting for a Believer, man or woman, when a matter has been decided by Allah and His Messenger, to have any option about their decision: if anyone disobeys Allah and His Messenger, he is indeed on a clearly wrong Path.[21]

Q33:36

This did not mean that there was no debate; indeed, throughout the course of Islamic history the debate has been ongoing between the adherents of Tradition, who claimed that established dogma should be accepted without question (*taqlid*) in interpreting the Law, and those advocating the use of reason (*ijtihad*) to question

---

[18] Heffening and Schacht 1979:163.
[19] Schacht 1964:65–7.
[20] Guillaume 1956:98.
[21] Ali 1989:1068 – "We must not put our own wisdom in competition with Allah's wisdom."

and re-examine established dogma. This debate has ebbed and flowed in its intensity.

Much of the *fiqh* came to be seen by some Muslims as remote from their daily lives. Developed largely by pious specialists and academic lawyers, a gap developed between law as written and law in actual practice. It was in the law of family relations – marriage, divorce, guardianship and succession – that the *fiqh* found its fullest expression. Nevertheless, Islamic communities around the world frequently adapted *fiqh* to their customary law in its daily application. Examples of this will be seen in the case of certain Malay–Indonesian communities in later chapters.

A feature of Western colonial rule in Muslim areas was that the colonial authorities often introduced reform of local legal systems, which had hitherto been based on *fiqh*. This had the effect of creating dual systems which ran concurrently; legal systems applying to matters of state administration which were based on Western civil-law codes, and *fiqh*-based systems which applied in the private domain. After the departure of the colonial powers, certain newly independent states of the Middle East, such as Egypt, Syria, Libya and Iraq, maintained elements of the civil codes at the level of state, but also introduced reforms to *fiqh*-based systems in the personal domain. For example, in 1953 Syria's new Law of Personal Status[22] required judicial permission for a polygamous marriage, and four years later the practice of polygamy was banned in Tunisia.[23] However, throughout most of the Arabian peninsula, local interpretations of Islamic law reign supreme, as they do in Iran. Only in Turkey has Islamic law been completely displaced before the courts since 1926, in favour of codes adopted from the West. Nevertheless, the drift towards modernisation of Islamic law and its partial displacement has been an essential ingredient in the rise of Islamist revivalism during the latter decades of the 20th century. This will be explored in more detail later in this present study.

---

[22] Commins 1995:159.
[23] Entelis 1995:236.

PROPHETHOOD AND ITS STORIES

In the area of prophethood and stories about prophets, there are striking parallels between Islam and its Semitic faith predecessors. For this reason, the following discussion will make reference to all three Semitic faiths, as this will provide crucial information for understanding certain tensions within Islam itself.

There is considerable overlap in the function of prophets within the biblical and Qur'anic contexts. Both depict the prophet as being a spokesman for God, whereby what the prophet says is actually of God, not of man.[24] The medieval scholar Ibn Khaldun portrays this prophetic role as mediator in the following terms:

Allah ... has ... chosen individuals from among mankind whom He has honoured by Himself speaking to them to mold [*sic*] them according to His understanding, and to make them the mediators between Himself and His servants.[25]

Moreover, in Islam, as in the Bible, the foretelling of future events was only an incidental part of the prophetic office, with the principal functions being to proclaim moral and religious truths and to correct abuses of which the religious community was guilty.

Islam teaches that prophets have been sent by God to all communities throughout the course of history. Three words are used in the Qur'an to refer to people designated by God to carry his message to humanity: *mursal* (envoy), *rasul* (apostle, messenger) and *nabi* (prophet). Some Muslim theologians distinguish between the latter two, and consider the former as a generic term. In commenting on Q22:52, the great Mu'tazilite exegete al-Zamakhshari (d. 1144) identifies messengers as those prophets who bear a new book from God, whereas non-messenger prophets are considered to bear no new revelation in book form but are sent to confirm the pre-existing *shari'a*.[26] All prophets, whether messengers or not, are considered to perform miracles. Likewise, in commenting on Q33:40, the great Traditionist and historian Ibn Kathir (d. 1373) makes the following statement:

---

24 Exodus 7:1, Jeremiah 1:9, Isaiah 51:16; Qur'an 96.
25 Ibn Khaldun *Muqaddimah*, translated in part in Jeffery 1958:134–6.
26 Al-Zamakhshari n.d. vol. 3, 18–19 – *wa al-farq baynahuma anna al-rasul min al-anbiya' man jam' ila al-mu'jiza al-kitab al-munzal 'alayhi, wa al-nabi ghayr al-rasul man lam yunzal 'alayhi kitab wa innama umira an yad'u al-nas ila shari'a min qablihi.*

Table 5.1. PROPHETS MENTIONED IN THE QUR'AN

Possible equivalent	Qur'anic prophet	Qur'anic reference
Adam	Adam	Q2:34; Q3:33; Q15:26–9 etc.
Enoch	Idris	Q19:56; 21:85
Noah	Nuh	Q7; Q10; Q11 etc.
	Hud	Q7; Q11; Q50
	Salih	Q11:61–68
Abraham	Ibrahim	Q2:125; Q3:96
Lot	Lut	Q7:80–4; Q27:54–8
Ishmael	Ismail	Q2:125–7
Isaac	Ishaq	Q2:136; Q2:140; Q3:84 etc.
Jacob	Ya'qub	Q2:132–3; Q2:136 etc.
Joseph	Yusuf	Q12
Jethro[a]	Shu'ayb	Q7:85
	Luqman[b]	Q31:12–19
Job	Ayyub	Q21:81–4; Q38:41–4
Moses	Musa	Q20:9–76
Aaron	Harun	Q7:111–51
Ezekiel[c]	Dhu'l-Kifl	Q21:85–6; Q38:48
Alexander the Great	Dhu'l-Qarnayn[d]	Q18:83–98
Samuel	Shamu'il	Q2:246–7
David	Dawud	Q38:17–30
Solomon	Sulayman	Q2:102; Q21:78–82 etc.
Elijah	Ilyas	Q37:123–32
Elisha	Al-Yasa'	Q6:86; Q38:48
Ezra	'Uzayr[e]	Q9:30
Jonah	Yunus	Q10
Zacharias	Zakariyya	Q3:37–41; Q19:2–11 etc.
John the Baptist	Yahya	Q3:38–41; Q19:7–15 etc.
Jesus	'Isa	Q3:45–59; Q19:16–34 etc.
	Muhammad	

Source: The information in this table represents an expansion of that presented in Knappert 1985:7–10.

Notes to Table 5.1

[a] The identification of Shu'ayb with Jethro is a matter of debate.

[b] Luqman's prophetic credentials are subject to debate (Jeffery 1958:130).

[c] The identification of Dhu'l-Kifl with Ezekiel is a matter of debate.

[d] Dhu'l-Qarnayn's prophetic credentials are subject to debate (Jeffery 1958:130).

[e] 'Uzayr's prophetic credentials are subject to debate (Jeffery 1958:130). Hamka refers to him as a prophet while Juwayni (cited in Peters 1990: vol. 1, 15) clearly does not.

This is the verse which stipulates that there will be no prophet after Muhammad; if no prophets are to come after him, then there will be no messengers after him, because the function of being a messenger is a specialised part of the function of prophethood. Every messenger is a prophet but not vice versa.[27]

However, some western scholars of the Qur'an pose searching challenges to this distinction. Jeffery[28] suggests that it was developed by later Muslim theologians, while Wansbrough comments similarly that 'rigorous and consistent distinction between the designations *nabi* and *rasul* is not justified by Quranic usage'.[29] The relatively late dates of al-Zamakhshari and Ibn Kathir seem to bear out these claims.

Table 5.1 lists the small number of prophets identified by name within the Qur'an, including Muhammad, and also identifies biblical and other equivalents advanced by some scholars.

Several points should be noted when examining this table:

1. Adam is the father of all in both Qur'anic and biblical traditions, being the first man created by God.
2. Abraham's two sons, Isaac and Ishmael, are both identified as prophets within the Qur'an. Ishmael is considered as the forefather of the Arabs, the race which took Islam throughout the world.

[27] Rippin and Knappert 1986:47.
[28] Jeffery 1958:30.
[29] Wansbrough 1977:54.

3. While most prophets named in the Qur'an have biblical counterparts, there are a number of significant biblical prophets who
   do not feature in the Islamic list, such as Amos, Isaiah, Jeremiah, and a number of others. It should also be noted that some
   equivalents drawn in this table, such as the identification of the
   Islamic prophet Dhu'l-Kifl with Ezekiel, are tenuous and open
   to debate.
4. Some Islamic prophets do not appear in the Bible, such as
   Hud, Salih and Luqman, who are all considered as Arabian
   prophets. Moreover, the prophetic credentials of some of the
   biblical equivalents listed are open to question; in the biblical
   tradition, David and Solomon function more as great kings
   than prophets, and John the Baptist's role appears to be somewhat enhanced in the Qur'anic view of prophecy compared
   with that of the Gospels. Alexander the Great has never been
   accorded prophetic status of any form within the biblical
   tradition.

Certain of the Islamic prophets are more prominent than others.
Nasr underlines this in saying, 'Jesus joins with Moses and Abraham to represent the ternary aspect of the monotheistic tradition
whose summation is to be found in the Prophet of Islam. In this
perspective, Abraham represents faith, Moses law and Christ the
spiritual way.'[30]

Christianity and Islam differ significantly with regard to the
role of Muhammad. As indicated in Table 5.1, Muhammad has
been allocated the status of final and greatest prophet within normative Islam. Wansbrough states on the basis of his detailed study
of the Qur'anic text that the Qur'an does not support a claim of
Muhammad's superiority over other prophets, saying that 'the
portrait of Muhammad emerged gradually and in response to the
needs of a religious community.'[31] However, such a view has no
currency among mainstream Muslim scholarship. Precedence is
allocated to Qur'anic verses which refer to Muhammad as 'the seal
of the prophets', and to Hadith accounts such as the following from
Muslim and Bukhari:

[30] Nasr 1981a:210.
[31] Wansbrough 1977:56.

It is related from Jabir that, 'The Apostle of God said, "I have been given five (qualities) which were not given to any before me. I have been given victory through fear (inspired by me) at a distance of a month's journey; and the world has been made a pure place of prayer for me … ; and plunder has been made lawful for me, and it was not made lawful for anyone before me; and I have been given intercession; and (formerly) a prophet was sent especially to his own nation, but I have been sent to all men generally."'[32]

Moreover, Muslims consider that the revelation of the Qur'an which was given to humanity through Muhammad served to supplant all revelations which preceded it; namely that given to Adam, the scrolls of Abraham, the Torah, the Psalms, and the Gospel.

Because of its entrenched suspicion of extant Christianity and Judaism, Islam rigorously avoids any attempt to portray it as derived from, or an offshoot of, those religions. Islam claims that all the prophets, going back to the time of Adam, were in fact Muslim, based on the notion that in Arabic the word 'Muslim' means 'one who submits (to the will of God)'. Islam teaches that the early Jewish communities did in fact hold a covenant with God, but forfeited God's favour by their continuous rebellion against God's wishes and commands. Islam claims a unique right to represent God's wishes through reference to the final revelation, the Qur'an and the prophetic Traditions (the *Hadith*).

Islamic prophets are assigned a regular set of characteristics. They are depicted as appointees of God, who are sent by him to engage with and, above all, to guide his community. Ibn Khaldun identifies four major hallmarks of prophets: the first and second relate to withdrawal and physical discomfort which characterise their receiving of divine revelation; the third is their integrity and wisdom, and the fourth is the 'wondrous signs (*khawariq*) … wrought by their hands as testimony to their truthfulness.'[33] A normative view adheres to a doctrine of prophetic impeccability (*'isma*). Al-Juwayni explains this by saying

---

[32] Goldsack 1923:285–6. Cf. also Rippin and Knappert 1986:48.
[33] Ibn Khaldun *Muqaddimah*, translated in part in Jeffery 1958:134–6.

that 'they should be impeccable ... to prevent there being anything to contradict what is indicated by [their] miracle[s]'.[34] Al-Juwayni goes on to qualify this somewhat to allow for the possibility of prophets committing venial sins. Support for this is provided in a number of Hadith accounts, such as the following from the collections of Bukhari and Muslim:

It is related from Abu Hurairah that, 'The Apostle of God said, "Abraham did not lie except on three occasions: two of them for the sake of God ..."'[35]

A number of 20th-century Qur'anic commentators develop this theme, and engage in rationalisation of prophetic oversights, such as Azad's treatment of Abraham and Jonah, and Chiragh 'Ali's exposition of passages relating to Solomon.[36]

Typically, Islamic prophets in the Qur'an encounter strong opposition from the majority of the community of which they are members, and this is also a feature of biblical prophethood.[37] This popular rejection leads to the downfall and destruction of the community in question. Only those few who are faithful to the prophets' injunctions and therefore to God's word find favour in the eyes of God.

The textual depiction of prophets within the Qur'an varies, with most accounts of Islamic prophets being rather telescopic compared to their biblical counterparts, though a small number are similar in length to their biblical equivalent. A particular case of lengthy Qur'anic prophetic narrative occurs with the story of the prophet Joseph, to whom an entire chapter of the Qur'an, Chapter 12, is devoted. The Joseph account is one of the most popular, colourful, and internally coherent of the Qur'anic prophetic narratives. Close examination reveals that the details of the Qur'anic account not only resemble those in the biblical account, but also include a range of extra information, drawn from non-biblical sources including presumably popular versions of this story from the Arabian community of the 7th century, including accounts found among the Jewish and Christian communities in that region. It is with this in mind that Rippin writes:

34 Al-Juwayni, *Kitab al-Irshad*, translated in part in Jeffery 1958:133–4.
35 Goldsack 1923:282.
36 Baljon 1968:71–2.
37 Wansbrough 1977:53.

… the context within which the Qur'an must be read is far more than the framework provided by the text of the Bible alone; rather, the living tradition of Judaism, Christianity and all the other faiths and folklore of the area are reflected in the Qur'an and provide the necessary background for its comprehension.[38]

Adang reaches a similar conclusion from her examination of Muslim writings on Judaism, and states:

… the biblical narratives in the Koran reflect the influence of apocrypha, pseudepigrapha, and *midrashim*, rather than canonical scripture, although some approximations to the biblical text do occur.[39]

Rippin conducts a comparative examination of the biblical and Qur'anic accounts of Abraham's attempted sacrifice of his son. The Bible presents this event at Genesis 22, allocating a total of nineteen verses to an account of the incident, which not only presents a moral but also contains the literary qualities required for an entertaining narrative. In contrast, the Qur'anic account, presented at Q37:101–9, devotes itself primarily to the presentation of the moral, summarising the event in a few brief verses and then devoting itself to statements of God's reward for goodness and kindness, and stating overtly that this event was designed as a test. Rippin also points to the ongoing debate within the Islamic tradition about the identity of the son who was the intended victim of sacrifice. A detailed examination of classical sources by Firestone reveals that some leading scholars such as al-Tabari favoured Isaac as the intended victim and others favoured Ishmael.[40] Whereas Isaac is clearly identified as the sacrificial offering in the Bible, modern Islamic scholars have reached unanimity on Ishmael as the offering when interpreting the Qur'anic passage, and generally ignore the debate which took place in classical Islamic sources.

The stories of the prophets

A key instrument throughout Islamic history for disseminating information about prophets is *Qisas al-anbiya'*, or the Stories of the (pre-Islamic) Prophets which abound in Islam. This title applies

---

[38] Rippin 1990:18.
[39] Adang 1996: 3–4.
[40] Firestone 1990: chapter 16.

to several collections of accounts dealing with the lives of many Old Testament prophets, Jesus, and various other figures.

The two principal collections were made by al-Kisa'i (d. 805) and al-Tha'labi (d. 1036),[41] the latter of whom was discussed earlier in the context of Qur'anic exegesis. These collections represented compilations of tales, both historical and legendary, originating from various groups in pre-Islamic Arabia, especially Jewish communities and Christian individuals and groups, who had long recounted Old Testament, New Testament and Apocryphal materials to Arab communities and probably to Muhammad himself. These prophetic stories gained a significant place in the corpus of Islamic literature because they resonated with the accounts of Muhammad's life, and he found the experiences of the earlier prophets to be relevant points of reference in his own ministry.

It is difficult to over-estimate the importance of the Stories of the Prophets as a device in the transmission of Islam across the centuries from the Middle East to outlying areas of the Muslim world. These Stories came to represent a particular genre, and popular storytellers throughout the Muslim world, including Southeast Asia, drew on the Stories of the Prophets in their activities.[42]

The Isra'iliyyat

An examination of prophetic narratives within the Qur'an with a simultaneous examination of parallel biblical passages reveals points both of intersection and of divergence. The explanation for these points of divergence predictably differs within the various faiths in question. Jews and Christians have traditionally accounted for a Qur'anic variation on a biblical theme by claiming this as evidence of Muhammad's imperfect knowledge of the biblical text.[43] Muslims, in response, claim that points of divergence are evidence of corruptions which have made their way into the biblical text and which, indeed, necessitated God's final revelation, the Qur'an.

---

[41] Nagel 1986:180.

[42] Knappert 1985:3.

[43] The Qur'an itself records that the Jewish contemporaries of Muhammad made this claim when his responses to their questions diverged from their own teachings.

It is important in this context to engage with the controversy surrounding the so-called *Isra'iliyyat*, or Judeo–Islamic traditions. These traditions refer broadly to stories brought into Islam either by former Jews who converted to the new faith, or by Muslims who gained access to these traditions through contact with Jewish and Christian communities.

There is evidence of early Jewish conversions to Islam during Muhammad's lifetime. Ibn Ishaq's record of the prophet's life indicates that a leading Medinan rabbi by the name of 'Abd Allah b. Salam accepted Muhammad's claim to be a prophet and exhorted his Jewish co-religionists to follow suit.[44] No doubt he brought a store of Jewish narratives with him into his adoptive faith. But the two principal names who acted as ultimate sources for the Judeo–Islamic traditions were Ka'b al-Ahbar (d. 652/3) who was born a Jew and converted to Islam in 638, and Wahb Ibn Munabbih (d. 728), a famous writer of the early Islamic period. There are conflicting accounts as to whether he was born a Muslim but had Jewish ancestry, or whether he was born a Jew and converted to Islam.[45]

Also important in the transmission of these accounts was Ibn 'Abbas, considered as the 'father of Qur'anic exegesis'.[46] Ibn 'Abbas' credentials as an orthodox Muslim are beyond question, in the eyes of orthodox scholars. Nevertheless, his own writings drew heavily on material obtained from Jewish converts to Islam,[47] including Ka'b al-Ahbar and Wahb b. Munabbih, and the very authority which accompanied his name ensured a smooth entry for many biblical and apocryphal stories into the emerging Islamic literary corpus in the formative period of Islam.

Reference to these traditions has most typically been called upon where Islamic scriptures, be they the Qur'anic text itself or the Traditions, have appeared to raise questions without providing answers, thus posing a challenge for scholars wishing to write commentaries upon the scriptural text in question. In order to fill the gaps, as it were, Islamic commentators sought explanatory

---

[44] Adang 1996:5.
[45] Adang (1996:11) concludes that he was born a Muslim, but a significant group of Islamic scholars, whom Adang identifies in a footnote to her study, considered that Wahb was born Jewish.
[46] Adang 1996:13; Peters 1994:13.
[47] Firestone 1990:9.

information from appropriate sources and these were at times provided by Jewish and Christian narrative materials. But such narrative accounts served a second purpose to supplement that of scriptural exegesis; they also provided an important and very successful mechanism of entertainment for Muslim communities around the world.[48] In this latter respect, the potential for imaginative expansion of the stories by skilled storytellers was to play a crucial role.

The stories which constitute the *Isra'iliyyat* are by no means uniform in form or style or, indeed, in subject matter. There are several different ways of categorising the *Isra'iliyyat*. The Encyclopedia of Islam identifies three types of narratives within these Judeo–Islamic traditions, as follows:[49]

1. Those presented for their historical value, which are relevant to particular Qur'anic passages, and which relate to biblical figures and especially prophets.
2. Narratives which relate to the *ahd bani Isra'il*, i.e. particularly to the period of the ancient Israelites, without necessarily placing any emphasis on particular prophets.
3. Fables based in folklore, often borrowed from Jewish or Christian sources.

The *Isra'iliyyat* can also be categorised along different lines. Some Muslim scholars take a different approach, distinguishing between the various *Isra'iliyyat* in terms of their relationship to the Qur'an, as follows:[50]

1. Those stories which are consistent in every way with the content of the Qur'an itself.
2. Those stories which are demonstrably false in that they are clearly seen to be at variance with Qur'anic content.
3. Those which add nothing of substance to the text of the Qur'an. A case in point is the story of the Seven Sleepers which occurs in Chapter 18 of the Qur'an and which is embellished by many Qur'anic commentators with details regarded by many to be of no relevance, such as the colour of the Sleepers'

48 Adang 1996:9.
49 Vajda 1978:211–12.
50 Hamka 1967:30.

dog. Ibn Taymiyya was particularly critical of this approach to exegesis.

Many of the narratives categorised as *Isra'iliyyat* came to be rejected after some time by many Muslim scholars for a variety of reasons; either they were clothed in folklore and fantasy, they were at variance with the Qur'an, or they added nothing of substance to the Qur'an. The reaction commenced during the latter half of the 8th century, when the most prominent religious scholars in the 'Abbassid Caliphate started proscribing Traditions which were considered to derive from foreign sources.[51] This was all part of the process which eventually led to the formulation of the canonical Hadith collections. The term *Isra'iliyyat* came to serve as a term of literary abuse, as it were. Firestone comments that, 'Labelling certain traditions as Israelite Tales eventually came to be a simple way of discounting their worth.'[52]

However, material deriving from biblical and extra-biblical resources had become thoroughly integrated into Islamic literature by this time, so much so that it was 'included in the most respected collections and cited freely in authoritative exegesis of the Qur'an'.[53] Firestone further argues that the degree of integration between biblical and apocryphal materials and the evolving corpus of Islamic literature merely reflected the considerable degree of cultural and ethnic assimilation between Jews, Christians and Arabs, which existed at the outset of Islamic history. He argues importantly as follows:

The Qur'an often makes reference to stories and legends of biblical characters ... without actually providing the narratives in the text. It assumes in homiletic fashion that the listener is already familiar with the broad topics being discussed.[54]

Throughout Islamic history, many great writers have continued to decry what they saw as the impregnation of Islamic scholarship by unreliable materials of foreign (mostly Jewish and Christian) origin. Such a practice was condemned by names as illustrious as

---

[51] Firestone 1990:9.
[52] Firestone 1990:13.
[53] Firestone 1990:10.
[54] Firestone 1990:9.

the great historian Ibn Khaldun, who pioneered modern historiographical method and who wrote:

> Historians, Qur'an commentators and leading transmitters have committed frequent errors in the stories and events they reported ... they did not probe with the yardstick of philosophy, with the help of knowledge of the nature of things, or with the help of speculation and historical insight. Therefore, they strayed from the truth ...[55]

But such statements never succeeded in eradicating the appeal of these stories for the Muslim masses throughout the world. These Judeo–Islamic traditions continued to serve an important interpretive function through a range of literary media, summed up well by Firestone who writes that 'they function as narrative exegesis to the Qur'an by interpretation through the medium of the story of legend'.[56]

[55] Ibn Khaldun 1967:11.
[56] Firestone 1990:14.

6

MYSTICAL BELIEF AND PRACTICE

Mysticism, or *tasawwuf*, is one of the principal subjects of study in the Islamic sciences undertaken by students in Islamic religious schools around the world. It has also long attracted the attention of Western scholars of Islam.

An examination of the verses of the Qur'an which are testimony to Muhammad's early experiences led some to conclude that he was in a trance-like state, perhaps similar to mystical trances and ecstasies, at the time that the Qur'anic text came to him. Muhammad came thus to be seen as the first Sufi by many mystics,[1] and he was to serve as a model for subsequent generations of spiritual seekers. In the decades following his death groups of Muslims inclined to ascetic practice emerged throughout the Arabian peninsula, drawing for their inspiration both on the prophetic model, but also possibly on mystical practices undertaken by Christian communities with whom they had contact.

A wave of asceticism developed during the early period of 'Abbasid rule, following the victory of this dynasty over the Umayyads in 750. Among the most famous of these early ascetics was the female saint Rabi'a (d. 801), who is most famous for her poetic focus upon the love and mercy of God.[2] Contemporary with her were many other great ascetics who came to be viewed as saints and whose tombs, like that of Rabi'a, in time came to represent sites for pilgrimage of their followers, for the primary purpose of seeking their intercession with God.[3]

---

[1] Knysh 2000:5.
[2] Williams 1961:142–3.
[3] Clarke 1995: vol. 3, 461.

The influence of Christianity upon early Muslim mystics is suggested by many scholars. This is based on a number of factors, including the choice of these early ascetics to wear woollen garments as a distinctive mark of their group identity, which was also a feature of Christian monks of the period. Moreover, the identification in the course of time of the prophet Muhammad with 'the Light of God', which appeared at an early point of Islamic history,[4] may have had a Christian source; he came to be regarded by some mystics as existing prior to the creation, as the Perfect Man in whom all the divine attributes are manifested, and as being the window through which the believer could see God himself.[5] This theme is picked up regularly by Southeast Asian Sufi writers between the 16th and the 18th centuries.

In time asceticism gave way to ecstatic mystical experience among Muslims inclined towards Sufism, with this new phenomenon first attributed to the Egyptian Sufi Dhu'l-Nun (d. 861).[6] Such ecstatic states were considered as a means to search for and find the divine being and to engage in a love relationship with God. In the process, the individual would aim to follow a path leading to the metaphorical death of his material self and worldly desires in favour of attaining a state of *fana'*, representing the extinction of the personal self. The early Sufi Junayd (d. 910) articulates this well in writing, 'Sufism means that God makes you to die to yourself and makes you alive in Him.'[7]

The transition from initial asceticism to ecstatic trances, in search of knowledge of God, as described above, was inevitably to lead to further developments in mystical thinking which came to be regarded by some authorities as pantheistic and heterodox. The most famous early name in this tendency was that of al-Hallaj (d. 922) who taught that in seeking to know God the believer could in fact attain a measure of union with the divine via the God in himself. Al-Hallaj was executed for such statements, which were

---

[4] Hermansen 1998:224. Hermansen provides a fascinating discussion of this concept in Sufi exegesis.

[5] Nicholson 1914:82ff.

[6] Knysh 2000:40.

[7] Williams 1961:146.

considered by the authorities as heretical. However, his execution did not mean the end of the movement which he represented. Many Sufis continued along the path made famous by al-Hallaj and identified themselves with his doctrine of *Wahdat al-shuhud*, meaning 'Unity of Witness', signifying the identification of and witness to God within the heart of the believer.[8] Indeed, al-Hallaj himself was directly involved in the spread of Islam to India and his name is venerated greatly by Muslims in Gujerat, which played an important role in the spread of Islam to Indonesia. Hence Zoetmulder speculates that al-Hallaj's mystical ideas may well have been of particular significance to the Southeast Asian face of Islam.[9]

The adherents of the *Wahdat al-shuhud* doctrine in time came to encounter competition from adherents of a doctrine which was accused of being even more heterodox; namely that of *Wahdat al-wujud* (the 'Unity of Being') which dominated Islamic mysticism in the 12th and 13th centuries. This doctrine rejected the implicit dualism contained in the *Wahdat al-shuhud* doctrine, which had seen the mystic following a path which led to a union of sorts with the creator, but only after a period of dualistic separation.[10] Rather the adherents of the Unity of Being doctrine took a monistic view of the creation whereby all creation was seen as an inevitable manifestation and component part of the deity, and the mystical experience merely accentuated the individual's realisation of this fact and his discovery of his own godly attributes. In this view adherents sought and found support from certain cryptic Qur'anic verses such as the following:

And call not, besides God, on another god. There is no god but He. Everything (that exists) will perish except His own Face, to Him belongs the Command, and to Him will ye (all) be brought back.

Q28:88

Discussion thus far has touched upon the monism–dualism dichotomy, and any examination of Sufism will inevitably encounter discussion of the phenomenon of pantheism. Before proceeding further, it would be of benefit to distinguish between

---

8 Williams 1961:148.
9 Zoetmulder 1995:28.
10 Anderson 1990:75.

these terms. Zoetmulder conducted a valuable examination of the phenomena of pantheism and monism within Islam and distinguished between them by relating them to God: in pantheism, the world is seen to merge with God, or to become part of God's being (unity in diversity), whereas in monism God merges with the world (diversity in unity). Zoetmulder points out, however, that both phenomena have their roots in the tenet of the oneness of all Being; he suggests that in order to assess whether a particular doctrine is pantheist or monist, one should determine whether the starting point is the world or God.[11]

An examination of three prominent Islamic mystics – al-Hallaj, al-Ghazali and Ibn al-'Arabi – lead Zoetmulder to reach some important conclusions, namely that al-Hallaj was not in fact heretic or pantheist or monist; the union of God and mankind as he conceived it was 'a wonderfully close one, but there is no question of achieving identification'.[12] Thus even in his most advanced form of mystical ecstasy, al-Hallaj still envisaged a broader context of dualistic separation between Creator and creature. Al-Ghazali, famous for his role in cementing Sufism within Islamic orthodoxy by reinforcing the essential separation between Creator and creature in Sufi teaching, avoids any accusations of being pantheist or monist.

Ibn al-'Arabi (d. 1240), however, does not escape so lightly, and Zoetmulder demonstrates through an examination of his teachings that the great 12th-century Spanish mystic was monist to the core.[13] This is clearly evident when he writes '... when you know yourself, your "I" ness vanishes and you know that you and God are One and the Same'.[14] To him, Muslim mystics as far afield as India and the Malay–Indonesian world were to look for their inspiration and indeed were to base many of their writings upon his own prolific literary works. Ibn al-'Arabi's acknowledgment of the other monotheistic faiths of Judaism and Christianity, as well as his conviction that his way was the True Way, is clear from the following quotation from his writings:

---

[11] Zoetmulder 1995:3.

[12] Zoetmulder 1995:36. Williams (1961:148) agrees with this assessment of al-Hallaj.

[13] Zoetmulder 1995:46. Williams (1961:152) also agrees with Zoetmulder's assessment of Ibn al-'Arabi.

[14] Williams 1961:155.

My heart has become capable of every form: it is a
pasture for gazelles and a convent for Christian monks,
And a temple for idols, and the pilgrim's Ka'ba
    and the tables of the Tora and the book of the Qur'an
I follow the religion of Love, whichever way his camels take.
My religion and my faith is the true religion.[15]

Another important name to mention in this context is Jamal al-
Din al-Rumi (d. 1273), the founder of the Mawlawiyya, known in
the west as the 'Whirling Dervishes'. The predominant theme in
Rumi's writings is the creatorship of God.[16] His view of the creation is encapsulated in the following quotation, which has distinctly monistic overtones:

Ye who in search of God, of God, pursue,
Ye need not search for God for god is you, is you!
Why seek ye something that was missing ne'er?
Save you none is, but you are – where, o, where?[17]

The mystical lyric poet of Persia, Hafiz (d. 1389/90), lived more
than a century after his Persian compatriot, al-Rumi, but his conviction in the unity of Creator and created was no less certain than
that of his predecessor, as seen in the following passage:

There was a man that God loved well;
In every motion of his mind, God dwelt;
And yet he could not tell
That God was in him, being blind:
Wherefore as if afar he stood
And cried, 'Have mercy, O my God!'[18]

Some Sufi groups became so bound up in their own search for
divine enlightenment that they neglected the basic requirements
of Islamic ritual, such as the Five Pillars of Islam and other aspects
of the *shari'a*. This was to provide ammunition for their opponents
in later polemics which were to break out throughout the Muslim
world from the 14th century onwards. One location where there

---

15 Nicholson 1914:105.
16 Schimmel 1978:226.
17 Nicholson 1914:119.
18 Arberry n.d.:83.

was a tendency to compromise orthodox Islamic practice with local pre-Islamic belief was in the Indian sub-continent, where Hindu traditions represented fertile ground for more mystically-inclined Muslims.

With time there was an increasing degree of fragmentation among Sufi trends. Some were accepted as falling within the bounds of orthodoxy, while others were accused of heterodoxy. The most significant name in the history of Sufism in terms of ensuring its place within orthodox Islamic thought was the afore-mentioned al-Ghazali (d. 1111). After studying various Islamic sciences in depth and attaching himself to various groups – groups which included philosophers, scholastic theologians, and Sufis – in his own personal search for the truth, al-Ghazali decided to follow the Sufi path himself. After spending a long period of time studying in a Sufi monastery, al-Ghazali came to the conclusion that the mystical path provided the surest way to attain a knowledge of God's love for his creation, but he stressed that this did not exempt the individual Sufi from performing the fixed Islamic rit-ualistic requirements. After reaching an enlightened mystical view of the faith, al-Ghazali felt better equipped to return to the Islamic sources – the Qur'an and the Traditions – to ensure that he was fulfilling all the requirements of the faith. He defined two key aspects of the duty of a Muslim: first, to fulfil the pillars of the faith laid down by the *shari'a*, and second, to search 'to be near the Almighty and to acquire the rank of the highest religious person-alities' – i.e. those Sufis who had come close to a knowledge of God. This twin concern is captured in the following quotation from al-Ghazali's writings:

… that man who only considers valid knowledge to be jurisprudence, theology, and exegesis of mass appeal, it is as if he does not know the var-ious kinds of knowledge, their elaborations, levels, truths, and their outer and inner dimensions. It is customary, however, that one who is ignorant of something rejects it. And that so-called scholar has not tasted the wine of the Truth and is not cognizant of direct knowledge from God …[19]

Thus al-Ghazali's great contribution is in providing Islamic mys-ticism with a framework for continuing to grow and develop yet

[19] Al-Ghazali, *al-Risalah al-laduniyah*, pp. 87–8, translation A. Godlas, 1998, [www.arches. uga.edu/~godlas].

remain in large part within the orthodox fold. However, as we have seen above, certain post-Ghazali Sufis such as Ibn al-'Arabi developed theosophies which subjected the relationship between Sufism and orthodoxy to severe trials.

A further key name in this context is 'Abd al-Karim al-Jili (d. *c.* 1410). This figure took the concept of the Perfect Man, pioneered by Ibn al-'Arabi and others, and developed it to its highest point in his work entitled 'The Perfect Man'. Al-Jili defined this concept as follows:

The Perfect Man is the Pole on which the spheres of existence revolve from first to last ... He has various guises and appears in diverse bodily tabernacles ... His original name is Muhammad ... In every age he bears a name suitable to his guide in that age ... I mean that the Prophet is able to assume whatever form he wishes ... [The Perfect Man's] heart is identified with the Throne of God, his mind with the Pen, his soul with the Well Guarded Tablet ... You must know that the Perfect Man is a copy of God ... As a mirror in which a person sees the form of himself, and cannot see it without the mirror, such is the relation of God to the Perfect Man ...[20]

Such thinking provided fertile ground to popular veneration of Muhammad, which in turn provoked a negative response from orthodox doctrine that Muhammad, though the greatest prophet, was nevertheless human in all respects. The concept of the Perfect Man was to be very influential in Sufism in the Indian subcontinent, and in turn, in Southeast Asia.

THE PRACTICE OF SUFISM

Unlike the case with certain Catholic orders, full withdrawal from the world is not encouraged within Islam; moreover celibacy is similarly discouraged as unnatural. There are, however, instances where Sufis withdraw from the world for limited periods to concentrate on the remembrance of God and to follow the path towards knowledge of God.

Given that the goal of the Sufi is to seek a personal knowledge of God, the stages to be followed in reaching this goal are clearly defined, though there is some difference between various Sufi groups. Typically, a seven-stage path is set for the aspiring Sufi

[20] Peters 1994:349–51.

initiate. After attaching himself to a recognised Sufi scholar, the initiate will be led along the various stages. The first stage for all the different Sufi groups is that of repentance for past sins and errors. Al-Ghazali has the following to say:

Tauba means repentance for a sin by taking promise not to do the same evil again and to return to God. Repentance is the beginning in the life of a person who intends to walk in the path of religion.[21]

There is considerable variety among groups regarding the stages following the initial stage of repentance. Many define subsequent stages in terms of abstinence, renunciation, poverty, patience, trust in God, and acquiescence or satisfaction.[22] While the aspiring Sufi is progressing along these stages under the guidance of his teacher, attention is given throughout to the mortification of his material self, which is regarded as essentially evil and the source of passion and lust; it is broadly equivalent to the Christian notion of 'the flesh'.[23]

In addition to progressing through the above-mentioned stages under the guidance of his teacher, the Sufi initiate will also encounter various states of being, though unlike the stages, the teacher is not in control of which states of being the initiate encounters; rather that occurs through the grace of God, according to Sufi belief.[24] These states include a variety of experiences, such as meditation, love, fear, hope, contemplation, and certainty.

Essential to the experience of the Sufi student in travelling the mystical path is the technique of *dhikr*, which consists of the repetition of the name of God or a particular religious formulaic expression including the name of God until the student falls into a state of trance, encapsulated by the notion of *fana'*. Again, there are various stages of *dhikr*, and these have been summarised by Louis Gardet[25] into three generic stages. The first of these, *dhikr* of the

---

21 Karim 1982: vol. 4, 1.
22 A clear set of guidelines for initiates is provided by Ibn al-'Arabi in his *Risala fi kunhi ma la budda minhu li al-murid* (Jeffery 1962:640–55). In this work none of Ibn al-'Arabi's monistic inclinations are evident. Rather the guidelines focus on a depiction of a transcendent God, a call for observance of the *shari'a*, and personal renunciation and control. This demonstrates the breadth of Ibn al-'Arabi's theology, and provides ingredients to those who argue that this classical scholar was not the unambiguous monist which some claim him to have been.
23 Anderson 1990:82ff.
24 Knysh 2000:304.
25 Gardet 1965:223.

tongue, focuses upon the physical activity of repeating the name of God. The second of these, *dhikr* of the heart, no longer has a focus upon physical articulation of the name of God, but represents the process of focusing upon God within the heart. By this stage the student is into the trance state. The final of the three stages, *dhikr* of the innermost being, is considered to be the point at which the unification of the self with God takes place. This final stage was not accepted by al-Ghazali and tends to be rejected by orthodox Sufism.

SUFI BROTHERHOODS

When the developing mystical tendencies in Islam moved from the stage of ascetic withdrawal to ecstatic seeking to know God in trance-like states, there was a simultaneous streaming into schools or brotherhoods. Groups of Sufis who had similar inclinations in their preferred practice and doctrine collected into schools and established convents or monasteries (known variously as *zawiyya* or *khanqa* depending on location in the Muslim world) which were reminiscent of Christian convents for monks. In this way, Sufi orders (or brotherhoods) developed, with each tracing itself back through successive generations of scholarly masters via a continuous spiritual chain to the message transmitted by Muhammad. Many saw this relationship in the form of a tree, with the knowledge revealed to Muhammad being transmitted through the tree of Sufism, with each brotherhood representing a leaf.[26]

In time, certain of the brotherhoods came to be more prominent than others within the Sufi fold. The most famous of these is arguably the Qadiriyya, which had adherents right throughout the Muslim world and still has a substantial following in many Muslim countries, especially in India. Another famous group, the Naqshbandiyya, was, like the Qadiriyya, taken to the Malay–Indonesian world by Malay scholars returning from a period of studies in the Arab world, and these brotherhoods subsequently spread throughout the Indonesian archipelago.

Sufi brotherhoods are in fact far too numerous to list, except in a specialist study such as the excellent works by Nicholson and Trimingham.[27] The differences were not only regional, although

[26] Cf. diagram in Stoddart 1979:43.

the different geographical location was often a cause for the development of a distinctive brotherhood. However, other distinctive characteristics for each brotherhood related to the worship practices of the particular brotherhood, especially in the area of *dhikr*, with distinctive approaches to physical posture, breathing technique, use of music, etc. Sometimes particular communities and whole cities have grown up about the tomb of a saint, such as the city of Fez in Morocco which developed around the shrine of its founder and patron saint, Mullah Idris.

The title of saint (*wali*) was accorded to those who, in popular perception, were possessed by God.[28] Such saints often became famous for their performance of miracles, such as walking on water, appearing in various places at the same time, healing by the breath, and bringing the dead to life.[29] The veneration in which tombs of saints are held is an extension of the veneration accorded to Muhammad's tomb at Medina, where pilgrims can obtain blessings, or *barakat*, to assist them in their daily living and help them overcome hurdles. Such *barakat* are seen as deriving not from the master but from God.

Sufism is not the preserve of male Muslims; the early saint Rabi'a was testimony to this. Many women chose the Sufi path because of its relatively liberal approach to female participation.[30] There have been a significant number of female saints throughout the course of Islamic history, as well as countless individual female Muslims who have travelled the mystical path. Mention may be made of Shaikha Sultana of the Hadhramaut[31] and Jahanara Begum, the daughter of the Mughal Emperor Shah Jahan, whose tomb carries the following inscription and identifies her as an active member of the Chishtiyya order:

> Let nothing but plants cover my grave,
> For this is enough to cover the tomb of a stranger,
> The transient beggar woman Jahanara,
> Disciple of a Chishti master and daughter of Shah Jahan,
> The glorious ruler whose mind may God illumine.

[27] Nicholson 1914; Trimingham 1971.
[28] Nicholson 1914:125.
[29] Nicholson 1914:139.
[30] Jackson 1988:251.
[31] Stark 1936:207.

POPULAR SUFISM

Sufism represented a response by many Muslims throughout history to what they perceived as a dry orthodox practice of the faith, devoid of spirituality. The leading Sufis throughout the ages – al-Hallaj, al-Ghazali, Ibn al-'Arabi, Rumi, etc. – tended to be gifted intellectually and spiritually. Some of the greatest Islamic thinkers throughout the ages have been Sufis. But it was not only the intellectuals and spiritually gifted who were attracted to the mystical phenomenon. Indeed, vast numbers of Muslims who were never to leave a lasting mark on the world were also drawn to the spiritual quest, as is evidenced by the popularity of the various Sufi brotherhoods among the masses.

The popularisation of Sufism has been given various names by scholars and researchers. Some use the term 'Folk Islam', while others prefer to refer to the phenomenon as 'Popular Islam'.[32] The problem with either term is that each seems to draw a line between that term and Sufism. The resulting risk is that observers can miss the key fact that both Sufism and Folk or Popular Islam represent different dimensions to the same mystical quest. Therefore, this present study opts for the distinction between 'high' and 'popular' Sufism developed by Nicholson,[33] which effectively maintains a clear link between related phenomena.

Throughout Islamic history, a significant portion of the populations of Muslim communities world-wide has participated in worship practices which many Muslims consider to be beyond the boundaries of orthodoxy. For example:

- pilgrimage to graves of saints
- placing keys on the graves of saints in the belief that these keys will be endowed with the saint's *baraka* (blessing)
- praying to deceased saints
- seeking protection from jinn and the evil eye through the wearing of charms and amulets
- using the Qur'an as a physical remedy for illness (e.g. through drinking water in which a page of the Qur'anic text has been left to soak)

---

[32] Cf. Sikand 1996:16.
[33] Nicholson 1914:131, 139.

The occurrence of such practices throughout the Muslim world is widespread and in fact serves as a unifying thread at the level of popular Sufism throughout the far-flung corners of the Muslim world. Such practices were to provide grist to the mill of Islamic reformism, to which our attention is turned in the next chapter.

7

20TH-CENTURY ISLAMIC REFORMISM AND REVOLUTION

During the latter half of the 19th century, a new wave of theological and intellectual thinking swept through the Arab world in response to the perceived decline of Islam in the face of expanding European power. The cycle of Islamic reformist thought, which had so often come to the fore in the Muslim world during previous periods of decline, once again asserted itself as European domination seemed unstoppable. These currents were to unleash diverse reactions among Muslims during the 20th century.

A TYPOLOGY OF MUSLIM RESPONSES TO THE MODERN WORLD

Rippin and Knappert developed a very useful three-fold typology of these different Muslim responses to the challenges of modernity, as follows:[1]

1. A *Normative/Orthodox* group, which 'sees the past (as they [*sic*] envisage it) as legitimately leading to the present and that the past is sufficient to guide people today'.
2. A *Neo-normative/Revivalist* group which 'demands a reinterpretation of the present through a re-evaluation and recreation of the past such that it fits within the modern context'.
3. *Acculturationists/Modernisers* who 'tend to legitimise the modern context by reference to the past'.

---

[1] Rippin and Knappert 1986:29.

Such typologies are much disputed among scholars. Indeed, those typologies which are developed are usually subject to adjustment by their own authors. Thus Rippin subsequently refined the above classification, while in the process drawing heavily on the more specific typology of Muslims by Shepard.[2] The hybrid result includes the following broad categories:[3]

- *Traditionalists* are those who conceive of a continuum between the past and the present, with the past serving as a sufficient guide to deal with present issues and contexts. They see Westernisation as a threat but accept that established traditions can deal with this threat without needing to develop dynamic new responses.

- *Radical Islamists* insist on a reinterpretation of the present through a recreation of the past. Such groups wish to return to what they see as a model Medinan community established by Muhammad, but are suspicious of associations with and influences of the modern West. They long for an idealised, past 'Golden Age', and for them, the Qur'an and *Sunna* represent the central points of reference in all aspects of their worldview. It is to this group that the term 'fundamentalist' is best applied; this is because scripturalism represents the foundation of their approach.

- *Modernists* wish to maintain the unity of religion and politics but believe in the need to draw on elements of modern Western culture and lifestyle which could facilitate this overall goal. The influence of a westernised modern life is clear with this group. This particular approach has generated much intra-Islamic opposition, due to its development of controversial recommendations regarding the primary Islamic texts, such as the proposal by Ghulam Ahmad Parwez and his Pakistani research centre to demote the importance of Hadith as a tool for interpreting the Qur'an.[4]

- *Secularists* argue for the separation of religion and politics and in doing so are influenced by the modern West. Evidence of this approach can be seen particularly in modern Turkey. For such Muslims, Islam often becomes primarily a feature of cultural identity, rather than the essence of every aspect of their being.

---

[2] Shepard 1987.
[3] Rippin 1993:34-43.
[4] Baljon 1968:13.

In broad terms, the above typologies can be readily reconciled with each other. Traditionalists fall within Rippin's original Normative/Orthodox category, Radical Islamists are synonymous with Rippin's Neo-Normative/Revivalist category, while both Modernists and Secularists would fit under his original Acculturationist/Moderniser category. To this extent, a primary three-fold classification is arguably the most convenient for our purposes.[5]

Perhaps the key point of differentiation between the first two groups and the third is their angles of approach to the past and the present. Traditionalists and Radical Islamists see the answers to present problems being found in the past, and place a primary focus on an idealised past, though they would differ regarding methodology, with the latter group tending more towards revolutionary methods, while the former would incline more towards achieving their goals through established religious authority systems and structures. Modernists and Secularists, on the other hand, place a primary focus more on the present, and merely draw on the past as and when appropriate to inform their approach to present challenges. Like Radical Islamists, Modernists tend to eschew the existing religious authority structures which are so highly affirmed by Traditionalists, but unlike Radical Islamists, the Modernist agenda is one more of reform than revolution.

The evolution and manifestations of the above phenomena will now be examined through the lives and thought of key figures who have lived in the late 19th and 20th centuries.

PAN-ISLAM: JAMAL AL-DIN AL-AFGHANI

Arguably the great instigator of the Islamic reformist movement of a modernising type was Sayyid Jamal al-Din al-Afghani (1838–97). He was born and educated in Afghanistan, and by his twentieth birthday he had made the pilgrimage to Mecca. He spent time in India in these early years, where he was closely watched by the British administration, who saw him as a potential subversive because of his increasingly ardent Islamic activism and criticism of

---

5 Kurzman (1998:5-6) similarly employs a threefold typology which closely parallels that of Rippin and Knappert, though using different labels. Thus he identifies Customary Islam (= Orthodox Traditionalism), Revivalist Islam (= Neo-normative Radicalism) and Liberal Islam (= Modernising approaches).

colonialism. He left the British-controlled dominions and moved to Istanbul, arriving there in 1870. Al-Afghani soon made enemies, however, with the vested interest groups among traditionalists in the Ottoman capital, and he left shortly afterwards.[6] Al-Afghani had thus, by the age of thirty-five, developed an antipathy to core policies of the two greatest powers in the Muslim lands: Britain and Turkey.

Al-Afghani arrived in Cairo in March 1871, and this was to mark the beginning of a lengthy and productive period for him. He was enthusiastically welcomed by the Egyptian government of the time, which awarded him a generous annuity. He remained there until September 1879, during which time he met with and greatly influenced such future great Islamic scholars as Muhammad 'Abduh, who was subsequently to become the Grand Mufti of Egypt, and the nationalist leader Sa'ad Zaghloul. Al-Afghani collected around him a group of leading Muslim thinkers. He forcefully encouraged the local press to oppose colonialism, he helped found journals, and he helped encourage young thinkers to publish pamphlets and various forms of printed media criticising the western colonial powers. However, he also made enemies among the traditionalist scholars of al-Azhar and the Council of Ministers. He was again closely watched by the British, and was ultimately expelled from Egypt in 1879.

From there he returned to India, where he wrote his famous work *The Refutation of the Materialists*. A large part of this work was devoted to attacking the Darwinian theory of evolution. Al-Afghani praised religious faith and claimed that secularist atheistic materialism led to decadence, debasement and decay.

From India, al-Afghani progressed to London and Paris in 1883. While there he campaigned actively against the policies of the British in Muslim countries. He met up once again while there with Muhammad 'Abduh, and together they established an Arabic weekly, entitled *al-'Urwa al-wuthqa*, in which they attacked British policies and actions in the Muslim world, and emphasised the doctrinal grounds on which Islam should base itself in order to recover its previous greatness and strength. This journal served above all to outline the framework of Muslim reformist thinking

6 Goldziher and Jomier 1965:417.

of the Salafi movement.[7] It was banned in Egypt and India by the British authorities.[8]

In 1885 there was a parting of the ways between al-Afghani and 'Abduh. The former stayed on in Europe while 'Abduh went to Beirut. In subsequent years, al-Afghani spent time in both Persia and Russia. It was in a sanctuary near Tehran, where he spent a period of seven months, that he further developed and taught his theories of political reform to interested groups and young Islamic thinkers. The Shah of Persia, increasingly concerned by al-Afghani's potential for stirring up unrest, had him expelled, which was to cause a lasting sense of acrimony on the part of al-Afghani towards the Shah.

He launched into a period of denunciation of the policies of the Shah, such as the granting of tobacco rights to a British firm. This criticism was to have fruitful results, as the ensuing pressure forced the Persian government to cancel the contract and to compensate the British firm concerned. Al-Afghani then went to London for one year, and from there continued his vitriolic campaign against the Shah, demanding his deposition.

The last years of his life were spent in Istanbul on the invitation of Sultan Abdul Hamid. However, after a short time the relations between the two soured. On a number of occasions al-Afghani requested permission to leave but his requests were refused. Al-Afghani died on 9 March 1897; controversy surrounds his death, with some suggesting he was poisoned, others that he died from cancer.[9]

The ultimate objective of Jamal al-Din al-Afghani was to unite the Muslim states, both Shi'ite and Sunni, into a single Caliphate which would be strong enough to expel the Europeans and to destroy what he saw as the decadence that the Europeans had brought with them.[10] Rather than rejecting everything Western outright, he sought to draw on Western strengths and to express them within an Islamic framework, considering these strengths to have been integral to the periods of Islamic greatness throughout history.[11] In this, he laid firm foundations for 20th-century Islamic

---

[7] Shahin 1995:410.
[8] Goldziher and Jomier 1965:418.
[9] Goldziher and Jomier 1965:419.
[10] Rippin 1993:31.

modernist thinking. He pointed to Islam as a religion based on reason and science, and argued forcefully that Islam itself was ideally equipped to engage with modern civilisation on its own terms.

In addition to denouncing foreign powers and their control of Muslim countries, al-Afghani attacked Muslim rulers who opposed reforms, such as the Shah of Persia, and those who did not actively resist European encroachments. He preached a Muslim resurgence by use of the spoken and written word; indeed not only were his words and thoughts to exert a powerful influence throughout the Muslim world, but his actions, such as founding journals for the dissemination of his ideas, were to serve as a model for later generations of reformers throughout the Muslim world, including the Malay–Indonesian region.

MUSLIM MODERNISM: MUHAMMAD 'ABDUH AND RASHID RIDA

Muhammad 'Abduh (1849–1905) was, as we have seen, greatly influenced by his former mentor al-Afghani. He too observed a Muslim world faced with the clear dominance of the non-Muslim world via colonialism and deduced that the subjugation of Islam by the West was the direct result of the position of weakness in which Islam found itself and its penetration by non-Islamic principles. In his view God had deserted the Muslim world because it had allowed itself to become corrupted and polluted.

'Abduh's most influential written work is his *Theology of Unity*,[12] in which he reviews fundamental Islamic theological principles from a reformist standpoint. In this work he sought to reconcile Islam with reason and science, in order to develop al-Afghani's claim that Islam was in fact consistent with modern thought and discovery, rather than being in opposition to it as many claimed. He sought to demonstrate in this work that Islam was dynamic, rather than static; he did this by arguing that Islam made a fundamental distinction between core principles which were unchanging and external concepts which could adapt to changing circumstances. In this way he argued that Islam and modern civilisation were not mutually exclusive; rather Islam could and

[11] Esposito 1991:127.
[12] Abduh 1966.

should underpin modern advancements, while at the same time affirming its eternal premises, and that reformist modernising should be an ongoing process.

Another important forum which 'Abduh used to develop his ideology was provided by his lectures at al-Azhar university, where he had previously been a student. Between 1899 and 1905 'Abduh lectured on a range of topics, including exegesis of the Qur'an, and these lectures on exegesis were published in the periodical *al-Manar*. The various focuses of 'Abduh's commentary writing picked up on his key preoccupations discussed above, and were as follows:[13]

- Reassertion of the inimitability of the Qur'an.
- Presentation of the Qur'an as essentially consistent with modern science, though he carefully avoided suggesting that the Qur'an contained concealed references to later scientific discoveries.
- An avoidance of philological and syntactic analysis, thus discarding the practices of classical commentaries such as that of al-Baydawi.
- An avoidance of obscure terms.

In presenting his exegesis, 'Abduh was to apply modern practices of scriptural analysis focusing upon a concern for the reader, rather than an exclusive preoccupation with the text itself. His was the earliest of the modern commentaries to number each Qur'anic verse. Moreover, he demonstrated a concern for opening his reader's perceptions to the dimension of discourse. He did not limit himself to phrase-by-phrase exegesis, as was the case with al-Baydawi and other classical commentators, and he also sought to establish thematic connections among the chapters of the Qur'an.

Another great name in the modernist movement in Egypt who had considerable influence beyond the Arab world was Rashid Rida (1865–1935). Born and educated in Syria and Lebanon, he migrated to Egypt in 1897 for the express purpose of studying with Muhammad 'Abduh.[14] He served as editor of the reformist journal *al-Manar*, which gave him direct access to 'Abduh's

---

[13] McAuliffe 1991:84.
[14] McAuliffe 1991:81.

exegetical writings, which he revised, expanded and presented in the form of a published commentary, *Tafsir al-Manar*. In this he performed a crucial task in terms of developing modernist thinking. Only the commentary on the first one-and-a-half chapters of the Qur'an was printed at the time of 'Abduh's death,[15] so Rida's role in carrying on this task was invaluable. Rida's additions to 'Abduh's core commentary included addition of *asbab al-nuzul* tradition materials, some polemical material attacking Christian doctrines relating to the crucifixion of Christ and the Trinity,[16] as well as insertion of philological and syntactic discussion which 'Abduh had originally excluded. However, these additions did not significantly alter the accessibility of the work to non-specialist readers, as a lay audience remained the primary target of the *Tafsir al-Manar*.[17]

Rida stressed in his own writing that if the precepts of the Qur'an were not followed and implemented in Muslim life, weakness and decay would be the result, but that this Qur'anic living should be couched within a modern framework. Rida developed 'Abduh's thinking on the issue of *ijtihad*. He further clarified the distinction between acts of worship (*ibadat*), which were clearly set out in the Islamic scriptures and therefore were not subject to change, and matters concerning human interaction (*mu'amalat*), which were subject to reappraisal according to changing circumstances.[18] In the context of facilitating the engagement of Islam with modern science, Rida turned his attention to education and founded the School of Propagation and Guidance in 1912.[19] In this he served as an important model for the activities of contemporary and later reformists in the Malay–Indonesian world.

Thus, the modernist reformers, the movement deriving from the teachings of al-Afghani, 'Abduh and Rida, concluded that God would only permit a renaissance of Islam and a return to former glories when Muslims reformed themselves, with the reforms based on the Qur'an and the *Sunna*.[20] This reformism echoed

---

15 McAuliffe 1991:79.
16 Seferta 1986:10–15.
17 Seferta 1986:1, 15.
18 Shahin 1995:411.
19 Shahin 1995:411.
20 Rippin 1993:37.

ancient tensions between reason and revelation which had emerged in the early period of Islam. But the answer of the modernists was not to prioritise one at the expense of the other – though their emergence did represent a revival of the fortunes of the pro-reason camp – but was rather to seek a balance between the two, much as early reforming scholars such as al-Shafi'i and al-Ash'ari had done.

The 20th-century modernists advocated a four-fold programme:[21]

- a purification of Islam by eradicating western accretions.
- a reformation of the education system to re-establish Islamic principles.
- a greater emphasis on *ijtihad* rather than *taqlid*, or uncritical acceptance of religious dictates pronounced by religious authorities.
- and a reformation of Islamic doctrine to eliminate the increasing influence of the secular world.

According to the modernists, only if the above four goals were met would Muslims be able to participate and compete successfully in the modern secular world and still remain Muslim. Theirs was a reasoned response to the challenge from the West.

ISLAMIC RESPONSES TO DECOLONISATION AND BEYOND

In some Muslim states, wars of independence were fought while in others this did not occur. The former was the case in Indonesia, while the State of Malaysia in contrast achieved its independence through a peaceful process of transference of power from the British to local authorities. Nevertheless, whatever the means of obtaining independence, a need to define one's national, cultural and religious identity was felt among both Indonesian and Malay Muslims in order to identify their place in the modern world.

Even after independence, however, a sense of lingering subjugation was felt by many nationalities which had formerly experienced colonisation, due to the continuing state of overwhelming economic, technological and military superiority of the non-Muslim western powers. The initial sense of optimism and expectation which accompanied independence was not to last, as many

---

[21] Gibb 1947:33.

Muslim countries found the process of adaptation to the indus-trial world of the 20th-century with modern international eco-nomic systems a difficult hurdle to surmount.

In response, Muslim authorities in many countries adopted political, social and economic methods which were based on non-Muslim western models in an attempt to catch up with the West, as it were. In this, they were influenced in part by Muslim mod-ernist thinking, and in part by more secularist models of organisa-tion borrowed from the West. This was to prove a controversial approach which did not achieve the degree of success hoped for by the authorities concerned, inasmuch as such Muslim countries (e.g. Egypt, Turkey, Indonesia) have remained economically underdevel-oped compared to the prosperity enjoyed by the former colonial powers in the West. The effect of this perceived failure was dissat-isfaction amongst sections of the populations of Muslim countries and calls for a return to 'true' Islam. Such reactions were the breeding ground for the religious fundamentalism and political radicalism which has manifested itself in different ways through-out the Muslim world since the Second World War.

THE RADICAL ISLAMIST DIMENSION

Radical Islamism, or revivalism according to the Rippin typology, has flourished among the disadvantaged and have-nots through-out the Muslim world during the latter decades of the 20th cen-tury. It has based itself on an idealisation of early Islamic history, particularly as it related to the community of Muslims alive during Muhammad's prophethood. Radical Islamism has also been characteristically more revolutionary than reformist, seeing existing structures as inherently corrupt and therefore beyond redemption. Ayubi points out that the term 'political Islam' is best applied to radical Islamists as they 'are the ones that tend to emphasise the political nature of Islam, and to engage themselves in direct anti-State activities'.[22] He adds: '... political Islamists want to reverse the traditional relationship ... so that politics becomes subservient to religion, and not the other way round, as was the case historically.' [23]

---

[22] Ayubi 1991:69.
[23] Ayubi 1991:3.

Two leading radical Islamist thinkers of the modern era were Abul A'la Mawdudi and Sayyid Qutb.

Sayyid Abul A'la Mawdudi (1903–79)

The Indian subcontinent has produced a number of leading Islamic thinkers. One of the greatest names is the Pakistani scholar Sayyid Abul A'la Mawdudi, who has been described as 'one of the leading interpreters of Islam in the twentieth century'.[24] He not only distinguished himself in the field of exegesis, but more broadly his ideology came to pose one of the most potent challenges to Islamic modernism from the radical Islamist camp this century.[25]

Mawdudi was a prolific writer, but also distinguished himself as an editor, spending much of his working life editing the monthly journal *Tarjuman al-Qur'an*. Like Sayyid Qutb, he was preoccupied with challenging the influence of the West upon the world of Islam. In 1941, he founded the radical *Jama'at-i-Islami*, an Islamist group that shared much of its ideology with the Egyptian Muslim Brotherhood, and which called for the establishment of an Islamic state after the forthcoming independence of India. Thus, like Sayyid Qutb and other radical Islamists, he saw independence from colonial rule as an essential step in reviving the predominance of Islam in the modern world. He was to exert a powerful influence on the new state of Pakistan after it was formed in 1947.

His principle work is his commentary, entitled 'Towards Understanding the Qur'an' (*Tafhim al-Qur'an*). It took him thirty years to complete it. The key ideas which manifest themselves in this commentary include the notion that God alone is sovereign, and that mankind has gone astray because he has lost his vision. This can be seen in his commentary on Q3:117:

God is the Lord and Master of man as well as of all that man owns, and the world in which he lives. If a man either does not recognize the sovereignty of his Lord and unlawfully serves others or disobeys God's Laws then his actions become crimes for which he deserves to be tried ...[26]

---

[24] Robinson 1991:872.
[25] Ahmad 1967:208.
[26] Mawdudi 1988: vol. 1, 280.

The above reference to the primacy of 'God's Laws' demonstrates Mawdudi's conviction that all necessary guidance required by mankind is be found in the *shari'a*. His view that Islamic laws could not be outdated brought him into conflict with modernist thinkers for whom legislation, whether human or divine in origin, had to allow for varying degrees of dynamic evolution. Here we find echoes of the revelation-versus-reason debate from the earliest centuries of Islam.

Mawdudi strongly advocated that political power was necessary to put God's divine plan into effect. In other words, the Islamic state has a missionary purpose. Moreover, the Islamic state should be all embracing, but run by Muslims, though non-Muslims would be permitted to live within it as *dhimmis*. His conviction of the appropriateness of a subservient role for non-Muslims is drawn from Qur'anic pronouncements on power and on the People of the Book. This comes through in his discussion of Q3:118, which demonstrates his clear belief in the scales of justice being tilted heavily towards the Muslims in their interaction with Jews:

It is strange that although the Muslims had reason to feel aggrieved by the Jews it was the latter who felt aggrieved by the Muslims. Since the Muslims believed in the Torah along with the Qur'an the Jews had no justifiable ground for complaint. If anyone had cause to complain it was the Muslims for the Jews did not believe in the Qur'an.[27]

Mawdudi is a seminal figure in terms of 20th-century radical Islamist thinking, and his writings have helped to crystallise approaches by millions of Muslims to the issue of how to apply Islamic thinking in the modern world. As Robinson says of Mawdudi's ideology, 'the outcome is the most comprehensive statement of the nature of the Islamic state in modern times'.[28] Along with Sayyid Qutb, Mawdudi has become the spiritual and political guide for countless Islamists in the late 20th century.

Sayyid Qutb (1906–66)

This figure is considered as the main ideologue of modern Muslim Sunni fundamentalism.[29] He spent the period between

[27] Mawdudi 1988: vol. 1, 281.
[28] Robinson 1991:873.
[29] Jansen 1997:117.

1948 and 1950 in the USA, and this was to prove crucial in the formulation of his ideology, as it served to affirm his radical opposition to the influence of the increasingly secular West upon the
Muslim world. On his return to Egypt, he joined the Muslim
Brotherhood, which had been founded in Cairo in 1928 by
Hassan al-Banna and which was committed to spreading radical
Islamist ideologies. The principal focus of his opposition for the
remainder of his life was the regime of President Nasser of Egypt,
who had taken power during the military coup in Egypt in 1952,
and who championed pan-Arab nationalism as the basis of the
republic of Egypt, rather than an Islamic state based on the *shari'a*.
Over the next fourteen years, Sayyid Qutb was arrested and
imprisoned on several occasions by the Nasser regime, and was
eventually accused of sedition and executed in August 1966.

'In the Shade of the Qur'an' (*Fi zilal al-Qur'an*) is arguably his
most important piece of writing. The work extends to thirty volumes, with one devoted to each of the volumes (*juz'*) of the
Qur'an. Much of the text was written during his lengthy sojourns
in the prisons of the Nasser regime.

This work is considered by many as 'activist exegesis', for it
encapsulates a very single-minded, black and white approach to
the issues being addressed. His commentary on Sura 109, for
example, abounds with terminology which portrays the viewpoints of his opponents as beneath contempt. Examples of such
terms are 'fouled their conceptions',[30] 'all was polytheism', 'confusion in their concepts', 'this muddle', 'wrangling or vain arguments',[31] 'ignorant concepts', 'deviated', 'they grow more and
more completely perverse'.[32] Implicit in this interpretation is that
although the pre-Islamic Arab communities are the subject of discussion in this instance, the same is said by radical Islamists about
modern Muslims who drift away from the true path and who
enter a latter-day *jahiliyya* (age of ignorance).

Absent from Sayyid Qutb's commentary is the meticulous listing of alternative interpretations characteristic of the exegesis of
al-Tabari or al-Razi, accompanied by an unemotional statement
indicating the preferred interpretation of the author concerned.

---

[30] Qutb 1979: vol. 30, 328.
[31] Qutb 1979: vol. 30, 329.
[32] Qutb 1979: vol. 30, 330.

For Sayyid Qutb, true Islam is synonymous with a scripturalist-based set of beliefs and practices which reflect 'the way adopted by the Islamic call in its early days.'[33] This is, in effect, the exegesis of intolerance, and one which is based on a utopian vision of the early community, in a way which is characteristic of radical Islamist thinking. There are clear Hanbalite influences here in the portrayal of the generations which produced the Islamic scriptures as having lived at the best of times. This refrain showed itself in medieval Hanbalite writing such as Ibn Qudama's creed, which states categorically that 'the best of all centuries was that of our Prophet and those who followed after that century'.[34]

This portrayal of a long-lost Golden Age recurs throughout Qutb's commentary; a clear example is provided in his commentary on Sura 96 when he writes of the period during which Muhammad received his revelations:

... twenty-three years of direct contact between the human race and the Highest Society. The true nature of this period cannot be recognised except by those who lived in that period and went through its experience, witnessed its start and end, relished the sweet flavour of that contact and felt the Divine hand guiding them along the road ... The people who lived in that period were fully aware of its uniqueness, recognised its special place in history and felt the great loss when the Prophet passed away to be in the company of the Supreme Companion. This marked the end of this remarkable period which our minds can hardly imagine but for its actual occurrence.[35]

Such a view provides fertile ground for a reductive approach to exegesis. For example, while al-Zamakhshari is concerned to report a debate among early Muslim theologians as to which was the earliest revelation received by Muhammad,[36] Qutb simply comments as follows:

It is universally agreed that the opening [of Sura 96] was the first Qur'anic revelation. The accounts stating that other verses were revealed first are not authentic.[37]

---

33 Qutb 1979: vol. 30, 332.
34 Rippin and Knappert 1986:125.
35 Qutb 1979: vol. 30, 221.
36 Peters 1990: vol. 2, 49–50.
37 Qutb 1979: vol. 30, 218.

Other features to note in Sayyid Qutb's commentary include his method of commenting on blocks of verses, or entire suras, rather than limiting himself to phrase-by-phrase or word-by-word exegesis, as was the practice of the classical commentators. Qutb had an awareness of discourse-level considerations, and his methodology of focusing on blocks of discourse rather than clause-based units represented a significant advancement on one of the important initiatives of Muhammad 'Abduh, as observed earlier. This can be clearly seen in his exegesis of Sura 96 (*al-alaq*), a structural analysis of which is given in the following table.

Table 7.1. COMPONENTS IN QUTB'S EXEGESIS OF SURA 96

1.	Qur'anic text of entire Sura in Arabic
2.	Presentation of two Hadith accounts describing the first encounter between Gabriel and Muhammad, to set the scene
3.	A lengthy reflection by Qutb on the significance of God's revelation to His Prophet
4.	A verse-based exegesis of verses 1–5
5.	A long citation from Ibn Qayyim al-Jawziyya* making heavy use of Hadith reports showing how Muhammad kept the remembrance of God in the forefront of his mind at all times
6.	Further Hadith reports on the same topic
7.	A reflection by Qutb lamenting that generally people think themselves self-sufficient and forget their Creator. A portrait of the typical transgressor is painted. Also included is Qutb's own structural analysis of this Sura.
8.	Qutb's conclusion

* Prominent Hanbali theologian and specialist in *fiqh*, lived 1292–1350. Cf. Laoust 1979:821–822.

Nowhere in his exegesis of this Sura is there a phrase-by-phrase analysis of the Qur'anic text, as was the exegetical technique of medieval commentators such as al-Baydawi. Qutb's main concern was more to do with the big issues of contemporary relevance at the macro level rather than the minutiae of linguistic analysis of the Qur'anic text.

His concern with allocating priority to the scriptural record in all areas, also characteristic of radical Islamists, is reflected in his own exegetical technique. Where possible he uses the Qur'anic text itself and the Hadith to comment on a Qur'anic verse. In this, he preserves the style followed by the medieval Islamist Ibn Taymiyya, who advocated that the only valid sources for Qur'anic interpretation, in order of priority were: first, the Qur'an itself; second, the prophetic traditions; third, the writings of the Companions; and finally, the writings of the Followers (*Tabi'un*).

Sayyid Qutb's polemical style extends beyond his primary targets – those Muslims who he considers to have betrayed the Islamic call – to Christians and Jews, especially the latter. He calls for Muslims to separate themselves from unbelievers, including those nominal Muslims who have become secularised. He also calls on all believing Muslims to fulfil the requirement of *jihad* by engaging in Islamic mission to nominal Muslims and non-Muslims:

The first step that should be taken in this field by the person calling on people to embrace Islam is to segregate himself from *Ignorance* ... no intermingling, no half measures or conciliation is permissible ... contemporary advocates of Islam ... badly need to realise that they are calling for Islam today in entirely *Ignorant* surroundings amongst ex-Muslim peoples ...[38]

In the radical Islamist writings, we again witness a surfacing of the ancient debate between reason and revelation. But in their case, revelation is clearly predominant, as it had been with radical activist thinkers from earlier times, such as Ibn Hanbal and Ibn Taymiyya.

ISLAM AND OTHER FAITHS IN THE MODERN WORLD

Previous discussion in this chapter has touched upon the attitude to other faiths which has developed within Islam both during the early formative stages and in subsequent centuries. Muhammad's contacts with Jews and Christians were vitally important in laying a blueprint for later contacts between Muslims and followers of these two earlier Semitic faiths.

---

[38] Qutb 1979: vol. 30, 331.

A challenge for modernising Muslims and Jews and Christians in the pluralist context of the late 20th century lies in the landscape presented by the Qur'an. The Islamic Holy Book serves as a window into the Meccan and Medinan communities of early 7th-century Arabia. Thus we learn much from it about the nature of the interaction between Muhammad and Jews and Christians. But for many late-20th-century Muslims, especially radical Islamists, the Qur'an also serves as the divine blueprint of what the relationship between Islam, Judaism and Christianity should be for all time.

The same applies with the Hadith collections. On the one hand they reflect events and attitudes prevalent among Muhammad's community in the 620s. On the other hand, they serve for many Muslims today as the instruction book for how a 'right' life should be lived. The result is that there is a fundamental tension between the pluralist relativism which has come to prevail in much of the West in the late 20th century and a single-minded exclusivism which is found in much of Islamic scripture and classical scholarly writing. For example, a view which would be widely accepted by Muslims today about the fate awaiting unbelievers is that articulated with great clarity by Ibn al-Jama'a in the late 9th century:

Men fall into two categories, believers and unbelievers, and that unbelievers will be in the Fire is unanimously agreed. Believers are also of two categories, the obedient and the disobedient, and that the obedient will be in Paradise is unanimously agreed. The disobedient again are in two categories, the repentant and the unrepentant. That the repentant will get to Paradise is unanimously agreed, but [the fate of] the unrepentant is as Allah – exalted be He – may will.[39]

The preoccupation of some Muslim writers with giving a scriptural spin to their views on appropriate relations between Muslims and non-Muslims will be addressed within a Southeast Asian context in chapter 11.

Part I of this study has thus presented us with a plethora of theological reference points to assist our primary study of Malay–

---

[39] From 'Ali al-Qari's *Daw' al-Ma'ali*, cited in Jeffery 1958:216–17.

Indonesian Islam. We have considered a range of key issues relating to Islamic sacred scripture – Qur'an and Hadith – and the matter of variant readings upon the Qur'anic text. We have touched upon significant debates within the Islamic community, and how these debates informed, and were informed by, commentary upon scripture, the emergence of Islamic law, accounts of Islamic prophets and the phenomenon of Sufism. Finally we surveyed developments in the 20th century, focusing upon modernising voices and the response from radical Islamists to modernising tendencies.

All the above discussion has been underpinned by a debate at the macro level. On one side of the debate have been conservative forces committed to giving absolute priority to Islamic scripture and law in the formation of attitudes and policy in all areas. On the other side have been, first, those arguing for a prime position for human powers of reason and rational thinking, most recently realised in modernising tendencies in the 20th-century, and second, those engaged in the spiritual quest, who considered a focus on matters of ritual and law to be only part of their search for knowledge of and communication with God.

Our investigation of the Southeast Asian Muslim world will refer back to this contextual theological discussion. This will assist us to identify points of convergence, areas of divergence, and the nature of the transmission of Islamic thought from the Muslim heartlands to an area on the geographical periphery of the Muslim world.

PART II

MALAY ISLAMIC THINKING TO 1900

8

THE 16TH AND 17TH CENTURIES

SUFIS IN CONFLICT

THE BIRTH OF MALAY ISLAMIC LITERATURE

The Malay world in the early Islamic period in Southeast Asia focused upon a series of local rulers and city states, most with cosmopolitan populations derived mainly from the immediate region but also from as far afield as the Arab world, Persia, India and China. The newly arriving Islamic faith came to represent the latest element in a melting pot of cultures and creeds. The nature of the arrival of Islam, being predominantly through peaceful means, meant that the host societies which adopted it in fact fostered a new offspring: a Muslim progeny with strong pre-Islamic cultural and religious roots. In time, the various social and religious layers which constituted the different Malay societies merged to an increasing degree, producing a distinctive expression of the Islamic faith.

The process of integration experienced by Islam was translated into the literature of the Malay societies in question. The Malay world witnessed a body of Islamic literature being grafted on to the literary expression of the existing Malay society. In the process, stories were adapted, adopted and extensively recast. Hindu–Buddhist literature which had long existed in the Malay world prior to the arrival of Islam was subjected to new demands to adapt to the changing times. A number of pre-Islamic Hindu stories were reprocessed to fit an Islamic mould. This was supplemented by the importation to the Malay world of a considerable body of Islamic stories deriving from the Arab world and Persia.

Islamic works imported

The imported stories were diverse in character. Some concerned
the prophet Muhammad and were often impregnated with folklore or mystical belief. These include the *Hikayat Nur Muhammad*
(The Story of the Mystic Light of Muhammad), which dates from
no later than the middle of the 17th century and reflects the mystical inclinations of Malay Muslims of that time. The Malay interest
in the theme of Muhammad's light represented the end point of a
long process of transmission from the early Islamic period, with
writers such as the early Sufi hagiographer and exegete Abu 'Abd
al-Rahman al-Sulami (d. 1021) writing as follows in his *Haqa'iq al-
tafsir*:

When God willed to create Muhammad, He made appear a light from
His light. When it reached the veil of the majesty it bowed in prostration
before God.[1]

Other early Malay stories were also often concerned with the
prophets of Islam and drew on the traditional *Qisas al-Anbiya'*
(Stories of the Prophets) which had gained great currency in the
Arab world. These included a Malay rendering of the *Qisas al-
Anbiya'* as well as other works such as *Hikayat Iskandar Zulkarnain*
(The Story of Alexander the Great). These stories were characteristically graphic in their imagery, entertaining in their narrative
qualities, and captivating in their appeal to Malay societies accus-
tomed to colourful epic narratives.

Another category of story which appealed to Malay audiences
dealt with significant non-prophetic figures from the period of
the Companions of the Prophet or the following generation. An
example is the *Hikayat Muhammad Hanafiyyah*, which dealt with
the military campaigns of a half-brother of Hasan and Husain, the
sons of the assassinated Caliph 'Ali. This work was translated into
Malay around the 15th century and quickly assumed a significant
position within the corpus of Malay literature. Other such stories
are *Hikayat Tamim al-Dari*, a story about a Christian who converted to Islam soon after the *hijra*, and *Hikayat Amir Hamzah*, a
narrative romance of legendary proportions based on the character of Hamza ibn 'Abd al-Mutallib, the uncle of the prophet
Muhammad. All the above categories of stories were guaranteed a

---

1 Cited in Hermansen 1998:224.

receptive audience among Malays of the early Islamic period who had for centuries been drawing on colourful and lengthy Hindu epics for didactic and entertainment purposes.

A melting pot

The intermixing of religious and literary traditions, so much a characteristic of this early period, was mirrored in other ways. One of the most prominent Islamic scholars in the court Malay world, Nur al-Din al-Raniri, was of mixed Indian and Malay extraction and exemplified the considerable racial integration taking place at the time. Moreover, intermixing was also evident in the language of Islamic texts. Court Malay, the language of the great narrative and historical classics of the pre-Colonial era, underwent a remarkable transformation in many works focusing on specifically religious issues as a result of a technique of literal translation being used in rendering the work into Malay from its Arabic original. The resulting style of Malay, known as *Kitab* Malay is noticeably influenced by Arabic grammar because of this translation technique.

PROMINENT MALAY RELIGIOUS SCHOLARS AND THEIR WRITINGS

In order to gain an insight into the religious doctrines which were predominant in the pre-colonial Malay Muslim states, it is necessary to look closely at the Sultanate of Aceh during the latter part of the 16th and all of the 17th century. Acehnese scholars have not only left us almost all the evidence of theological activity which survives from this period, but indeed it seems that they were in the vanguard of Malay Islamic thought at the time. We can confidently draw conclusions about Malay religious activity in general in the pre-colonial era by taking Aceh as our case study. Not only do we learn much about Malay Islamic theology during the late 16th and 17th centuries by examining the products of Acehnese Islamic scholarship at the time, but a dissection of works written during this era also helps us to identify Islamic currents which must have been significant during the formative period of the 13th to 15th centuries in the Malay world.

The early years of the 17th century in Aceh were characterised by profound social and religious change. Sultan Iskandar Muda had placed great importance upon the strengthening of the Islamic faith both within and without the territory of Aceh proper.

Many mosques were built, including the famous *Bayt al-Rahman* mosque in Aceh, later to be destroyed by fire.

Turkish archives record the presence of Acehnese pilgrims in Arabia during this time,[2] and it had become common for Acehnese scholars of Islam to spend a period of their lives studying at various centres of Islamic learning in the Arabian peninsula. The earliest documented case we have of a Malay scholar travelling to the Arab world to undertake studies of the Islamic sciences is that of Hamzah Fansuri, the great mystic of the late 16th century.[3] He was initiated into the Qadiriyya Sufi Order in Arabia, and in doing so established, or perhaps continued, a tradition which many Malay religious scholars were later to follow.

Islamic theosophical doctrines relating to the nature of God and Man's relationship to the Creator were a major focal point of religious teaching and writing in Aceh during this period. Sufi schools of thought were flourishing throughout the Muslim world, and in India and Aceh various competing schools, some of which denounced the others as heretical, flourished during this period.

Hamzah Fansuri

Very little is known about the life of Hamzah Fansuri.[4] However, an examination of his writings provides essential insights to his theology, and also serves as a resource from which certain biographical indicators can be extracted.

Hamzah originated from Fansur, also known as Barus, on the west coast of Sumatra. Barus was an important and prosperous trading port in the early 16th century, of which testimony is found in both Asian and European historical sources. Barus' greatness was not to last, however, as the rise of the Sultanate of Aceh on the northern tip of Sumatra led to a decline in Barus' importance as a trading post. It seems likely that Hamzah was born at a time that Barus was fast becoming a declining backwater and was probably living on its memories.

---

2 Djajadiningrat 1911:178.
3 This practice was also followed by Indian Muslim scholars; the founder of the Chishti Sufi order, Mu'inuddin Chishti, is reputed to have travelled extensively throughout the Muslim world, learning from leading Sufis. Cf. Jackson 1988:264.
4 The details of Hamzah's life have been a matter of considerable debate among scholars. See, for example, Brakel 1969, responding to research by Al-Attas.

Hamzah lived most, and possibly all, of his life in the 16th century. The date of his death is controversial; Drewes and Brakel argue that he must have died around 1590 on the basis of his demonstrated theological doctrines and his writings.[5] Other scholars conclude that Hamzah's life extended into the 17th century, and he lived during a significant part of the reign of Sultan 'Ala al-din Ri'ayat Shah, who ruled Aceh from 1589–1604.[6]

Hamzah appears to have travelled fairly widely. Among his likely destinations were the Malay peninsula, Siam and various points in Arabia, where he studied a variety of mystical schools of thought and where he was initiated into the Qadiriyya order.[7] His stay in Siam was also significant since it was probably there that he learned Persian and adopted doctrines which were later to be considered heretical by subsequent Islamic scholars. There was a substantial Muslim community that was living in Siam at the time, which drew heavily on Islam in India for its theological orientations, and this community appears to have been significant in influencing Hamzah's own brand of theology.[8]

After his travels to Siam and Arabia, Hamzah returned to Aceh and taught in that location as well as in Barus. Some speculate that the influence which his doctrines evidently exerted on Shams al-Din al-Sumatrani indicate that Hamzah was Shams al-Din's teacher. This may well have been the case, though we will never be able to confirm it. Nevertheless, there is little doubt that Hamzah's doctrinal approach was a significant factor in the formation of Shams al-Din's theology. However, they were not identical; Hamzah drew on Ibn al-'Arabi's five grades of being[9] between the pluriformity of creation and Absolute Unity, whereas Shams al-Din's teachings were based on a doctrine of seven grades, and were influenced by al-Burhanpuri's *al-Tuhfa al-mursala ila ruh al-nabi* (The Gift addressed to the Spirit of the Prophet). See Tables 8.1 and 8.2.

---

[5] Drewes and Brakel 1986:3.

[6] Nasution *et al.* 1992:296.

[7] Winstedt 1923:312; Al-Attas 1963:22. Vakily 1997:119 claims that this initiation took place in Baghdad, while Winstedt implies that it occurred at Mecca or Medina.

[8] Drewes and Brakel 1986:5; Vakily 1997:119.

[9] Al-Attas 1963:23. Al-Attas also points to Jami's *Lawa'ih* as being a significant source for Hamzah's ideas, while Moris (1999) points to Ibn al-'Arabi and 'Abd al-Karim al-Jili as being the principal influences upon the teachings of Hamzah.

It is also argued that Hamzah's writings represent the commencement of Islamic writing in Malay. Again this is difficult to
confirm, because of the lack of surviving records pre-dating
Hamzah, which points either to their non-existence in the first
place or to the fact that they once existed but decayed over time or
were destroyed. Nevertheless, Moris is probably correct when she
makes the more circumspect claim that 'he was the first Malay
thinker to have penned down [sic] lofty and abstract metaphysical
principles and ideas in the Malay language'.[10]

His literary works.   Though Hamzah's greatest legacy rests in his
poetry, he also wrote various prose works: *Asrar al-'arifin* (The
secrets of the gnostics), *Sharab al-'ashiqin* (The drink of lovers) and
al-Muntahi (The adept). Hamzah uses his prose works to clearly
articulate and systematise his framework of five grades of being,
the outward self-manifestations of the divine Unity. A summary
of this system is given at Table 8.1.[11]

While Hamzah uses prose to articulate his theosophical system,
he uses his poetry to give rapturous expression to this theosophy.
An examination of this poetry readily demonstrates Hamzah's
concern with exhorting Muslims to identify the presence of God
within themselves, and by doing so, coming to an understanding
of their place in God's overall oneness. This can be seen in the following excerpts from his Poem XXII: [12]

> The dervishes proclaim
> Your Lord is most clearly manifest
> If you really have eyes to see
> Then equally look upon yourself.

Rather than God being presented as transcendent and unattain-
able for the individual believer, as was the image portrayed by
more orthodox *shari'a*-minded Malay Islamic teachers, Hamzah
gives an insight here into his monistic view where God is identified with all elements in the universe, even the ordinary individual.

---

[10] Moris 1999.
[11] Cf. also Winstedt 1923:315; Johns 1955a:75; Johns 1957:102–3; Bousfield 1985: 201–
2; Bousfield 1988:116ff; Moris 1999.
[12] These quotations from Hamzah's poem XXII are drawn from Drewes and Brakel
1986:109–11.

Table 8.1. HAMZAH FANSURI'S FIVE GRADES OF BEING

Grade	Name	Nature
1.	Non-determination (*Huwa/la ta'ayyun*)	Innermost Essence of God, beyond knowledge, inconceivable, indeterminate, non-manifest
2.	1st determination: Individualised Essence (*Ahad/Wahid*)	Knowledge (*'ilm*), being (*wujud*), vision (*shuhud*), light (*nur*), balance of opposites
3.	2nd determination: Inclusive Unity (*Wahidiyya*)	Fixed prototypes, Reality of things, Forms of knowledge, Spirit of relationships. Unity in diversity
4.	3rd determination: the Relational Spirit (*ruh idafi*)	Human spirit, animal spirit, vegetable spirit
5.	4th determination	Relational spirit separates from the divine Essence; Materialisation of all created things

Bousfield encapsulates this in referring to Hamzah's mystical path 'that leads from the realization that everything depends on God for its existence through to the realization that, not only is there no God but the One God, but there is naught *but* God.'[13] God is the only true Reality and the multitude of evident other realities represented by the various determinations are merely self-manifestations of the one true Reality, God. Hamzah is concerned to impart this to his readers. By following the path of Sufi exercise and knowledge, the gap perceived by his readers between God and themselves can be breached and they can come to an understanding of true Reality:

---

[13] Bousfield 1985:196.

> Should you only know your self, dear sir
> Your beauty is without compeer
> Between servant and Lord there is a constant bond
> So do not fail to attend to yourself.

Hamzah presented himself as a model for his disciples, whereby if they followed his example, they could realise union with the Almighty as he had done:

> Hamzah is poor and naked
> A sacrifice, just as Isma'il
> Neither Persian nor Arab
> Yet in constant union with the Eternal One.

One of the spin-offs of the monistic approach of the Wujudiyya is what Bousfield refers to as 'savage determinism'. If God is all and all is God, then there can be no place for human free-will as was so vociferously argued for by the Mu'tazila. God determines all things, all events, all actions. This is articulated clearly in a passage from Hamzah's prose, as follows:

One He causes to believe; one He causes to disbelieve; one He causes to be rich; one He causes to be poor; one He allows always to transgress; one He allows always to do good; one He allows to do evil; one He causes to enter Heaven; one He causes to enter Hell ...[14]

Hamzah's view of various stages on the path to attaining mystical knowledge (*ma'rifa*) is well encapsulated elsewhere in his poetry. Speaking in metaphorical terms, he refers to 'the Four Gates of the Castle' as being in the first instance *shari'a*, or the outward prescriptions of Law; second, *tariqa*, learning from a Sufi master; third, *haqiqa*, or a love-relationship between a Sufi seeker and God; and finally *sirr*, or the secret mystery of God's essence which is the ultimate goal.[15] It is in the context of the transition from the third to the fourth 'gate' that accusations of heresy could particularly arise.

Drewes and Brakel's detailed study of Hamzah's writings allocate numbers to his poems for ease of reference. A close

---

[14] Bousfield 1985:197–8, citing Al-Attas 1970.
[15] Reijn 1983:16.

examination of Poem XXXI[16] is instructive, as it provides an understanding of Hamzah's multiple perspectives: poetic style, theosophy, method of appeal to his readers, and his self image.

Poem XXXI clearly demonstrates Hamzah's love of metaphor. The primary theme of this poem is the Light of Muhammad, which he refers to variously as a unique fish, a royal fish, and a whale. At times the Light is 'deaf', at times 'dumb'. Similarly Hamzah portrays the omnipresence of God as the water, or ocean. Thus elements of the fourth determination are linked with the first determination, the initial manifestation of the divine Essence.

Structurally, Hamzah achieves a delicate sense of balance in his poetry. He does this in part by sometimes repeating key notions in the first and last lines of successive stanzas. For example, in terms of content Stanza 1 is structured by line as ABCD, while Stanza 2 is structured as AEFD. Similarly Stanza 3 appears as GHIJ, while Stanza 4 as GKLJ. This repetition of content is effective in contributing to the overall cohesion of the poem.

Cohesion through the poem is also achieved at a more macro level by repeating key themes in different stanzas. For example, a reinforcement of the al-Hallaj theme is provided in Stanza 7 after having been introduced in Stanza 6. Likewise, in Stanza 8 Hamzah further demonstrates his eye for poetic cohesion by reminding his reader of the central theme of the quest for immersion in 'the sea called the Creator'. This is reinforced in Stanza 9 with the reference to the fish being 'in constant union, in the currents of the Sea'.

In terms of his theosophy, Poem XXXI manifests strong monistic flavours. A recurring theme that the Light of Muhammad is of the Light of God avoids any sense of dualism. Moreover, Stanza 6 reflects a strong influence of the al-Hallaj story, eulogising the very phrase 'I am God' which led to his execution, and identifying *fana'* (self-effacement into God's being) as the desirable model provided by the Light of Muhammad.[17]

---

[16] Drewes and Brakel 1986:137–41.

[17] Elsewhere in his poetry Hamzah makes overt reference in laudatory terms to al-Hallaj, calling on mystics to be 'like Mansur (al-Hallaj)'; cf. Reijn 1983:16.

However, this poem is not merely a contemplation of the nature of being. Hamzah is concerned with practice, and with giving guidance to his readers. In this he demonstrates that he is as much teacher as littérateur. Stanza 8 emphasises that Hamzah is a devotee of ecstatic Sufi practice, not merely ascetic withdrawal, with his reference to 'ebriety and rapture'. In Stanza 11 Hamzah turns to a direct address to his reader using second person address forms. He exhorts the reader not to look far and wide for God, and in a clearly monistic statement, he reminds his reader: 'You are in constant union with the pure Ocean.' Hamzah uses graphic terms to impress on his reader that one must shun worldly matters and relationships. He calls on his reader to 'leave your mother and father'. In Stanza 10 Hamzah is scathing of those Muslims who seek spiritual truth in the wrong places, referring to them as 'stupid fish'. He takes them to task for not attaching themselves to a Sufi shaykh, a spiritual guide, who can lead them in the right path.

In the final stanza, like a good teacher concerned with helping his students to identify with him, Hamzah brings the focus around to himself. He states that he is 'of low descent', thus stressing for his readers that worldly titles and status are no guarantee of spiritual insight.

Hamzah was clearly an influential force within the Acehnese religious world during the late 16th century. It is possible that he held a high official position within the bureaucracy. He may well have been the 'chiefe bishope' (*shaykh al-islam*) described by the English mariner Sir James Lancaster as having represented the Acehnese Sultan in negotiations in 1602.[18] However, his monistic notions were enlarged upon and formed the central core of the teaching and writing of Shams al-Din al-Sumatrani (d. 1630), *shaykh al-islam* during the rule of Iskandar Muda.[19]

Shams al-Din al-Sumatrani

Shams al-Din al-Sumatrani was born before 1575 and died on 25 February 1630.[20] Little is known about his life, and what is

---

[18] Azra 1992:348.
[19] Juynboll and Voorhoeve 1960:741.
[20] Johns 1997b:296.

recorded must be gleaned from fragmentary evidence present in the remnants of his writings, in those of his posthumous antagonist, Nur al-Din al-Raniri, and in the records of European seafarers.

He may have occupied a central role in the power structure of the Sultanate of Aceh even before Sultan Iskandar Muda's accession to power in 1607.[21] His most important work, the *Mir'at al-Mu'minin*, that contains the core of his monistic teachings and in which he expounds upon a system of seven grades of being, was composed in 1601 during the rule of, and probably sponsored by, Sultan 'Ala al-Din Ri'ayat Shah al-Mukammil (r. 1589–1604).[22]

When Iskandar Muda succeeded to the throne, the official standing of Islamic theosophy in the Sultanate was evidently well established. Hamzah Fansuri had formulated key theosophical doctrines in the region, but we must turn to Shams al-Din to find evidence of these doctrines receiving official sanction from the Acehnese Sultan. Shams al-Din received the direct patronage of Sultan Iskandar Muda and served as *Shaykh al-Islam*, the supreme spiritual guide, in the Sultanate. Moreover, Shams al-Din initiated Sultan Iskandar Muda into the Naqshbandiyya order.[23] Thus we can conclude that the study of Islam throughout the Sultanate during this period was oriented towards speculative theosophical doctrines which were initially expounded by Hamzah, consolidated by Shams al-Din and his followers, and were later to be condemned as heretical.

Why did Iskandar Muda patronise such a particular theosophy? The answer to this question may lie in part in the Sultan's own view of himself and his role. Iskandar Muda seems to have sensed the stamp of destiny upon him, in the form of greatness and renown. This is reflected in his choice of names once he ascended the throne. Lombard[24] argues convincingly that the Sultan assumed the name Iskandar Muda during his lifetime, possibly even on the day of his assumption of power. Attempts to compare Iskandar Muda to Alexander the Great are

---

[21] Lombard 1967:162.

[22] Djajadiningrat 1911:182.

[23] Johns 1997b:296.

[24] Lombard 1967:169–70. Cf. Lombard for a detailed account of the rule of Sultan Iskandar Muda.

contained in the *Hikayat Aceh* and *Adat Aceh*,[25] no doubt included to earn the pleasure of the Sultan. His other names, Perkasa Alam Johan and Makuta Alam, also suggest a central figure on the world stage and give us a clear insight into the Acehnese idea of kingship and the role of the king. Iskandar Muda clearly saw himself as another all-conquering hero, and this no doubt partially accounts for his external policy of expansion of Aceh's domains.

Such a self image may well have been boosted by the Sufi doctrines he endorsed. For if God were present in all creatures and things, and Man were merely a manifestation of God, is it not possible that a great sovereign be elevated to semi-divine heights in the eyes of his subjects? It is not difficult to imagine the degree of awe in which Iskandar Muda must have been held by his subjects after the first period of great Acehnese military victories. He indeed must have been likened to Alexander the Great. Moreover, just as the arrival of the Hindu and Buddhist faiths in Southeast Asia had offered Malay rulers an option for identifying with new gods and for claiming a degree of divine sanction to their rule, it is quite possible that Iskandar Muda, who already felt the stamp of destiny upon him, saw in pantheistic Sufism a means for enhancing the popular perception of his kingship as one sanctioned, blessed and in-dwelt by God.

Thus the doctrines taught by Shams al-Din served the purposes of a ruler preoccupied with self-glorification, and Shams al-Din clearly had an instinct for 'scratching where the Sultan itched', as it were. It was little wonder that Shams al-Din's reputation flourished during the reign of Iskandar Muda.

His literary works.   Shams al-Din had the gift of linguistic ability, and wrote in both Malay and Arabic. His principal work in Arabic was *Jawhar al-haqa'iq* (Jewel of True Realities), in which he manifested influence from various sources, including the thought of Ibn al-'Arabi, the poetry of Ibn al-Farid, and the structure of al-Burhanpuri's *Tuhfa*.[26] As Johns observes,[27] comparative study of Hamzah and Shams al-Din's writings points to a shift in influence

---

[25] Lombard 1967:170–1.
[26] Johns 1997b:296.
[27] Johns 1995:177.

upon Acehnese mystical thinking from Arab writers (Ibn al-'Arabi and al-Jili upon Hamzah) to Indian writers (al-Burhanpuri upon Shams al-Din).

Shams al-Din's system of seven grades of being is articulated in various of his works, including *Mir'at al-mu'minin*. It also appears in very succinct form in his shorter work *Nur al-daqa'iq*.[28] Shams al-Din clearly draws on al-Burhanpuri's *Tuhfa al-mursala ila ruh al-nabi* in formulating his system, though his presentation in the *Nur al-daqa'iq* is somewhat more lucid than al-Burhanpuri's presentations. Shams al-Din's seven grades are shown in summary below:

Table 8.2. SHAMS AL-DIN AL-SUMATRANI'S
SEVEN GRADES OF BEING

Grade	Name	Content	Characteristic
1.	*Ahadiyya*	The Essence of God	Uncreated and eternal
2.	*Wahda*	The Attributes of God (the Reality that is Muhammad)	Uncreated and eternal – multiplicity in unity
3.	*Wahidiyya*	The Names of God (the Reality of Man)	Uncreated and eternal – unity in multiplicity
4.	*'Alam al-arwah*	The World of Spirits	Created and particular – God's Being manifested
5.	*'Alam al-mithal*	The World of Ideas	Created and particular – God's Being manifested
6.	*'Alam al-ajsam*	The World of Bodies	Created and particular – God's Being manifested
7.	*'Alam al-insan*	The World of Man	Created and particular – God's Being manifested

This seven-grade structure of emanation should not be understood as a time line. Rather it refers to 'different structures of consciousness' which Sufis who follow this particular path may

---

[28] Johns 1953.

attain. Success in achieving all grades makes the seeker a 'Perfect Man'.[29]

A further insight into Shams al-Din's style as an author and his theological position can be obtained by examining his Commentary on Hamzah Fansuri's Poem XXXI which was discussed previously.[30] This shows the degree of influence that Hamzah exerted on Shams al-Din, as well as the features of the theology of these two Sufis which were so vehemently attacked at a later point by Nur al-Din al-Raniri. We will examine this commentary from the point of view of the goal which Shams al-Din identifies for the faithful, the method to attain that goal, and miscellaneous issues arising in his work.

Shams al-Din identifies the goal for the faithful as being to reach an understanding of the divine oneness of all existence. He propounds a notion of an 'inward eye' which enables those possessing it to understand the nature of the union between Creator and creature. He stresses throughout this commentary that 'God's Essence is not different from one's self; the difference is owing to the diverse manifestations'.[31] Even the *nur Muhammad* is a manifestation of God's Being, not a difference in essence, but merely a difference in appearance, or manifestation.

Shams al-Din's ultimate monist beliefs are encapsulated when he says:

the essence of man is God most high; essentially man is the Only Lord ... there is no question of return to Him, nor in fact of coming (from Him), for coming and return presuppose two entities. How could there be any question of return and coming, since we and God most high are of one being?

Shams al-Din's declaration that 'all that exists derives its existence from the Light of God' was to provide fuel for the accusations of Nur al-Din al-Raniri in the late 1630s and early 1640s.

Following Hamzah's poetic method, Shams al-Din was not content to merely identify the goal for the believer, but was concerned to equip the faithful with the tools to achieve that goal. In this context, Shams al-Din presents Love as a core theme in his

---

29 Bousfield 1988:116.
30 Drewes & Brakel 1986:195–207.
31 Drewes & Brakel 1986:195.

theosophy. He suggests that it is through Love of God that we can attain perfection and come to an understanding of the union between Creator and creature. However, this Love for the Creator needs to be accompanied by complete renunciation of worldly concerns in order to maximise the possibility of realising union with God. Moreover, Shams al-Din reiterates the concept of extinction in God (*fana' fi'llah*) which the faithful must seek, saying 'for only God is and there is nothing besides Him'. The outward sign of this is a type of inebriation, mentioned by Hamzah in his poem. Shams al-Din clarifies the concept of being inebriated by saying, 'One is enraptured and inebriate when one makes no difference whatever ... between one's own being and God's Being.' Again this was targeted for vehement criticism by al-Raniri.

A plethora of miscellaneous themes and features can be found in Shams al-Din's commentary, echoing elements found in Hamzah's original poem. Like Hamzah, Shams al-Din responds well to metaphorical writing. He explains Hamzah's preference for the metaphor of the China Sea over that of Mount Sinai by suggesting that a Holy Land does not capture the omnipresence of a Holy Sea.

Furthermore, in the preface to this work, Shams al-Din alludes to the doctrine of the Perfect Man by referring to Muhammad as 'the best of mankind'. This reflects the influence of a doctrine developed by medieval theologians, including Ibn al-'Arabi, and made famous by al-Jili's classic work on the subject, entitled 'The Perfect Man'.[32] This doctrine had considerable impact on views of kingship in Court Malay texts,[33] and Shams al-Din was no doubt aware of its perceived relevance to the Malay world context.

This commentary demonstrates very clearly the line of transmission ending with Shams al-Din, who based himself upon Hamzah Fansuri, with both ultimately drawing upon famous Arab Sufis, including Ibn al-'Arabi and al-Jili. Hamzah and Shams al-Din should be seen primarily as transmitters, rather than innovators. They took Sufi teachings circulating in the Arab world and India and caste them in a Malay mould for the benefit of Malay Muslims. However, their primary

---

[32] Peters 1994:349–51.
[33] Milner 1988:39ff.

function as transmitters was not to protect them from scathing polemical attacks, as we shall see.

Nur al-Din al-Raniri

The death of Iskandar Muda in 1636 led to an about face in the religious and doctrinal orientation of the Sultanate. Shortly after Iskandar Thani's succession to power, Nur al-Din al-Raniri, an Islamic scholar originating from Gujerat in India, arrived in Aceh. He was appointed as *shaykh al-islam* under the patronage of the new Sultan, and during the next seven years, he devoted his energies to writing works aimed at refuting what he considered to be the heretical teachings of Hamzah and Shams al-Din.

Al-Raniri's full name was Nur al-Din Muhammad b. 'Ali al-Hamid al-Shafi'i al-Ash'ari al-'Aydarusi al-Raniri al-Surati. Though the details of his early life are sketchy, much can be gleaned from his name. He was born into a diaspora Hadhrami family of the Hamid clan in Ranir (present day Rander) in Gujerat, India. He received training in Islamic mysticism from Sayyid 'Umar b. 'Abd Allah Ba Shayban al-'Aydarusi,[34] a scholar living in India who had originated from Terim in the Hadhramaut and who was versed in the 'Aydarusiyya Sufi order. Sayyid 'Umar had himself studied with Muhammad al-'Aydarus (b. 1562), who like al-Raniri and Sayyid 'Umar, was the offspring of a mixed Hadhrami/Indian family.[35] Thus al-Raniri represented a link in the strong relationship between Hadhrami initiates of the 'Aydarusiyya Order and India.[36]

Al-Raniri's early study of Islam in India may have been accompanied by a study of Malay with the significant Malay community resident in Gujerat.[37] Various suggestions have been made regarding al-Raniri's early contacts with the Malay world; it has also been suggested that his mother was a Malay,[38] though the evidence for this is inconclusive. It is, however, well established that al-Raniri's uncle, Muhammad Jailani Hamid, visited Aceh during the 1580s for the purpose of teaching the

---

34 Voorhoeve 1959:90.
35 Tudjimah 1961:2.
36 Drewes 1955:150.
37 Iskandar 1966:2.
38 Al-Attas 1966:12.

Islamic sciences. Initially, his intention was to teach theology and Islamic law, but after encountering limited interest in these fields, he travelled to Mecca to study Islamic mysticism, a field which attracted greater interest in Aceh at the time. After detailed studies in this field, Muhammad Jailani Hamid returned to Aceh to teach Sufism to a substantial number of students.[39]

In 1620/1, al-Raniri made the pilgrimage to Mecca and Medina, which perhaps afforded the opportunity to further perfect his Malay through contact with the Malay community established in Mecca.[40] Al-Raniri in all likelihood took advantage of his presence in the Arabian peninsula to pay a visit to the place of origin of his ancestors, the Hadhramaut; this would be consistent with the custom among members of diaspora Hadhrami sayyid families to keep contact with their country of origin.[41] He may even have studied in the Hadhramaut during this period.

His whereabouts over the next fifteen years are uncertain, though scholars have suggested that he spent some time during this period in various parts of the Malay peninsula, including Pahang. Various factors suggest this:

1. His extensive knowledge of the *Sejarah Melayu* which acts as a source for his work *Bustan al-Salatin*.
2. His detailed knowledge of the kings of Pahang, referred to in *Bustan al-Salatin*.
3. His excellent relationship with Sultan Iskandar Thani of Aceh, who originated from Pahang, and who welcomed him warmly when al-Raniri arrived later in Aceh, which suggests that the relationship had existed some time prior to his arrival in that state.[42]

It has also been suggested that al-Raniri visited Aceh during the rule of Sultan Iskandar Muda prior to 1636, but because of his discomfort with the predominance of the highly speculative approach to Sufism within the kingdom at the time, he left

---

[39] Tudjimah 1961:3.
[40] Voorhoeve 1951:357.
[41] Al-Attas 1986:4.
[42] Iskandar 1966:3; al-Attas 1986:7.

disenchanted.[43] Though there is some doubt about this initial visit, it is accepted that al-Raniri arrived in Aceh after the death of Iskandar Muda, on the basis of information provided by *Bustan al-Salatin*, which mentions his arrival in that port city on 31 May 1637.[44] His appointment as Chief Judge by Sultan Iskandar Thani soon after his arrival placed him in a position to greatly influence the theological life of the kingdom, and during the next seven years he wrote a total of fourteen works on various subjects.[45]

With the death of Iskandar Thani in 1641, al-Raniri initially found favour with the new Sultanah Safiyyat al-Din, and remained in the post of Chief Judge. However, his star was to set soon afterwards. Al-Raniri was forced to leave Aceh in disgrace in 1644, driven out by a grouping of the followers of Shams al-Din who were championing the cause of a new Minangkabau scholar named Sayf al-Rijal.[46] Al-Raniri returned to India where he died on 21 September 1658.[47]

The importance of Raniri in the history of the Sultanate should not be underestimated. Although he appears to have spent barely seven years there as a resident, he ignited a doctrinal dispute, and initiated a process of reform, that was to have a significant impact on Acehnese religious circles and, indeed, on the whole region.

His literary works.   Al-Raniri's literary works have been listed by several scholars in recent decades: Voorhoeve,[48] Tudjimah,[49] Daudy[50] and Al-Attas.[51] The most comprehensive list, that drawn up by Daudy, indicates that in all al-Raniri produced twenty-nine works, some of which have been edited and published and many which have not but which exist in manuscript form in various parts of the world. A measure of al-Raniri's significance is provided by the fact that his writings alone constitute almost 4 per cent of the approximately 800 titles contained in Malay language

---

43   Tudjimah 1961:4.
44   Voorhoeve 1951:357.
45   Iskandar 1964:440.
46   Ito 1978:491; Azra 1992:362–5.
47   Voorhoeve 1959:91.
48   Voorhoeve 1955:152ff.
49   Tudjimah 1961:9ff.
50   Daudy 1983:48ff.
51   Al-Attas 1986:24ff.

manuscript collections world-wide,[52] with his *Bustan al-Salatin* representing probably the longest work in this corpus.

Al-Raniri's writings serve as a testimony to his breadth of knowledge and abundance of talent in wide-ranging fields. His areas of specialisation in the Islamic sciences were comprehensive. He wrote on theology, Islamic law, the Traditions and Sufism. A number of his writings, such as *Sirat al-mustaqim*, dealing with the rules of Islamic ritual, are still studied in Indonesian Islamic schools some 350 years after their composition.[53] Moreover, he wrote about history and demonstrated himself to be an expert in language style, and possessed a command of many languages: Persian, Arabic, Urdu, Malay and Acehnese.[54] Doubts have been expressed as to his command of Arabic[55] on the basis of grammatical errors in the Arabic texts of some of his works. However, Daudy[56] has challenged this claim, pointing out that the nature of the errors suggests faults by the copyist rather than the original author. Furthermore, al-Raniri was versatile not only in terms of fields of learning mastered and various language skills, but also in that he was able to adjust his writing style to suit diverse audiences; some of his works were addressed to scholarly specialists, others to non-specialist lay readers.[57]

It would be useful to briefly examine the content of several of al-Raniri's works at this juncture in order to gain an understanding of the thoughts and motivations driving him in his writing.

In his work *Hujjat al-siddiq li-daf' al-zindiq*, which is designed to serve as a specific refutation of what he considered as the pantheistic teachings of his two predecessors, Raniri clarifies his concerns, and warns of violent retribution which will befall those who engage in heretical practices and beliefs. He intended this to represent the response of orthodoxy to the monistic notions of Hamzah and Shams al-Din. Ahmad Daudy, who conducted a detailed study of the doctrines of both al-Raniri and his earlier Acehnese adversaries, concluded that all lay outside the boundaries of orthodox Islamic doctrine,

---

[52] Steenbrink 1990:192.

[53] Steenbrink 1990:193.

[54] Daudy 1983:58.

[55] Tudjimah 1961:8.

[56] Daudy 1983:58.

[57] Steenbrink 1990:197.

while Al-Attas, in contrast, argued strongly for al-Raniri having misunderstood the essential orthodoxy of Hamzah's position.[58] Regardless of the views of modern scholars, there is no doubt that the views of Hamzah and Shams al-Din were subjected to accusations of heresy by al-Raniri and others claiming to represent orthodoxy. Central to the orthodox concerns was strong opposition to the suggestion by the monistic Sufis of the individual Muslim realising his essential union with the Creator. Many more orthodox Islamic scholars regarded this as heresy, and al-Raniri speaks clearly in these terms in *Hujjat al-siddiq*.

Al-Raniri presents a skilful summary of the core beliefs regarding the being of God as held by four schools of Islamic thought: the Theologians; the Sufis; the Philosophers; and the Wujudiyya, or those adhering to the doctrine of *wahdat al-wujud*. Al-Raniri endorses the view of the Theologians, who he says base themselves upon reason and revelation and 'affirm [the existence] of two beings: the one Contingent Being and the other Necessary Being'.[59] He also endorses the approach of the Sufis, indicating that they base their views on reason, revelation, insight and experience. Al-Raniri levels criticism at the Philosophers who 'say that God has no power whatsoever over all … , and that He has no power to create anything other than and apart from that which emanates from Him'.[60]

But al-Raniri reserves his most scathing criticism for some of the Wujudiyya. He argues that there are two groups of Wujudiyya: the true and the heretical. Ibn al-'Arabi belongs to the former, according to al-Raniri, as the great medieval thinker wrote that '… the Being of God is that upon which [all other] beings depend for their existence'.[61] Al-Raniri argues that the true Wujudiyya in fact belong with the Sufis. The heretical Wujudiyya are distinguishable as those who affirm that '… the creatures are God's Being and the Being of God is the being of the creatures … nothing exists but God'.[62] The key difference, according to al-Raniri, is that the true Wujudiyya

58 Al-Attas 1963:28.
59 Al-Attas 1966:101.
60 Al-Attas 1966:102.
61 Al-Attas 1966:104.
62 Al-Attas 1966:103.

see it as a vain exercise to strive to know God, as only God can will that. However, the heretical Wujudiyya, in al-Raniri's view, consider that human effort under appropriate guidance can unlock the secrets of the divine unity.

This work constitutes a climax to al-Raniri's attack on the 'heretical' Wujudiyya, identified with Hamzah Fansuri and Shams al-Din of Pasai. Among al-Raniri's principal accusations in this work are the following:

1. The equating of the Creator and the created is a heresy.
2. Those Sufis who make such claims are in a state of involuntary intoxication (a theme which appeared clearly in the writings of Hamzah and Shams al-Din examined earlier).
3. These monistic Sufis believe that entering such a state frees them from their obligations to the behavioural norms of Islamic law, as recorded in the *shari'a*.
4. In this the monistic Sufis are mistaken. All Muslims are obliged to perform their ritual obligations at all times.
5. Such Sufis who continue on the path of heresy, and ignore the warnings, are deserving of death and fire.[63]

A significant number of al-Raniri's writings were devoted to addressing this polemic and to refuting what he considered as the heretical writings of Hamzah Fansuri and Shams al-Din al-Sumatrani and their followers. Another work to consider is *Jawahir al-'ulum fi kash al-ma'lum*, which includes a clear articulation by al-Raniri of his position and a sharp denunciation of the teachings of his predecessors.[64] Al-Raniri identifies one of his sources in compiling this work as *Lawa'ih fi bayan ma'ani 'urfaniya* by the great Sufi scholar 'Abd al-Rahman Jami (d. 1492). Al-Raniri is concerned to establish a frame of reference in his writing which would be considered as orthodox. In this context, he clearly states in this work that all things return to God. Though the statement is short and concise, it serves to establish a sense of divine otherness which is a key plank of al-Raniri's attack upon the teachings of Hamzah and Shams al-Din. This framework is reinforced by statements such as 'whatever anyone knows is by virtue of His knowledge', which again serves to affirm a sense of

---

[63] Al-Attas 1966:110–12.
[64] Johns 1957:105–6.

God's omnipotence, supplemented by a hint of God's predestination of events – i.e. a transcendent God of majesty and power.

However, al-Raniri himself does not eschew Sufi teachings. Indeed, he himself was a Sufi, having been initiated into the Rifa'iyya order and also being affiliated with the 'Aydarusiyya and Qadiriyya orders.[65] Rather, he seeks to present what he considers as a Sufi orthodoxy, with statements such as the following:

> The Essence of God is One, in it there is no multiplicity or plurality, it is only substances and accidents that are manifold, i.e. visible things. … The Essence of God considered as absolute and void of determinations and limitations is called *Haqq*, but from the standpoint of the multiplicity of visible manifestations and determinations is called *khalq* and the world, for the world is the exterior of God, i.e. a manifestation of Him, and God the hidden reality (*batin*) of the world, i.e. He manifests it.[66]

Anticipating reader confusion with his presentation of the *Haqq/khalq* dichotomy, al-Raniri then presents an analogy of multiple mirrors reflecting the one source, representing multiple manifestations of the one unity. Having thus articulated what he sees as correct Sufi teaching, based on multiplicity within unity, al-Raniri launches an attack on the Wujudiyya, targeting (though not identifying) Hamzah Fansuri and Shams al-Din. He accuses them of collapsing the correct multiplicity-within-unity view into a simple equation of God and the world by saying 'the world is God and God is the world'. He attributes their perceived errors to a misunderstanding on their part of technical terminology of Sufism and to an imperfect understanding of 'the sciences of exegesis and tradition'. In this, al-Raniri implies, they commit the ultimate calumny of distorting the word of God, the Qur'an.

One of the many reasons that al-Raniri's writings are so valuable is that they identify important literary sources used by Hamzah Fansuri and Shams al-Din. Given the destruction of many of their writings in the purges during al-Raniri's period in Aceh, much can thus be gleaned about external influences upon Hamzah and Shams al-Din through the pages of al-Raniri's writings. *Jawahir al-'ulum fi kash al-ma'lum* identifies their sources as follows: Muhyi'l-Din ibn al-'Arabi's *Fusus al-Hikam*; 'Abd al-

65 Azra 1992:367; Vakily 1997:120.
66 Johns 1957:105.

Karim al-Jili's *Sharh Mishkat Futuhat*; the writings of Muhammad ibn Fadl Allah al-Burhanpuri.[67]

Moreover, al-Raniri not only identifies the sources used by Hamzah and Shams al-Din, but he also methodically repeats some of the core statements made in their sources, and demonstrates how Hamzah and Shams al-Din have incorrectly (in his view) interpreted these statements. Al-Raniri's own response is based on the notion articulated above, that his predecessors were confusing the multiplicity-in-unity theme with a much more reduced monism which saw all existence as God, rather than as an outward manifestation of God.

Other works composed by al-Raniri for the purpose of attacking the teachings of Hamzah and Shams al-Din were *Nubdhah fi da'wa al-zill ma'a sahibihi* (in Arabic) and *Hall al-zill*. Other shorter works were devoted to specific polemical issues such as *al-Lama'an bi takfir man qala bi khalq al-Qur'an*, in which al-Raniri attacks those who consider the Qur'an to have been created.[68]

In his work *Tibyan fi ma'rifat al-adayn*, for which he drew extensively from the *Kitab al-tamhid fi bayan al-tawhid* of Abu Shakur al-Salimi,[69] al-Raniri describes quite graphically a debate which took place between the followers of Shams al-Din and himself in the presence of Sultan Iskandar Thani. The debate lasted for several days and both sides presented their case to the Sultan, clearly seeking his endorsement. Al-Raniri accused his opponents of effectively claiming divinity for themselves in asserting that they had attained union with God. This is reminiscent of the accusation which led to the execution of al-Hallaj in 922. Al-Raniri's arguments won on the day, and the *'Ulama'* pronounced a *fatwa* of unbelief and condemned the followers of Shams al-Din to death. It is related that some renounced their previous doctrines and returned to the orthodox line, while others did not. Al-Raniri describes that a period of executions followed this incident, no doubt justified by reference to the sentence passed on al-Hallaj.

It is important to understand the significance of the topic of debate. Al-Raniri's stress upon a differentiation between God and his earthly manifestations, between *Haqq* and *khalq*, was directly

<hr>

[67] Johns 1957:105–6.
[68] Al-Attas 1986:28.
[69] Steenbrink 1990:198.

relevant to the temporal context. The implication of such a line of argument was that ordinary individuals should acknowledge the authority of, and respect and revere, the Sultan, as the head of the temporal kingdom. The followers of Shams al-Din, according to al-Raniri's line of argument, were destined to incur the wrath of the Sultan, by suggesting that they as ordinary individuals could realise communion, and indeed union, with almighty God, thus placing them closer to the Creator than the Sultan himself.

It should also be remembered that the above-mentioned polemic in Aceh had occurred along similar lines in India some decades earlier. Sufis who had held sway in the Mughal court in India during the latter part of the 16th century fell out of favour during the reign of Jahangir,[70] who was greatly influenced by the head of the Naqshbandi order, Ahmad Sirhindi. This latter figure, though himself a Sufi, also affirmed the distinction mentioned above between creature and Creator, and his attack on Sufis whom he considered inclined to pantheism resembled in content the stance of al-Raniri. In the same way as occurred in Aceh some decades later, Sirhindi's influence brought about a great narrowing in the religious perspective of the court, and led to widespread persecution, murders, and destruction of literary works.

The exact manner of influence of these developments in India upon those in Aceh is difficult to determine. It is likely that the transmission of these conflicting theological standpoints was via the well established lines of communication between India and the Malay world which had been in existence for over a millennium. This ensured that polemics preoccupying competing schools of thought within Indian Islamic communities would surface in a similar form within Muslim Southeast Asia. Moreover, the fact that al-Raniri grew up in India and undertook most of his education there meant inevitably that he too served as a conduit for Indian Islamic doctrines and reformist thinking. Mention should also be made of the role of the Arabian scholarly networks in this period in stimulating a reformist surge in the far corners of the Muslim world. Azra identifies al-Raniri as 'one of the most important early *mujaddids* in the archipelago'.[71] In fulfilling this role, al-Raniri was transmitting reformist pulses originating in

---

[70] Ruled 1605–27.
[71] Azra 1992:351.

both Arabia and India, and thereby stimulating the Islamisation of the archipelago.

An additional perspective relating to al-Raniri's inclination towards polemics concerns his portrayal of Jewish and Christian scriptures and belief. In his *Hujjat al-siddiq li daf' al-zindiq*, al-Raniri groups the heretical Wujudiyya with the Jews and the Christians, dismissing Jewish and Christian belief by stating 'such sayings and beliefs are a rejection of the truth'.[72] Steenbrink has identified a number of strongly anti-Christian statements in Raniri's diverse writings. In one instance al-Raniri portrays the biblical materials as falsified, and therefore suitable for being used as toilet paper. His choice of terminology to describe Jews and Christians favours the term *kuffar* (infidels) over *ahl al-kitab* (People of the Book).[73] In this way he echoes certain anti-Jewish and anti-Christian polemical approaches which he no doubt encountered in Arabia and which were perhaps fuelled by conflicts between Muslims and early European colonial expansion into Asia.

'Abd al-Ra'uf al-Singkili

The main Islamic scholar to dominate the religious life of the Acehnese sultanate during the latter half of the 17th century was 'Abd al-Ra'uf b. Ali al-Fansuri al-Singkili (*c.* 1615–93). He was born in the West Sumatran coastal town of Singkel, which was a vassal state of the Sultanate of Aceh. His early years must have been spent studying the Islamic sciences during the period of predominance of the monistic Sufis. There is some evidence that he may have been a blood relative of Hamzah Fansuri.[74] 'Abd al-Ra'uf's childhood coincided with the years of great external expansion of the Sultanate. Virtually nothing is known about this period of his life, though legends concerning his ancestry and childhood abound.

At twenty-six or twenty-seven years of age, 'Abd al-Ra'uf departed for Arabia to further his study of the Islamic sciences, as had Hamzah Fansuri some sixty or so years before. Our knowledge of 'Abd al-Ra'uf's experiences in Arabia is based on his work

---

[72] Al-Attas 1966:105.
[73] Steenbrink 1990:194–5.
[74] Azra 1992:383–4.

'Umdat al-muhtajin (The Support of the Needy), which contains a codicil, apparently composed by the author himself, which details his years of study at various centres of Islamic learning in the Arabian Peninsula. In this codicil,[75] 'Abd al-Ra'uf makes a list of some fifteen teachers with whom he studied, in addition to listing other scholars and students with whom he had varying degrees of contact in centres such as Mecca, Jeddah, Bayt al-Faqih, Zabid, and Medina during his nineteen-year stay there. The most important of his contacts were clearly Ahmad al-Qushashi (d. 1660) of Medina, the spiritual father of many 17th-century Indian mystics, and his successor Ibrahim al-Kurani (d. 1690), who authorised 'Abd al-Ra'uf to establish a school of mysticism in Aceh. This school was to contribute greatly to the spread of the Shattariyya Order throughout the archipelago,[76] though this order was not to survive in the Arabian peninsula.[77]

The importance of this codicil in *'Umdat al-muhtajin* is that it provides us with a spiritual genealogical tree for the mystical order which 'Abd al-Ra'uf did so much to establish in the Malay world. Johns points out that 'Abd al-Ra'uf is the first of the great Malay Islamic scholars for whom a line of transmission is traceable.[78] It is perhaps to this fact that much of his subsequent reputation can be attributed, as the importance of lines of transmission (*isnad*) as evidence of authority within Islam is well established.

This codicil provides crucial insights into the pattern followed by Malay Islamic scholars in undertaking their training in the Islamic sciences. The term codicil in fact conceals its true form; it is, in essence, a very user-friendly travel diary in which the author outlined for his readers the principal focuses of his nineteen-year sojourn in Arabia. The travel diary identifies the priorities for such visits by early Malay scholars as follows:

• The necessity of undertaking wide-ranging study in the Islamic sciences, covering topics such as law, dogma, the Traditions, history, Qur'anic recitation, Sufism, and other subjects.

---

[75] For the Malay transliterated text and an English translation of this codicil, cf. Riddell 1990a:223–38.

[76] Trimingham 1971:130.

[77] Snouck Hurgronje 1906:II, 18.

[78] Johns 1975:46.

- The need to pass through various stages of learning. For example, 'Abd al-Ra'uf initially studied with Ibrahim b. 'Abd Allah Jam'an (d. 1672) who referred him on after a time to Ahmad al-Qushashi.
- The need for the scholar in question to be mobile, progressing from location to location. As indicated above, 'Abd al-Ra'uf studied in a variety of centres in the Arabian peninsula as did, no doubt, his successors.
- The need to study for a recognised qualification, not merely undertake studies for personal fulfilment. Ahmad al-Qushashi initiated 'Abd al-Ra'uf into the mystical path, and after the former's death Ibrahim al-Kurani completed 'Abd al-Ra'uf's instruction, and awarded him the licence which gave him authority to propagate the mystical teachings he had acquired.
- The need to be eclectic in undertaking the study of Sufism. 'Abd al-Ra'uf did not only study with one Sufi order, but he studied with teachers following the systems of the Shattariyya, Qadiriyya, Habashiyya, Firdawsiyya, Tinuriyya, Khalwatiyya, Hamadaniyya and the famous Naqshbandiyya Orders.

There seems little doubt that 'Abd al-Ra'uf would have sought answers to the issues arising from the violent polemic that had filled centre stage in Aceh prior to his departure in 1642. That news of this polemic had reached Arabia is recorded in the preface to Ibrahim al-Kurani's *Ithaf al-dhaki bi-sharh al-tuhfa al-mursala ila al-nabi* (A Presentation to the discriminating in explanation of the Gift addressed to the prophet), where the author states:

We have had reliable information from a company of Jawi, that there have spread among the inhabitants of the lands of 'Java' some books on Realities, and esoteric teachings by men attributed with knowledge because of their study and the teaching of others, but who lack any understanding of the Law of (Muhammad) the Chosen, the Elect (of God), and even less of an awareness of the knowledge of Realities bestowed upon those who follow God's path, may He be exalted; this has led many of them to deviate from the right path, and given rise to faulty belief, in fact they have been attracted to camp in the valleys of unbelief and heresy ...[79]

---

[79] Johns 1975:51; 1978:479.

This work was ostensibly composed to resolve some of the contentious issues arising from the conflict in Aceh. It is probable that 'Abd al-Ra'uf himself was one of those who brought news of this conflict to Arabia. It is equally probable that 'Abd al-Ra'uf was committed to resolving the conflict that had been so harmful to religious life in Aceh. However, his methods were considerably more irenic than those of al-Raniri, as is indicated by his statement that:

If [a] man is a *kafir* why waste words on it? And if he is not the saying will come back upon ourselves, for the Prophet said: 'Let no man accuse another of leading a sinful life or of infidelity, for the accusation will turn back upon himself if it is false.' Such is the danger of accusing another of infidelity; we take refuge with God from such.[80]

'Abd al-Ra'uf returned to Aceh in 1661 after the death of his master Ahmad al-Qushashi. Biographical details relating to that part of 'Abd al-Ra'uf's life between his return to Aceh and his death are scarce. The last thirty years of his life can only be glimpsed through fragmentary comments made in manuscripts of his works copied by certain of his students. It was during the rule of the last female Sultan of Aceh, Kamalat Shah, that we find the last piece of evidence that 'Abd al-Ra'uf was still alive. In a colophon to a manuscript of *Mir'at al-Tullab* copied by one of his students, mention is made that at the time of copying (1693), 'Abd al-Ra'uf was living in Peunayong,[81] now a section of Banda Aceh, and scholars are generally agreed that 'Abd al-Ra'uf must have died around this time.

His literary works.   In an appendix to his edited text of 'Abd al-Ra'uf's *Bayan Tajalli*, Voorhoeve[82] makes a meticulous listing of all the works which can be attributed to 'Abd al-Ra'uf and the locations of the various extant manuscripts of these works. A perusal of the subjects of his writings helps us to understand the manner and degree of education of 'Abd al-Ra'uf. His written works include various of the traditional Islamic disciplines, with a special feature of both his and Ibrahim al-Kurani's writings being that they taught both the *zahir* (exoteric) and the *batin*

---

[80] Johns 1955b:153–4.
[81] Voorhoeve 1952:88.
[82] Voorhoeve 1952.

(esoteric) sciences, reflecting his concern to reconcile *shari'a* and Sufism. The subjects of his writings include:

1. Jurisprudence (*fiqh*)
2. Sufism (*tasawwuf*)
3. Qur'anic exegesis (*tafsir*)
4. Islamic Law (*shari'a*)
5. Eschatology (*sakharat al-maut*)
6. The purpose of prayer
7. The doctrines of Ibn al-'Arabi
8. The duties of teacher and student

Soon after his return to Aceh from Arabia, 'Abd al-Ra'uf was commissioned by the Sultana Safiyat al-Din Shah (1641–75) to write *Mir'at al-Tullab*, a work on jurisprudence. This work was completed in 1663.[83] Sultana Inayat Shah Zakiyat al-Din Shah (1678–88) commissioned 'Abd al-Ra'uf to write at least two works. The first of these was *Risalat adab murid akan shaykh*, which deals with the respective duties of teacher and student.

The second work commissioned by Sultana Zakiyat al-Din Shah was a commentary upon the famous *Arba'ina Hadith* by al-Nawawi (d. 1277).[84] Al-Nawawi's original work had a major impact upon Islamic communities around the world throughout history, as it included a concise presentation of forty Hadith accounts addressing fundamental but key issues in Islamic belief and practice. Al-Nawawi indicated in the preface to his work that 'every person wishing to attain the Hereafter should know these Hadith',[85] thus the work came to be regarded by non-theologians among the Muslim populations as an important key for winning God's favour. Abd al-Ra'uf's selection of this work as a focus reflects its important role in the mass education of Muslims in the Malay–Indonesian world during the 17th century. Furthermore it points to his determination to address the legacy of the earlier polemics in Aceh by reaffirming the reformed Sufi approach initiated by al-Raniri, emphasising the place of the *shari'a* after its neglect during the long period of dominance of Hamzah and Shams al-Din.

---

[83] Abdurrauf 1971:foreword.
[84] Voorhoeve 1952:111.
[85] Ibrahim and Johnson-Davies 1977:22.

In addition to those works that clearly result from an official
commission, there are many others that were produced by this
prolific scholar, perhaps on his own initiative. The previously
mentioned *'Umdat al-muhtajin* provides directions for the practice
of wide-ranging methods of *dhikr* which 'Abd al-Ra'uf learned
from his many teachers in Arabia. It also contains sections
addressing ethical questions likely to be encountered by the Sufi
postulant.[86]

Another shorter work which deserves attention is *Lubb al-kashf
wa al-bayan lima yarahu al-muhtadar bi al-'iyan*[87] (Essential exposition and Clarification on the Visionary Experience of the Dying
and what Gladdens him) which describes the experience of the
dying. 'Abd al-Ra'uf wrote this as a reflection on a Jawi text he
encountered, which he described as being based on *Kitab al-
tadhkira bi-umur al-akhira* by the famous 13th-century Andalusian
Malikite scholar al-Qurtubi (d. 1272).

Lubb al-kashf engages with several issues of concern, in particular the experience of death which every individual must undergo
at some point and which is a source of anxious anticipation for
many. The author affirms the view that the dying experience a
series of visions as they depart this life. These visions tempt the
dying person to abandon Islam and to turn to other faiths. In this,
'Abd al-Ra'uf is affirming a view that the deceased are subjected to
a series of temptations and torments during and after death. As we
saw in Part I of this study, this issue was a matter of some debate in
the early centuries of Islam, with some groups such as the
Mu'tazila rejecting this. 'Abd al-Ra'uf is thus aligning himself
with the position which came to represent orthodoxy after the fall
from influence of the Mu'tazila.

Moreover, *Lubb al-kashf* addresses the matter of faiths 'of the
Book', namely Christianity and Judaism, which it presents
clearly as having strayed from the true path. The Christians and
Jews are presented, along with Satan, as those who tempt the
dying to abandon Islam during the dying process. In fact,
demons are portrayed as disguising themselves as relatives of the
dying in an attempt to lure the believer away from Islam. This
co-locating of Christianity and Judaism with demonic forces

---

[86] Cf. Rinkes (1909) for a study of this work.
[87] Voorhoeve 1952:91–3.

resonates with al-Raniri's portrayal of Christian belief discussed earlier in this present chapter. As with al-Raniri, it is likely that 'Abd al-Ra'uf absorbed such anti-Christian doctrines during his period of study in the Arabian peninsula, and they may have been exacerbated by unfavourable contacts with Christians after his return to the Malay world in the context of encroaching European colonial expansion.

Furthermore, *Lubb al-kashf* is strongly determinist in orientation, including phrases such as 'Allah inclines whoever He wishes towards faiths which have gone astray', providing Qur'anic references in support. Though only a short work, *Lubb al-kashf*'s significance should not be underestimated. First, it engages with matters of common concern to individuals. Second, it acts as a vehicle for the transmission of teachings by a major Islamic scholar from the late Abbasid period, whom it identifies for the edification of its readers. Third, it grounds itself at appropriate points in Qur'anic verse references, thus demonstrating a concern with appearing to be based on orthodoxy rather than a highly speculative approach.

Another work of considerable significance produced by 'Abd al-Ra'uf is his commentary on the Qur'an, *Tarjuman al-Mustafid*, which was written around 1675. This work is discussed in more detail in a later section.

In the previously mentioned *Bayan Tajalli*, 'Abd al-Ra'uf addresses the question of the nature of God, which was such a source of controversy among his scholarly predecessors in Aceh. He affirms a Sufi position, but eschews the degree of monistic unity embraced by Hamzah and Shams al-Din. God's uniqueness is affirmed, which sits well with *shari'a*-focused orthodoxy. Everything in the world is seen as belonging to God. God's seven principal attributes are articulated, and man is given seven faces which serve as a reflection of God. If man follows the *shari'a*, and partakes in *dhikr* 'both with the tongue and with the soul', and follows other mystical practices under the instruction of a teacher, he will reach an awareness of the Truth and will undergo a voluntary 'death' to the things of this world, resulting in true submission to God.

The vast scope of his writings is a mark of the overall dedication and determination of 'Abd al-Ra'uf, and it demonstrates several concerns:

- He was concerned with the personal virtue of individuals. He wanted to take them through the range from elementary principles to the highest level of mysticism.
- He aimed to clarify a range of issues which had previously been sources of contention.
- He wished to provide a broad framework for the expansion of his particular Sufi order, the Shattariiyya Order.
- Above all, he wished to affirm a reformed type of Sufism, promoted by al-Raniri, which emphasised the importance of adhering to the *shari'a* but still allowed room for following the mystical path.

It should also be noted that he was painstakingly accurate in his renderings, and did not add information to that drawn from his sources to nearly the same degree as did other Malay authors such as 'Abd al-Samad al-Palimbani. Though his methods were by no means characterised by the same degree of fervour and violence as those of al-Raniri, 'Abd al-Ra'uf's teachings were clearly perceived by his contemporaries and those who followed as falling within the bounds of orthodoxy. The star of the early monistic Sufis had set, and they were never to regain the same level of official support as had been the case during the rule of Iskandar Muda.

Other works

Malay translation of al-Nasafi's creed.   Another work which should be considered at this juncture is the Malay translation of the *'Aqa'id* (Creed) of al-Nasafi (d. 1142). Al-Attas has shown that the surviving manuscript which contains this text was copied in 1590, making it the oldest known Malay manuscript available today.[88] Al-Attas further identifies Aceh as the likely place where this manuscript was produced, given the degree to which the study of the Islamic sciences was flourishing there at that time. Indeed, there was a major Arab world input to Islamic studies in Aceh at the end of the 16th century, as we have seen in earlier discussion. During the rule of Acehnese Sultan 'Ali Ri'ayat Shah (1571-9), Islamic sciences were taught by the Meccan scholar Muhammad Azhari.[89] In the 1580s two more Arab scholars, Abu al-Khayr ibn

---

[88] Al-Attas 1988:6ff.
[89] Al-Attas 1988:32, citing the *Bustan al-Salatin*.

Shaykh ibn Hajar and Muhammad al-Yamani, came to play significant roles as Islamic teachers in Aceh, while Muhammad al-
Hamid, the paternal uncle of Nur al-Din al-Raniri, also taught
Islamic sciences at Aceh between 1580–3 and again from 1589–
1604. Al-Attas goes so far as to speculate that the Malay translation
of al-Nasafi's Creed may have been done by one of the students of
Muhammad al-Hamid.[90]

Of particular interest in the context of earlier discussion is the
'orthodoxy' of this text, in contrast with what Al-Attas points to
as the adaptations of Hamzah's teachings by pseudo-Sufis in
Aceh at the time. Al-Attas is a vigorous advocate for the orthodoxy of Hamzah's teachings, arguing that later accusations of
heresy against Hamzah were in fact undeserved. He asserts that
Hamzah's reputation had been sullied by eager disciples who had
taken Hamzah's monistic teachings much further than the great
writer himself would have agreed to.

Thus it may well be that introduction of a standard, uncontro-
versial text such as al-Nasafi's Creed had as its purpose to serve as
a corrective to the excesses of certain Sufis. It includes an accessible, yet sufficiently comprehensive statement of key Ash'arite
doctrines. It was produced during the latter years of Hamzah
Fansuri, and may have represented an opening shot in an emerging war of words between competing schools in Aceh, which was
to reach its peak in the late 1630s.

Tuhfa al-mursala ila ruh al-nabi. Another work which bears
examination at this point of our study is *Tuhfa al-mursala ila ruh al-
nabi*, to which reference has been made in previous discussion. This
work provides a particularly good example of transmission of
Islamic thought from India to the Malay–Indonesian world, and
relates closely to the theological polemic in Aceh in the 1630s
referred to earlier.

The Arabic text of this work was completed in 1590[91] and was
written in India by Muhammad ibn Fadl Allah al-Burhanpuri (d.
1620). It was written primarily as a rebuttal to speculative views
circulating in India which were considered as heterodox by the

---

[90] Al-Attas 1988:34.
[91] Johns 1998a:283.

Islamic authorities at the time. The polemic in India resembled in certain respects that which occured in Aceh in the 1630s.

Al-Burhanpuri based his theological framework on a system of seven grades of being, on which Shams al-Din drew directly. The work had reached Sumatra by 1610, and proceeded to become a core text in religious schools throughout the Indonesian archipelago.[92] Ibrahim al-Kurani composed a commentary on the *Tuhfa* prior to 1661 to inform the Indonesian situation and resolve the al-Raniri versus Hamzah and Shams al-Din polemic. Johns proposes that the Javanese version of the *Tuhfa*, rendered by an anonymous court poet, was completed by 1680 at the latest,[93] so the significance of the work for Malay–Indonesian Islam should not be underestimated, as it appeared in the region when the reforming efforts to reconcile *shari'a* and Sufism were underway.

With regard to the mystical framework presented in the original *Tuhfa*, in spite of Shams al-Din's use of it for his own writing, it appears to differ from Shams al-Din's approach in a significant way. The work begins by explaining the seven grades of being, with the same categories, titles and characteristics articulated by Shams al-Din in *Nur al-Daqa'iq* discussed previously. However, the author is at pains to stress the point made by al-Raniri that knowledge of the Essence of God – the ultimate goal of the Wujudiyya – is a gift of the grace of God, not the result of human effort: '... one who desires a knowledge of Him from this aspect, and strives for it (by these created means) wastes his time.'[94] This is re-stated throughout. In fact, the work's parting statement in the final paragraph reiterates that falling into ecstasy occurs through the Grace of God, not through one's own effort.

Al-Burhanpuri was also conscious in his writing of the need to strike a balance between mystical pursuits and observance of the outward rules of the faith. He stresses the importance of observing the *shari'a*, saying that it should not be neglected in favour of mystical pursuits. Furthermore, he stresses the role of revelation by ample quotes from the Qur'an in support of the mystical system proposed by this work. In other words, he affirms the balance between the spiritual quest and observance

---

[92] Johns 1998a:283.
[93] Johns 1965:12.
[94] Johns 1965:140.

of the revealed law, which represented the approaches of al-Raniri and 'Abd al-Ra'uf. This is further emphasised by the presentation of Hadith reports in support of the mystical system offered to the reader.

Crucially, near the end of the work, the author articulates in clear terms the sequence which the seeker should follow: '… first you must follow the practice of the prophet … in word and deed, inwardly and outwardly. Secondly, meditate on the Unity of Being …'[95] Furthermore, the concept of Unity is expressed in terms which eschew the radical monist approach. This is captured in the following section from the Javanese *Tuhfa*, which explains the expression 'return to the Reality':

Do not claim to become God, for this is wrong according to all four [Sunni legal] schools. The meaning of 'return' is, as one says, 'go back to a prior state.'[96]

It is clear from the content of this work that the authors, both of the original Arabic text and of the Javanese rendering, were writing for a specific didactic purpose. They were not merely engaging in mystical contemplation. They not only outline opportunities for Sufi fulfilment, but also identify taboos: neglecting the *shari'a*, overlooking the primacy of God's grace in successful mystical practice, putting meditation before imitating the prophet's model, and equating oneself with God. This approach ensured that the *Tuhfa* was to be as valuable in the Malay–Indonesian world as it was in India in contributing to the gradual emergence of a reformed Sufism. The date of its appearance in Southeast Asia is clearly significant, as it made its mark in the same late 17th-century period as 'Abd al-Ra'uf's great literary activity, similarly designed to re-establish theological stability after the turmoil of the 1630s and 1640s.

A 16th-century Javanese anthology.   Another work which is significant for our understanding of early Islam in the Malay–Indonesian world is a 16th-century Javanese anthology which was taken back in manuscript form to Holland by the earliest Dutch seafarers to Southeast Asia. This anthology was studied in detail by Kraemer for his Doctorate in 1921, and a condensed translation

---

[95] Johns 1965:147.
[96] Johns 1998a:284.

into English was made in 1986 by Andrew Rippin and Jan Knappert.[97] Just as occurred with Cambridge MS Or. Ii.6.45 discussed in the next chapter, this Javanese anthology probably owes its survival to a European penchant for preserving unusual literary records.

The main subject addressed in the anthology is mysticism, touching on various aspects of this field. A range of sources are mentioned by the author or authors – 'Ali, Muhammad, Husayn ibn 'Umar, the Traditionist Muslim and al-Hasan al-Basri – representing a veritable Who's Who of early Islamic sources.

The anthology is concerned with external symbols of the faith, and includes calls for devout observance – 'we must praise God from the evening prayers to the morning prayers'.[98] Priority is given to using revelation to guide behaviour. For example, the anthology advises against making friends of women, on the basis of Hadith reports from the Traditionist Muslim. The work also advises against listening to modernisers on the basis of Muslim's Hadith accounts. The significance of this seems to be a desire to affirm the timelessness of the content of revelation, rather than seeing revelation as something that should move with the times.

With regard to the mystical dimension to faith, the anthology addresses a range of perspectives. It provides detail on *dhikr*, indicating there are six degrees of this: *dhikr* of the mouth, soul, heart, interior, spirit, subtle being. This reference points to the prevalence of the practice of *dhikr* within the 16th-century Javanese Islamic community from which this manuscript originates, as well as further afield in the Malay–Indonesian Islamic community.

The work idealises the state of discarding cares for worldly things, and prioritises self-effacement, or *fana'*. Seekers are exhorted to be gentle, humble, compassionate, conscientious, meek, wise, kind, and meditative. The anthology also indicates that it is by God's grace that servants are favoured, saved, and enlightened.

The selection ends on an eschatological note. It presents a list of gifts to be taken by the dying Muslim for the death journey, to be given to Gabriel, the grave, the Place of Judgement, Munkar and Nakir, the Angel of the Record, the Narrow Bridge, and the

[97] Rippin and Knappert 1986:166–70.
[98] Rippin and Knappert 1986:167.

guardian of Hell. Each of these recipients is to be given four presents. The number four is significant given the centrality of the four elements (earth, fire, wind, water) in Javanese cosmology. The presents to be taken by the dying include many related to outward observance of the faith, rather than inner knowledge: regular prayer, regular study of the Qur'an, repeating the *shahada*, and avoidance of forbidden things.

This work provides a window into popular Islamic mystical belief in Java in the late 16th century. It does not engage with the detailed mystical speculation of the contemporaneous Acehnese mystics, namely Hamzah Fansuri and Shams al-Din al Sumatrani. This fact may point to Java having been behind Aceh at that time in terms of engaging with sophisticated theological and mystical thought. Alternatively it may simply point to the fact that the author/s of this anthology intended to produce a work which was accessible to as wide an audience as possible.

As we conclude this chapter, several issues stand out from our survey of theological writing in the Malay world, principally Aceh, during the 16th and 17th centuries.

First, one is struck by the need to commence our study at around the middle of the 16th century, rather than at the time of the establishment of Islamic kingdoms in the Malay world around 1300. This is due to the absence of surviving theological writings in Malay from the earliest period of Islam in the region. We will attempt to address this gap in part in the next chapter.

Second, note should be taken of the degree of external sourcing of both principal ideas and reactions to those ideas. We have seen the degree of dependence of the early writers upon Islamic thought originating from the Arab world and India. This dependence was in terms of both transmitting theosophical speculation from thinkers such as Ibn al-'Arabi and al-Jili and reforming reactions to this theosophy by al-Raniri, drawing on earlier Indian ideas. Moreover, 'Abd al-Ra'uf turned for advice to an Arab scholar, Ibrahim al-Kurani, in attempting to resolve the great theological conflict of 17th-century Aceh.

In connection with the above point, one is struck by the primacy of theosophical speculative ideas during the period under examination. Theosophy – which bases the knowledge of the world upon the knowledge of God, and which ultimately says that if we know God then we will know everything because God is everything – is most evident in the writings of Hamzah Fansuri and Shams al-Din al-Sumatrani. Their theosophy was the driving force of the 16th- and 17th-century Malay world in two ways: first, in terms of being dominant for the first part of the period; and second, in terms of being the target of reforming activity by al-Raniri and 'Abd al-Ra'uf – attracting a hostile reaction from the former and a more irenic response from the latter.

Moreover, it is striking that Sufism was the theological default, or the mainstream, during the period under examination. A non-Sufi *shari'a*-focused orthodoxy was always running to catch up, as it were, and it was to take several centuries more before Sufism was to be pushed to the margins in the way that non-Sufi thinking was in these early centuries.

9

EARLY MALAY QUR'ANIC
EXEGETICAL ACTIVITY

The prominent position enjoyed by the Sultanate of Aceh within
the Malay world during the pre-colonial era in both the political
and religious spheres is clearly demonstrated by surviving literary
records. The vast majority of theological texts from the pre-
colonial Malay world which are still extant originate from Aceh.
Thus, if we are to obtain an insight into theological life and orientation in the pre-colonial Malay world, it is to the Sultanate of
Aceh that we must direct our attention.

Our task is hampered by the absence of literary records from
the very earliest period of Islam in the region (i.e. 14th – 16th centuries), caused by several factors. The most pervasive relates to the
climate of the Malay archipelago; quite simply, the humidity of
the equatorial regions works very much against the survival of
paper for long periods of time. This means that we would not
expect to find manuscripts which survive from the early period of
Islam, and indeed, no examples of any manuscripts from the
Malay world pre-dating the late 16th century are surviving today
in the archipelago itself.

Another factor works against us finding literary records dating
from the early Islamic period in the Malay world; this is connected with the absence of a long-established tradition of preser-
vation of texts in the archipelago. It is likely that old texts were not
venerated; they were merely copied and left to wither away. This
is no doubt a result of the difficulty of preserving paper described
above.

The theological works that have survived from the pre-colonial
era cover a broad span of the Islamic sciences: philosophy, dogma,

jurisprudence, mysticism, exegesis and other fields. These are in the form of hand-written manuscripts; some are later copies of works written in the period under examination, while a few are much older manuscripts which were actually written by the author or copied by disciples of the author one or two generations after his death.

Our examination of selected writers and works originating from Aceh in the previous chapter has provided us with a useful insight into religious thought in the 16th and 17th centuries. However, as the earliest manuscripts from this region can be dated to the turn of the 17th century, scholars of early Malay Islam must address a gap in knowledge. Quite simply, we do not have a body of surviving documents representing the focus of theological activity during the first three hundred years of Islam in the Malay world.

In this context, it is important to identify techniques to fill this gap in our knowledge. Fortunately, such techniques exist, and depend on an examination of works written in the latter stages of the pre-colonial era. If we conduct an analysis of later works, in particular an identification of the sources used in their composition, we are provided with reliable indicators as to the Arabic works used by and the theological orientations of the earliest Malay Islamic scholars. In other words, in order to gain an insight into Islam in the earliest period, we need to identify Arabic works referred to by these early Malay scholars in a range of fields.

We should not be deterred by the fact that the works identified in this way were written in Arabic by Islamic scholars originating from the Middle East. Such works have played a crucial role throughout the history of Southeast Asian Islam in determining its theological directions and orientations. Indeed, such works should not be viewed as belonging to the Middle East; rather they belong to the Muslim world in its entirety because of the degree to which they are used throughout this world. The Arabic language works which will be discussed in the following pages will therefore be viewed as playing as integral a role in the formation of Southeast Asian Islam as did later works penned in Malay by scholars originating from the Malay world.

The field of Qur'anic exegesis represents one of the most important branches of the Islamic sciences, and it will be crucial for our purposes. As it deals with the sacred text of Islam considered by Muslims to be the exact word of God, it addresses wide-ranging issues which inform other components of the Islamic sciences. Qur'anic exegesis is a compulsory part of all specialist studies in Islam undertaken in both Muslim and non-Muslim countries, and the body of literature available on this subject is wide-ranging and rich in variety and approach.

In this particular branch of Islamic studies, there is a relative abundance of evidence as to the activity of the early Malay scholars. This evidence takes the form of both Arabic-language commentaries originating from the Arab world but used by the early Malay scholars, as well as remnants of early exegetical writing in Malay language produced by Malay scholars. The discussion which follows will consider relevant works in that order; namely, Arabic-language works referred to by Malay scholars in the pre-colonial era, and Malay-language works based upon and derived from them. In the process, our examination of Qur'anic exegetical activity will serve to inform our exploration of early Malay Islamic scholars and their literary activity.

MA'ALIM AL-TANZIL

Attention was devoted in chapter 4 to this Arabic-language commentary, produced by al-Baghawi (d. 1122). It represents one of the stream of commentaries which base themselves predominantly on a narrative approach, presenting detailed and colourful stories to elucidate the Qur'anic text, and avoiding more philological, philosophical or mystical elements. Al-Baghawi's commentary is significant in terms of Southeast Asian Islamic exegetical activity in the early period of Islam as it served as a source for the earliest surviving commentary on the Qur'anic text in Malay, namely the commentary on *Sura al-Kahf*, which is held by the Cambridge University library. This is examined in greater detail in the following pages.

THE COMMENTARY BY AL-BAYDAWI

The *Anwar al-tanzil* by al-Baydawi (d. 1286) seems to have been held in high regard by early Southeast Asian Islamic scholars, and this is still the case. This commentary served as an important source for 'Abd al-Ra'uf's Malay commentary upon the whole Qur'an, which is examined in some detail in a later section.

It is not surprising that the early Malay scholars decided to draw upon al-Baydawi's commentary as a source. It has a high reputation in the Arab world, but of perhaps greater significance is the fact that it presents concise exegetical comment drawing on a range of approaches, including narrative, philological, philosophical and other elements. In other words, it presents a smorgasbord of exegetical styles to its readers, and thus was ideally suited to the Malay context during the stage of consolidation and expansion of Islam in the region.

LUBAB AL-TA'WIL

This commentary, compiled by al-Khazin (d. 1340), was similarly examined earlier. It was seen to be a focus of controversy in the Arab world, owing to its recourse to stories of dubious reliability. This commentary was closely based on al-Baghawi's *Ma'alim al-tanzil*, and similarly serves as an important source for the Cambridge Malay commentary on *Sura al-Kahf*. However, Southeast Asian interest in and reference to al-Khazin's commentary seems to have far surpassed the case of al-Baghawi's commentary. We find direct references to al-Khazin's commentary in the seminal exegetical work by 'Abd al-Ra'uf discussed later. Moreover, al-Khazin's work continues to be widely referred to by Southeast Asian Muslims right up to the present era.

How can we reconcile the criticism which al-Khazin's commentary received from Muslim scholars in the Arab world and its lack of popularity there, on the one hand, with the seeming fundamental role it played in the development of the study of Qur'anic exegesis in Southeast Asia and its popularity there, on the other? In order to answer this question, it is necessary to place the criticisms levelled against the *Lubab* within a Southeast Asian context. The *Lubab* has been accused of the following:[1]

1. Drawing on miraculous, strange stories, more akin to superstition.
2. Presenting stories that denigrate the good name of prophets.

---

[1] Al-Dhahabi 1985: vol. 1, 294–300.

3. Being unnecessarily verbose in presentation of minute detail.
4. Presenting detailed stories without commenting upon their accuracy or reliability.

With respect to the first of these criticisms, Islam in the Malay-Indonesian world came to represent the most recent layer of a religious consciousness that had its roots in animistic belief. Moreover, for centuries the communities of Southeast Asia had practised various forms of Hindu and Buddhist worship, which came to permeate their perception of their world in minute detail. Although we have evidence of Muslim communities existing in Southeast Asia from the 12th to 13th centuries, the process of adoption of the Islamic faith was gradual, and previous practices continued alongside new beliefs.

It has been argued that the popularity of Sufi mystical practices throughout the Malay archipelago is a legacy of Hindu mystical elements, and, indeed, of an inclination towards belief in magic remaining from the pre-Hindu animistic period.[2] Whatever the case, such inclinations are fertile ground for tales of the fantastic. This may well explain the evident popularity in the medieval Malay world of stories such as the *Hikayat Muhammad Hanafiyyah*, which is ostensibly an Islamic story about the military campaign led by Muhammad Hanafiyyah against the forces of Yazid to avenge the murders of Hasan and Husain. This account is full of the fantastic; the heroic depiction of the battle exploits of the sons of Ali under Muhammad Hanafiyyah's command is reminiscent of the idealisation of heroes and rulers in Malay historiography as can be seen in works such as the *Sejarah Melayu* and the *Bustan al-Salatin*. Indeed the hero and his underlings seem to be endowed with supernatural powers to enable them to overcome their evil foes.

Thus, it is likely that miraculous, superstitious influences in a work such as al-Khazin's commentary would not have aroused as much ire in Southeast Asia as was the case in the Arab world; on the contrary, it may have appealed to the religious eclecticism of many a Southeast Asian Muslim. Moreover, the inclusion of magical, fantastic details in the commentary would have served to add

---

[2] Kahane 1984:168–9.

flavour to the work for Malay readers raised on a diet of stories such as that of Muhammad Hanafiyyah.

The second, third and fourth criticisms cited above all relate to stories: denigrating the good name of prophets, being unnecessarily verbose, and being presented without comment by the narrator. Again, one needs to consider that the reader of the Court Malay era, i.e. 14th–17th centuries, was brought up on a diet of very lengthy epics and *hikayat*. Some originated from their Hindu-Buddhist past, such as the *Ramayana* Epic, and others were home-grown, such as the chronicles of the various rulers, and the tales, many of which were legendary and exaggerated, which surrounded them. It is most unlikely that Malay readers of al-Khazin would have been dissuaded by the length of his anecdotes or the fact that they were presented without comment, as this was very much the style of their own folk stories.

Moreover, these lengthy stories presented by al-Khazin were often connected with a king or ruler, which were often also the focus of Malay story-telling. An example is the story of King David and Bathsheba, which is a colourful depiction of the account of how the King sent one of his generals to certain death in battle in order to be able to marry his widow. Though al-Dhahabi is highly critical of al-Khazin for presenting this story and debasing the memory of the Prophet David,[3] it does serve two functions which are consistent with Malay accounts of kings and rulers. First, it presents an image of a just and fair king, who falls to temptation, but later acknowledges the error of his ways and chooses a new and even more just way of life. Second, it contains a heavy didactic element, in which the King is ultimately the model of good behaviour for his subjects.

Taufik Abdullah has provided an enlightening overview of the Malay classic *Taj al-Salatin*,[4] and has clearly shown how that particular work uses the device of story-telling – be it normative myths, hagiographies of prophets, or Islamic myths – to transmit certain concepts and morals. For example, it is shown that the hagiographies of prophets are designed to provide models of just behaviour to local rulers. The *Taj al-Salatin* further demonstrates via the story-telling device how an unjust king, Fir'aun,

3 Al-Dhahabi 1985: vol. 1, 297.
4 Abdullah 1993.

is punished by God. This device, so much a part of traditional Malay literary works, is also found throughout al-Khazin's commentary, and explains its popularity among the Malays of the early centuries of Islam. A parallel example of the punishment of an unjust king found in al-Khazin's work is his lengthy exegetical comment on the 18th Chapter of the Qur'an relating to the tyrannical ruler Daqyanus. This Roman emperor persecuted the seven sleepers for their monotheism, but ultimately failed to capture them and force them to pay homage to him as divine ruler. This particular account comes in for severe criticism in some modern Arabic critiques of al-Khazin, but it constitutes a solid core of the Cambridge Malay commentary on *Sura al-Kahf*, and thus evidently enjoyed a certain appeal among the Malay Islamic audience before and leading up to the 17th century.

The specific accusation sometimes heard, that al-Khazin's recourse to the *Isra'iliyyat* diminished the value of his commentary, appears to be somewhat irrelevant to the Malay–Indonesian context. The absence of significant Jewish communities in the region, with the resulting lack of direct exposure to the controversy regarding the Jews' supposed distortion of the original Torah, meant that for most Malay Muslims, issues of Jewish–Muslim conflict and controversy about the *Isra'iliyyat* would not have had the immediate relevance that would have been the case in the Arab world. Therefore, their assessment of the value of al-Khazin's commentary would not have been so much determined by the issue of the *Isra'iliyyat*.

Nevertheless, there is evidence that theological polemics that erupted from time to time in the Malay world did derive in part from disputes originating in the Arab world. The use of the *Isra'iliyyat* by certain Muslim scholars may have been a factor in the conflict between Nur al-Din al-Raniri and the monistic Sufis in the 17th century. Likewise, some 20th-century scholars have drawn attention to this issue.[5] However, such issues do not appear to have taken hold of popular Islamic practice or perceptions in the region in the earliest period.

It is not surprising that al-Khazin was well received in Southeast Asia. The fact is that he was a good story-teller, and his stories are very readable. Moreover, they are couched in a style, and at a

---

5 This is examined in chapter 12.

linguistic level, which makes them accessible to a non-specialist reader with a knowledge of Arabic, unlike other commentaries which require more of a background in reading exegesis, such as that by al-Baydawi.

Thus an examination of the reception of al-Khazin's commentary in Southeast Asia suggests that controversy in Qur'anic exegesis which sprang from a Middle East environment was not automatically transferred to a Malay environment. It was as if there was a process of filtration, whereby particular commentaries were subjected to a balance-sheet evaluation; the issues at dispute were measured against the strengths of the particular work in terms of its local relevance. Where a work was particularly relevant, in meeting Malay needs with respect to story telling, depiction of rulers, or miracle and magic, then negative characteristics of this work did not receive the same degree of attention as was the case in other parts of the Muslim world.

THE JALALAYN

No examples of the *Jalalayn* in Arabic dating from the early Islamic period are to be found in the Malay archipelago. Nevertheless, we can gain an insight into the degree of use of this commentary in the early Southeast Asian Islamic period from other sources.

The very fact that the earliest commentary on the whole Qur'an in Malay, *Tarjuman al-Mustafid*, is a selective rendering of the *Jalalayn*, as is seen in subsequent discussion, suggests strongly that the Arabic *Jalalayn* itself must have been widely referred to. Its reputation must have been of the highest order for it to be chosen as the principal point of reference for Malay students of Qur'anic exegesis.

Moreover, it is ideally suited for pedagogical purposes, particularly at the introductory level. It provides an invaluable overview of the science of Qur'anic exegesis, it draws on a range of classical exegetical sources, and above all, it is quite manageable from a linguistic point of view for Malay-speaking students with an intermediate grasp of the Arabic language.

We find further evidence as time goes by of reference to the *Jalalayn* as an exegetical source by Malay writers. A striking example is the commentary *Marah Labid*, which was the first commentary on the whole Qur'an written in Arabic by a Malay scholar, Muhammad Nawawi al-Jawi. This commentary was published in Cairo in 1897, and the author used the *Jalalayn* as one of his sources in compiling this work.[6]

The final piece of evidence of the important place of the *Jalalayn* in Malay exegetical tradition is to be found in collections of manuscripts in the region. Though dating from a comparatively recent period, copies of the *Jalalayn* are to be found in collections through the Malay–Indonesian region, and they point to its popularity from earliest times. At the National Museum in Jakarta, which contains the most substantial manuscript collection in the archipelago, eight of the twenty-four manuscripts which represent commentaries upon the Qur'an are either copies of the *Jalalayn* (5) or are commentaries upon the *Jalalayn* (3). Its clear popularity in recent times is no doubt an indicator of the prominent role it fulfilled in earlier times in the area.

The *Jalalayn* is published in Malaysia and Indonesia and is sold throughout these countries. It is in widespread use in the various types of Islamic schools and other places of Islamic learning. This commentary is arguably the most important work of Qur'anic exegesis in the archipelago in terms of its past and present contribution to the spread of Islam in the region.

EARLY MALAY EXEGETICAL ACTIVITY

When one considers the eminent position and prolific literary activity of the early Acehnese Islamic scholars, i.e. Hamzah Fansuri, Shams al-Din al-Sumatrani and Nur al-Din al-Raniri, it seems unlikely that not one of them attempted even a partial rendering of or commentary upon the Qur'an in Malay.

Those writings by Hamzah which survive contain many Qur'anic quotations rendered into Malay, and these renderings fall into two general categories:

1. Renderings or paraphrases presented in classical Malay poetic form found within his thirty-two surviving poems. These are spread unevenly, with only fifteen of these poems containing excerpts from the Qur'an. Brakel explains this by saying that '… the less esoteric the poems, and the more they are directed towards a larger audience, in other words: the stronger

---

[6] Johns 1997a:9.

rhetorical effect is required, the more likelihood there is that the Qur'an is resorted to'.[7]

2. Renderings not bound by such poetic metrical limitations contained within his prose works. The following rendering of Q20:76, taken from *Asrar al-'arifin* provides an interesting point of comparison when held against 'Abd al-Ra'uf's far more literal rendering of the same verse. Notice Hamzah's reversal of the Qur'anic word order in this verse:

(Dibalaskan mereka itu) yang Islam (daripada Tuhan mereka itu: tempatnya syurga, lalu di bawahnya sungai, masuk mereka itu dalamnya kekal.)[8]

Translation:

(Those) faithful Muslims (are rewarded by their Lord with a place in Paradise with running streams below, where they remain for eternity.)

'Abd al-Ra'uf's version:

yaitu (segala syurga yang tempat tetap yang berlalu dari bawahnya segala sungai padahal mereka itu kekal dalamnya. Dan adalah yang demikian itu balas orang yang menyucikan dirinya) daripada segala dosya.

Translation:

i.e. (the Gardens of perpetual abode with running streams below, where they will remain forever. Such is the reward for those who cleanse themselves) from sin.[9]

In selecting which Qur'anic verses to include in his writings, Hamzah leans towards those which lend themselves to mystical interpretation and are widely used within Muslim mystical literature. Thus, the limited evidence available suggests that Hamzah saw nothing wrong with translating Qur'anic passages into Malay, and indeed that he was inclined to a freer style of translation than that adopted almost a century later by 'Abd al-Ra'uf.

Those few works by Shams al-Din which survive indicate that this early Malay mystic was also favourably disposed towards translating individual Qur'anic passages into Malay for the benefit

---

[7] Brakel 1980:3. Cf. Drewes and Brakel [1986:189] for a concise list of those Qur'anic verses which appear in Hamzah's poetry.

[8] Al-Attas 1970:270. The Qur'anic text is as follows: *Jannatu 'adnin tajri min tahtiha al-anharu, khalidina fiha wa dhalika jaza'u man tazakka.*

[9] Riddell 1990a:212.

of his readers. Van Nieuwenhuijze[10] records this somewhat free rendering of part of Q3:19 by Shams al-Din:

Kebaktian berkenan kepada Allah itu Islam.[11]

Translation:

Devotion to Allah is synonymous with Islam.

Other than isolated Qur'anic verse renderings such as those cited above, no more substantial rendering of or commentary upon the Qur'an bears the name of Hamzah or Shams al-Din. This somewhat puzzling fact may be accounted for when we consider the volumes of their writings destroyed by the followers of al-Raniri after 1637. If indeed either Hamzah or Shams al-Din undertook the writing of an exegetical work upon the Qur'an, such a work dealing with so sensitive an issue as interpretation of the meaning of the Qur'an may well have been among the first writings cast into the fire.

No substantial works of Qur'anic exegesis can be attributed to al-Raniri. As there was no post-Raniri purge of his works, we may deduce that he did not undertake such a work. What remains is merely the usual run of Qur'anic citations and Malay renderings within the larger body of his works. The following example is taken from al-Raniri's *Hujjat al-siddiq li-daf' al-zindiq* and is a rendering of Q19:90–1:

Hampirlah tujuh petala langit belah-belah, cerak-ceraklah tujuh petala bumi, dan runtuhlah segala bukit berhamburan tatkala mendengar kata Yahudi dan Nasara ada bagi Tuhan yang bernama Rahman itu anak.[12]

Translation:

The Heavens are apt to split asunder and the earth crack and the mountains to fall apart when they hear the sayings of the Jews and Christians that the God who is called the Merciful begat a son.[13]

Al-Raniri demonstrated an inclination for placing Qur'anic quotations early in his various writings, to set the scene as it were. Thus he commences Section 1 of Book 4 of his *Bustan al-Salatin* with a quotation from Q51:50, as follows:[14]

---

10 Van Nieuwenhuijze 1945:36.

11 The Qur'anic text is *inna al-din 'inda Allah al-islam*.

12 Al-Attas 1966:89. The Qur'anic text is as follows: *Takadu al-samawatu yatafattarna minhu wa tanshaqqu al-ardu wa takhirru al-jibalu haddan an da'au lil-rahman waladan.*

13 Al-Attas 1966:106.

14 Jones 1974:10–11.

Fa firru ila Allah inni lakum minhu nadhir mubin.
Larilah kamu kepada Allah, bahwasanya aku bagimu menakuti yang amat nyata.

Translation:

Flee unto God, for I am a manifest warner to you from him.

The Cambridge Malay commentary

The most important key to solving this puzzle is provided by a little-known manuscript containing Malay-language commentary on the 18th Chapter of the Qur'an (*Sura al-Kahf*), which is now held in the Cambridge University Library collection and is catalogued as MS Or. Ii.6.45. It is of value to examine briefly the life of this manuscript, as it provides a glimpse into the nature of early contacts between Dutch adventurers and Muslims from the Malay world.[15]

This manuscript was part of the collection of the Dutch orientalist Erpenius, who died in November 1624. The oration by G.J. Vossius at Erpenius' funeral indicates that Erpenius had been planning to publish a Malay text; this suggests that Erpenius, who was a prominent Arabist, also understood Malay. Though it is impossible to determine how he obtained MS Or. Ii.6.45, some idea may be gleaned by seeing how he obtained several other Malay manuscripts from the Malay world.

Three Malay manuscripts from the Erpenius collection bear the signature of a certain Pieter Willemszoon van Elbinck. This figure was a merchant who visited the Indonesian archipelago on various occasions between 1604 and 1615. He was initially in the service of the Dutch East India Company, but evidently became disenchanted with the Dutch because of restrictive trade practices imposed on Dutch merchants such as himself, and subsequently returned to the Indies with British expeditions. It was after the completion of one such English voyage that Van Elbinck died in London in 1615.

During his visits to the Indies, Van Elbinck procured, and copied, several Malay manuscripts. He may have been doing this specifically on behalf of Erpenius, or with a view to general sale once he returned to Europe. Whatever may have been the case,

---

15 It was initially examined by Van Ronkel [1896] at the end of the 19th century; he provides some important insights into the history of the manuscript which are summarised in the following paragraphs.

Van Elbinck's manuscripts came into Erpenius' hands, including the following:

1. The story of Joseph, copied 1 October 1604 by Van Elbinck. The tale presented in this manuscript is based on the Qur'anic account. It was subsequently printed as *Hikayat Yusuf* in Batavia in 1871 (using other MSS).
2. A composite manuscript, including the 58th Sura of the Qur'an; instruction on good government for princes and rulers, in the style of mirrors for princes; and a Dutch–Malay vocabulary, compiled by Van Elbinck.

It was most likely by a similar process that Erpenius obtained the manuscript containing the commentary on *Sura al-Kahf*.[16]

It had been Erpenius' wish that his library, including his manuscript collection, would eventually be taken over by the University of Leiden. After his death in 1624, the University entered negotiations with his widow about purchase of the library, but they were unable to come to an agreement. In due course, Erpenius' manuscripts were put up for sale in Antwerp, where some were bought by the English Duke of Buckingham for £500. After the Duke's death,[17] his widow donated the manuscripts, which included the commentary on *Sura al-Kahf*, to the University of Cambridge, where they have remained ever since.

This information helps us to ascribe a date to the manuscript with some degree of confidence. Working backwards from the death of Erpenius (and using Van Elbinck's manuscript procurements as a point of reference) we might estimate that the manuscript was obtained on his behalf in the first decade of the 17th century. Even if it was a comparatively fresh copy, it would be fair to assume that the work was produced sometime around 1600.

---

[16] As this manuscript bears no signature, we will probably never know its exact provenance.

[17] The Duke of Buckingham was assassinated by a certain Felton on 23 August 1628. A portrait of the Duke held by the National Portrait Gallery in London as exhibit no. 3840 records the following: 'George Villiers, 1st Duke of Buckingham 1592–1628. Favourite and leading minister of both James I and Charles I, he was charming and ambitious, but lacked the stature to hold high office. As Lord High Admiral he bungled the expeditions to Cadiz and La Rochelle and became the Commons' "grievance of grievances". Assassinated by a fanatic in Portsmouth.'

The importance of MS Or. Ii.6.45 lies in the fact that its date of composition can be conclusively fixed to the period in which Shams al-Din, and possibly Hamzah Fansuri, lived. The fact that no other copies of this work are extant suggests that its own survival may be due to its being transported away from Aceh prior to the fires of al-Raniri some four decades later which probably destroyed other copies of the same work and other similar exegetical works. This also suggests that works of Qur'anic exegesis were on the top of al-Raniri's 'hit-list', and so thorough was the implementation of their destruction that no survivors can be found in Aceh. It also means of course that MS Or. Ii.6.45 is an extremely valuable manuscript in its own right, as it is the sole remaining key to an understanding of Acehnese Qur'anic exegetical activity prior to the appearance of 'Abd al-Ra'uf's *Tarjuman al-Mustafid* some seventy-five years later.

An examination of Cambridge MS Or. Ii.6.45 with a view to identifying Arabic sources reveals that this manuscript was primarily based upon the narrative commentaries by al-Baghawi and al-Khazin discussed earlier. However, other commentaries, including al-Baydawi's *Anwar al-tanzil*, were also drawn upon for both the phrase-by-phrase comments on the Qur'anic verses and the narrative interpolations between the verses.[18] Considering that European seafarers to Aceh in all likelihood obtained their mementoes and souvenirs from officially-sanctioned outlets, and possibly from the Court itself, it may be deduced that at the time of compilation of this Malay manuscript around 1600, the commentaries by al-Baghawi, al-Baydawi and al-Khazin had sufficient prestige within the Kingdom of Aceh, then the foremost power among the Malay states, to be considered worthy as a source of instruction in Qur'anic exegesis for Malay Muslims. This also enables us to conclude with some confidence that these three Arabic-language commentaries had enjoyed a degree of popularity in the Malay world for some time. They may well have served as basic texts for students of Qur'anic exegesis during the preceding centuries which have hitherto provided little hard evidence of the nature of Islamic studies in the region.

---

[18] Riddell 1990b:11–12.

Content and style of the Cambridge Malay commentary. A close examination of this Malay commentary suggests that the anonymous
author did exactly what was by now standard practice for exegetes;
that is, he built his work around a core drawn from another commentary. Al-Baghawi had used al-Tha'labi's commentary in this
way, and al-Khazin had done the same with al-Baghawi's work.
We shall see in later discussion that Muhammad Nawawi al-
Banteni used the great commentary by Fakhr al-Din al-Razi in
this way. The author of Cambridge MS Or. Ii.6.45 based his core
upon the narrative commentaries, especially al-Baghawi and al-
Khazin, to which he added selections drawn from other sources.
However, unlike al-Baghawi and al-Khazin before him, he did
not identify his principal source in a preface, thus leaving us the
task of dissecting his work to reconstruct the research and writing
technique employed by the Malay author.

This work appears to have been written by the Malay author as
he scanned the various sources which must have been laid out
before him. He presents the text of the Qur'an in Arabic in red letters, and follows each Qur'anic phrase with a section in Malay –
sometimes long, sometimes short – which represents a literal
translation of the particular source used.

His heavy dependence upon al-Baghawi and al-Khazin meant
that the Malay commentary is narrative-based in exegetical
approach. Indeed, it could be considered as a Malay descendent of
the Arabic trilogy examined earlier. It thus follows that, not only
did the Malay author transfer to his work the rich and colourful
stories contained in the works of his predecessors, but he also
unconsciously transferred some of the characteristics of those earlier works which had attracted criticism from certain Muslim
scholars.

Though only one copy of the Cambridge Malay commentary
survives, its use of the narrative commentaries for source material
was repeated in the compilation of *Tarjuman al-Mustafid* by 'Abd
al-Ra'uf al-Singkili (d. 1693), the first Malay-language commentary on the whole Qur'an, and which itself drew upon the work by
al-Khazin. Thus the evidence for an interest on the part of Malay
Muslim scholars during the early period of Islamisation in narrative-based exegesis is considerable.

Narrative as exegesis.   A detailed examination of this commentary's exegetical discussion of Q18:9 has been undertaken in previous scholarship.[19] It revealed a series of features which characterise the text of this commentary, including:

• rich narrative detail, pointing to the author's concern to tell a good story.
• an interest in presenting real-life situations in the narrative.
• contextualisation of what was originally a Christian tale to an Islamic framework. In this the commentator reflects the approach of his source texts.
• a predeterminist approach, with God involved in the lives of his creatures, but nevertheless clearly transcendent and sovereign. In this, the theology is orthodox; there is no evidence of the monistic approach which is seen in the writing of leading Acehnese Islamic scholars contemporaneous with the author of this commentary, namely Hamzah Fansuri and Shams al-Din al-Sumatrani.

It would be of benefit at this juncture to pay this commentary another visit, given its importance in the development of Malay Islamic thinking. We shall examine the text of the commentary on Q:18:75–9 in the following paragraphs.

These verses focus upon the encounter between Moses and Khidr, in particular the rupture in their relationship resulting from Moses' constant questioning of Khidr about the motives behind his actions. In the comment on verse 75, Yusha' (Joshua) plays a role in the developing crisis:

Then Yusha' said: 'Moses! Adhere to your promise to be patient with him. Do not challenge his actions, so that you will be allowed to accompany him.'

The ultimate source of this comment is clearly al-Baghawi's *Ma'alim al-tanzil*, which is as follows:

It is related that Yusha' said to Moses: 'O Prophet of God! Remember the promise by which you are bound.'

---

[19] Riddell 1997a.

The commentator may have taken it directly from al-Baghawi, or from al-Khazin's commentary on the same verse, which itself drew on al-Baghawi.

In his treatment of verse 76, the Malay commentator again bases himself upon the narrative exegetes, but a comparison with the commentary of al-Baghawi on the same verse demonstrates the practice of summary translation employed by the Malay commentator. He chooses to delete al-Baghawi's discussion of the variant readings, as well as the lengthy chain of authorities (*isnad*) provided in the Arabic commentary. This may well have been done to maintain the impetus of the narrative, and to prevent it being disrupted by philological detail.

In commenting on verse 77, the Malay commentator once again bases himself upon al-Baghawi's discussion. He provides various opinions about the identity of the town encountered by Khidr and Moses, though like al-Baghawi, he does not indicate his preferred option, as might have been expected of al-Tabari. The Malay commentator also draws on al-Baghawi to provide an account of how the pair were shunned by the inhabitants.

In certain respects, however, the Malay commentator is not entirely faithful to al-Baghawi's record in commenting on this verse. First, al-Baghawi specifies that the woman who showed them kindness was a Berber, but the Malay commentator makes no mention of this. This can be seen as an example of contextualisation, presumably occurring because the Malay commentator considered the Berber identity of the woman to be of no relevance to his Malay audience. This reflects al-Baghawi's original contextualisation of the Christian story to an Islamic context. Second, al-Baghawi indicates that the pair blessed the women and cursed the men of that town, whereas the Malay commentator indicates that it was Khidr who did so. In fact, the latter version seems more plausible, given that Khidr was the clear authority among the two, so it is possible that the Malay commentary more accurately preserves the original record of this anecdote. Third, al-Baghawi provides the sources for the report that Khidr erected the collapsing wall with his bare hands, whereas the Malay commentator makes no mention of the sources for this account.

In his commentary on verses 78 and 79, it can clearly be seen that the Malay commentator has based himself again upon the narrative comment ultimately attributable to al-Baghawi. In the process, he partially condenses al-Baghawi's text but is faithful to the core content.

A translation of the Malay commentary on verse 78 is as follows:

Khidr (said: 'This is the [point of] separation between us), which I predicted would happen as you could not be patient watching my actions. How could you accompany me [any further]? (I will clarify for you my actions which you were unable to patiently) observe.'

Baghawi reads as follows on the same verse:

(Said) Khidr: ('This is the parting between you and me.) i.e. this is the time of parting between us. Some say: this rejection of taking a wage is the parting between us. Al-Zajaj said: the meaning is that this is the parting between us, i.e. the termination of our contact, and *bayna* is repeated for emphasis. (Now I will tell you) i.e. I will relate to you (what you could not bear with patience).' In some commentaries Moses took his cloak and said: "Tell me the meaning of your actions before you separate from me."'

These few verses again demonstrate the process of transmission from the Islamic heartland to the Malay world. In this case, the role of narrative has been significant in theological exposition, a feature that recurs frequently in our study of Islam in the Malay–Indonesian world.

Perspectives on eschatology.   The three verses contained in Q18:47–9 are important for understanding eschatology in the Qur'an, in particular the methodology of the Judgement to be employed by God on the Day of Resurrection.

Again we find that the author of the Cambridge Malay commentary was determined to present rich narrative in support of his exegetical goals. And the way to do this, on the subject of the final Judgement, was to engage with Hadith reports. As we saw in Part I of this study, the Hadith fill out the Qur'anic eschatological framework by proving minute detail of the most graphic kind relating to the punishments awaiting the wicked and the rewards awaiting the blessed.

The anonymous author of the Cambridge Malay Commentary, in drawing on the narrative exegetes for these particular verses, is able to point to original writers with considerable reputations: Qatada and Dahhak. But the ultimate source used to fill out the Qur'anic detail by the author enjoys a greater level of authority than either of these two writers; namely, the prophetic Traditions themselves.

Verse 48 indicates that on the Day of Judgement, all people will be aligned in rows before God, awaiting judgement. The Qur'an does not elaborate on the physical presentation of the people, but the commentaries, based on the Hadith, suggest that all will be naked. Clearly our author was intrigued by this, as in his own social environment (and indeed today) people would have felt ashamed to be naked in front of other people. The Hadith account selected, ultimately attributable to 'Aisha, reassures the reader that on that Day a sense of personal privacy will be far from people's minds.

I asked: 'O Prophet of God! Won't all the women feel ashamed?' The Prophet of God replied: 'The events at the time will be so important, that no-one will be concerned with other people, nor will anyone even notice other people. Each will be concerned with themselves; no-one will feel any curiosity towards other people.'

Thus this Hadith has captured graphic detail as well as a sense of real-life context, and this is transferred to the Malay commentary on Sura 18 verse 48 as follows:

(And they will be brought) by the angels, O Muhammad, (unto your Lord), and they will be (standing in lines), and they will see that there is no-one for protection. (So truly) a decree pronounced for the unbelievers who deny the Day of Judgement: (you have come before Us) on this day naked, with nothing to your name (just as We originally made you) when you came from the earth alone, without any clothes or wealth. (But you thought that We would not fulfil) Our (promise to you) which was said to you by the prophets. And We will resurrect you from the grave, assemble you in the field of Mahshar, cause you to be fearful, and criticise your actions.

An account from 'Aisya, may God be pleased with her: one day I asked the Prophet of God SAW: 'Prophet of God! How will the people appear who are resurrected from the grave on the Day of Judgement, when they are assembled in the field of Mahshar?' The Prophet of God SAW said: 'All those resurrected from the grave to the field of Mahshar will be naked.' So I said: 'Will all the women be naked too, O Prophet of God?' The Prophet of God replied: 'All the women will be completely naked.' So I asked: 'O Prophet of God! Won't all the women feel ashamed ... .'

The commentator's treatment of this verse shows his sensitivity to the concerns of ordinary people. Indeed, it suggests that the audience of this commentary had some of the same kinds of questions and were puzzled by some of the same kinds of situations as were the original audiences of the Hadith reports themselves.

MS Or. Ii.6.45 and the Qira'at.   If the angle of approach by this commentator to the *qira'at* is compared with later periods, we would have to conclude that the author of MS Or. Ii.6.45 only had a passing interest in this issue. The commentary does not provide copious amounts of detail on this subject, nor does it rigorously examine the full range of variants. There are several possible reasons for this:

- It may reflect the fact that the variants themselves were not significant to meaning. If the commentator prioritised meaning rather than philological detail, he may have considered discussion of the *qira'at* to be less crucial than other subjects.
- It is possible that the commentator did not have detailed information on all readings to hand, and therefore merely included a token amount of information on this subject to flag the existence of the *qira'at* for the benefit of his readers.
- Perhaps the most likely reason is that the commentator was concerned to produce a commentary that was user-friendly and accessible to non-specialist readers. This would account for his choice of narrative-based exegetical sources, such as al-Baghawi and al-Khazin, and his avoidance of very specialised subject matter, such as the *qira'at*.

Nevertheless, the fact that the author of MS Or. Ii.6.45 did address the *qira'at* at all demonstrates that he wished to make his readers aware of the subject, albeit not to any great degree. In doing so, the author has left a crucial record for later researchers seeking to understand the dynamics of early Islamisation in the Malay world.

The following discussion will present the small amount of information in MS Or. Ii.6.45 on the *qira'at*, in the order that it occurs in the commentary.

Verse 17 – The commentary includes the following:

'Amir and Ya'qub read this as *tazawwar* with a vowelless *ra'* and a doubled *waw* ...

The Malay commentator seems to have based himself on al-Baghawi and not al-Khazin in drawing up this record, as the latter makes no mention of these *qira'at*. In contrast, al-Baghawi addresses this instance of the variant readings by drawing on Ibn 'Amir and Ya'qub. However, al-Baghawi's record of their readings is at variance with the account in MS Or. Ii.6.45, as follows:

qara'a Ibn 'Amir wa Ya'qub bi sukun al-zay' wa tashdid al-ra' 'ala w.z.n.t.h.m.r.'.

The record of al-Baghawi agrees with the reading in Ibn Mujahid.[20]

Verse 34 – The commentary includes the following:

Some read this as *wa kana la-hu thumurun* with a *dammah* over the *tha'* and *mim*.

Ibn Mujahid attributes this reading to Abu 'Amr.[21]

Verse 47 – The commentary includes the following:

Ibn Kathir and Ibn 'Amir read this as *wa tusayyaru al-jibal*. With the *ta'* the meaning is 'on the day the mountains moved from one place to another'.

This comment represents a direct rendering of the record of al-Baghawi. The above information is summarised below:

Table 9.1. *QIRA'AT* FROM *SURA AL-KAHF* PRESENTED IN
CAMBRIDGE MS OR. II.6.45

Verses	Ibn 'Amir	Ya'qub	Abu 'Amr	Ibn Kathir
18:17	*tazawwar*	*tazawwar*		
18:34			*thumurun*	
18:47	*tusayyaru*			*tusayyaru*

Several observations should be made about this commentator's treatment of the *qira'at*. First, at no stage does he seek to compare systematically different *qira'at*. When he does present them, he merely provides one version, recorded by either one or two readers. Thus he is avoiding a focus on difference, which may well be deliberate if he was addressing a non-specialist audience who he

20 Dif 1988:388.
21 Dif 1988:390.

felt may have been confused by a discussion of different readings of the Qur'anic text.

Furthermore, the commentator only makes reference to three of the canonical seven readers: Ibn 'Amir, Abu 'Amr (though without mentioning his name), and Ibn Kathir. As his discussion of the *qira'at* is so superficial, we cannot infer that his choice of readings reflects relative popularity of the seven either in Southeast Asia or the Arab world at the time.

Moreover, he also makes reference to one of the additional readers constituting the Ten readings, namely that of Ya'qub al-Hadhrami. The reasons for his choice of one of the additional readers is unclear. We might speculate that the Hadhrami origins of this reader may have had some relevance to the choice by the commentator to include him, given the significant role which immigrants from the Hadhramaut played in the Islamisation of the Malay world from the earliest period.[22]

Finally, the difference noted between the Cambridge commentary's record of *qira'at* for Q18:17 and that of al-Baghawi could be due to several factors. It could reflect an error on the part of the author of the commentary. It could also reflect an error on the part of the copyist of the manuscript, if the extant MS does not represent the original text. It could also reflect variations in the manuscript traditions of al-Baghawi's commentary, with the version available for the present study coming from a different stream from that referred to by the Malay commentator some four hundred years ago.

Although the commentator who produced Cambridge MS Or. Ii.6.45 may not have regarded himself as a specialist on the *qira'at*, and nor should he be regarded as such, nevertheless he has made a significant contribution to our understanding of early Malay Islam by providing us with the earliest record of Malay Muslims addressing the issue of the *qira'at*. He thus laid the foundations for the examination of an important area of Qur'anic studies which was to be addressed again in a much more scientific way by 'Abd al-Ra'uf less than one hundred years later.

---

22 Riddell 1997b:220.

Tarjuman al-Mustafid

The first Malay commentary on the whole Qur'an was *Tarjuman al-Mustafid* by 'Abd al-Ra'uf al-Singkili. This work was compiled around 1675.

Tarjuman al-Mustafid has been traditionally regarded throughout the Malay world as a translation of the authoritative Arabic commentary *Anwar al-Tanzil wa Asrar al-Ta'wil* by al-Baydawi (d. 1286). This has been shown conclusively to be incorrect.[23] In fact, the text of *Tarjuman al-Mustafid* is composite in two ways. First, its sources are composite; the Jalalayn commentary provides the majority of the exegetical information contained in *Tarjuman al-Mustafid*, while the commentaries by al-Baydawi and al-Khazin are drawn on to a lesser extent. Second, the authorship is composite; 'Abd al-Ra'uf composed the core of the work, using the Jalalayn as his source text, while his student Da'ud Rumi later added anecdotal interpolations and information on the variant readings, drawing from al-Baydawi, al-Khazin and other sources, including the Jalalayn.

A detailed breakdown of the work suggests clearly that 'Abd al-Ra'uf regarded *Tarjuman al-Mustafid* predominantly as a Malay rendering of the Jalalayn.

It would be of benefit to examine a short sample of Qur'anic exegetical comment by 'Abd al-Ra'uf in order to gain an insight into his style. For this purpose we shall focus upon the commentary on Q38:17–26 drawn from *Tarjuman al-Mustafid*. The Qur'anic text seems somewhat cryptic on its own, and for readers familiar with the biblical text, the Qur'anic version seems to point to the story of David and Bathsheba presented in 2 Samuel 11–12.

'Abd al-Ra'uf was clearly concerned to take the skeletal outline of the particular Qur'anic text used as a base and convert it into a comprehensive narrative account which could stand alone.

For example, the staccato-like sentence presented in Q38:20 is followed in 'Abd al-Ra'uf's commentary by a short yet vivid description of the large numbers of guardsmen posted around the kingdom each night.

(And We strengthened his kingdom with wisdom and knowledge.) Some of the commentators say that the kingdom was guarded each night

---

[23] Riddell 1984 and 1990a.

by thirty thousand men. We gave him clear signs in all that he did, and We gave him wisdom which extended [from him] to all who sought it.

This exegetical interpolation is not necessary for theological purposes, but it assists the reader to visualise the scene and it appeals to the narrative inclinations of readers. It thus serves as an exegetical gloss designed for narrative effect; in other words, it serves dual purposes of both adding information and entertaining.

'Abd al-Ra'uf's treatment of Q38:23 is deserving of close attention. The commentator has taken it upon himself to play with the Qur'anic text to the point where he discards all reference to 'ewes', replacing it with references to 'wives'.

('My brother here has ninety-nine wives, while I only have one wife.' He said) i.e. the one who had ninety-nine wives said: ('Give her into my care) and I will marry her'. (And he imposed himself upon me in this dispute.) *Pericope* Khazin reports that Ibn 'Abbas said that 'Give her into my care' was actually stated as 'Divorce her so that I can marry her.'

Such an overt pronouncement that this whole matter concerns wives, not ewes, serves to cement the link between the Qur'anic account and the biblical account of David and Bathsheba.[24] In this, the commentator has risked arousing the ire of a more literalist approach to exegesis which foregrounds the doctrine of prophetic impeccability, and which is sensitive to any suggestion of Qur'anic exegetes drawing on the isra'iliyyat. Nevertheless, 'Abd al-Ra'uf does not seem daunted. He identifies al-Khazin as his source for this account, and quotes al-Khazin's source in turn as Ibn 'Abbas, one of the greatest authorities among the Companions of Muhammad. This verse demonstrates clearly the point that though some of the detail may differ, a combination of Qur'an plus exegetical commentary in this case is needed to approach the level of literary dynamism offered by the standalone biblical text.

In his treatment of Q38:24, 'Abd al-Ra'uf reverts to talking about sheep rather than wives. Nevertheless, he has made his point in the previous verse, and his concern at this point is not with that particular issue but rather with the reason for God's testing of David. He calls upon various accounts explaining the reasons for the test and his interpolation is lengthy, explanatory, and

---

[24] For a fuller discussion of this matter, refer Riddell 1997c.

entertaining in its vivid language. For example, the scene of the two angels looking at each other with a knowing smile and ascending to Heaven is graphic in its simplicity and most effective. At the end of the same verse, 'Abd al-Ra'uf further consolidates the link with the biblical David and Bathsheba story by adding the phrase 'because of his love for the woman' in explaining the test.

There can be little doubt that for the story-based stream of exegesis, centred upon scholars such as al-Tha'labi and al-Khazin, the outline account found in Q38:17–26 needed to be filled out with details of the David and Bathsheba story for readers to properly understand the context and import of this Qur'anic story. Without these exegetical contributions, the Qur'an itself begs more questions than it answers in terms of this particular story. Throughout his commentary, 'Abd al-Ra'uf took full advantage of the narrative additions presented by exegetes such as al-Khazin, without being unduly concerned by the possibility of such additions being derived from Jewish sources.

Information on the variant readings. Throughout the body of *Tarjuman al-Mustafid*, Da'ud Rumi, the student of 'Abd al-Ra'uf, inserted explanatory paragraphs in which he presented recitation variants taken from the canonical readings (*qira'at*) which we discussed earlier. For these variants he undoubtedly drew on the knowledge acquired by his master, 'Abd al-Ra'uf, during nineteen years of study in Arabia. 'Abd al-Ra'uf had made a broad study of various exegetical writings, including those containing information on the canonical readings, and would have consulted Ibn Mujahid's *al-Qira'at al-Sab'*, arguably the major classical work on the canonical readings. Moreover, it is recorded that 'Abd al-Ra'uf's teacher, Ibrahim al-Kurani had studied al-Qurtubi's *Taysir fi al-Qira'at al-Sab'* and the *Tayyibat al-Nashr fi al-Qira'at al-'Ashr* during a three-month period at al-Azhar in Cairo in 1650.[25] Ibrahim would undoubtedly have instructed 'Abd al-Ra'uf in the science of the variant readings, and 'Abd al-Ra'uf would have in turn passed on the fruits of Ibrahim's study at Cairo to his own student, Da'ud Rumi.

Each of the explanatory paragraphs containing discussion of the variant readings begins with the following words:

---

[25] Johns 1980:5.

Concerning the differences among the three readers …

His selection of 'three readers' may well show which of the seven canonical readers were regarded as most significant in the Muslim world in the 17th century. The primary readers and their recorders referred to in *Tarjuman al-Mustafīd* are the following:

1. Hafs b. Sulayman b. al-Mughira (*c.* 90/709–180/796). He was the son-in-law and transmitter of the reading of 'Asim. He lived initially in Baghdad, then moved to Mecca where he popularised 'Asim's reading.[26]
2. Abu 'Amr b. al-'Ala (70/689–154/770). Of uncertain origins, either Arab or Iranian, he spent time in Medina, Mecca, Kufa and Basra, studying various readings from these centres, then established himself in Basra for the remainder of his life. He is as well known as a grammarian as he is a reader. His system of reading was greatly influenced by that of Nafi' of Medina and Ibn Kathir of Mecca, and it became established as the standard reading in Basra.
3. Hafs b. 'Umar al-Duri (*c.*150/767–246/860). He was an indirect disciple of Abu 'Amr, in addition to being a direct disciple of al-Kisa'i. Al-Duri transmitted both systems. He was born in Samarra' and died in Baghdad.
4. Nafi' b. 'Abd al-Rahman b. Abi Nu'aym al-Madani (d. 169/785). His family originated from Isfahan though he himself was born and died in Medina. His chain of transmission going back to the Companions is well attested. His system established itself in Medina, supplanting those of his teachers.
5. Abu Musa 'Isa b. Mina b. Wirdan (120/738–220/835). Better known by his pseudonym of Qalun, he was born and died in Medina. He was one of the main transmitters of Nafi' of Medina.

The system of 'Asim transmitted by Hafs was adopted in Cairo in 1923 under the auspices of King Fu'ad as the basis of the Egyptian standard edition of the Qur'an. The fact that this system was referred to in *Tarjuman al-Mustafīd* and was associated with the name of Hafs and not 'Asim indicates the degree to which it had already established itself in the Arab world by

---

26 The readings of 'Asim and Hafs are identical except for one word in Q30:53, which the former reads as *du'f* and the latter as *da'f*.

the time of 'Abd al-Ra'uf's sojourn there in the 17th century. Moreover, in the Malay commentary the Hafs reading is implicitly regarded as the norm in relation to which the readings of Abu 'Amr/al-Duri and Nafi'/Qalun are given as variants. This is no doubt due to the fact that the differences between the canonical schools only attain a degree of significance when those of the Hijaz and Basra are held up against those of Kufa.[27] In this particular instance, it is worthwhile remembering the influence of the reading of Nafi' upon that of Abu 'Amr. An investigation of data on the readings reveals a high degree of resemblance between readings of these two, and fewer instances of agreement between either of them and the reading of Hafs.

The significance of Tarjuman al-Mustafid. *Tarjuman al-Mustafid* has played an important role in the history of Malay Islamic education. For almost three hundred years it was the only commentary in Malay on the Qur'an as a whole. Although other commentaries in Malay and Indonesian have appeared during the last forty years, nevertheless *Tarjuman al-Mustafid* continues to be printed and widely used throughout Malaysia, Sumatra and Java. Not only has it greatly influenced the nature of Qur'anic studies in the region, but it has also undoubtedly greatly contributed to the study of exegetical works in Arabic. A perusal of Van Ronkel's catalogue of Arabic MSS held by the Batavia Society Museum (now the National Museum in Jakarta) shows to what extent the *Tafsir al-Jalalayn* had come to occupy centre stage in Islamic schools in the archipelago,[28] a position it holds to this very day in Indonesia as well as Malaysia.[29] It is possible that 'Abd al-Ra'uf's rendering of this work reflects the extent of its popularity in the region prior to the compiling of *Tarjuman al-Mustafid*.

In summarising our principal observations from this examination of early exegetical activity in the Malay world, several things are striking.

In the first instance, a source analysis of the earliest exegesis in Malay helps us address a problem highlighted at the end of

---

[27] Blachère 1977:132.
[28] Ronkel 1913:12–31.
[29] Nor Bin Ngah 1983:2.

chapter 8. Such an analysis suggests which Arabic-language exegetical works were popular among the Malays before the 16th century, and we thus have found one piece for the puzzle of Malay theological activity in the 13th to 15th centuries.

Most striking perhaps is the total absence of Sufi exegesis. Given the predominance of Sufi writing in other fields which we saw in chapter 8, we must seek explanations for this curious state of affairs.

One possible explanation is provided by the compensating dominance of narrative/story-based exegesis. It seems that narrative is to Malay exegetical activity what Sufism is to activity by Malays in other Islamic fields in this early period. This dominance of story in the exegetical genre suggests that exegesis in Malay was designed substantially for the masses rather than exclusively for the educated religious elite.

An alternative explanation is that there were exegetical writings produced by the monistic Sufis which were destroyed by al-Raniri and his followers. The presence of Qur'anic verses and exegetical comment on an *ad hoc* basis in the writings of both Hamzah Fansuri and Shams al-Din provides support for this theory. However, the only way to prove it would be to discover some as yet unknown commentary by the early Sufis or their disciples. For the moment, this question must remain unanswered.

Also striking from our study of early exegesis is the disregard of the *Isra'iliyyat* issue, which had aroused such emotion in the Arab world among exegetes in an earlier period. The reason for this has been identified as the lack of immediate relevance of the Jewish–Muslim dispute to the Malay environment.

We should also note in concluding that the early Malay exegetes showed a clear interest in the *qira'at*, or variant readings of the Qur'anic text. This provides evidence that Islamic scholars in the 15th- and 16th-century Malay world were committed to teaching the full range of Islamic sciences, in spite of the dominance of Sufism.

We commented at the end of the previous chapter that the non-Sufi *shari'a*-based orthodoxy were pushed to the margins of the Malay Islamic stage during the 16th and 17th centuries. Nevertheless, we could argue that in exegesis, this group found its voice in this early period. Here was a field of Islamic learning where Sufi approaches were not the default; on the contrary, none of the Arabic or Malay commentaries examined in this chapter gave priority to allegorical interpretation of Qur'anic verses. Exegesis thus provided one of the key channels for the transmission of non-Sufi thinking which was to assume centre stage in a later period of Malay Islamic history.

10

THE 18TH AND 19TH CENTURIES

FROM SUFISM TO REFORM

By the end of the 18th century, Islam in the Malay world had reached the limits of its geographical expansion, and was undergoing a phase of consolidation in the various regions where it had been adopted. The process of consolidation was facilitated by an extensive network of Islamic study centres, known by various names depending upon the geographical location, including *madrasah, pondok* and *pesantren*. There was much interaction between these centres, and the scholars who graduated from them produced an impressive literary output in various fields of the Islamic sciences.

In this chapter, we will continue with an examination of key themes and writers who influenced Islamic thought in the Malay world during the 18th and 19th centuries.

SUFI THEMES: MONIST AND MAINSTREAM

Previous discussion identified the importance of Sufis in the early period of Malay Islam. Scholars such as Hamzah Fansuri, Shams al-Din al-Sumatrani and 'Abd al-Ra'uf al-Singkili ensured that Sufi thought was to play a central role in defining the face of Islam in Southeast Asia. Indeed, in this way the Malay world has played a unique role in terms of the wider Muslim world. Whereas in the Middle East, Sufism had only emerged in a systematic way several centuries after the Islamisation process of the Arab world was complete, in the Malay world Sufism came to be normative during the formative years. As Bakar says, 'Sufism's greatest contribution to Malay civilization lies in shaping and crystallizing its intellectual and spiritual milieu during the later phase of the

168

Islamisation process, from the ninth/fifteenth century until about the end of the twelfth/eighteenth century.'[1]

While the colonial powers were entrenching themselves in the Malay world, a plethora of Sufi orders were also penetrating the region and consolidating their presence. The principal orders in this regard were the Qadiriyya, Chishtiyya, Shadhiliyya, Rifa'iyya, Naqshbandiyya, Shattariyya and the Ahmadiyya.[2] We have encountered some of these orders in earlier discussion. Hamzah Fansuri was initiated into the Qadiriyya, Shams al-Din initiated Sultan Iskandar Muda into the Naqshbandiyya, Nur al-Din al-Raniri was a member of the Rifa'iyya, while 'Abd al-Ra'uf al-Singkili is the great pioneer of the Shattariyya in the Malay world.

Rituals and practices

As they spread throughout the region, the various orders took with them a variety of practices, rituals, and written materials which served to maintain links with other branches of the same orders in other parts of the Muslim lands. In this way, the Sufi orders played an important role in consolidating the sense of a world-wide Islamic community (the *umma*). Furthermore, the practices which emerged gave a unique profile to the local face of Islam.

Sufi rituals emerged which aimed to provide adherents of the various orders with an opportunity to demonstrate that they had gained control over their physical natures. The Rifa'iyya order in the Malay world practised a series of rituals which it had drawn from other parts of the Muslim world. These included practices which entailed considerable physical danger or discomfort, such as the *dabbus* ceremony, during which Sufis inflicted wounds on themselves while in a state of trance, as well as the eating of live snakes, sitting in heated ovens, and riding lions.[3] Rifa'iyya adepts believed that by participating in events which included such physical hardship, they could prove to themselves and to others that they were able to endure these physical challenges but still remain

---

[1] Bakar 1991:259.
[2] Bakar 1991:271.
[3] Bakar 1991:272.

focused on their spiritual interactions with the Creator in trance-induced states.

Though such practices were associated with the Rifaʿiyya order by followers in the Malay world, some leading early Sufis, such as the famous Persian Sufi Jami, had long claimed they were innovations which could not be traced back to the founder of the order, al-Rifaʿi. In fact, such rituals represent manifestations of popular Sufism, as they provided vehicles for the masses to engage in the spiritual quest. They sit in contrast to the more esoteric thinking of 'High' Sufism in the region, promoted by scholars such as the great Acehnese thinkers previously discussed who applied Sufi perspectives to the Islamic sciences in their writings on *kalam, fiqh* and other fields of learning.

Also famous as examples of popular Sufism were the *ratib* ceremonies practised by various Sufi groups. These events typically included a combination of *dhikr* rituals, interspersed with fragments from poetic odes (*qasidah*) and songs of divine love (*nashid*),[4] with these practices undertaken in various states of trance. Among the most famous of the *ratib* ceremonies were those practiced by the ʿAlawiyya order, which was brought to the Malay world by immigrants from the Hadhramaut, and which played an important role in the spread of Islam in the region.[5]

Snouck Hurgronje included a detailed description of *ratib* ceremonies in Aceh in his monumental two-volume study of the Acehnese. He speaks of the popularity of the *ratib samman* throughout the archipelago. This *ratib* had fixed rules and postures, and Snouck Hurgronje observes that Shaykh Samman, the supposed originator of this *ratib*, 'held noise and motion to be powerful agents for producing the desired state of mystic transport'.[6]

The practitioners of the *ratib samman* in Aceh neglected some of the strict requirements laid down for the event in the Arab world, according to Snouck Hurgronje. He observes that in Arabia participants were required to clearly and correctly pronounce the names and attributes of God and the *shahada* while taking part in the *ratib*. However, in the archipelago practitioners did not always

4 Bakar 1991:278.
5 Alatas 1997.
6 Snouck Hurgronje 1906: vol. 2, 217.

observe this requirement, and sometimes their pronunciation of these references was incoherent, and mixed up with senseless ramblings of a type discouraged in Arab contexts.[7] Likewise Malay observance of bodily postures for this *ratib* was described as being much less exact than that required in the Arab world.

Elsewhere in the Malay archipelago, Sufi orders also introduced practices which were of mixed Islamic and pre-Islamic origin. In the Moluccas, an elaborate set of prayer litanies for the dead was developed by adherents of the Qadiriyya in the region. These litanies included prayers for the spirit of Muhammad, then for the spirit of the ancestors of the family hosting the event of commemoration, including those recently deceased, and also prayers for the ancestors of those present.[8] Such litanies were recited at regular intervals after the death of someone. Thus they represented an adaptation of Islamic ritual norm to local ancestor-veneration practice.

Perhaps the most widespread local adaptation of world-wide Sufi ritual surrounded ceremonies conducted in association with visitations to saints' graves. An example is the annual pilgrimage to the grave (in the Javanese village of Kajen) of Haji Mutamakin, the personality made famous by the *Serat Cabolek*. Clothes are laid upon this grave, others are auctioned for a considerable sum, and the biography in narrative form of 'Abd al-Qadir Jailani is recited.[9]

Modern scholars and writers regard such localised variations as worthy of study and respect. However, for increasing numbers of Islamic scholars during the 18th and 19th centuries who saw themselves as representing Islamic orthodoxy, such local adaptations were none other than corruptions, polluting true Islamic practice as they viewed it. As Milner observes, 'It is in the eighteenth and nineteenth centuries that the influence of the "*sharia*-minded" fundamentalists is constantly evident in Southeast Asia.'[10] Local practices such as those described above were to provide considerable fuel for later reformist campaigns.

---

[7] Snouck Hurgronje 1906: Vol. 2, 217–8.
[8] Reid 1984:18.
[9] Wieringa 1998:36–7.
[10] Milner 1988:46.

Selected thinkers and writings

The mystical quest continued to permeate the writings of the majority of Malay theologians during the 18th and 19th centuries, just as had been the case in previous centuries. We will now examine selected writings from this period in order to gain additional perspectives on how Southeast Asian Muslims were responding to and adapting Islamic thought originating from outside the region.

Javanese suluk literature.   Mention should be made at this juncture of *suluks*, or Javanese verse works concerning religious subjects composed subsequent to the Old Javanese literary era. Though most of these made their initial appearance in the pre-colonial era, their circulation and popularisation was consolidated during the period of Dutch colonialism in Java. Hence their inclusion at this point of our study, as they provide an important window into Javanese Islamic belief and practice during the 18th and 19th centuries.

Zoetmulder based his doctoral study of monism and pantheism in *suluk* literature upon a considerable number of excerpts from various *suluk* works. His principal focus was the *Centini*, but he also examined other texts such as the *Seh Bari*, *Suluk Samsu Tabarit*, *Suluk Kadis* and the *Serat Siti Jenar*. He concluded that, by and large, the *Seh Bari* text was not pantheistic, as the work maintains a clear distance between Creator and creature. In examining certain segments from the *Centini*, Zoetmulder reached the same conclusion, but added that both should be viewed as lying on the boundaries of orthodoxy, saying that they came close to being pantheistic and that 'immanence is so pressing that a feeling of oneness arises, but the quality of this oneness cannot be expressed'.[11]

Many *suluk* works include Sufi doctrines which drew accusations of heterodoxy, such as the doctrine of seven grades of emanation of the Wujudiyya,[12] encountered previously in our discussion of 17th-century Acehnese mystics. Zoetmulder argued that the emanation doctrine had great appeal to Javanese Muslims because of their penchant for doctrines which are

---

11 Zoetmulder 1995:95. Soebardi's (1975) view is that the composition of this work had among its goals the encouragement of the study of *shari'a* and orthodox theology.
12 Ricklefs 1997:245.

pragmatic and which could be used as a practical means to achieve mystical ecstasy. He drew on texts from the *Centini* to demonstrate this.

There are clear examples within *suluk* literature which demonstrate a kind of 'radical' monist teaching which goes beyond the thought of Hamzah Fansuri and Shams al-Din al-Sumatrani. This can be seen in the *Suluk Samsu Tabarit*, which contains passages rejecting and ridiculing a legalistic approach to religion, tending to portray good works as of little benefit, and encouraging neglect of the obligatory duties of Islam.[13] The figure of Lebe Lontang is portrayed in a positive light as an ecstatic who intentionally behaves in a manner contrary to the norms of orthodox Islamic practice and shows contempt for the Qur'an and prayer. This approach of setting *shari'a* and *tasawwuf* in tension is also evident in certain writings ascribed to the Javanese saints (*walis*) who are credited with having brought Islam to Java.[14] In certain *Siti Jenar* stories, for example, the main character manifests certain radical doctrines, rejecting Islamic law and showing himself to be unambiguously monist in orientation.[15] Woodward made a detailed study of this fundamental opposition within Java, concluding that Javanese Muslims' 'views of the relative significance of mysticism and normative piety range from those of strict *shari'a* minded Sufis, to those of the most extreme radicals denouncing all aspects of normative piety and openly preaching the doctrine of the unity of Allah and the human soul'.[16] *Suluk* literature played a crucial role in articulating this basic opposition and embedding it within the Javanese psyche.

The continuing circulation of these works during the 18th and 19th centuries ensured that popular Javanese mystical practice remained on a collision course with the reformist thinking which was gradually penetrating the region following the early reforming activities of al-Raniri and 'Abd al-Ra'uf.

Ratu Pakubuwana (d. 1732). A name worthy of note in the context of Islam in central Java during the early part of the 18th

---

[13] Zoetmulder 1995:230.

[14] Cf. Rinkes 1996.

[15] Cf. the 18th-century Javanese commentary *Kitab Patahulrahman* in Beatty 1998:21.

[16] Woodward 1985:82.

century was Ratu Pakubuwana, the wife of the Javanese ruler Pakubuwana I. She outlived her husband, and was to exert a significant influence on her grandson, Pakubuwana II, who ascended the Javanese throne of Mataram in 1726 at the age of sixteen. Her contribution was more via promotion of others than in direct writing herself. In 1729–30, barely two years before her death, she set upon sponsoring a series of pious Islamic works, *Carita Sultan Iskandar, Carita Nabi Yusuf,* and the *Kitab Usulbiyah.*[17]

The first two of these works dealt with Islamic prophetic figures. The *Carita Sultan Iskandar* commences with the most lavish praise of Ratu Pakubuwana, stating that she is beloved of God and has received intercession from the prophet Muhammad. The story thus loses no time in establishing the religious credentials of its promoter, the Queen. It moves from the spiritual to the temporal realm by painting a graphic picture of how Ratu Pakubuwana is greatly esteemed within the Javanese kingdom. Having thus paid due regard to Ratu Pakubuwana, the author of the story then proceeds to explain that this *Carita* was translated into Javanese from the Malay version, which is helpful for our search for lines of transmission of Islamic thought. The author then engages with the story of the prophet Iskandar, but it is no mere re-run of a standard Islamic account. There is a strongly contextualised flavour to the work, with the Islamic tale firmly set within a Javanese context.[18]

Kitab Usulbiyah, while singing the praise of Javanese rulers, sets itself in a distinctly Javanese royal environment while addressing Islamic themes in a contextualised manner. The *Kitab Usulbiyah* relates that Jesus met Muhammad on earth, an assertion which is clearly not based on Islamic sacred scripture but which serves the needs of the Javanese audience for evocative narrative tales which fire up the imagination. Muhammad is depicted as wearing what appears to be the golden crown of Majapahit, a further sign of adaptation of Islamic belief to local history. The work itself came to assume extraordinary proportions; the *Kitab Usulbiyah* was depicted as being so valuable that copying it would equal a thousand pilgrimages to Mecca or a thousand recitations of the

[17] Ricklefs 1997:237.

[18] Ricklefs 1998:40–53. Ricklefs bases his excellent analysis upon the 1995 study of *Serat Iskandar* by Alex Sudewa.

Qur'an. Carrying it into battle was seen as a guarantee of victory and, indeed, the book was portrayed as having mystical powers, even to the point where it was overtly equated with the Qur'an in that it was said to contain God's words.[19]

Thus these two works also played their part in affirming unique Javanese perspectives on Islamic belief and practice, as well as subtly undermining certain exoteric aspects of scriptural Islam, such as performance of the pilgrimage to the holy sites in Arabia.

Raden Ngabehi Yasadipura I (1729–1803). This important writer was born in Surakarta/Solo, Central Java, in 1729, and died in the same town at the age of seventy-four. He was one of the most famous writers and thinkers to emerge from Central Java. He was prolific in literary output, and has left at least ten books.[20] Among the works usually ascribed to Yasadipura I is the *Serat Cabolek.* Recent scholarship has cast doubt on whether Yasadipura I was the author of this work, and has raised issues which require further attention by scholars.[21] Wieringa emphasises the likelihood of Soebardi's text of the *Serat Cabolek* as being a hybrid of several different versions.[22] As our primary interest is in theological thinking rather than historical facts and figures, we will accept that *Serat Cabolek* reflects a type of mystical thought in circulation at the time of Yasadipura I's life, and we will leave the final ascription of authorship to other scholars to resolve.

Yasadipura's prolific output included several tales of Islamic origin, including the *Menak, Tajusalatin* and *Ambiya.* Soebardi described the second of these works as 'a free adaptation of the Malay version of a work apparently of Persian origin'.[23] Mention of the Malay version was made earlier in this present study in the context of Islamic writings produced by religious scholars during the heyday of the Sultanate of Aceh in the 16th and 17th centuries. Yasadipura's *Ambiya* is his Javanese adaptation of the famous Stories of the Prophets,[24] which has been mentioned frequently in

[19] Ricklefs 1997:238–9; Ricklefs 1998:62–91.
[20] Shadily *et al.* 1984: Vol. 7, 3977.
[21] Ricklefs 1998:128ff; Wieringa 1998:31–2.
[22] Wieringa 1998:31.
[23] Soebardi 1975:24.
[24] Soebardi 1975:25.

this present study and which played an important role in the spread of Islam beyond the Middle East.

Soebardi observes that this author 'may be studied equally as a poet, historian, religious teacher and mystic – although these various fields are not as disparate to a Javanese as they might appear to a European'.[25] This is indeed the case, though our interest in *Serat Cabolek* focuses more on Yasadipura I as religious teacher and mystic.

The discussion which follows is based upon Canto I of *Serat Cabolek*.[26] The excerpt focuses upon one of the main protagonists of the work, Haji Amad Mutamakin, who is typecast in a negative light from the outset for preaching the Science of Reality (*ilmu hakekat/ haqiqa*) at the expense of observing the *shari'a*. Soebardi indicates that Mutamakin was a mid-18th-century scholar who had studied the Islamic sciences in Yemen, like many of his Malay world scholarly forbears and successors.[27] The *Serat Cabolek* suggests that Mutamakin learned the Science of Reality from his Yemeni teacher, Shaykh Zayn. However, Ricklefs points out that no other references can be found to Mutamakin in 18th-century Javanese or Dutch East India Company (VOC) records.[28] Whether he is a historical personality or fictitious figure is open to debate. Wieringa suggests that more research needs to be done before this question can be resolved, whereas Ricklefs errs on the side of accepting the historicity of the story, saying 'The grounds for rejecting the tale are, in this writer's opinion, weaker than the grounds for believing that *Serat Cabolek* refers to an actual episode at Kartasura *c.* 1731.'[29]

This story encapsulates a debate which took place throughout the Muslim world over many centuries regarding the respective place of the exoteric and esoteric sciences. In al-Burhanpuri's *Tuhfa* we encountered this issue, with an affirmation of the Sufi quest being mixed with a loud exhortation to observe the *shari'a*. Those who demoted the place of *shari'a* were often portrayed as possessed of demonic forces. And indeed, Mutamakin's demotion

---

25 Soebardi 1975:20.

26 Soebardi 1975: 66–70.

27 Soebardi 1975:26–7.

28 Ricklefs 1998:131.

29 Ricklefs 1998:140. Ricklefs (1998:132) further records that there is a grave near the northern Javanese village of Cabolek which locals believe to contain the remains of Mutamakin, who is regarded as a saint. The grave is a site for pilgrimage.

of the *shari'a* bounced back on him, with the result that his understanding of *haqiqa* became incorrect. In other words, Yasadipura I includes the clear moral in the story that the *shari'a* cannot be sidelined with impunity.

Mutamakin fell upon personal misfortune. But he also seduced many by his eloquent exposition of mystical knowledge. Paragraph six of the excerpt suggests that a key ingredient in the dispute relates to Mutakim's method of expounding his convictions, which he did 'loudly and coarsely'. Javanese culture expects subtlety in interpersonal relations, with coarseness frowned upon. Perhaps part of the reason for the rejection of Mutamakin's theology was less to do with what he said and more to do with the way that he said it. In this context, it is important to note the stress later placed on politeness in paragraph sixteen of the excerpt.

The King is called upon to intervene. Demoting the *shari'a* was considered as treason against the King, pointing to a Javanese view of the king as both temporal ruler and also the representative of Muhammad. Woodward argues that this story records a new stage in Javanese views of kingship, as the King has come to be seen as having 'replaced the *walis* as the arbitrator of religious disputes and as the authority on what constitutes heresy', with the King ultimately responsible in the area of mysticism and the *santri* scholars in the area of normative piety.[30] Day adds that orthodoxy in this text is defined in terms of its identification with Javanese kingship, rather than in terms of specific theological statements.[31]

Paragraph ten introduces an important new element. Haji Mutamakin is reported as claiming 'to be the Reality that is Muhammad'. This represents the second grade in the seven grades of emanation, and suggests influence from al-Burhanpuri's Javanese version of the *Tuhfa*.[32]

This claim by Haji Mutamakin serves as a direct challenge to the role of the King, who himself does not claim such an elevated status. Note that Yasadipura I, and the society he describes, accept the phenomenon of 'the Reality that is Muhammad'. What they reject is Mutamakin's attempts to claim such elevated status.

---

[30] Woodward 1985:125.
[31] Day 1988:145, 147.
[32] Johns 1965:42–3.

Mutamakin has triggered the combining of powerful conservative forces opposed to his claims of mystical union with the Creator.

The remainder of the excerpt describes the process of selecting a jury for Mutamakin's trial, and then the trial itself provides the platform for the expounding of various theological viewpoints in the remainder of *Serat Cabolek*. Soebardi sums up his view of the key lessons of the story as follows:

> The writer's partiality towards the *santri* group is particularly obvious in the praise and respect shown to the *'ulama'* ... Yasadipura I has made skilful use of a common motif in the Javanese literary tradition, that of conflict between pantheistic Javanese mysticism and orthodox, legalistic Islam ... Yasadipura I has attempted to play the role of an al-Ghazali, presenting a harmonization of these two religious currents in Javanese society, by projecting the image of one who valued *shari'a* ... and by condemning the teaching of the Science of Reality to the uninitiated public. He regarded the *shari'a* as the vessel ... and esoteric knowledge as the *contents* [of the spiritual life].[33]

Thus the key idea is that mystical knowledge without *shari'a* is just a fraud, or 'a pretence'. Mystical pursuits stand affirmed, indeed encouraged for some, but only on condition that they represent a part of a holistic approach to devotional life by a Muslim. The *Serat Cabolek* has played its part within the broader Javanese *suluk* corpus of engaging with the key debate regarding the role of *shari'a, vis-à-vis* Sufi practice,[34] coming down on the side of affirming Law but simultaneously encouraging the mystical quest. In this it adds weight to the reformed Sufism promoted by al-Raniri and 'Abd al-Ra'uf.

Raden Ngabehi Yasadipura II.   In an important contribution to the study of the Islamic element in Javanese literature, Kumar[35] examined the hitherto little-studied *Sasana Sunu* by Yasadipura II, which was written during the 1820s.[36] This writer was the son of Yasadipura I, and served as a functionary in the Sultan's palace in Surakarta. Yasadipura II often wrote jointly with his father, with

---

[33] Soebardi 1975:42–4.

[34] Day (1988:144) refers to this issue as 'the perennial subject of debate in Javanese Islamic *suluk* literature'.

[35] Kumar 1997.

[36] Yasadipura II 1980.

the result that works attributed to the one often contain significant elements produced by the other.[37] The second Yasadipura's writings include *Serat Darmasunya* (1820), *Serat Arjuna Sasrabahu utawi Lokapala* (1824) and *Sasana Sunu* (1825).

The *Sasana Sunu* had as its primary objective moral guidance for the Javanese upper class, and Islam is allocated a major role in this process. The work is divided into twelve chapters, addressing wide-ranging issues. It saw itself as presenting an Islam which was essentially orthodox in its orientation; the text is damning of Sufis, such as al-Hallaj, and the Javanese Seh Siti Jenar, both of whom were executed for mystical beliefs considered as heterodox by the authorities of their times.

The *Sasana Sunu* exhorts young members of the Javanese elite, who are the principal audience addressed by the writer, to follow the *shari'a* in their daily lives. The author calls for adherence to the five pillars, obedience to the dietary laws, and abstinence from alcohol and other standard Islamic prohibitions. For example, Yasadipura II warns his readers on things which can cause 'drunkenness', namely beauty, material goods, national fervour, youth as well as rice wine and other alcoholic drinks. He defines a person of superior quality as one who is possessed of all of the above but who does not allow himself to become intoxicated by them.

Thus again the issue of observance of the external precepts of Islam has arisen as an issue, and its recurrent mention in the literature of the period points to the widespread neglect of the *shari'a* among 18th- and 19th-century Javanese society. Yasidapura II's exhortations are articulated with regard to financial affairs in the following excerpt:

It should always be remembered that money or possessions obtained illegitimately should never be accepted, no matter how large the sum. Likewise with illegal income, it should not be taken. It is better to earn a little which is legal. Pursuit of profit should be with appropriate means. The meaning of 'appropriate' is that which is legitimate and according to law ... in seeking livelihood for life's needs, do not lend money with interest.[38]

However, this work is not a purely Islamic treatise untouched by the Hindu-Javanese roots of the author or his audience. Kumar

---

[37] Shadily *et al.* 1984: vol. 7, 3977.

[38] Yasadipura II 1980:11.

comments that 'In general ... Islamic concepts are combined with or glossed by Javanese ones and the overall framework seems clearly Javanese rather than Islamic'.[39] Indeed, throughout the text some interesting parallels are drawn by Kumar between Hindu-Javanese traditions and the Islamic teachings which are presented as goals by the author. For example, the audience is exhorted by the author to read both pre-Islamic texts, including the Old Javanese *Ramayana* and other works based on the Hindu-Javanese tradition, as well as Islamic texts, such as the Javanese version of the Stories of the Prophets. This no doubt reflects the fact that during the 18th and 19th centuries pre-Islamic *wayang* (traditional Javanese drama) stories were generally preferred by the general Javanese population to stories based on Muslim texts. Indeed, evidence of accommodation by Islamic scholars of Java's pre-Islamic past is also seen in reports that those scholars were versed in both Islamic and traditional Javanese literature.[40]

At certain points there appear to be some syncretistic elements in the practices advocated by the author, such as in the commendation of restraint in food, drink and sleep, which while being characteristic of some of the practices of Muhammad described in the prophetic Traditions, are also reminiscent of Javanese ascetic practices (*tapa*) which are designed to enhance the individual's spiritual powers.

The work encourages young males to come to grips with the daily life of the peasantry as well as urging them to provide facilities for devout Muslims, by way of setting up mosques and providing rice fields for *santri* Muslims.[41] These urgings are designed to emphasise the social benefits of a strong religious commitment. The text itself is very consciously observant of Hindu–Javanese social structures, by being targeted at the traditional elite, yet it also attempts to place these structures within an Islamic context by making references to Qur'anic verses, such as Q4:59, which call for obedience to rulers in authority.

---

[39] Kumar 1997:257.

[40] Supomo 1997:220.

[41] Cf. Carey 1981:XLV for information on these *santri* communities set up before and during the Java War.

One of the most interesting examples of adaptation of Islamic concepts to a Javanese environment is addressed by Kumar in her analysis of the understanding of the term *wahyu* in the text. In Arabic the term means revelation and is associated with the prophets, especially Muhammad. However, in the *Sasana Sunu* the term *wahyu* is presented as a quality which all members of the Javanese elite can hope to attain and by thus hijacking a prophetic quality for the ruling class, the Javanese elite seemed to be placing themselves as nearer to God.

Thus although an Islamic term is used, the social implications are distinctly unislamic. Moreover, in spite of including an Islamic flavour in his writings, Yasadipura II also allocated due recognition to the importance of traditional Javanese *adat* or custom, and urges that young Javanese should observe this traditional custom.

Ranggawarsita (1802–73). This famous Javanese writer's birth name was Bagus Burhan. In early adulthood he quickly established a reputation for learning in the city of Surakarta, where he became the last of the great Court poets.[42] He frequently interacted with Dutch residents of the city, and jointly authored, with the Dutchman C.F. Winter, a book on Javanese grammar. Ranggawarsita also served as redactor for the periodical *Bromartani*, edited by Jonas Portier.

Ranggawarsita became a prolific writer in Javanese on wideranging subjects.[43] His poetry addressed didactic, moralistic themes (*Serat Wirit Sopanalaya*), and a range of ethical issues (*Serat Candrarani*). He also engaged with Javanese mysticism and prophecy in poetic form (*Sapta dharma*). His theological eclecticism, reflecting his Javanese context, can be seen in his poetry, which also drew on Hindu themes, such as *Sri Kresna Barata* which is a poem about the Hindu deity Krishna. His works also included the *Paramayoga* and the *Pustakaraja Purwa* presenting a legendary history of Java covering the period from Adam to the middle of the 7th century CE.[44]

---

[42] Cribb 1992:408.
[43] *Ensiklopedi Nasional Indonesia* 1990: Vol. 14, 250.
[44] Cribb 1992:409.

For the purposes of the present study, one of Ranggawarsita's most interesting works is *Wirid Hidayat Jati*. This work was published in 1908 by the publishers Jawi Kandha in Surakarta.[45] In it Ranggawarsita claims to have assembled the accumulated mystical teachings of the Javanese *wali* who purportedly spread Islam throughout the island. Ranggawarsita begins by listing several generations of Javanese saints on whom he has drawn. He states at the outset that the teachings were based on the four sources of the *shari'a*: the Qur'an; the traditions of the Prophet; the consensus of the scholars; and analogy. Thus from the beginning he seeks to achieve a reconciliation between *shari'a* and the Sufi records he is transmitting.

However, in his introduction, Ranggawarsita quickly unveils his monistic orientation in saying '... man is a manifestation of the Divine Essence which is One in nature. This is the core of gnosis as taught by the prophets and saints of old ...'

The first chapter includes detailed instructions as to how the aspiring Sufi must prepare himself for study of the teachings of the saints. He must wear clean clothes free of gold thread, cover his head and adorn his left ear with flowers in a specific Javanese pattern. He must wear strands of flowers prepared in a particular way. Furthermore the room must be prepared according to similarly specific instructions. A dowry of coins must be placed in the room with perfume and incense grains, and covered with a white cloth. The aspiring Sufi must face westward, and study the teachings in eight parts.[46]

Ranggawarsita then proceeds with an explanation of the teachings themselves. At one level, the author takes the role of God, speaking in the first person:

In truth there was nothing, for when there was the great void, before anything existed, there was I beforehand, in truth the Essence of the Most Holy encompassed My attributes, accompanied My name, characterised my actions.[47]

There are certain elements in this work designed to please those Muslims more concerned with the exterior (*zahir*) sciences: God

---

[45] Cf. Simuh 1987; Ranggawarsita 1908; Ranggawarsita and Medeiros 1999.

[46] Ranggawarsita and Medeiros 1999.

[47] Simuh 1987:66.

is Creator, God is omnipotent, God is One. God creates on account of His will, not on account of any obligation. This echoes Ranggawarsita's attempt to keep the *shari'a*-minded on side, as we saw in the introduction.

Truly I, the Essence Most Powerful, have the power to create all things in an instant, complete in form, on account of My omnipotence, thereby to become evidential proof of My action which represents the embodiment of My will. In the beginning I created *Hayyu* (the wood) called *Shajara al-Yaqin*, which grew in the realm of the eternal non-existence; then the radiance called *Nur Muhammad*; then the mirror called *Mir'a al-Hayya'i* [?]; then the spirit called *Ruh Idafi*; then the torch called *Kandil*; then the jewel called *Darrah*; then the great wall called *Hijab*, which represents the partition from My presence ...[48]

However, the mystical flavour of this excerpt is paramount. Again the framework of the seven grades of being appears, pointing to the continuing influence of the Javanese translation of al-Burhanpuri's *Tuhfa*.

The first excerpt cited above resonates with the first grade of non-determination. Then the next excerpt speaks of the Creation, and the sequence of created things – in order: the tree; the radiance (the Light of Muhammad); the mirror; the spirit; the torch; the jewel; and finally the great wall which separates the world from God's essence – are presented as seven stages, with the number seven allocated the importance found in much mystical thought.

Note that similarities can also be found with the Ibn al-'Arabi five-fold scheme followed by Hamzah Fansuri, with the fourth created element, the *Ruh Idafi*, also appearing as Hamzah's second determination.[49]

Of further interest is the following paragraph:

The Essence of the Lord Most Holy sees through our eyes; He hears through our ears; He smells through our noses; He speaks through our tongues, He feels all feelings through using all of our senses ...[50]

A question posed by less mystically-inclined Muslims is whether God is denying his transcendent self-sufficiency by depending on

---

[48] Simuh 1987:68.
[49] Johns 1957:103.
[50] Simuh 1987:72.

us for seeing, hearing, smelling, speaking and feeling. However, the monistic Sufi response is to say that God's interlinking with the human senses points to the oneness of all creation. Thus here are further ingredients for conflict between monistic Sufis and the '*shari'a*-minded'.

Elsewhere in this work, Hindu flavours are sensed by references such as '*atma*, namely pure essence with the attribute of one-ness ... .' The author's comfort in using Sanskrit terminology points to the gradual assimilation of pre-Islamic and Islamic belief systems.

This work, though not specifically representative of Ranggawar-sita's broader writing, is valuable in that it shows that this major literary figure was in step with a more monistic Javanese mystical context. It serves to provide a further important window into that context, in the lead-up to the growing mood of reformist thinking which was to culminate in the modernist movement of the 20th century.

'Abd al-Samad al-Palimbani (c. 1704–89).   'Abd al-Samad al-Palim-bani originated from the Palembang region of Sumatra, as indi-cated by the *nisba* in his name. His father, Sayyid 'Abd al-Jalil b. Shaykh 'Abd al-Wahab, originated from San'a, Yemen,[51] and taught the Islamic sciences in Palembang before moving to Kedah where he became Mufti in 1700.[52] 'Abd al-Samad went to Arabia to further his studies as a young man. He studied with several Malay scholars based in Arabia, including Muhammad Arshad al-Banjari and 'Abd al-Wahab Bugis.[53] His studies also included a period spent as a pupil of Muhammad al-Sammani (d. 1776), the founder of the Sammaniyya order, and the supposed source of the *ratib samman* discussed earlier. It was largely due to 'Abd al-Samad's indirect influence that the Sammaniyya came to be firmly established in Palembang and elsewhere in the archi-pelago.[54]

During his life he composed at least eight works, of which six survive in published or manuscript form. His greatest

[51] Azra 1992:494.
[52] Nasution *et al.* 1992:33.
[53] Ibid.
[54] Voorhoeve 1960:92.

contribution to Malay Islam took the form of adaptations into Malay of classical Arabic works. His *magnum opus* was his rendering of al-Ghazali's *Ihya' 'Ulum al-Din* into Malay, which he completed in 1789 after ten years' work, and which is still reprinted and used in various parts of Malaysia and Indonesia today.[55] His work took an Arabic title, *Sayr al-Salikin ila 'Ibadat Rabb al-'Alamin.* True to translation norms current among Malay scholars for centuries, 'Abd al-Samad did not limit himself to producing a faithful rendering of the original text alone, but at times produced a very free rendering, seeing fit both to reduce or expand the original, drawing on various Arabic commentaries as the occasion demanded. However, unlike some of his fellow Malay scholars, he meticulously identified the sources of his additions to al-Ghazali's work, drawn from the works of Ibn al-'Arabi, al-Jili, al-Burhanpuri, al-Qushashi, al-Kurani, al-Sammani and others.[56]

'Abd al-Samad's interest in al-Ghazali was not limited to rendering the *Ihya'*. He also wrote a Malay adaptation of al-Ghazali's *Bidayat al-hidaya*, which he again gave a title in Arabic, *Hidayat al-Salikin fi Suluk Maslak al-Muttakin.* These two adaptations of al-Ghazali's writing also served as vehicles for presenting the thought of other Sufi writers, including Ibn al-'Arabi. 'Abd al-Samad saw al-Ghazali and Ibn al-'Arabi as providing two complementary paths in the mystical quest, with the former leading the Sufi seeker towards knowledge of God, and the latter providing metaphysical insights into the nature of the Divine and the relationship between Creator and creation.[57]

Perhaps his choice to maintain Arabic titles for Malay works reflected his living context, as 'Abd al-Samad lived most of his life in Arabia, like Muhammad al-Nawawi al-Jawi almost one hundred years later. It should be noted that the latter also gave his Malay works Arabic titles.

'Abd al-Samad was also inclined to anti-'infidel' polemic. In this context, *jihad* formed the basis of his work *Nasihat al-Muslimin*, which inspired the author of the Acehnese poem 'Hikayat prang sabi',[58] which was widely circulated during the Aceh war against the Dutch in the late 19th century.

---

[55] Johns 1987b:417.
[56] Azra 1992:534.
[57] Nasution *et al.* 1992:34.

Azra describes 'Abd al-Samad as 'the most prominent Malay–Indonesian scholar in the 18th-century networks.'[59] His importance lies not only in his role as transmitter of Islamic thought and texts to Southeast Asia from his base in Arabia. Of significance is the fact that he provided a Malay voice focusing on more *shari'a*-conscious Sufi thinking at a time when debates about radical monism were increasingly taking place in the Malay world. Indeed, 'Abd al-Samad himself criticised the speculative monist teachings of the earlier Wujudiyya, echoing al-Raniri's division between believing Wujudiyya and atheistic Wujudiyya approaches.[60]

His works were to be promoted by reformist-minded Malay Muslims over a hundred years after his death through publishing and distribution. An example is *Hidayat al-Salikin fi Suluk Maslak al-Muttakin*, which deals with orthodox belief and ritual, *dhikr*, and a range of other subjects, and draws upon 'Abd al-Ra'uf's *'Umdat al-muhtajin* as one of its sources. It was lithographed in Singapore in 1873, some ninety-five years after its original composition.[61]

Leiden Cod. Or. 2222 (c. 1840).   We saw earlier how examination of specific manuscripts can inform the search for Malay Islamic history. The Cambridge University manuscript containing commentary on the 18th Chapter of the Qur'an, MS Ii.6.45, serves as a crucial pointer to early activity by Malay Islamic scholars in the field of Qur'anic exegesis.

Similarly, much can be gleaned from considering Leiden Cod. Or. 2222, held by the library of Leiden University. This manuscript was most likely obtained by a Dutch officer participating in the Dutch attack on Aceh in 1873. It seems hitherto to have been held in the library of the fourteen-year-old Sultan Mahmud Shah, who assumed the Acehnese throne in 1870. Examination of the manuscript paper has led scholars to propose a date sometime after 1840 for production of the MS, on paper manufactured in Indonesia.[62] This is crucial, as it provides valuable data on the activities and theological interests of Acehnese religious scholars

58   Voorhoeve 1960:92; Azra 1992:499–500.
59   Azra 1992:501.
60   Azra 1992:540.
61   Winstedt 1969:152.
62   Janson *et al.* 1995.

connected with the court just prior to the commencement of the Aceh War.

Furthermore, the work attributes its theological basis to the teachings of Ahmad al-Qushashi (1583–1661). As we have seen, al-Qushashi taught 'Abd al-Ra'uf al-Singkili during his nineteen-year stay in Arabia. Snouck Hurgronje observed in 'The Acehnese' that most chains of transmission for mystical orders in Aceh traced themselves back to al-Qushashi in his time. Rinkes records the existence of a branch of the Shattariyya called the Qushashiyya in the Bencoolen area of West Sumatra, as well as in other parts of the archipelago.[63]

Though al-Qushashi, a 17th-century figure, serves as the inspiration of Leiden Cod. Or. 2222, we must not be distracted from the fact that the manuscript itself opens a window into 19th-century Malay thought, especially in Aceh. The text was produced by a particular mystical order, the Shattariyya, established in Sumatra by 'Abd al-Ra'uf and central to the formation of Malay Islam.

The manuscript was intended as a teaching text. It is based on a series of diagrams, rather than blocks of text, which would facilitate its overriding pedagogical function. Diagram 6 states the purpose overtly in saying 'This diagram is to teach the pupils the invocations from their teachers with the blessing of our Syaikh Ahmad al-Qusyasyi.'

The manuscript claims early on that al-Qushashi 'believes in the seven grades and the twenty attributes'. Thus the thinking contained therein is very much germane to the thinking of the 17th-century Acehnese mystics and Javanese mystical writers examined previously. Another resemblance to those earlier Malay writings occurs when Leiden Cod. Or. 2222 quotes al-Qushashi as saying that 'the most perfect is like a very deep sea, a sea of inconceivable depths … which even cannot be estimated by the prophet and the saints'. This statement clearly echoes the sea metaphor for the Divine used some 250 years earlier by Hamzah Fansuri. Furthermore, this very statement implies an elevated position for Sufi saints, supplementing the role of Muhammad. Thus prophethood and sainthood are depicted as firmly interlinked as instruments for the realisation of God's purposes.

---

[63] Rinkes 1909.

The text is pregnant with symbolism of Light, either the Light of God or the Light of Muhammad, with these terms being used interchangeably. In portraying a monistic view of the Creator and his creation, the author places stress upon the divine attributes, such as life, knowledge, wish, power, hearing, sight, word of God. The author also makes repeated references to the seven grades. The first three, referring to words of unity, are specified as *Ahadiyya* (associated with the Reality of God), *Wahda* (the Reality of Muhammad) and *Wahidiyya* (the Reality of Adam). The author also makes regular references to the other four grades: *'alam ruh,* the world of the spirit; *'alam mithal,* the world of the images; *'alam ajsam,* the world of the heavenly bodies; *'alam insan,* the world of mankind.

In seeking to expound on the incomprehensible for his students, the author uses diagram 20 to articulate al-Qushashi's thinking: 'the absolute essence means that which is hidden from everything (that is hidden), and that which is concealed from everything that is concealed, and that which is inside everything that is inside, and that which is far from everything that is far.' This echoes a statement from *Wirid Hidayat Jati* cited previously. Furthermore, the author's elevation of Muhammad is striking; diagram 23 includes a circle in red containing the words 'Allah Muhammad', into which are fed four other circles containing respectively the four elements: earth, wind, fire, water.

The production of a text such as this in the middle of the 19th century shows that the increasing influence of reformed Sufi thought, dating back to al-Raniri and 'Abd al-Ra'uf, had not fully asserted itself in the Malay world. This text provides evidence of a continuing tension between monist thought and reformed Sufism, which was to make a further upsurge of reformist thinking likely.

Raja Ali Haji of Riau (1808–70) and his writings.   Raja Ali Haji has been described as 'one of the greatest Malay writers of the 19th Century'.[64] He belonged to the Malay-Bugis royal house of Riau.

Raja Ali Haji underwent a broad education, which equipped him well to make a significant contribution to various areas of learning. His fame as a scholar spread throughout the region, and

---

[64] Winstedt, 1969:164.

by the age of thirty-two he had assumed significant responsibilities in acting as joint regent and ruling Lingga for the young Sultan Mahmud of Johor.[65] However, his fame was to be achieved, not so much as an administrator, but rather as a writer and thinker.

Raja Ali Haji is best known for his historical writings, principally the *Tuhfat al-Nafis* (The Precious Gift) and *Silsilah Melayu dan Bugis* (Malay and Bugis Genealogy). The former of these is his greatest work and represents a synthesis of various sources.[66] Raja Ali Haji's purposes in drawing up the *Tuhfat* were several; he was concerned not only to record the history of the Johor Empire's relationship with the Bugis, the other Malay states and the Dutch, but he also wrote for a didactic purpose, to enable his contemporary readers to learn lessons from the past.

In Raja Ali Haji's historical writing, the author was no longer preoccupied with propounding the view of Malay rulers' divine right to rule, as had been the case with earlier historical writing. Rather, his was a more critical world view necessary to support his quest for historical objectivity.[67] Another unique aspect of the *Tuhfat* was that in recording over 200 years of history and covering the entire Malay world in its scope, it added a new dimension to Malay historiography.[68] The result was to represent a watershed in Malay historical writing with the *Tuhfat* becoming the most important Malay historical work since the *Sejarah Melayu*.[69]

The diverse skills of Raja Ali Haji are reflected in the scope of his writings, covering theology, law, history, grammar, poetry and statecraft. In addition to the two historical works mentioned above, his principal writings include two works on grammar – the *Bustan al-Katibin* (Garden of Writers) and *Kitab Pengetahuan Bahasa* (Knowledge of Language) – two works on statecraft – *Intizam Waza'if al-Malik* (Systematic Arrangement of the Duties of Ruler) and *Thamarat al-Mahammah* (Benefits of Religious Duties) – as well as a range of poetic works written separately or embedded within his other writings. Nevertheless, all of these works are

---

[65] Andaya and Matheson, 1982:5.

[66] Osman, 1976:140.

[67] Osman, 1976:142.

[68] Andaya and Matheson, 1982:5.

[69] Winstedt, 1969:164.

notable in that they provide not only information on history, statecraft and poetic convention, but also provide an insight into Raja Ali Haji's theological thinking, which was an important part of his character.

In early adulthood, Raja Ali Haji came to be regarded as a religious authority, deriving from his extensive early education in the Islamic sciences and Arabic language.[70] He was instrumental in recruiting many teachers of Islam from outside the region to teach in Riau, and as a result of his efforts and those of his colleagues, Riau gained a reputation as a place where orthodox Islam flourished.[71] Raja Ali Haji became a very prominent member of the Riau branch of the Naqshbandiyya Sufi order,[72] and much of the focus within his writings was designed to urge pious living according to the precepts of Islam, and thus to promote reformed Sufism.

Raja Ali Haji was greatly influenced in terms of his theology by the classical Sufi al-Ghazali, whose seminal work *Ihya' 'ulum al-din* (Revitalisation of the Religious Sciences) had been translated into Malay by 'Abd al-Samad al-Palimbani in 1789 and again by Da'ud ibn 'Abd Allah ibn Idris al-Patani in 1824.[73] References to this work appear regularly in Raja Ali Haji's various writings. Another work by al-Ghazali to influence Raja Ali Haji was the former's *Nasihat al-Muluk* (Counsel for Kings), which had a great bearing on the *Thamarat al-Mahammah*. The central theme of these works was the importance of rulers serving as good models in religion for their subjects in order to prepare the common people for the Day of Judgement. These works stressed the notion that the degree of a leader's virtue would determine the well-being of the state itself. This theme also appeared in the *Tuhfat al-Nafis* where the successes and difficulties experienced by the Empire of Johor were seen to be directly connected with the virtuous (or otherwise) nature of its rulers.

Raja Ali Haji was not merely concerned with broad notions such as the above, but also engaged with specific doctrinal issues, such as the debate concerning predestination and human free will

---

[70] Andaya and Matheson, 1982:5; Osman, 1976:140.
[71] Andaya and Matheson, 1979:110.
[72] Abdullah, 1993:54.
[73] Andaya and Matheson, 1979:115.

discussed earlier in this present study. In the *Tuhfat al-Nafis*, Raja
Ali Haji portrayed the will of God as being crucial in determining
the outline of history and the framework of society, but the individual is made responsible for his own choices within that framework. Predestination rarely occurs as the central focus in this
work, and when it does it is only used to describe tragic events
which have certain didactic purposes.[74]

Raja Ali Haji was an arch-conservative in his views. He portrayed his society as in an advanced state of decay, and presented
the society of the prophet Muhammad as an ideal which individuals should strive to attain. He called for adherence to the *shari'a*,
serious study of religious literature, and obedience to established
scholarship. He called for the conduct of the state to be based on
social harmony in the name of God, and attributed the decline of
Riau to the failure of people – both rulers and subjects – to follow
the teachings of the Prophet. In this way, he made a contribution
to emerging reformist ideas which were spreading through the
Malay world.

Tuan Tabal. Another Islamic thinker and writer who left a mark
on Malay Islam during the colonial period was 'Abd al-Samad ibn
Muhammad Salih al-Kalantani. He died in 1891. He was a Sufi
notable, associated with the Ahmadiyya order, whose fame was
most pronounced in the areas of Kelantan and Patani, where he
was best known as Tuan Tabal, reflecting his village of origin in
South Patani. Unlike Ahmad Patani and Da'ud Patani discussed
below, Tuan Tabal made his mark from his base in the Malay
world. He was a prolific writer, and his literary legacy includes the
following works: [75]

- *Bab Harap*, concerned with Sufism.
- *Munyat ahli al-awbah fi bayan al-tauba*, a detailed investigation of
  Sufism.
- *Kifayya ta'lim al-'awam* (1878), concerning the twenty
  attributes.
- *Munabih al-ghafil*, concerning Sufism.

---

[74] Andaya and Matheson, 1979:117–18.
[75] Shadily *et al.* 1980: vol. 1, 56–7; Abd Rahim 1999:89.

- *Minhaj al-qarib al-mujib al-raghibin fi al-taqrib* (1878), concerning the unity of the Godhead, law and Sufism. This represents his most substantial work.
- *Bidaya al-ta'lim* (1890) concerning the five pillars and duties which must be fulfilled by devout Muslims.

His writing activities demonstrate his concern for achieving a reconciliation between the Law and the spiritual quest. In this way he too played a part in promoting the reformed brand of Sufism which had rehabilitated the place of *shari'a* within the practice of mysticism.

THE 19TH-CENTURY ARABIAN CONNECTION: INGREDIENTS FOR REFORM

In the 19th century the intellectual and social links between the Malay world and the Middle East were further consolidated. Students of Islam continued to travel from Southeast Asia to the Middle East, maintaining a tradition that dated back to at least the late 16th century, when the Acehnese scholar Hamzah Fansuri undertook studies in the Arab world. Furthermore, the century witnessed a surge in immigration to Southeast Asia from the Arab world, particularly from the Hadhramaut.[76] Finally, Arab scholars in Arabia issued increasing numbers of long-distance legal opinions, or *fatwas*, on wide-ranging topics in response to enquiries received from the Malay world.[77]

The result of such interaction between the geographical heart of the Muslim world and its geographical periphery was that major developments in Islamic thinking continued to penetrate the Malay world, as did various polemics. This can be seen in the writing of both Malays based in Arabia and Arabs based in the Malay world.

Of particular note is the contribution such voices made to a gradual restructuring of Malay Islamic thinking. We have seen how Sufi thinking, both a reformed variety and radical monist, dominated the Malay Islamic arena during the 16th, 17th and 18th centuries. The challenge to this status quo was to pick up momentum in the late 19th century, and assert itself in the 20th century.

---

[76] Kroef (1953:300) records that the Arab community in Indonesia more than trebled in number between 1860 (20,000) and 1900 (61,000).

[77] Cf. Kaptein 1995 and 1997a.

Muhammad al-Nawawi al-Jawi (1813–97)

Malay scholars responded to the dynamic interaction between the Middle East and Southeast Asia by producing their own literary contributions to Islamic studies. However, it is noticeable and somewhat surprising that the one major field of Islamic studies to receive a paucity of attention was Qur'anic exegesis. The earliest complete commentary on the Qur'an which we encountered was the *Tarjuman al-Mustafid* written by 'Abd al-Ra'uf around 1675, and a further two hundred years were to elapse before another Malay scholar produced a complete commentary upon the Qur'an.

The Malay scholar in question was Muhammad al-Nawawi al-Jawi, who was born in Banten in West Java, the son of a village religious official (*penghulu*).[78] He spent his early years on the island of Java studying in various locations. In his late teens, he undertook the pilgrimage to Arabia, following the footsteps of many of his earlier Malay co-religionists, and stayed there initially for three years before returning to Java. He returned to Mecca to settle permanently around 1855, establishing himself there as a teacher after undertaking further studies both in Mecca and in Egypt and Syria.[79]

The great Dutch scholar Snouck Hurgronje met al-Nawawi in Mecca in 1884–5, by which stage the latter was an old man. Snouck Hurgronje provides a graphic description of al-Nawawi as being small, bent, dirty and speaking a very formalised style of Arabic with a poor grasp of the colloquial language. This suggests that in spite of the length of time he had spent in the Arab world, a considerable proportion of his social contacts were with Malay speakers from the substantial Malay community in Mecca at that period. He earned the esteem of the local Malay community, and Snouck Hurgronje describes how al-Nawawi 'accepts the handkiss from almost all Jawah living in Mekka without false compliments as an obvious tribute to science ...'[80]

Al-Nawawi clearly had strong political views, though he does not appear to have involved himself in political movements. He was opposed to the Dutch presence in Indonesia. That presence

---

[78] Snouck Hurgronje 1931:268.
[79] Snouck Hurgronje 1931:268; Hafiduddin 1987:41.
[80] Snouck Hurgronje 1931:270.

was a key factor in his decision to settle in Mecca rather than inherit his father's mantle, as Snouck Hurgronje states forcefully that al-Nawawi would never have countenanced serving 'the infidel government even as *penghulu*'.[81]

While he does not appear to have shared the strong anti-Sufi views of some of his contemporaries, neither did he present Sufi approaches to the faith as normative, as did earlier teachers in the region such as Ahmad al-Qushashi. For example, he did not actively urge his students to join Sufi orders. Though his lessons included selections from the great Sufi masters, especially al-Ghazali, he avoided those writings which were inclined to attract accusations of heterodoxy, such as the writings of the leading monists. He was thus paying due respect to the Wahhabite Arabian environment in which he found himself. A change was taking place in terms of Malay Islamic education.

Though al-Nawawi was never to return to the Malay world, his influence was considerable in that part of the Muslim world by way of the instruction he provided to Malay scholars of Islam who had travelled to the Middle East to complete their training. They then returned to Southeast Asia and transmitted the results of their study in turn to their own students. Thus the stamp of al-Nawawi continued to fall upon the study of Islam in Southeast Asia via his own students and via his writings.

His literary works.   Al-Nawawi wrote exclusively in Arabic, and is reputed to have written at least ninety-nine works.[82] Hafiduddin has listed twenty-six of his most prominent works,[83] most of which are still included in the reading materials of reformist *pesantrens* in Indonesia.[84] This list demonstrates his breadth of knowledge in diverse fields, including Qur'anic exegesis, jurisprudence, dogmatics, rhetoric, ethics, history, linguistics and mysticism. Of particular note is that he wrote many commentaries on the works of other writers, and in this we see his primary role of teacher asserting itself. These include a commentary on al-Ghazali's *Bidayat al-hidaya*, addressing ethics and

[81] Snouck Hurgronje 1931:271; Hafiduddin 1987:41.
[82] Nasution *et al.* 1992:424.
[83] Hafiduddin 1987:42–3.
[84] Aboebakar 1957:88.

Sufism; a commentary on the Stories of the Prophets (*Qisas al-anbiya'*) and a commentary on a study of grammar. Al-Nawawi wrote commentaries on two leading works produced by Hadhrami immigrants to the Malay world: *Sullam al-munaja* (a commentary on *Safinat al-salah* by 'Abd Allah b. Yahya al-Hadhrami) and *Kashifat al-saja'* (a commentary on *Safinat al-najah* of Ibn Sumayr).[85] He also issued many *fatwas*, or legal judgements, for his Malay audience both in Mecca and in Southeast Asia. These included a *fatwa* against the pronouncements of Sayyid 'Uthman regarding use of the title of 'Sayyid'.[86]

His concern with imparting clear ethical guidance to his students can be clearly seen in his hermeneutical discussion of the *Asma' al-husna*, the names of God.[87] He uses this discussion to exhort religious leaders, the *'ulama'*, to embrace a list of qualities: firm faith, awe of God, uprightness of character, prophet-like qualities of behaviour, erudition, social concern, and lifelong devotion to Islam. This demonstrates a reformist spirit and concern with matters of Islam and this world, rather than the esoteric other-worldliness of many Malay scholars of previous centuries.

Hafiduddin points out that al-Nawawi's writings on jurisprudence were all based on Shafi'i sources, and suggests that this accounts in part for the strength of the Shafi'i school in Indonesia.[88] Johns takes this a step further by suggesting that al-Nawawi's loyalty to this particular legal school reflects his ultimate influence on the Nahdatul Ulama, with its own particular adherence to the Shafi'i school.[89]

His Qur'anic commentary. Undoubtedly his most famous work is *Marah Labid*, a two-volume commentary on the Qur'an written in Arabic, which represents the second complete commentary on the Qur'an written by a Malay scholar. This work was completed in 1886 and, after receiving the sanction of scholars in Mecca and Cairo, was first published in the latter city.[90] It has subsequently

---

[85] Brockelmann 1992:1040–1.
[86] Aboebakar 1957:88.
[87] This work is the last entry in Hafiduddin's list.
[88] Hafiduddin 1987:44.
[89] Johns 1995:181.
[90] Nasution *et al.* 1992:424.

been published on several occasions in both the Middle East and Southeast Asia.[91]

The fact that official sanction was obtained from religious authorities in Mecca and Cairo provides some insight into the character of this work. Both of these cities in the late 19th century had become dominated by reformist thinking which was opposed to many of the teachings and practices of Sufism. These new ideas were championed by Jamal al-Din al-Afghani and Muhammad 'Abduh in Cairo, discussed in Part I of our study, as well as Wahhabite scholars in Mecca. In order to obtain approval from the authorities in Mecca and Cairo, al-Nawawi needed to present an exegetical approach which was in harmony with the new reformist spirit of the region. An examination of this commentary reveals that *Marah Labid* did indeed embody the new spirit of reformism.[92] Moreover, the official sanction which he received even extended to his being accorded the title of *Sayyid 'ulama' al-Hijaz* (Chief Scholar of Arabia) by the shaykhs of al-Azhar.[93]

Though the sources which he has drawn on in compiling this work are composite, the principal source was *al-Tafsir al-Kabir* by the great medieval scholar Fakhr al-Din al-Razi (d. 1210). Indeed, Razi's work has provided up to 70 per cent of the commentary of al-Nawawi, leaving a mere 30 per cent to be divided between the other four sources used by al-Nawawi.[94] The commentary by the Jalalayn, so central to 'Abd al-Ra'uf's earlier commentary, again served as an important secondary source for al-Nawawi's work.[95]

In order to understand Nawawi's approach to writing a commentary on the Qur'an, it is necessary to view the approach of his principal source, al-Razi's *al-Tafsir al-Kabir*. This work is monumental both in size and in the range of subjects it addresses. Razi writes on theology, jurisprudence, philosophy, dogmatics, and also includes very colourful stories as a device for theological exposition. Razi is well known for his ideas on rationalist theology, and rejected a literalist approach to theology which was adopted by some of his contemporaries.[96] The content of al-Razi's

---

[91] Cf. Nawawi n.d.

[92] Cf. the discussion of several suras in Hafiduddin 1987:48.

[93] Hafiduddin 1987:44; Johns 1981:21.

[94] Johns 1997a:9.

[95] Hafiduddin 1987:54.

[96] Johns 1997a:13.

commentary is so diverse that there are in effect a number of simultaneous commentaries contained therein, addressing the popular level via the stories and dramas presented, but also addressing a more scholarly audience via lengthy and detailed discussion of philosophical issues.

Al-Nawawi's commentary picks up on a range of levels presented by al-Razi, though it is noticeable that al-Nawawi has particularly drawn upon the narrative elements of *al-Tafsir al-Kabir.*[97] In doing this, he manifested the penchant for narrative which had been demonstrated by earlier Qur'anic commentary writing in the Malay world, as represented by the Cambridge Malay commentary and that written by 'Abd al-Ra'uf al-Singkili. It is also important to note that despite al-Nawawi's heavy dependence on al-Razi, his methodology was one of selection and arrangement of al-Razi's ideas, thus ensuring a degree of originality in his own work. Sometimes al-Nawawi reduces the various approaches discussed by al-Razi, and sometimes he deletes them altogether. His purpose in selecting from al-Razi's work is for the sake of brevity, but also for other reasons, such as ensuring accessibility to a wider readership than al-Razi's monumental multi-volume commentary allowed for.

Al-Nawawi supplemented his presentation of stories drawn from al-Razi by mirroring al-Razi's leaning towards rationalist theology, and in doing so, al-Nawawi ensured that this approach was diffused via his students throughout the Malay–Indonesian world. Al-Nawawi thus ensured that the debate between the rationalists, represented by al-Razi on the one hand, and the literalists, represented by Ibn Taymiyya (d. 1328), was again transmitted to Southeast Asia.

Thus al-Nawawi contributed to a breaking of the Sufi mould, as it were. Though earlier Malay commentaries which we encountered had similarly not taken a Sufi approach with a focus on allegorical interpretation in commentary writing, their authors, principally 'Abd al-Ra'uf, had committed himself to the centrality of Sufi themes in many of his other writings. Al-Nawawi broke this pattern. His influence on Malay scholars returning to Southeast Asia contributed to the momentous changes which were about to take place in Southeast Asian Islam.

[97] Johns 1997a:12.

The Patani connection

During his visit to Mecca in the 1880s, Snouck Hurgronje had occasion to have extensive contacts with the Malay community there, and to observe who were the most influential writers living in that community at the time. One of his interesting observations was that the writings of scholars originating from the Patani area were significant, as measured by the regularity of their publication by the Meccan presses.[98] Thus those Patani thinkers who made a mark in Mecca must have left a legacy throughout the Malay world via returning students, just as was the case with Muhammad al-Nawawi.

Ahmad Patani (1856–1906) was notable in this regard. Born in Patani, he studied in both Cairo and Mecca, where by the mid-1880s he had risen to become supervisor of the Malay Printing Press under the Turkish authorities.[99] He taught many Malay students in Mecca, the most famous of whom was Muhammad Yusuf (1868–1933), later known as Tok Kenali. Of considerable significance was his letter-based dialogue with Malay Muslims on important issues relating to the faith,[100] a medium of communication which was to play a vital role in the spread of reformist thinking from Arabia to the Malay world.

His publications included a work on grammar, which appeared from a printing house in Cairo, as well as various items of poetry. His principal works included *Bahja al-mubtadin wa farha al-mujtadin* (1892) on legal statements regarding matters of ritual and social relations, and a series of legal rulings for the Patani region, entitled *Fatawa al-pattaniyya*, drawn up in response to questions from his country of origin. He was also the likely editor of works by earlier Patani Malay scholars, including an anthology of Traditions concerning the afterlife by Zayn al-'Abidin Patani, as well as a significant volume of works by Da'ud ibn 'Abd Allah Patani.

This latter figure was another Meccan-based Patani scholar who wrote in the first decades of the 19th century. There are few details available on his life.[101] A date of death around 1850 seems

---

98 Snouck Hurgronje 1931:286–7.

99 Matheson and Hooker 1988:28.

100 Matheson and Hooker 1988:29.

101 Nasution *et al.* (1992:203) records his birth as 1709, and Abd Rahim (1999:89) records his death as 1890! Given the reliable dates of his various writings, neither of these dates

plausible given that there is no surviving work by him after 1843. Some reports identify his birthplace as the village of Kresik in Patani, and record that he spent around thirty-five years studying and teaching in Mecca and Medina.[102] Matheson and Hooker suggest that he may have studied with 'Abd al-Samad al-Palimbani.[103]

He was a prolific writer, and many of his works, which altogether numbered at least fifty-seven,[104] are still widely printed and used in Southeast Asia. His writings covered wide-ranging topics.[105] His earliest work was a treatise on laws surrounding marriage, written in 1809 and based on various works by Shafi'i authors.[106] Other works address Muhammad's Night Journey (*Kifayat al-muhtaj*, written in 1809), matters relating to mysticism and other subjects (*Jam' al-fawa'id*), life after death (*Kashf al-Ghumma*), dogma (*Al-Durr al-thamin*, written in 1816), as well as legal matters (*Furu' al-masa'il*, completed in 1838). One of his most substantial works was his *Minhaj al-'abidin ila janna rabb al-'alamin*, published in Mecca in 1824, which is a rendering of al-Ghazali's *Ihya' 'ulum al-din* supplemented by sections drawn from other works. His series of tracts on *salat* were widely circulated in Mecca after 1880.[107]

There is further evidence of the high reputation enjoyed by both these Patani scholars. The preface to several modern published editions of *Tarjuman al-Mustafid* by 'Abd al-Ra'uf al-Singkili includes a statement attributed to these two scholars and Shaykh Idris Kelantani testifying (incorrectly) that the work was a faithful rendering of al-Baydawi's *Anwar al-tanzil*.[108] Though this statement appears to be a later addition to the work, and was probably not composed by the three scholars themselves,[109] the fact that their names were associated with such a process of authentication

---

seems likely. Azra (1992:516) suggests a birth year of 1740, which is probably thirty years earlier than the most likely date of birth, given Da'ud's first published work appeared in 1809.

[102] Nasution *et al.* 1992:203.
[103] Matheson and Hooker 1988:20.
[104] Azra 1992:522.
[105] Matheson and Hooker 1988:21–6.
[106] Winstedt 1969:153.
[107] Snouck Hurgronje 1931: 287.
[108] 'Abd al-Ra'uf 1951.
[109] Riddell 1990a:41.

points to the high regard in which Ahmad and Da'ud Patani must have been held in both Mecca and the Malay world.

Sayyid 'Uthman b. 'Abd Allah b. Yahya (1822–1913)

In preceding paragraphs we have explored the important contribution to Malay Islam made by Malay scholars resident in, or travelling to, Arabia. It would be appropriate at this juncture to refer to the significant contribution made by Arab immigrants to the Malay world.

The scholar who made the most significant contribution to literature from among the Hadhrami immigrant community in the Netherlands East Indies during the 19th century was Sayyid 'Uthman b. 'Abd Allah b. Yahya. This scholar was born in Batavia to a father born in Mecca of Hadhrami parentage.[110] His maternal grandfather was the Egyptian 'Abd al-Rahman b. Ahmad al-Misri (d. 1847) who, after amassing his wealth as a merchant in Batavia, devoted the remainder of his life to religious affairs, engaging in research and allocating funds to the construction of a mosque.[111]

Sayyid 'Uthman studied in Mecca and visited the Hadhramaut as well as other significant Islamic locations in the Arab world and Turkey, and in the process undertook specialist studies in theology and jurisprudence. Upon returning to the Netherlands East Indies, Sayyid 'Uthman devoted himself to writing works on various aspects of the Islamic sciences, and by the time Van den Berg carried out his important study of the Hadhramis in the Malay world in the 1880s, Sayyid 'Uthman had already composed thirty-eight literary works.

The subjects of these writings were various, and included the following:

- Attributes of God
- Jurisprudence
- The Muslim pilgrimage
- Genealogy of Hadhrami sayyids
- The five pillars of Islam
- Prayers in Arabic with explanation in Malay
- Laws of inheritance

[110] Azra 1997:250.
[111] Berg 1989:105.

- Language-learning exercises
- Group prayers
- Polemic against the Naqshbandi Sufi order
- Qur'anic recitation technique
- Arabic grammar
- Theology
- Marital laws (including partitioning of goods upon divorce)
- Arabic–Malay dictionary

Of the thirty-eight works listed by Van den Berg, eleven were written in Arabic and twenty-seven in Malay.[112] Though most of these works were only around twenty pages in length, the diversity of the subject matter is testimony to the breadth of knowledge and training of Sayyid 'Uthman and to the scope of his contribution to Islamic learning in the Malay world in his time. Indeed by the time of his death, in Batavia in 1913, Sayyid 'Uthman had written around 100 works in all, with the vast majority being in Malay.[113] This latter fact suggests that the audience for Hadhrami religious scholarship was not only the local Arab community but was primarily the Malay Muslim community as a whole.

Sayyid 'Uthman was to attract criticism from many Malays for two principal reasons. First, his belief that Muslims should obey European authority in the Netherlands East Indies while adhering strictly to Islam drew much criticism. He went so far as to issue a *fatwa* in 1890, entitled *Manhaj al-istiqama fi al-din bi al-salama*, in which he criticised the peasants' revolt in Banten of 1888. He claimed that the conditions for *jihad* were not present in Banten at the time of the revolt, and therefore those who proclaimed *jihad* in inappropriate conditions were 'foolish'.[114] Opposition to this view even came from as far afield as Muhammad al-Nawawi in Mecca, who Snouck Hurgronje records as disagreeing 'with those pensioned officials who hold that the Jawah lands must necessarily be governed by Europeans. The resurrection of the Banten sultanate, or of an independent Moslim state, in any other form, would be acclaimed by [al-Nawawi] joyously …'[115]

112 Berg 1989:106–8.
113 Azra 1997:252.
114 Amiq 1998:97ff.
115 Snouck Hurgronje 1931:270.

Sayyid 'Uthman was appointed as an advisor for Arab affairs by the Netherlands East Indies administration in 1889, an event seen by many Malay Muslims as collaboration with the colonial power and no doubt occurring because of his perceived sympathies with certain aspects of Dutch rule.

Second, opposition of another form from some Malays derived from Sayyid 'Uthman's vehement criticism of Sufi practice in the Malay world. He launched a highly polemical attack on the Naqshbandiyya Sufi order. In all, Sayyid 'Uthman wrote at least seven treatises on Sufism, in which he included much polemical, anti-Sufi comment. His attack centred upon the claim that the masses who joined the various orders were doing so without an adequate knowledge of the *shari'a*, and this was exacerbated by the fact that the leaders of the orders themselves were lacking in knowledge about the basics of Islam.[116] His view brought him into conflict with mystics among the local group of religious scholars who regarded his attacks as a threat to their position. He turned for support to Muhammad al-Nawawi in Mecca, but though the latter responded with sympathetic comments, his support for Sayyid 'Uthman's position was far weaker than the Hadhrami scholar took to be the case.[117]

Sayyid 'Uthman's prolific writing addressed matters of real-life concern to his fellow Muslims. For example, he provided input to a clarification of divorce law, particularly as it related to dividing up property accumulated during marriage. According to Javanese customary law, jointly-acquired goods should be distributed equally, or according to a split of two-thirds for the husband and one-third for the wife, if a marriage ends in divorce.[118] In contrast, the *shari'a* does not allow for the joint ownership of goods through marriage. This discrepancy was resolved by Sayyid 'Uthman by pushing for the recognition of the existence of a formal partnership between husband and wife, thus adjusting *shari'a* to account for local circumstances.[119]

---

[116] Amiq 1998:100.

[117] Snouck Hurgronje 1931:272.

[118] Javanese customary law allows goods brought into a marriage to remain with the original owner.

[119] Djajadiningrat 1958: 389.

Sayyid 'Uthman had not always demonstrated such flexibility with regard to the application of *shari'a*. In a case researched by Kaptein,[120] Sayyid 'Uthman upheld the strict guidelines of Islamic law in ruling that documentary evidence alone was inadmissible when a Javanese wife petitioned for divorce in 1881 after being deserted by her husband for a lengthy period. However, he seems to have revised his views in subsequent decades, on account of what Kaptein terms an 'increased orientation towards the interests of the colonial government'[121], reflecting his responsibilities as Advisor on Arab Affairs to the Dutch colonial administration.

Sayyid 'Uthman's reputation was controversial for a range of reasons. Indeed, in certain ways he was something of an enigma. On the one hand he manifested a reformist spirit by attacking Sufi practices which he saw as being un-Islamic. In contrast, he opposed the anti-Dutch struggle, advocating in its stead a policy of measured co-operation with colonial authorities. This was out of keeping with reformist thinking emerging from the Arab world. Moreover, he demonstrated flexibility regarding application of the *shari'a* in certain contexts, yet demonstrated inflexibility in other instances. On balance, it would appear that the *shari'a*-minded reformist tendencies which he may have had earlier in life waned as he aged, particularly under the influence of Dutch enticements in the form of an elevated position in the colonial administration.

Any study of human history, whether focusing upon society, religion, politics or other fields, will encounter a fundamental opposition between forces for continuity and forces for change. In Southeast Asia, the forces for continuity, for stability, and for maintenance of the status quo had long held sway. The various societies in the Malay world were conservative, and ruling structures and paradigms were firmly entrenched during the periods examined thus far in this present study.

In the Islamic theological arena, Sufis continued to hold centre stage during most of the 18th and 19th centuries, as had been the case during the previous two centuries. Old debates continued to

---

[120] Kaptein 1997b:87ff.
[121] Kaptein 1997b:94.

be played out, especially the tension between a reformed Sufism and radical theosophical doctrines. This was seen in many of the writers and works examined in this chapter.

However, the old world familiar to Southeast Asian Muslims was to undergo rapid change during the 19th century. Colonial powers gained varying degrees of control over the daily lives of Malay Muslims, with dramatic results. Old dogmas came to be increasingly put to the test and found wanting. As the 19th century closed, other solutions were sought for the new problem of external colonial domination. Furthermore, new theological approaches were explored as the dominance of a cult of continuity gave way to a new cult of change.

These dramatic changes resulting from colonialism heralded the end of the dominance of Sufism and the onset of a mood for theological reform. The process was still in its infancy in the last quarter of the 19th century, as we have seen in our examination of the later writers from that period. But as Kaptein says 'The latter part of the nineteenth century is particularly interesting because it was the period immediately prior to the rise of modernist Islamic thinking in Indonesia.'[122] In a sense, this period represents a bridge between two eras. So having painted the landscape of one era, where Sufism was predominant and Sufi debates filled centre-stage, and outlined the bridge represented by the last part of the 19th century, we will now proceed to the next era, the period of reform and modernising thought in Malay Islamic thinking.

[122] Kaptein 1997a:15.

PART III

MALAY ISLAMIC THINKING
IN THE 20TH CENTURY

11

MALAY ISLAMIC THOUGHT (c. 1900–98)

RESPONSES TO REFORMISM IN THE MALAY WORLD

The currents of new thinking in the Arab world which emerged in the latter part of the 19th century were to be felt with some force in Southeast Asia. In Part I, some attention was devoted to pan-Islam ideas promoted by Jamal al-Din al-Afghani, and the modernist thought of Muhammad 'Abduh and Rashid Rida. Whether in the Arab world or Southeast Asia, the catalyst for the spread of these new ideas was colonialism and the search for new Islamic solutions to the colonial presence.

There were various manifestations of pan-Islamic ideology in the Netherlands East Indies. Increasing contacts occurred between local rulers and the Ottoman Caliphate authorities in Turkey. Indonesian Muslims looked more and more to the religious authorities in the world-wide Islamic community for guidance as their active struggle against Dutch rule gained momentum. These external contacts surfaced in newspapers and periodicals. Moreover, larger payments were made to charities to assist external Muslim causes. In addition, greater numbers of Muslim children were sent to Turkey for their education from the Malay world around the turn of the 20th century.[1] The extent of Turkish influence was even in evidence in Friday mosque services in the Malay world, where sometimes a *doa* (prayer) was given for the Ottoman Sultan, read from a printed version imported from the Middle East.[2]

---

[1] Dijk 1997.
[2] N. Kaptein, personal communication.

207

This sense of pan-Islamic identity, being felt by Muslims in the Malay world around this time, is described by Snouck Hurgronje as follows:

The feeling of belonging together which to a greater or lesser extent is active or easy to evoke from its latent situation among all professors [sic] of Islam; the awareness of belonging to a powerful unity, which plead or ought to plead the cause of each of her parts when their threatened political, social or economic interests had to be defended.[3]

It is interesting that the above description plays down a theological dimension to the pan-Islamic identity. That such a dimension was present cannot be doubted. The transmission of theological reflection to the region, on topics other than Sufism, had picked up pace during the 19th century, as we have seen. Further evidence is found in the popularity of the famous catechism by Muhammad al-Fadali al-Shafiʻi (d. 1821), former rector of al-Azhar University in Cairo, which was translated into Malay and Javanese[4] and served as a vehicle for transmitting non-Sufi theological perspectives to the Malay world.

Modernist ideas[5] were to extend to and implant themselves in the Malay–Indonesian world by the end of the 19th century. There is considerable evidence for this, and indeed the transmission was not merely to be a transferral of ideas which then developed in isolation in Southeast Asia, but rather it was to take the form of a continuing dialogue between Malay Muslims and those of the Middle East where the modernist ideas had originated.

An important tool for the dissemination of reformist thought was the distribution of the Egyptian journal *al-Manar* in the Malay world. Not only did it establish its own readership in Southeast Asia, but it also prompted the establishment of reformist-based journals in the Malay language in the area, including *al Imam*, *al-Munir* (published in Padang in West Sumatra, 1911–16), and *Azzachierah al-islamiyyah*. Indeed, the idea of founding journals

---

[3] Jonge 1997.

[4] Rippin & Knappert 1986:20.

[5] The appropriateness of the term 'modernism' has been challenged by Johns (Riddell and Street 1997:xvii), on the basis of its not being 'a term in the Islamic tradition'. Nevertheless, the widespread currency of this term, and its relevance to Rippin's typology used for this present study, leads us to make use of it, though Johns' point is well taken.

and periodicals for the specific purpose of disseminating modernist thinking can be traced back to Jamal al-Din al-Afghani, whose pioneering role in modern reformism was discussed earlier in chapter 7.

Bluhm-Warn[6] has established that there was a continuing dialogue between Malay Muslims and the editors of *al-Manar* in Egypt, in which the Malay individuals in question wrote seeking advice and legal judgements on a range of theological issues, economic and environmental matters, technological advances, issues of current political concern such as patriotism and nationalism, and a range of other matters. Kaptein has devoted attention to a similar phenomenon between the Malay world and Mecca.[7]

Letters to the editor of *al-Manar* from individuals in Southeast Asia pointed to the same sorts of debates, regarding *ijtihad* and *taqlid* for example, as were occurring in the Middle East. Moreover, such letters sought guidance on specifics such as the reputation and value of Islamic leaders of former times, such as Ibn Taymiyya. The responses from *al-Manar* to these Southeast Asian correspondents did not limit themselves to a Middle Eastern context; in one case cited by Bluhm-Warn, the editor of *al-Manar* specifically attacked the teachings of Sayyid 'Uthman, the Hadhrami scholar in Java we encountered previously who had found favour with the Dutch administration and particularly with Snouck Hurgronje, the Advisor on Islamic Affairs to the Dutch Governor General.

The concern of the Southeast Asian writers in addressing these issues for resolution to the Middle East demonstrates two things: first, the perception from Southeast Asia of authority lying in the Arab world, and second a confidence in seeking and obtaining support from fellow Muslims in the face of conflict with non-Muslim authorities as well as with traditional Muslim leaders.

The direction of the guidance provided was very clearly from West to East, in the form of Middle Eastern instructions for application to Southeast Asian Muslim contexts. This ongoing Middle Eastern influence upon reformist developments in Southeast Asia was reinforced by the arrival in the Malay world of Ahmad

---

6   Bluhm-Warn 1997:295ff.

7   Kaptein 1997a.

Surkati, a Sudanese who had studied in both Mecca and Medina and who came to Java in 1911 as the inspector of Islamic schools as part of a scholarship programme sponsored by the Ottoman authorities and available for Indonesian Muslims to study in the Middle East.

Surkati had a major impact upon the developments within the modernist movement in Indonesia, and was prepared to challenge many traditionally accepted values, as seen in his rejection of traditional royal lineage within Javanese society in favour of equality of all classes and races according to Islam and in the spirit of modernist doctrine. Surkati was a close associate of Ahmad Dachlan, who founded the Muhammadiyah in 1912, and indeed Surkati had a great influence upon the Muhammadiyah during its early period. Both Surkati and Dachlan were in favour of promoting the ideas of Muhammad 'Abduh, and co-operated in this respect.

Surkati also employed the media for the dissemination of modernist ideas, by establishing the journal *Azzachierah al-islamiyya* which was devoted to discussion of values considered important by the modernist movement and which carried on the style of modernist debate established by *al-Manar*. In his capacity as inspector of Islamic schools, Surkati was successful in disseminating modernist ideas throughout the network of Islamic schools under his control, which were established by the al-Irshad group, which was itself initiated by Surkati. Indeed, Surkati's influence has lived on through his students, many of whom became prominent Islamic leaders, such as Iskandar Idris.

Another of the modernist magazines to emerge from the Malay world, *al Imam*, was published in Singapore between 1906 and 1908, initially under the editorship of Tahir Jalaluddin. It acted as an important vehicle for modernist ideas emanating from the Middle East in that among its pages were included translations into Malay of articles originally published in Arabic in *al-Manar* and other journals.[8] *Al Imam* was vigorous in its criticism of the royal courts in both the Malay peninsula and the Indonesian archipelago. It depicted the courts as representing the subjugation of Islamic values to Western decadence and secularism. *Al Imam*'s concern was first and foremost for the *umma*, or the Islamic community,

---

8 Bluhm 1983:35.

rather than placing its primary focus on an ethnic focus *vis-à-vis* the Malay race.

The traditional leaders of Malay society, the Sultans, were not the only group to be targeted for criticism by the young modernists, who termed themselves the *Kaum Muda* (Young Generation). They also directed strong and sustained criticism towards the *Kaum Tua* (Old Generation) traditionalists who appeared to them to protect and defend unquestioningly the domination of conservative religious scholars in the sphere of Islamic worship and belief. The journal *al-Ikhwan*, a mouthpiece of the *Kaum Muda*, commented in 1929:

> The *Kaum Tua* behave as if it were necessary to accept every single word of the writings of the *'Ulama'*, as if they were equal to the Qur'an ... while the *Kaum Muda* consider that the Qur'an and Hadith alone have this authority, that no *'Ulama'* is infallible, and that God provided us with reason and intelligence to enable us to critically examine the statements of the *'Ulama'*.[9]

The influence of modernist reformism in the Malay–Indonesian world was not limited to journals alone. Indeed, the modernist ideology manifests itself very clearly in many novels which were written during the early part of the 20th century in Islamic Southeast Asia. It is of interest to note that some writers of these novels, such as Sayyid Shaykh al-Hadi, had studied in the Middle East under Muhammad 'Abduh; Sayyid Shaykh's influence was to extend beyond the world of fiction writing to the print media; he played a prominent role in the establishment of the modernist journal *Al Imam*.[10] His novel *Farida Hanom* is written in Malay for a Malay audience. However, he uses it as a device to set his readers within a Middle Eastern context; the setting is in Cairo, the principal characters are Egyptian, references are made to leading vehicles of the modernist movement such as *al-Manar* and Muhammad 'Abduh, and the narrative is located within a modernist stream. However, the author adjusts the language of the Middle Eastern setting to make it accessible to a Malay audience. This author uses his novel as a platform for presenting modernist

---

[9] De Beer 1983–4:45.
[10] Azra 1999:86.

ideology, such as his criticism of studying Western scholarship in place of studying Islamic law.

Other writers did not have the Middle Eastern experience such as that enjoyed by Sayyid Shaykh, but nevertheless managed to transmit some of the core modernist principles in their works. An example is Ahmad Kotot's *Hikayat Percintaan Kasih Kemudaan*. This author was a Malay schoolteacher who never visited the Middle East and this resulted in his setting being firmly located within the context of a Malay village. Nevertheless, the influence of modernism is stamped very clearly on his writings.[11]

In the Sundanese area of West Java, the debate between modernists and conservative traditionalists also manifested itself in the literature of the region. These works were written in the local language, Sundanese. The young generation of modernists, known as the *Kaum Muda* like their counterparts on the Malay peninsula, took up the principles proposed by Muhammad 'Abduh and addressed a range of issues in their literary activities by way of both newspaper articles and novels. It is noticeable that novels written by the generation of Sundanese modernists did not demonstrate any sympathy for mystical practices or Sufi orders. The issues which novels written by these young modernists addressed were, in particular: freedom to choose a marriage partner; and the rejection of inherited privilege traditionally allocated to the class of Sayyids, or descendants of the family of the prophet Muhammad, a class which had grown in numbers and influence through substantial immigration to the Malay world from the Hadhramaut.[12]

In response, the conservative older generation, the *Kaum Tua*, continued to call in its writings for traditional values as represented by arranged marriages and veneration of the class of Sayyids, Hadhramis and their mixed-race descendants. This group of conservatives, after losing ground during the first two decades of the 20th century, reasserted its dominance in West Javanese novels from the 1930s, focusing on traditional values and addressing such issues as folk medicine and mystical practice.[13]

Another region which deserves special mention in the context of modernist reformism is the Minangkabau area of Sumatra. This

---

11 Cf. Hooker (1994) for a detailed study of these works.
12 Mukherjee 1997:311ff.
13 Cf. discussion of themes in Kaum Tua novels in Sundanese in Mukherjee 1997.

region had long served as a channel for new ideas coming from the Middle East into the Malay world. A number of leading Minang scholars based themselves in Mecca, such as Shaykh Ahmad Khatib (1852–1916), and exerted the kind of influence on visiting Malay students as we saw earlier with Muhammad al-Nawawi. Ahmad Khatib, who held the position of Shafi'i Imam at the Great Mosque in Mecca,[14] was outspoken in criticising Sufi orders, such as the Naqshbandiyya, which he accused of being a source of pantheism. He also attacked features of Minang customary law which he considered as un-Islamic, such as the inheritance law within the matrilineal structure of Minang society.[15]

Ahmad Khatib's students went on to make profound contributions to the change in the Islamic intellectual dialogue in Southeast Asia. Chief among these was the previously mentioned Minangkabau scholar Shaykh Mohammed Tahir bin Jalaluddin Al-Azhari (1869–1957), the first editor of *Al-Imam*. He had lived and studied in Mecca with Ahmad Khatib, his first cousin, from the age of twelve, before taking a degree in astronomy at al-Azhar University in Cairo. While there he was greatly influenced by the reformist ideas of Muhammad 'Abduh, and formed a strong friendship with Rashid Rida, which provided the opportunity to write a number of columns for the periodical *al-Manar*. He was thus well equipped to transmit the spirit and technical know-how of Islamic modernism to Southeast Asia when he returned to the region to settle in 1906. Roff rightly speaks of him in the following terms: '... of all the reform group probably the most notable in intellect and scholarly achievement ...'[16]

Other important Minang students who benefited from Ahmad Khatib's instruction were Shaykh Abbas Abdullah (1883–1957) and Haji Agus Salim (1884–1954). The former spent eight years in Mecca between 1896 and 1904, and upon his return to Sumatra he involved himself on the side of the *Kaum Muda* in their debates with traditionalist groups. He was instrumental with other Minang modernists in establishing a new school system in 1918, the *Sumatera Thawalib*, which combined the study of classical Islamic subjects with modern

---

[14] Roff 1994:60.
[15] Djamal 1998:6ff; Noer 1973:31–3.
[16] Roff 1994:60.

secular subjects, and included activities such as debating to train its students to engage with contemporary issues.[17] Haji Agus Salim, like Mohammed Tahir bin Jalaluddin Al-Azhari, was related to Ahmad Khatib, and studied with him while posted to the Dutch Consulate in Jeddah during the period 1904–13. Upon his return to the Netherlands East Indies in the latter year, Agus Salim became involved in the emerging nationalist movement, and in 1915 joined Sarekat Islam, the first Muslim nationalist organisation in the archipelago. His involvement in nationalist politics in subsequent decades was to add another modernist voice to the local Islamic scene. He led the opposition to the involvement of traditionalist *kyai* scholars in building up the support for the Sarekat Islam Party in the mid-1930s, fearing erosion of modernist values in the Party. He was appointed as Foreign Minister in the Republican government in 1946, in which capacity he visited Islamic countries seeking support in the struggle against the Dutch. He served in ministerial positions in several post-independence cabinets, before spending 1952–3 lecturing on Islam and politics in universities in the USA.[18]

Of course not all leading modernists were from the Minangkabau region or were students of Ahmad Khatib. A number of names have already been mentioned, but it is necessary at this juncture to add that of Ahmad Hassan, who was born in Singapore in 1887 of mixed Indian–Javanese parentage. He acquired his modernist leanings not from a teacher based in the Middle East, but rather from Muhammad Yunus and other leading modernists in Bandung. But whatever the sources of influence or locations of study, powerful forces were at work in the Malay–Indonesian world, challenging the political and religious status quo. The mood of continuity was being taken over by a new mood for change.

The spirit for change attained its most perceptible realisation after the Second World War, when the colonies of the Malay–Indonesian world were transformed into the independent nations of Indonesian, Malaya, Malaysia and Singapore. The pre-independence nationalist movements were then faced with the task of

[17] Nasution 1992:2-3.
[18] Sastrawiria & Wirasutisna 1955: 282-293; Kahin 1970:94-5.

translating ideologies into structures of state, and several features are worthy of note at this juncture in connection with the themes discussed in previous paragraphs.

First, in contrast with efforts to break the link between ethnicity and religion by earlier modernist journals such as *Al-Imam*, Malaya, then Malaysia, enshrined this link in its 1957 constitution. This will be explored further in discussing Malay writers in a subsequent section. Second, the post-independence period witnessed ongoing rivalry between traditionalists and modernists in seeking to hold the centre of the Islamic stage. In the Malaysian context this was played out by the tension between the Parti Islam SeMalaysia and the United Malays Nationalist Organisation, while in Indonesia the principal actors were the Nahdatul Ulama and the Muhammadiyah.

Furthermore, the second half of the 20th century witnessed the evolution of neo-modernist Islamic thinking in Malaysia and Indonesia. Early signs of this were reflected in the struggle by some Indonesian Muslims, supported by Indonesian non-Muslim leaders, in favour of establishing the principle of an officially multi-religious state, arguing against the priority of Islam. This is most clearly seen in the *Pancasila* concept developed by Sukarno in 1945 and established as the philosophy of the Indonesian State. Neo-modernism asserted itself more markedly in the 1980s and 1990s, as will be seen in some of the writers examined.

Thus the old world was gradually being swept away by the new modes of Islamic thinking. Traditional authority structures were being challenged, as was the right of Sufi approaches to hold centre stage on the Malay theological arena. The Sufi star had set, because 'Sufism, particularly among modernist Muslims, [had come to be] regarded as one of the main causes of regression of the Muslim world'.[19] We will now turn our attention to Malay writers this century who have responded to, and helped define, new directions in Islamic thinking.

[19] Azra 1992:549.

VOICES OF MODERN SUFISM

In the face of the anti-Sufi onslaught by Islamic modernist writers both within the Malay world and without, it was inevitable that efforts would be made to restructure Sufism to ensure its ongoing existence but in a form which would be more palatable to new moods and ideologies. Many writers could be selected to demonstrate this. Our purposes will be well served by focusing on two writers, one giant of the 20th century whose literary output spanned the early and middle parts of the century, and another whose writing only began to make its mark towards the end of the century.

Hamka (1908–81)

Haji Abdul Malik Karim Amrullah has been referred to as the 'Hamzah Fansuri of the modern era'.[20] Hamka, as he came to be known, was born in the Minangkabau region of West Sumatra, and was the son of Haji Rasul, one of the key figures in introducing modernist ideas to the Minangkabau region. Haji Rasul's contribution to modernist thinking in Sumatra is well encapsulated in Hamka's book, *Ayahku* (My Father), which appeared in the mid-1950s.[21]

Hamka's formal education extended only as far as primary school level. However, he was able to benefit from his father's expertise in the area of Islamic studies to study a broad range of Islamic subjects with his father as a child, including the text of the Qur'an. Between the ages of eight and fifteen, Hamka attended several religious schools, and this pattern in his religious education, supplemented by the family environment in which he grew up, destined him to follow in his father's footsteps as a scholar of Islam. The varied nature of his Islamic education was also a significant factor in his later eclectic approach to Islamic practice and thought.

He was to become a prolific writer. As early as the age of twenty, he published his first novel in the local Minang language, and the following year he published a series of books on Islamic subjects, covering such issues as the role of women in religion, traditional custom and Islam, and a range of other matters. This

---

[20] Hamka 1990:XIX.
[21] Hamka 1958. Also cf. Djamal 1998, and Noer 1973:37–8.

writing activity had closely followed his participation in the pilgrimage to Mecca in 1927, and during the pilgrimage and in the years which followed he served as a correspondent for a number of daily and weekly publications, writing on a wide variety of Islamic subjects. He was thus closely involved in a principal medium for the spread of new modernist ideas, namely periodicals, which were expanding rapidly with the spread of printing presses.

Perhaps his most famous role as an editor and writer for journals was when he served as editor for the publication *Pedoman Masyarakat* from 1936 until the period of occupation by the Japanese during the Second World War. Much of his expository writing for this journal was later published in book form as *1001 Soal-Soal Hidup* in 1961. This work addresses issues such as the relationship between children and parents, attitudes to prostitution, friendship, etc.[22] These titles reflect a concern to apply Islamic principles to modern problems, a key factor in modernist reformism.

Simultaneously there appeared a number of popular novels, which were to be acclaimed as significant contributions to the development of modern Indonesian literature. However, these same works led to some controversy because of the claim by some Islamic scholars that it was inconsistent for a leading Islamic figure such as Hamka to engage in the writing of popular novels. This was in spite of the fact that these novels generally centred upon strongly Islamic themes. In this way, Hamka furthered the long tradition of Malay Islamic scholars using narrative as a device in theological exposition.

His experiences beyond the immediate region of his birth and upbringing extended to various parts of the Indonesian archipelago. In 1924 he had gone to central Java where he had closely observed the emergence of various Islamic movements. During this period he had close contact with the Muhammadiyah, which had been established in response to the modernist ideas coming into Indonesia from the Middle East, and he studied with the leading Islamic nationalist of the period, Tjokroaminoto. In the early 1930s, he moved to Makassar, where he taught until 1935, before returning to Sumatra.

---

[22] Hamka 1961.

During the Japanese occupation he continued to write, and produced a large number of essays on various fields of Islam, including theology, philosophy, history and Sufism. His international acclaim as a scholar of Islam was to lead to the award of an honorary doctorate from the Al-Azhar University in Cairo, and the same award from the National University of Malaya. As in the case of Muhammad al-Nawawi, we again find a Malay scholar receiving official sanction from the heart of reformist thinking in Cairo.

In 1962 he began to compile his most significant work, his commentary on the Qur'an, called *Tafsir al-Azhar*. This work drew heavily on morning lectures which he had delivered from 1959 to 1964 at the Al-Azhar mosque in Jakarta.[23] A multi-volume work, this writing task was to be carried out largely during a period of almost three years in prison from 1964 to 1966, resulting from the Sukarno regime's wariness of his wide influence and its perception of him as a potential opponent. A closer examination of *Tafsir al-Azhar* appears in chapter 12.

Hamka also wrote many essays and books on Islamic mysticism. These include *Tasawuf Perkembangan dan Pemurniaannya* (The Development and Perfecting of Mysticism) and *Tasawuf Modern* (Modern Mysticism). Indeed, his mystical inclinations coloured much of his approach to Islamic teaching. However, his was not the voice of Sufism which dominated the Malay Islamic stage during the 16th to 19th centuries. Rather, his was a voice of modernising Sufism, and in his *Tasawuf Modern* (1939) he parried the anti-Sufi statements of modernists by advocating a type of Sufism shorn of its perceived un-Islamic practices but still maintaining a solid mystical core. This contributed to his functioning, and being perceived, as a moderate who was widely respected among the various schools of Islamic teaching and thought in post-colonial Indonesia. His reputation led to him being elected Chairman of the *Majelis Ulama Indonesia* (Council of Islamic Scholars of Indonesia).

Nevertheless, his reputed moderation did not detract from his commitment to clear and strong principles and beliefs. One subject on which he held strong views and wrote consistently was in the area of Indonesian traditional custom (*adat*) and the influence

---

[23] Feener 1998:62; Jafar, 1998.

it exerted in certain ways upon Islamic practice in Indonesia. In concert with other modernist writers of his age, he strongly opposed and criticised what he regarded as a tendency towards syncretistic practice. In this he sought to draw a clear demarcation between orthodox Sufi belief and non-orthodox teaching, in an effort to shore up Sufi approaches at a time that the mystical quest was being increasingly marginalised.

An interesting example is provided in his work *Pelajaran Agama Islam* (Studying Islam). In one section, Hamka discusses the topic of angels, jinn and the spiritual realm.[24] The key components of Hamka's teaching evident in this section are rational argument, reference to scripture, relating his discussion to a modern context, defence of what he sees as orthodoxy, and attacking what he considers as non-orthodox teachings. Hamka initiates the discussion by rationally arguing why Muslims should not concern themselves with scientific proofs of the existence of angels. An awareness of angels, says Hamka, is an experiential rather than an intellectual matter. This serves as his foundational argument.

The matter of angels ... belongs in the area of the unseen world. Because of that, an approach to knowledge which demands material proof cannot be used to ascertain the 'where' or the 'who' [of angels]. They are a [rare] 'gem' which are not of the world. They are not something which is concerned with form, so that they do not demand space and time. So spiritual exercise and its experiences from time to time can lead to an awareness of the presence of angels around us.

He then proceeds by introducing Islamic scripture – in this case Q41:30 – to identify angelic functions, and he engages in exegesis of the verse to provide broader portrayal of these functions. Thus he has so far combined rational argument with scriptural reference, possibly in an attempt to appeal to both a modernist and a more conservative audience.

Hamka argues clearly for the relevance of these matters to modern times, stating that protecting angels and misleading evil spirits influence people no less today than they did in the past, with the success of the competing influences being determined by the strength of faith of the people concerned. This lays the groundwork for the last crucial subject of this discourse, namely

[24] Hamka 1956:122–4.

the clash between orthodoxy and non-orthodoxy. On the one hand, says Hamka, belief in angels and the spiritual realm belongs firmly within the six core articles of faith. But on the other hand, a wrong interpretation of this subject – namely a belief in the independent power of these spirits apart from God's overarching power – leads people to wrong practice and false paths. Such practices, designed to appease these spirits and effectively circumvent God, include burning candles at graves, giving livestock as presents to dead saints, making food offerings, and calling on angels without recognising that angels are mere functionaries of God.

Hamka concludes this discourse with a clear restatement of *Tauhid* monotheism.

In summary, belief in all which is unseen is not intended to increase one's doubt and superstition, but to reinforce our faith, exclusively intended for the One God, Allah. Nothing moves in this world if God does not wish it. Everything [only exists] with the permission of God.

He has thus affirmed what he sees as orthodox teaching, and attacked what he considers as a syncretistic combination of *adat* and Islamic orthodoxy.

Hamka died on 24 August 1981. The comparison between Hamka and Hamzah Fansuri should be seen to derive from the very significant role which each played within his respective Malay–Indonesian community in terms of determining the direction of theological thinking and activity. Unlike Hamzah Fansuri, Hamka was at no stage accused of embracing a heterodox or heretical theology.

Muhammad Zuhri (1939–)

Muhammad Zuhri was born in Kudus, Java. After completing his schooling, his first call was to the teaching profession, and after undergoing teacher-training, he worked as an elementary-school teacher from 1957 to 1964. During this period he also joined the largest Muslim modernist organisation in Indonesia, the Muhammadiyah.

He left the teaching profession and took to painting. He relates that he had a series of mystical experiences around this time, which led him to follow the Sufi path. He studied Sufism with Kiai Hamid from Pasuruan, who initiated Zuhri as a Sufi.

He settled with his family in Sekarjalak village, near the city of Pati, Java. There collected around him a group of disciples to whom he taught Sufism, and this group constituted itself as Pesantren Budaya Barzakh (Barzakh Cultural Pesantren), which was meeting on a bi-weekly basis in the 1990s. Zuhri also attracted disciples from further afield, principally from Jakarta and Bandung. His disciples were typically young intellectuals. Those in Jakarta set up a foundation, called Yayasan Barzakh, in August 1994 while those in Bandung formed an Islamic art and cultural organisation (Keluarga Budaya Barzakh or Barzakh Cultural Family).

Zuhri engages with the socially disadvantaged and with the sick, presenting his approach to Sufism as a remedy for personal problems. His disciples claim that he has had success turning prostitutes away from their ways, for example. They also claim that Zuhri has special gifts for healing by way of his Sufi healing method. As a result the Barzakh Foundation established an HIV/AIDS healing project in 1996 under Zuhri's guidance.[25]

The Barzakh Foundation sets the following as its main activities:[26]

1. Monthly discussions about Islam and Sufism under the guidance of Muhammad Zuhri.
2. Raising funds for orphanages, the homeless, the poor, victims of disasters, etc.
3. Providing treatment or counselling following Sufi methods to solve private (physical or mental illness), family, or social problems.

Zuhri has developed a method of Sufi healing based on earlier Sufi methods. He claims that 'the True Healer is God Himself, the Sufis acting only as mediators'. For this healing method Zuhri bases himself upon four elements: prayer; traditional medicine or therapy; fasting and *dhikr*; and specific objects.

With regard to *dhikr* as part of the healing process, Zuhri allows it to be performed, usually under his supervision, either individually or in a group with repeated recitation of sacred formulas or God's attributes. With regard to the role of specific objects

---

[25] [www.geocities.com/yayasan_barzakh/] copied 31 July 1999.
[26] Ibid.

mentioned above, it would be instructive to read the precise description provided by the Barzakh Foundation:

The Sufis also combine the recitation of God's attributes and holy verses with prayer in a specific and complex method. The formulations may be written on paper, bone, or leather as amulets called *wifq*. These objects may be placed in a glass of water to be drunk by the patient or they may be buried in the ground, or carried around on the patient's person. The formulations can also be recited aloud or silently, or used in many other ways not only to cure mental or physical illness, but also to solve family, financial, or social problems.

Thus in Muhammad Zuhri and his group we see an interesting nexus between traditional Sufism and the modern world. The goals set are communitarian rather than personal. Zuhri's activities are designed to help the sick and the underprivileged, in a way entirely in harmony with social action ideologies of the late 20th century. His concern is no longer the primary goal of personal communion, or union, with God as had been the case with many Sufi approaches in earlier centuries.

But the tools of the trade are, in many respects, traditionally Sufi. Observance of the Islamic rituals is central, as is the age-old Sufi practice of *dhikr*. Moreover, we also find evidence of traditional folk Islamic, or popular Islamic instruments such as amulets, water in which scriptural verses had been soaking, and the like.

Finally, although Zuhri eschews joining a Sufi order in his public statements, the early signs are that his activities bear resemblance to the early stages of the formation of a new order: Sufi master at the head, disciples gathered who learn from the master, organisations founded and identifiable with the group. Time will tell if we are witnessing a modern, probably localised, Sufi order in the making.

His writings.   Zuhri has written a range of materials.[27] These include two books, *Qasidah Cinta* (1993) and *Langit-langit Desa* (1993), both of which represent collections of shorter poetic or prose pieces by Zuhri addressing a range of Sufi, ethical or philosophical themes. He has also written a number of articles which have appeared in national newspapers and other periodicals. His

---

27 For a study of a selection of Zuhri's writings, cf. Lee 1999.

writings also include a series written for the *Harian Terbit* newspaper, which focuses on a fictional character, Si Ubaid, and various situations of daily life he finds himself in. He is also an active poet. Further evidence that Zuhri represents a meeting point between traditional Sufism and the modern world can be seen in the use by Zuhri and his disciples of the internet, with all of his writings either appearing or being destined for publishing on the World Wide Web.[28]

In Zuhri's short article, entitled 'Nobility of Character',[29] he addresses the issue of moral excellence. At several points he presents scriptural references based on both Qur'an and Hadith to provide a framework for his argument. He also affirms that Islam is essentially holistic, in opposition to the dualism prevailing in 'both Western and Eastern moral codes'. In this respect he resonates with the views of Al-Attas encountered below, though his tone is far less polemical than that of Al-Attas.

Yet the holism of which Zuhri speaks is not monistic. On the contrary, throughout his article one finds a clear duality maintained between Creator and creature. But he argues that those of moral excellence or noble character provide the bridge between the two, with the model *par excellence* of this being Muhammad, the *uswatun khasanah*. In this we hear echoes of the Perfect Man theme articulated by al-Jili and by the 17th-century Acehnese monistic Sufis encountered earlier.

The connection with Zuhri's own approach comes clearly in the last paragraph. In seeking to attain this intermediary state between God and mankind by attaining a noble character, the individual is exhorted to address one's 'social life'. In other words, the path to moral excellence, and thus greater closeness to God, comes not from personal and private meditation only, but it also crucially derives from social action, of the type followed by Zuhri and his Barzakh Foundation.

We thus see in the life and writings of Muhammad Zuhri a clear attempt to affirm the Sufi path but through late 20th-century social action approaches. This methodology is designed to make

---

[28] Indeed, Zuhri's use of information technology tools also extends to his HIV/AIDS treatment of sufferers, through offering this treatment free of charge via the internet, with instructions for healing practice being provided in distance mode.

[29] [www.geocities.com/Athens/5739/] copied on 10 December 1998.

Sufism appear relevant to modern times, and also, no doubt, to parry powerful modernist criticisms heard throughout the 20th century that Sufism was too 'other worldly', irrelevant, and indeed on a false path. In this, there is no doubt evidence of Zuhri having learned from his contact with the modernist Muhammadiyah.

VOICES OF ORTHODOX TRADITIONALISM

The surge in modernist thinking during the 20th century has contributed to a remarkable resurgence of Islam as a political and social force. This has been at the expense of some groups, especially popular Sufi approaches, but it has opened opportunities for various non-Sufi Islamic ideologies. Traditionalist voices in Islam, representing those which Rippin refers to as the Orthodox or Normatives, have benefited by association with the increase in Islamic identity. This will be examined via two Islamic scholars who are associated with the principal Islamic opposition party in Malaysia (PAS).

Nik Abdul Aziz Nik Mat (1931–)

A key name in the rise of PAS as a political force in Malaysia has been Nik Abdul Aziz Nik Mat. Born in a village near Kota Bharu in Kelantan, he gained his early education in the Islamic sciences from his father, who was a prominent religious scholar and founder of an Islamic school in the region. His father's instruction was supplemented by that of a number of local religious notables in Kelantan and Trengganu during Nik Abdul Aziz's childhood and adolescence.

At the age of nineteen, Nik Abdul Aziz was sent to India to study for around five years at a Deobandi school. From there he continued to Cairo, where he took Bachelor's and Master's degrees majoring in Islamic Law at Al-Azhar University. Upon his return to Malaysia in 1962, Nik Abdul Aziz devoted himself to full-time teaching of the religious sciences and preaching. Around the same time, he joined PAS.

His political career began in earnest in 1967, when he was elected to the state parliament as member for the seat of Kelantan Hilir, which he retained in subsequent elections until 1986. In the latter year he became member for Bachok, another seat in Kelantan. In October 1990, Nik Abdul Aziz was appointed as

Chief Minister for the State of Kelantan, a position which he still held at the time of writing this present study.[30]

Nik Abdul Aziz has not only been a powerful force in the rise of PAS to a position of political predominance in the Malaysian state of Kelantan, but he has also established himself as one of PAS's leading Islamic theologians. He is a prolific writer, with a particular focus upon educating the Muslim masses, rather than producing scholarly works only accessible to highly trained specialists. His writings typically take the form of tracts, press statements, devotional columns in various periodicals, and bulletins issued from his office as Kelantanese Chief Minister.

An example of his popular theological writing is his column *Tazkirah*, which addresses a range of subjects relevant to his mass Malay audience, and which appears in the PAS periodical, *Harakah*. We will briefly discuss one of Nik Abdul Aziz's *Tazkirah* columns,[31] which provides us with a taste of this figure's concerns in educating his audience, and also with an insight into his preaching style.

In the article in question, entitled *Mukjizat Israk dan Mikraj* (The Miracle of [Muhammad's] Night Journey and Ascension), several key characteristics can be identified.

First, Nik Abdul Aziz is in part interested in reporting matters of debate between the Islamic scholars. For example, he reports the debate about the date of Muhammad's ascension. There are several aspects to this debate, but the author guides his audience to the crucial issue which he identifies as 'whether the ascension occurred to the Prophet before the Prophet's *hijra* to Medina'. This same debate is reported by al-Zamakhshari[32], whose work may well have served as the Malaysian author's source. Like al-Zamakhshari, Nik Abdul Aziz does not offer his opinion as to which is the correct view on this point.

Another debate reported, about which the Malay author is prepared to identify his opinion, surrounds the question of whether Muhammad ascended in a dream only, or whether the ascension of his physical body occurred. Nik Abdul Aziz comments that 'Almost the entire Islamic *umma* and its religious scholars concur that

---

[30] [www.bernama.com/infolink/toc/Who/] copied 29 July 1999.
[31] Nik Mat 1998.
[32] Gatje 1996:76.

the Prophet's ascension was carried out by God involving both his body and spirit ...' He does not indicate that contrary views were held by scholars as notable as Hasan al-Basri,[33] but seems rather dismissive of views inconsistent with his own on this point.

A second characteristic feature of his writing evident in this article is his commitment to affirming the prophetic credentials of Muhammad. He expends considerable effort in pointing to the miraculous nature of the event of the ascension, in the process subtly consolidating Muhammad's claims to prophethood. This recognises that a key hallmark of Islamic prophets is their involvement in miraculous events.

At the same time, Nik Abdul Aziz is concerned not to include materials which might undermine Muhammad's claims. He makes no reference to the report that some of Muhammad's followers turned away from him as a result of his claimed ascension to meet God. Such reports, found in al-Zamakhshari[34] and other classical exegetical works, were perhaps considered as potentially confusing to Nik Abdul Aziz's audience and may have been deleted as a result.

A third characteristic feature is his recourse to narrative as a device in his expository writing. A key idea in this passage is the limit of human intellectual powers, and the inability of humans to comprehend the miraculous workings of God. To demonstrate this, Nik Abdul Aziz relates the story of Abraham emerging unharmed from the fire, as well as the principal story in this article about Muhammad's ascension. It demonstrates what we have seen elsewhere: that narrative is considered as a powerful tool in the process of theologically educating the Muslim masses in Southeast Asia.

The fourth feature of this article is Nik Abdul Aziz's attempt to relate an event from the life of Muhammad to modern scientific explanations. He poses the puzzle as to 'how it could be that the Prophet as a man could ascend to the highest Heaven without any preparation or instrumentation, except for a horse "Buraq" which served as the vehicle and "space shuttle"'. He goes on further to explain Buraq's reputed phenomenal speed in terms of scientific knowledge about the speed of light. 'Travelling as fast as light

---

[33] Gatje 1996:76.
[34] Gatje 1996:75.

enabled the Prophet to arrive in the al-Aqsa Mosque in Jerusalem in a short space of time.' Such statements indicate to his audience that far from science having displaced Islam, in fact scientific knowledge is just catching up with what has been accepted as Islamic belief for centuries.

The final feature is the author's emphasis on the severe limitations of human powers of rational thinking:

One of many instances which mankind has never been capable of understanding is the ascension of the physical body of Prophet Muhammad. ... Human intellect struggled to understand the miracle of this ascension. The meaning of *isra'* is a journey which God brought about for the Prophet as a sign of recognition ... The meaning of *mi'raj* is the event following the *isra'*, namely the ascension from al-Aqsa through various heavenly layers to the highest level ... where the knowledge and intellect of humans or jinn cannot reach.

This short passage shows Nik Abdul Aziz's central concerns in his theological writing. He is concerned to address the Muslim masses, affirming key aspects of Islamic belief, only reporting those debates between theologians which will not undermine the belief of the masses, and trying to affirm the widely heard claim among Muslim apologists in the 20th century that Islam is entirely consistent with modern scientific discoveries. In this, one can see traces of his period of study at Al-Azhar, where the effort to reconcile Islam with modern science dates from the time of the early 20th-century modernists.

Furthermore, he is concerned to affirm the priority of revelation over reason. In an overall sense, Nik Abdul Aziz does not sit well in the modernist camp. Rather, he seems to be more appropriately seen within the Orthodox/Traditionalist group. The spirit of his writing is based on an assurance to his readers that the scholars know best. 'Trust us', could be his catch call.

Abdul Hadi Awang (1947–)

Another important Islamic figure and thinker in contemporary Malaysia is PAS's Haji Abdul Hadi Awang. Hadi Awang was born in Kampung Rusila, Marang, in the state of Trengganu. He attended both state and Islamic schools in Trengganu. In 1973 he graduated in Islamic Law at the Islamic University of Medina and two years later took a Master's degree in Politics at Al-Azhar University in Cairo.

He then returned to Malaysia to take up an active role in politics. His entry to PAS coincided with the ABIM (Malaysian Islamic Youth Movement)–PAS alliance in the late 1970s. His charismatic nature, fluency in Arabic, and eloquence in expounding Islamic doctrine and theology earned him a substantial following among PAS supporters. In July 1977 he became Head of the Trengganu Youth wing of PAS, and the following year he unsuccessfully contested the Marang state seat in the Malaysian General Elections. From 1981 he served as Deputy President of PAS, and during this period he won various parliamentary contests. His initial victory was in winning the Trengganu state seat of Marang for PAS in the 1982 General Elections, a victory which he repeated in subsequent elections.

He aggressively engages directly with his opponents in speeches and writing, which are liberally interspersed with Qur'anic quotations and excerpts from the Stories of the Prophets.[35] His approach is one of Islamic holism, whereby he perceives Islam to be the ultimate answer to both social and individual needs. He therefore advocates the establishment of an Islamic State for all Malaysians, seeing it as to the advantage of all races,[36] and has spoken and written favourably about the Iranian revolution and the resulting regime. His opposition to, and clashes with, modernist UMNO Islamologues, including Anwar Ibrahim, are legendary, and his rejection of the UMNO argument that Islam needs to be interpreted in contemporary terms serves as the defining difference between these two political parties.

Hadi Awang is very active in preaching both orally and via the written word. He attracts thousands to his weekly sermons at the Dar al-'Ulum mosque near his modest home, and he preaches on a monthly basis in Kuala Lumpur. Moreover, his sermons are published and distributed, and one of the most popular forums for his various theological comments is the PAS newspaper, *Harakah*. This periodical includes in each issue a column written by Hadi Awang, in which he provides a commentary on select verses from the Qur'an. It would be instructive for our purposes

---

35 Sundaram and Cheek 1988:852.
36 Milner 1993:116.

to examine one such column in which he provides exegetical comment on verse 86 of *Sura al-Nisa'*.[37]

In this comment Hadi Awang addresses the issue of Muslims giving greetings to non-Muslims. From the outset he indicates his scripturalist approach by making reference to a Hadith account from Bukhari which calls on young people to respectfully greet their elders. Hadi Awang proceeds to engage in the minutiae of giving greetings in wide-ranging contexts, discussing this in the context of what is proper and what is not.

He then addresses the following situation. It is clear that if a Muslim is greeted by another Muslim, a return greeting should be issued. What if a Muslim is greeted by a non-Muslim?

Hadi Awang approaches this question through reference to the Hadith, which record that Muhammad used to only give shortened greetings in response to greetings he received from Jews, because of the supposedly insincere nature of the initial greeting by the Jews.

He then proceeds to the next question: what was the norm during the Caliphate when Muslims were greeted by *dhimmis*? Hadi Awang cites a difference among classical scholars on this score, with Ibn 'Abbas, al-Sha'abi and Qatada saying a return greeting should be issued, while Imam Malik and Ashhab Ibn Wahab were of the opinion that a return greeting need not be issued. Hadi Awang adds that some scholars felt a return greeting by the Muslim with an implicit insult was the way to respond, especially where the *dhimmis* issued the initial greeting in a mocking tone.

Hadi Awang concludes this exegetical column by adding that it is not appropriate to greet somebody who is occupied in the toilet, as a Hadith account records that such were Muhammad's instructions.

A clear statement as to why these two PAS scholars, Nik Abdul Aziz and Abdul Hadi Awang, should be considered as orthodox traditionalists rather than neo-normative revivalists would be helpful.

First, both come from rural rather than urban modernist origins. Because of this, their education in early formative years was undertaken in a context of conservative traditionalism, with due authority accorded to a scholarly elite and the body of literature

---

[37] [members.xoom.com/harakah2/semasa/] copied 31 July 1999.

accumulated over centuries of scholarly thinking. This is a context which lends itself more to *taqlid* than *ijtihad*.

Second, the tertiary education which both men acquired at reputable Middle Eastern centres of Islamic learning produced in them a clear affirmation of the primacy of *'ulama'*-based authority. They regard the masses as needing clear leadership and guidance from the clerical class.

Third, both men chose to join the political system rather than preach revolution against it. Both have risen through the ranks of their party to assume positions of political leadership. Both seem committed to the democratic political process, which allows for their appointment as Chief Ministers of Malaysian states through elections, but also allows for them to lose such positions through elections. Once in power, there is no evidence that either has sought to alter democratic structures in an effort to perpetuate the dominance of Islamic political groups.

Finally, certain characteristic features of their writing point to Nik Abdul Aziz and Abdul Hadi Awang as orthodox traditionalists. They seem to be primarily concerned to address and educate the masses rather than the empowered educated class. They tend to present a range of scholarly opinions in their writing, drawing on the broad corpus of Islamic thinking by the *'ulama'*, rather than pronouncing single-minded scripturally driven injunctions as one finds in the writing of Sayyid Qutb and other neo-normative revivalists. Furthermore, Nik Abdul Aziz and Abdul Hadi Awang show concern for entertainment as well as education in their writing, by using devices such as colourful narrative and discussion of miracles.

MODERNISING VOICES

Rippin's category of modernisers among contemporary Islamic thinkers covers a variety of sub-groups. These will be explored by looking at a selection of Malaysian and Indonesian writers active in the second half of the 20th century. The factor which unites them all is that in spite of their drawing on 7th-century scripture as a tool to address modern issues, their feet are firmly planted in modern times and their focus is on the present and the future, rather than the past. They are even prepared to subject 7th-century Islamic texts and dogmas to scrutiny and discuss

adaptation to modern contexts, in a way not contemplated by traditionalists or neo-normative revivalists.

Harun Nasution (1919–98)

This prominent thinker was born in Pematang Siantar, Sumatra,
into the Mandeling Batak ethnic group, the principal Muslim
group among the predominantly Christian Batak.[38] His school
education consisted of periods in both Dutch- and Islamic-system
schools, after which he was sent to the Middle East to study, initially in Saudi Arabia and then in Cairo. Dissatisfied with studies
of the Islamic sciences at Al-Azhar University, Nasution transferred himself to the American University of Cairo, where he
found far greater fulfilment in completing undergraduate studies
with majors in education and sociology.

Upon completion of these studies, Nasution entered the diplo-
matic service of the government of the newly independent
Republic of Indonesia, and served in embassies in Cairo and
Brussels. However, he was drawn to further studies, and in 1960
returned to Cairo to undertake studies in Islamic Law. He then
won a scholarship to McGill University in Canada, where he
completed Master's and Doctoral degrees, with a dissertation
focusing upon rational thought in the writings of Muhammad
'Abduh.

The remainder of his working life was spent with the IAIN
(State Institute of Islamic Studies) Syarif Hidayatullah in Jakarta,
where he served as Dean of the Graduate School and as Rector. In
these roles he was able to make a significant contribution to modernist thinking in Indonesia. At the same time he took the IAIN
along a path which was consistent with New Order Government
goals to develop the IAIN as a vehicle for achieving a modern,
depoliticised Islamic presence in Indonesia. Under his leadership,
the IAIN in Jakarta developed a dynamic, modern curriculum,
combining studies of the traditional Islamic sciences with subjects
drawn from modern western educational models, such as Sociology, Anthropology, Comparative Religion and secular Philosophy.[39] In doing so, he was contributing to a process which moved
Indonesian Islamic attitudes away from prevailing attitudes in

---

[38] The biographical details presented here are drawn from Nasution 1995.
[39] Saeed 1999.

many other Muslim communities based on knee-jerk hostility and suspicion of all things western. Moreover, the curriculum at IAIN Jakarta incorporated the study of streams of Islamic thought which were regarded with suspicion by many orthodox Islamic theologians, such as certain of the writings of Ibn al-'Arabi and Mu'tazilite theology.

Nasution wrote prolifically, and his many books were concerned primarily with philosophy and rational thought, modernism, and the theology of the Mu'tazila.

Martin, Woodward and Atmaja undertook a study of Nasution's essay entitled *Kaum Mu'tazilah dan Pandangan Rasionalnya* (The Mu'tazila and Rational Philosophy), in the process identifying Nasution's sympathies for certain aspects of Mu'tazilite thought.[40] Nasution begins this work by providing a brief survey of events leading up to the emergence of the Mu'tazila, with special reference to the debate in the 8th and 9th centuries surrounding the status of a Muslim who commits sin. At an early point in his essay, he signals that his interest does not lie in making an excursion through early Islamic theological thinking; rather his focus is on the relevance of such thinking for Indonesia in the late 20th century. He observes:

In Indonesia, Mu'tazili thought is not well known or appreciated, because ... it is thought to be based on opinions which deviate from correct Islamic teachings ... some groups within the Muslim community have asserted that they value rationality more than revelation ... Not a small number within the Muslim community are of the opinion that [the Mu'tazila] do not believe in revelation at all ...[41]

This harks back directly to the debate within early Islam concerning the respective priority allocated to reason versus revelation. Nasution's comment at this early point of his essay lays the groundwork for his subsequent defence of Mu'tazilite thinking.

Nasution proceeds to examine the key aspects of Mu'tazilite thought, discussed earlier in this present study. He focuses closely on their view of the respective roles of reason and revelation, and concludes as follows:

---

[40] Martin *et al.* 1997.
[41] Martin *et al.* 1997:183–4.

Even though they give reason a very high place, the Mu'tazila consider revelation to be very important. It is not true that they consider reason to be more important than revelation.[42]

In fact, argues Nasution, the Mu'tazila consider that one of reason's principal functions is to identify general truths, but revelation is needed to fill in the details, as it were. For example, reason can be used to deduce that there will be a Day of Judgement in the future, but only revelation can determine 'the exact nature of the rewards and punishments that humans will be given at that time'. [43]

The other key function of reason, according to Nasution's account of Mu'tazilite thinking, relates to exegesis of the Qur'an. Mu'tazilite exegesis affirms the distinction between external and internal meanings of Qur'anic verses, discussed earlier in this present study. Nasution points out that where there appears to be a conflict between reason and the external or surface meaning of a Qur'anic verse, then this conflict will be resolved by a search for the internal meaning of the verse concerned. This internal meaning will be identified by, and accord with, reason.

Nasution concludes his study with a stout defence of the orthodox nature of Mu'tazilite thinking. He summarises it as 'a form of rationalism which is in accord with, and defines itself in terms of, the truth of revelation'.[44] He then points to a process of rehabilitation of Mu'tazilite thinking which commenced with the Islamic reformist movement of the late 19th century, saying that Jamal al-Din al-Afghani and Muhammad 'Abduh had 'perspectives identical to those of the Mu'tazila'.[45]

Nasution clearly identifies himself with such a school of thought. In embracing Mu'tazilite thought in so overt a manner, he is demonstrating a certain measure of courage which characterised his writing throughout his long career. Furthermore, the fact that Nasution could so identify himself and remain a powerful force on the Indonesian Islamic stage for so long is a testimony to the eclectic nature of Indonesian Islam and the relatively tolerant spirit resulting from the Indonesian state philosophy of *Pancasila*.

---

[42] Martin *et al*. 1997:188.
[43] Ibid.
[44] Martin *et al*. 1997:191.
[45] Martin *et al*. 1997:192. 'Abduh had long been reviled as a covert Mu'tazili in certain radical Islamist circles.

S.M.N. Al-Attas (1931–)

Syed Muhammad Naguib Al-Attas is clearly one of the foremost Islamic thinkers to emerge from the Malay–Indonesian world during the last half of the 20th century. His family was of Hadhrami origin, migrating to Southeast Asia along with the waves of Arab migrants to the region arriving around the turn of the 20th century. Though born in the Dutch East Indies, the major part of his working life and its principal literary output has been associated with Malaysia, where he was long on the academic staff of the National University of Malaysia.

Al-Attas has been a prolific writer on wide-ranging fields. His early works were chiefly concerned with Islamic history, addressing issues such as Malay Sufism, doctrinal conflict among competing Sufi groups and scholars, and the transmission of Islamic thinking from the Arab world to Southeast Asia. These early writings include the following:

- *Some Aspects of Sufism as known and practised among the Malays* (1963)
- *Raniri and the Wujudiyyah of 17th-century Acheh* (1966)
- *The Islamisation of the Malay–Indonesian Archipelago* (1969)
- *The Mysticism of Hamzah Fansuri* (1970)
- *The correct date of the Trengganu inscription* (1970)
- *The origin of the Malay sha'ir* (1971)
- *Islam dalam sejarah dan kebudayaan Melayu* (1972)

In later years Al-Attas turned his attention to arguing the case for Islam being a rich storehouse of modern scientific knowledge and method. He showed a particular interest in matters philosophical. The following list demonstrates this, though we can also see that he did not lose interest in the subjects of his earlier research:

- *Aims and objectives of Islamic education* (1979)
- *Islam, Secularism and the Philosophy of the Future* (1985)
- *A Commentary on the Hujjat al-siddiq of Nur al-Din al-Raniri* (1986)
- *The Oldest Known Malay Manuscript* (1988)
- *On quiddity and essence: an outline of the basic structure of reality in Islamic metaphysics* (1990)

The above writings address, among other things, the subject of Islam's relation to other faiths, principally Christianity. We will briefly examine his ideas on this subject at this juncture, to supplement his perspectives on various issues to do with Islam and Sufism which appear at various other points of this study.

In a chapter concerning Christianity and secularism,[46] Al-Attas's voice is one based on religious exclusivism. His great eclecticism can be further seen in his evident familiarity with both Christian history and with the biblical text. However, many would see his argumentation as somewhat tendentious.

In his view modern Christianity has become corrupted by drifting from its early roots and practices, and this has happened because of Western Christianity's embracing of a dichotomy between the sacred and the secular. He comments:

The claim that secularization has its roots in biblical faith and that it is the fruit of the Gospel has no substance in historical fact. Secularization has its roots not in biblical faith, but in the *interpretation* of biblical faith by Western man ...[47]

Al-Attas thus places the fault for modern Christianity's supposed straying from the truth squarely at the feet of the West. He says that while original Christianity was a revealed faith, Christianity in its modern western guise 'is for the most part a sophisticated form of culture religion'.[48] In his view the rot set in when the apostle Paul misrepresented the original revealed message and set Christianity off on a wrong path.[49] Dualism, based on the sacred and secular distinction, was the result of the assimilation of Aristotelian philosophy and Cartesian thought. In contrast, says Al-Attas, Islam has maintained its focus on the essentially holistic nature of God's creation.

Al-Attas' disdain for the West is highly visible in this writing. He speaks in a stereotyping way, negatively portraying 'Western man' as:

... always inclined to regard his culture and civilization as man's cultural vanguard ... We reject the validity of the truth of their assertion ...[50]

---

[46] Al-Attas 1990. This is based on his *Islam, Secularism and the Philosophy of the Future* (1985).

[47] Al-Attas 1990:114.

[48] Al-Attas 1990:120.

[49] This claim is not original. Paul has long been denounced by Muslim polemicists as one who set out to pervert the Christian revelation.

[50] Al-Attas 1990:117.

But his tendency to stereotype is not restricted to his portrayal of the West. He also depicts Islam as a monolith, and speaks on behalf of the faith as follows:

Islam totally rejects any application to itself of the concepts secular, or secularization, or secularism as they do not belong and are alien to it in every respect; and they belong and are natural only to the intellectual history of Western-Christian religious experience and consciousness. [51]

In contrast with much of his earlier writing, Al-Attas allows his own views in his study of secularism/secularisation to be very visible. This work is representative of both latter-day Islamic apologetics and polemics. It is apologetics in as much as it seeks to respond to charges that Islam is medieval, by portraying Islam as a rich source of answers to situations in modern life. It is simultaneously polemical in that it seeks clearly to attack Christianity as it supposedly exists in its Western guise. Thus this work shows Al-Attas the scholar co-existing with Al-Attas the Muslim apologist/polemicist.

Al-Attas's voice on this subject is somewhat at odds with more pluralist approaches of other modern Islamic thinkers such as Anwar Ibrahim, Mohamed Talbi and Seyyed Hossein Nasr. In fact, his approach converges in many respects with the view of Christianity held by more radical Islamists such as Sayyid Qutb.[52] It demonstrates his concern to prioritise the consolidation of the Islamic community in Southeast Asia, with less interest on his part in inter-faith relations based on pluralist approaches to multi-faith issues.

In this work, Al-Attas has added his voice to the spirit of 20th-century Islamic reformism, by developing new apologetic and polemical approaches to challenge Western influence. His concern is not with esoteric discussion of Sufi issues of the immanence of God, or with the debate between *shari'a*-mindedness versus theosophical inclinations. His focus is clearly on problems he perceives with the modern world, and his methodology is to draw on wide-ranging materials, including the knowledge of the

---

[51] Al-Attas 1990:118.
[52] Refer to articles by Talbi, Nasr and Qutb on this subject in the same volume as that containing Al-Attas 1990.

ancients, to engage with modern debates. This is the essence of modernist reformism.

Nurcholish Madjid (1939–)

Nurcholish Madjid was born in Jombang to a family of religious scholars associated with the local pesantren. His early education included both government and pesantren schools, followed by undergraduate studies at the IAIN Syarif Hidayatullah in Jakarta, majoring in Arab literature. He took his PhD in Islamic Thought under the famous Muslim modernist Fazlur Rahman at the University of Chicago, Illinois, graduating in 1984.

During his studies, Nurcholish played an active part in student politics, demonstrating the inclination for leadership and activism which would equip him well to play an influential role during the momentous events of 1998, including a period as Deputy Chairman of the IIFSO (International Islamic Federation of Students Organizations) from 1969 to 1971.

Nurcholish spent much of the time from 1975 to 1998 teaching at various levels at IAIN Jakarta. In addition, he was associated with various research institutes, and spent a period as visiting professor at McGill University, Montreal, in 1991/2. He has had various other involvements, in recognition of his position as one of Indonesia's foremost Islamic thinkers. These have included membership of the Advisory Council of *Ikatan Cendekiawan Muslim Se-Indonesia* (ICMI) from 1995, membership of the Indonesian Press Council during the 1990s, and membership of the National Commission for Human Rights from 1993.

However, Nurcholish is not only a participant in groups initiated by others. Arguably his most influential initiative has been his establishment in 1986 of the Paramadina Foundation (*Yayasan Wakaf Paramadina*), for which he is Chairman. Paramadina serves as a think-tank, issuing press statements, speeches and a range of published materials via hardcopy, audio and internet media, commenting on wide-ranging issues related to Islam and the modern world. The scope of Paramadina's interests are reflected in the discussion of Nurcholish's writings below.

His writings. Nurcholish has been a prolific writer, producing various books and a vast number of published articles. His books include *Islam, Kemodernan, dan Ke-Indonesiaan* (1987), *Islam, Kerakyatan, dan Keindonesiaan* (1993) and *30 Sajian Ruhani* (1998).

Islam, Kerakyatan, dan Keindonesiaan represents a collection of Nurcholish's writings dating mostly from the period between 1970 and 1972. His concern in these writings is with the underclasses, the little people who are disempowered by social and political structures. He speaks with the voice of the student activist who has taken on the duty of representing the disempowered in confronting the structures of state. These writings present him at the stage before he had begun his detailed engagement with theological and philosophical thought.

Islam, Kemodernan, dan Ke-Indonesiaan represents an anthology of Nurcholish's thinking. In this work Nurcholish provides an insight into his self-styled neo-modernist views. He gives support to the established modernist call for Islam to engage with modern times. However, he diverges from this modernist approach by proclaiming that this engagement should be done on the basis of the rich resources of traditional Islamic thought, rather than being founded on a dramatic latter-day reinterpretation of the sources, as was the approach of 'Abduh, Rida and their Malay–Indonesian disciples. Further, he calls for the Islamic basis of the modern framework to be expressed within a national context – 'keIndonesiaan'. This represents another plank of his neo-modernist approach.

30 Sajian Ruhani demonstrates his concern to reach out to the Muslim masses, rather than merely address Islamic scholars. In this work, Nurcholish presents thirty daily readings for Muslims engaged in the Ramadan fast. He points out how fasting provides an opportunity for reflection on faith, revelation and God, as well as a worthwhile exercise in personal self-restraint. In this way, fasting leads to greater devotion to Islam, rather than a merely mechanical exercise followed without thought.

A key theme to emerge clearly from his writings is Nurcholish's strong commitment to a democratic society. His favouring of individual rights as the ultimate measure of democracy rather than 'collectivist convergence' places him somewhat at odds with the traditional Indonesian approach to discussion and debate based on consultation (*musyawara*) and consensus (*mufakat*).

Furthermore, Nurcholish argues for the ultimate separation of Islam and politics. His famous statement dating from 1970, 'Islam yes; Islamic party no',[53] has often been quoted, particularly after the collapse of Suharto's New Order Government in May 1998. Nurcholish's statements at this time showed that he advocated the relegation of Islam to the private domain, and stood against increasing the role of *shari'a* in matters of state.[54] This is a view which dates back to his student days, as reflected in the following statement taken from a speech in 1972:

the concept of 'Islamic state' is a distortion of the [properly] proportioned relationship between state and religion. The state is one of the aspects of worldly life whose dimension is rational and collective, while religion is an aspect of another kind of life whose dimension is spiritual and personal.[55]

This attracted criticism from some modernist groups, who see him as being too close in his thinking to the liberal West.

The tag 'liberal' has often been applied to Nurcholish. He is a contributor to the recent study edited by Charles Kurzman entitled *Liberal Islam*, and the publisher's summary of this work helps us to understand how Nurcholish is viewed in the context of world Islamic thinking:

'Liberal Islam' is not a contradiction in terms; it is a thriving tradition and undergoing a revival within the last generation. This anthology presents the work of 32 prominent Muslims who share parallel concerns with Western liberalism: separation of church and state, democracy, the rights of women and minorities, freedom of thought, and human progress. Although the West has largely ignored the liberal tradition within Islam, many of these authors are well-known in their own countries as advocates of democracy and tolerance.[56]

The above issues are indeed close to Nurcholish's heart. He has often indicated in interview that he is an advocate for the rights of minorities, saying 'We cannot allow the minorities to continuously feel threatened.'[57] The issue of minority rights is germane to the broader issues of pluralism and democracy which are key

---

[53] Madjid 1998b:285.
[54] *Asiaweek*, 19 June 1998.
[55] Madjid 1998b:294.
[56] Kurzman 1998:back cover.
[57] Interview with *Ummat*, No. 29 Tahun IV, 1 February 1999, 39.

concerns for Nurcholish, and he engages with them from the standpoint of his neo-modernist view of Islam.

On a related point, the issue of the relation between Muslims and the People of the Book is the subject of several of his essays. This leads him on to address the thorny question of *Jihad, Dar al-Islam* and *Dar al-Harb* in another essay which bears a brief examination.

In the essay *Dar al-Islam dan Dar al-Harb*, Nurcholish's expansive spirit and inclusivist approach provides the framework for his overview of Islamic history. He stresses the diversity of viewpoints circulating during the formative period of Islam, suggesting that 'orthodoxy' was in a state of flux: 'the diversity of viewpoints with respect to orthodoxy was great, though those which converged were equally numerous.' But he affirms that the early success of Islamic expansion was due to Islam's openness, rather than to any oppressive spirit:

> Of great interest is that the Islamic *umma* in the classical period has been noted by reliable scholars of history, both from the West and the East, for its good treatment of (non-Muslim) enemies. Because of this, the Muslims succeeded, in a relatively short period of time, in creating the most progressive empire at that time, extending from the Atlantic Ocean to the Gobi Desert. It is relevant to reflect that this expansion was not achieved by means of subjugation (*qahr*), but rather by means of liberation (*fath*) of the populations from oppression. In this way it was consistent with the fundamental view of Islam regarding war and peace.[58]

Nurcholish is committed to affirming the Qur'an as a valid foundation for examining the issue in focus: 'the Qur'an instructs us to study history in detail, view the world and observe the experiences of past communities.'[59] However, this is no mere revivalist call to return to the early scriptural sources. Rather, the student can learn much from the rich tapestry of Islamic history.

In the final paragraph, Nurcholish also affirms the sixth article of faith by saying that all events are part of God's divine plan. Though this is a somewhat predeterminist statement, Nurcholish is no mere fatalist, as he stresses that humans have been given reason to enable them to understand the divine plan.

---

[58] Madjid 1995:91.
[59] Madjid 1995:91.

Anwar Ibrahim (1947–)

Anwar Ibrahim is one of the leading figures on the Malaysian Islamic stage in the modern era. In 1971 he founded the Malaysian Islamic Youth Movement (ABIM) and became President at its inception. He remained in this position until he joined the ruling United Malays National Organisation in 1982. An examination of ABIM's priorities provides an insight into Anwar's beliefs and methodologies.

After its establishment ABIM quickly engaged in reformist activities, calling on individuals to adhere to Qur'anic example and for society to adhere to Islamic practices and procedures in addressing modern-day issues and problems.[60] During the 1970s ABIM sought to identify itself with various overseas movements, including the Muslim Brotherhood. ABIM's policies found fertile ground with a university student body which was increasingly Malay in make-up as a result of the New Economic Policy.

ABIM sought to establish and run a network of independent schools as a vehicle for disseminating its Islamic programme. In this it reflected the policies of leading modernist groups in the Malay world during the 20th century, such as the Muhammadiyah and al-Irshad. Indeed, it was motivated by modernist reformism, rather than traditionalist or revivalist approaches. For example, ABIM was much more cautious about calls for the establishment of an Islamic State in Malaysia which came increasingly from the main opposition party, PAS.

Nash[61] cites Anwar's reminiscences in 1987 concerning the beginning of the *da'wa* revival:

It was an explosive time. There were lots of issues … Malay poverty, language, corruption. And after May 13 [1969 riots], you just got hooked on [*sic*] immediately. It was all a question of the survival of the *umma,* of the Malay race. Previously we had been thinking about all these problems outside Islam, when actually we could have solved them through Islam.

This statement indicates how clearly Anwar equated the concept of *umma* with the Malay race, rather than with the worldwide Islamic community; i.e. his focus in using the term was ethnic rather than religious, which is the more common usage.

---

[60] Lapidus 1988:782.
[61] Nash 1991:705.

Moreover, Islam is presented by Anwar as a powerful tool for asserting Malay rights, rather than being an end in itself. In Anwar's schema, Islam is a means to an end, rather than an end in itself. In this he shares much with the neo-modernism of Nurcolish Madjid.

Nevertheless, Anwar's commitment to his vision of Islam is beyond question. At no stage did Anwar Ibrahim become so embroiled in his increasing political responsibilities as a government Minister that he neglected his religious duties or ceased to promote what he considered to be worthy Islamic causes. An example is provided by his becoming patron of the Al-Quran Mushaf Malaysia Project which he launched in January 1997. This project was based on the artistic illumination of hundreds of handcopied pages of the Qur'an. It was the product of a specialist group of dedicated Muslim artisans and professionals, skilled in the various aspects of Islamic calligraphy, art and design. The projected completion date for the project was the year 2000.

Anwar was one of the principal driving forces behind the success of the National Front at the polls between 1982 and 1998. Moreover, his stamp was firmly placed on the policy of Islamisation which was adopted by the National Front and was designed to steal a march on PAS, the principal Islamic opposition group.

His writings. Anwar wrote extensively in the period between 1975 and 1998, using published articles in journals, newspapers and speeches as forums for expounding his evolving Islamic thinking.

Arguably the high-water mark for Anwar came in the mid-1990s. By this stage he was heir apparent for the Malaysian Prime Ministership. Malaysia was riding the crest of an economic wave, leading the Southeast Asian economic boom with Singapore, and Anwar had widespread support from various sections of society. He wielded enormous influence from his position as Minister of Finance in the Malaysian Government and Deputy Prime Minister. He was ranked forty-first in the 1996 *Asiaweek* listing of the fifty most powerful people in Asia.[62] An examination of speeches and interviews which he gave around this time

---

[62] [http://wisdom.psinet.net.au/~lani/asia.html] copied 30 July 1999.

will give us an insight into the thought of this leading Islamic figure, and will also provide instructive points of contrast for our discussion of PAS leaders.

Perceived by many as having become merely an UMNO spokesman for a liberal or moderate view of Islam – until his political demise in 1998 – Anwar was strongly criticised by more conservative Malay groups, who saw him as having sold out when he joined UMNO.

Anwar responded to these criticisms in a television interview,[63] and took the opportunity to articulate a sophisticated understanding of his view of pluralism within an Islamic context.

Anwar was in turn heavily critical of what he perceived as fundamentalism, and sought to differentiate between various approaches to Islam in the modern world, saying:

> ... we have aberrations, we have radicals, we have militants, we have extremists. You shouldn't lump all [Muslims] together ... we have a problem with Islamic radicals, extremists and aberrations within Islamic movements ... We represent a moderate brand of Islam. We represent Muslims who believe that the success of Muslims in Malaysia will depend to a large extent on our ability to work, collaborate and trust [*sic*] the non-Muslims.

Unlike the *da'wa* revivalists in Malaysia, such as the Darul Arqam group, who characteristically withdrew from a society they perceived as corrupt in favour of establishing an Islamic ghetto along the lines of the Medinan community, Anwar stresses that it is possible for Islam to thrive in a multicultural and multi-religious community. Anwar dismisses the calls of Islamic radicals as hollow and irrelevant to the modern world:

> I do accept that some [radicals] have an understanding of some facets of Islam in a traditional context. The problem remains their relevance to a contemporary society. It is essentially popular appeals, exhortations without substance, without a clear agenda. We differ with them substantially because of their failure to relate Islam with the contemporary modern setting ... There cannot be an Islamic agenda devoid of and oblivious to the realities of a multi-racial society.

Anwar's belief in the need to separate religious issues and observance from the workings of the modern state is similar to the

---

63 Jamal 1993.

separation between Church and State observed in the West. They also resonate with the neo-modernist views of Nurcholish Madjid encountered earlier. He rejects the call by groups such as PAS for the establishment of an Islamic State in Malaysia as being anachronistic in the late 20th century:

Spiritualism and morality ... should be in the various confines of each individual and the family. That is again a point of departure between us and the extremists in the Islamic Party, because I think we should not promote their brand of spiritualism as a state agenda to force down the throats of everybody.

Nevertheless Anwar seeks to insure himself against accusations that he is a Western lackey by strategically-placed statements designed to criticise Western values. He believes that Malays can learn from others, but that does not mean they should become like others:

We are able to learn much from the West – a lot of positive counsel, civilisational experience in the West that we choose to import ... but we differ essentially from how [Westerners] perceive the world, society, life. We have to be rooted to our own cultural tradition but open enough to allow for all positive elements of other cultures and civilisations.

Another forum where Anwar was able to expound on his neo-modernist views of Islam and society was via his speeches given as Finance Minister or Deputy Prime Minister. The year 1995 represented a high point in this regard, and it would be instructive to briefly comment on the key elements of several of his speeches given at this time.

In his Opening Address at the Third International Convention of the Islamic Medical Association of North America in Kuala Lumpur in July 1995,[64] Anwar clearly demonstrated his skill at engaging with issues of the modern day within an Islamic framework. He makes regular references to the *umma* in discussing the need to devote attention to health care throughout the Muslim world, saying:

To my mind, the discourse on health care should rank high among our many concerns because the overall health condition is one of the criteria

---

[64] Opening address by Anwar Ibrahim, Deputy Prime Minister of Malaysia, at the Third International Convention of Islamic Medical Association of North America, Kuala Lumpur, 10 July 1995, [www.ikd.org.my] copied 28 July 1999.

for measuring the well-being of the Ummah. In this regard, a large part of the Muslim world today would be able to make rapid strides in social and economic development if there is a concerted effort to raise public awareness on hygiene, a better knowledge on nutrition and no effort is spared to institute preventive medicine to eliminate curable contagious diseases.

Anwar confirms the Islamic basis of his call by expressing it in terms of Islamic scripture, claiming that scripture is entirely consistent with his call for better health:

From the perspective of the Islamic tradition, healing of the sick was generally regarded as the highest form of 'service to God' after the prescribed rituals. Health and medical concerns in Islam were shot through with religio-ethical motivation and valuation. Islamic physicians regarded medicine as a religious calling because it helped men and women to help others preserve and restore their health.

Another of his important speeches from 1995 is entitled 'The Celebration of Reason over Passion',[65] Anwar takes the opportunity to laud the modern Muslim scholar Muhammad al-Ghazali for always having championed 'a rational, moderate and tolerant Islam', thus indirectly affirming what he views as the approach to Islam championed by the Malaysian government of which he was a member. As he did in the television interview discussed earlier, Anwar points out the difference between European secularisation and Islamic holism by saying 'Secularization demands a separation between public space and private sphere, while the vision of Islam encompasses both, guided by supreme moral authority.'

But Anwar's call is no mere call for a revivalist, Islamist state. He calls for reform in social and political affairs, with an emphasis on attaining 'a civil society'. This is the language of the neo-modernist, affirming that Islam contains the answers but calling for an Islam which prioritises human rights, democracy and civil society. He defines the latter as:

… a flourishing of social intermediaries between the family and the state, a social order founded upon moral rules rather than individual fancy, a governance based on popular participation rather than elitist imposition,

---

[65] Speech by Anwar Ibrahim, Deputy Prime Minister of Malaysia and President of International Islamic University at the IIU President's Conferment Award for Sheikh Muhammad Al-Ghazali, 22 August 1995, [www.ikd.org.my] copied 28 July 1999.

rule of law instead of human capriciousness, respect for individual freedom and the freedom of expression within the bounds of morality and
decency.

Anwar then laments the degree to which so many Muslims in the
modern day are preoccupied with 'forms' and 'trivialities', such as
the call in the *Sunna* for men to wear a beard. Here he is alluding
to Islamist groups such as PAS, in a way which is consistent with
his attack on opposition groups in his television interview discussed earlier.

Hasbullah Bakry (1926–)

Hasbullah Bakry was born in Palembang. As was the case with
other leading Islamic thinkers such as Hamka and Nik Abdul Aziz
Nik Mat, his appetite for studying Islam was nurtured in a
strongly religious family, with a father who was a local Islamic
notable. Bakry studied in his father's *pesantren* in Palembang, as
well as at a local junior high school. He then continued study of
the Islamic sciences at the State Centre for Higher Education in
Islamic Studies in Jogjakarta.[66]

During his work career he served in a variety of positions. He
was engaged as a lecturer in comparative religion at the National
Islamic Judicial School of Jogjakarta, and also served for many
years as Councillor for the Centre for Spiritual Care of the Indonesian Police in Jogjakarta. Both of these positions provided him
with an environment conducive to writing.

He produced several books and articles in periodicals. The
most important were *Nabi Isa dalam al-Qur'an dan Nabi Muhammad dalam Bijbel* (1959), *Al-Qur'an Sebagai Korektor terhadap Taurat
dan Injil* (The Qur'an as a Correction of the Torah and the
Gospel) (1966), and *Pandangan Islam Tentang Kristen di Indonesia*
(The Islamic Viewpoint Regarding Christianity in Indonesia)
(1984). The first of these represents his principal work, and it was
written as a polemical response to F.L. Bakker's *Lord Jesus in the
Religion of Islam* (1957). The impact of Bakry's response was
increased through the English translation as *Jesus Christ in the
Qur'an, Muhammad in the Bible* (1990). It has been the most significant polemical work by an Indonesian Muslim in the modern era.

---

[66] Ropi 1998:222, 228.

In his 1959 work[67] Bakry was motivated to lessen the impact of Christian mission activities among Indonesian Muslims. His writing demonstrates a good knowledge of the biblical text; his focus is on textual rather than sociological issues. Thus Bakry draws extensively on the biblical text, from both Old and New Testaments.

The Christians always claim that Mary is the descendent of David (of the tribe of Judah) but they are never able to demonstrate her line of descent. As for the genealogy from David which appears in the Gospel of Matthew 1:1–17 and Luke 3:23–8, it provides a line of descent from David to Joseph, the husband of Mary, but not to Mary herself. And although Joseph was (possibly) Mary's husband according to the Gospel, nevertheless the Gospel itself says (Matthew 1:25) that 'Joseph did not have intercourse with Mary before Jesus was born'.

Ropi comments that Bakry's method of using biblical verses to undermine the claims of Christianity was 'no more than the continuation of a medieval polemic that had started centuries before him'.[68] Bakry shows that he has learned the art of polemics well, by skilfully, though somewhat tendentiously, using the biblical text to undermine its own authority. He makes statements such as the following:

… the degree of inaccuracy increases when we consider that much of the contents of the Gospel of Luke are considered as weak traditions.

In one summary statement, he has challenged the reliability of the biblical record as presented in Luke's Gospel, and he has done so in a way which would resonate with Muslim readers, by referring to 'weak traditions' – a term taken directly from the language of the prophetic Traditions.

His two key concerns in his writing are what he sees as the false doctrine of the Trinity and the supposed predictions of the coming of Muhammad in the Bible.[69] He uses the biblical text to argue that Jesus could not have been the Messianic figure long awaited by the Jewish people. In this Bakry is clearly influenced by the non-canonical Gospel of Barnabas, which denies the

---

[67] The following discussion is based upon Bakry 1968:43–6.

[68] Ropi 1998:223.

[69] Ropi 1998:222.

messiahship of Jesus. He then proceeds to identify Muhammad clearly as the fulfilment of the messianic hope:

However, in fact the Messiah who was promised by Moses has already appeared; namely Prophet Muhammad. ... And the kingdom of God which was promised by Prophet John the Baptist in Matthew 3:2 and by Prophet Jesus in Matthew 4:17 has in fact already appeared; namely the kingdom of Islam which was brought by Prophet Muhammad.

Thus his writing is quite polemical, and sets out to undermine the fundamental tenets of Christian belief, and to portray established Christianity as a false, corrupt creed, in terms reminiscent of Al-Attas's anti-Christian writing encountered earlier. At the same time Bakry is committed to affirming the claims of Islam regarding Muhammad as the final prophet.

In this task Bakry belongs within the tradition of Muslim polemicists going back to the classical period, and indeed he appears to have drawn upon classical sources in developing his own polemical style. His contribution fits within the broadly reformist spirit of the 20th century, identifying the West and its religion as the adversary and seeking to knock it down in order to enhance the claims of Islam.

Djarnawi Hadikusuma (D. 1993)

In the study by Martin, Woodward and Atmaja encountered earlier, the authors supplement their detailed study of Harun Nasution with reference to other Southeast Asian Islamic authors. These include Djarnawi Hadikusuma, a theologian and writer who played a prominent role in the modernist Muhammadiyah organisation in Yogyakarta until his death in 1993. It would be useful for our purposes to briefly examine an excerpt from Hadikusuma's work *Kitab Tauhid* (The book of the unity of God) which is translated by Martin *et al.*[70]

In this excerpt Hadikusuma addresses the issue of the divine decree and predestination, which recurs at different points of this present study. His concern is to ensure that his audience has a correct understanding of this fundamental doctrine. He warns that 'if a person has an incorrect understanding of *qadla* and *qadar*, it is easy for him to slip into the incorrect view that it is not

---

[70] Martin *et al.* 1997:143–5.

necessary for him to make serious efforts ...'.[71] In other words, Hadikusuma is concerned that an orthodox viewpoint which gives primary weighting to God's predestination of events can lead individuals to succumb to a kind of lazy fatalism. He therefore exhorts his readers to be energetic in their life's efforts, rather than responding merely as passive passengers to what comes their way in life.

His is a skilful blending of an orthodox portrayal of God's overarching omnipotence and a call for an active human response to God's plan. He says 'Knowledge of *qadla* and *qadar* is reserved for God alone. It is not our affair. We cannot know *takdir* before it unfolds. Our lack of knowledge gives us the freedom and courage to exert ourselves. What is our affair is to work and to exert ourselves and to choose the road of the good life and to reject the path of evil.'[72]

Hadikusuma is thus playing his part in emphasising a theme common to Malay–Indonesian Islamic scholars in the late 20th century; namely that Muslims have choices available to them, not in a way which undermines God's ultimate sovereignty, but rather of a type which affirm a belief in God's plan for the world. His is not the message of traditionalist dependence upon scholarly authorities, as we heard from the pen of Nik Abdul Aziz Nik Mat earlier. Rather, it is a modernist message for Indonesian Muslims to see themselves as having choices and a measure of freedom to make those choices.

Abdurrahman Wahid (1940–)

In many respects this figure is a giant on the Islamic stage in modern Indonesia and his election as Indonesia's fourth president in 1999 will only enhance his already substantial profile. However, in spite of the fact that he has written many columns and articles in various periodicals, he has not devoted his energies to producing substantial monographs focusing on Islamic theological thought.

Better known by his familiar name Gus Dur, he was born in East Java into a famous family; his grandfather being Kiai Haji Hasyim Asy'ari (1871–1947) who studied Jurisprudence,

---

[71] Martin *et al.* 1997:144.
[72] Martin *et al.* 1997:145.

Tradition and Sufism with both Shaykh Ahmad Khatib and Muhammad al-Nawawi during a period of seven years in Mecca in the 1890s, before returning to become famous as the *kyai* at the Pondok Pesantren Tebuireng. His greatest legacy lies in his foundational role in establishing the Nahdatul Ulama (NU) in 1926.[73]

Abdurrahman Wahid's father was A. Wahid Hasyim, who also became prominent in the NU, and then served as Minister of Religious Affairs in the Indonesian government from 1949 to 1951.[74]

Abdurrahman Wahid's childhood years were spent in both state schools and *pesantren* Islamic schools. At the age of twenty-four he went to Cairo to study at al-Azhar University, following a well-worn path of young Indonesian Muslim intellectuals, including Harun Nasution. Also like Nasution, Abdurrahman Wahid was dissatisfied at al-Azhar, finding it outmoded in terms of its educational approaches, so he transferred to the University of Baghdad where he took a degree in Arabic literature.[75]

After making a number of visits to Europe in the early 1970s, Abdurrahman Wahid returned to Indonesia where he initially taught at Hasyim Asy'ari University in Jombang. He quickly involved himself in the NU, and by 1984 had attained the supreme position as Chairman of that organisation, a position to which he was re-elected in 1989 and 1994. He was also prominent in other bodies and won a number of significant awards, both domestic and international.

Abdurrahman Wahid has become a powerful voice on the political stage, though not holding specific political office or being associated with a political party during the New Order Government. He was ranked twenty-fourth in the 1996 *Asiaweek* listing of the fifty most powerful people in Asia, with his power measured on the basis of his chairmanship of the thirty-million-strong NU.[76] He has been described in the following terms:

---

[73] Khuluq 1998:46ff; Aboebakar 1957:69ff.

[74] Aboebakar 1957.

[75] Mujiburrahman 1999:341.

[76] [http://wisdom.psinet.net.au/~lani/asia.html] copied 30 July 1999.

a known champion of religious tolerance and democratization ... the most influential, enigmatic, fascinating and yet also vulnerable political player on the increasingly messy Indonesian political landscape.[77]

Abdurrahman Wahid is a strong advocate for the relevance of *Pancasila* (Indonesia's official state philosophy) for Islamic aspirations for Indonesia, and is a vocal opponent of Islamist calls for abandoning *Pancasila* in favour of Islamic *shari'a* as the basis of political organisations and the state. One of his much-quoted statements is the following:

Using religious politics is a dangerous tendency. Let the government govern and let the religious groups take care of their own affairs.[78]

He opposed the New Order Government's creation of ICMI (the Indonesian Association of Muslim Intellectuals) from the outset, saying that it could become the 'thin end of the wedge' as far as political Islam was concerned, leading to a threat from Islamist thinking to Indonesian democracy.[79] In a later interview, Abdurrahman Wahid explained his opposition to joining ICMI in the following terms: 'As long as they think Islam is an ideology, then I will not participate. Islam is a way of life. Its adherents should follow it voluntarily, not needing any legislation from the state.'[80] Articulating this opposition in further detail, Wahid wrote as follows in 1995:

I consider that groupings of intellectuals go nowhere. Intellectual groupings, especially those that fly the flag of religion, will [only] function effectively if they have a voice for the future. Struggles for human rights, democracy and the rule of law are universal struggles. Giving voice to these issues is the responsibility of the people vis-à-vis the state. In other words, such matters should not be enveloped by the flag of Islam. Islam can make a contribution, but it is not appropriate that it lay claim [to these issues]. At the moment it is as if Islam claims that the only valid contribution is the Islamic one. We must be thinking rather that all elements, both social-democrat and nationalist, can contribute to a united Indonesia.[81]

---

[77] *Indonesia Political Watch*, vol. 1 no. 4 (14 December 1998), [www.castleasia.com/ipw /covers/1998/ipw4.htm] copied 30 July 1999.

[78] Schwarz 1994:160, based on an interview with Abdurrahman Wahid on 9 July 1992.

[79] Mujiburrahman 1999:339.

[80] *The Australia/Israel Review*, 22/8 (6–26 June 1997).

[81] Wahid 1995:71.

He founded the Forum Demokrasi in 1991 essentially as a democratic response to ICMI's establishment just beforehand.

Central to the thinking of Abdurrahman Wahid is the notion of *pribumisasi*. This notion represents 'the domestication of Islam', which he describes as follows:

> The source of Islam is revelation which bears its own norms. Due to its normative character, it tends to be permanent. Culture, on the other hand, is a creation of human beings and therefore develops in accordance with social changes. This difference, however, does not prevent the manifestation of religious life in the form of culture.[82]

He affirms this process, unlike revivalist groups which reject such localisation of what they see as an eternal divine blueprint. He adds:

> Contextualisation of Islam is part of Islamic history ... the involvement of Islam in history did not change Islam itself, but only the manifestation of Islamic religious life.[83]

Abdurrahman Wahid does not see the details of *fiqh* as being permanent. Rather, these legal codes based on the divine law need to be dynamic to reflect changing times and circumstances. *Pancasila* represents just such an outcome of adaptation of the divine law to contemporary circumstances.

Abdurrahman Wahid's thinking demonstrates the process of transmission of Islamic thought. He draws on the Egyptian Islamic thinker, 'Ali 'Abd al-Raziq, in reconciling Islamic values with democratic values via *al-hurriyya* (freedom), *al-'adala* (justice) and *shura* (consultation).[84] Likewise, he is indebted to the medieval Maliki jurist Abu Ishaq al-Shatibi (d. 1388) in articulating a key to Islamic reform as being the protection of five basic needs: *hifz al-nafs* (the protection of self), *hifz al-din* (the protection of religion from forced conversion), *hifz al-nasl* (the protection of family), *hifz al-mal* (the protection of property), *hifz al-'aql* (the protection of intellect).[85] In formulating his thought, Abdurrahman Wahid is drawing in various ways on both

---

82 Mujiburrahman 1999:342.
83 Mujiburrahman 1999:342–3.
84 Mujiburrahman 1999:346.
85 Mujiburrahman 1999:342.

traditionalist and modernist thought to produce an outcome which neatly fits the neo-modernist paradigm.[86]

Amien Rais (1944–)

Amien Rais received his school education in a Muhammadiyah school in Solo. He undertook undergraduate studies in Political Science at Universitas Gajah Mada in Yogyakarta, after which he took a PhD at the University of Chicago, writing his thesis on the Muslim Brotherhood in Egypt.[87]

He returned to Indonesia to take up a lectureship in International Relations at Gajah Mada University. He became an increasingly vocal critic of the New Order Government. Though he was co-opted by the government to join ICMI in 1990, he was forced to withdraw after a dispute with President Suharto. This did not cause him to oppose ICMI, however. Indeed, he remained a strong supporter of the ICMI concept, and refuted the anti-ICMI critique from people such as Abdurrahman Wahid in the following terms:

> ... since the formation of ICMI, attacks and criticisms have been non-stop until now. In my opinion, this is a good sign. Because if ICMI came into being without any reaction from anyone, the ICMI infant could become stunted ... I always say that our friends in ICMI do not need to tremble from the external attacks and criticisms, because we have to take heart from the Sunna of the Prophet ...[88]

Rais thus regarded ICMI, taking a modernist view, as an expression of scriptural truth in modern form.

Rais's power base was consolidated in 1993 when he was elected as Chairman of the Muhammadiyah. After the fall of Suharto in May 1998, Rais formed the Partai Amanat Nasional (National Mandate Party), which endorsed Rais as its candidate for the Presidency.

Amien Rais played a key role in precipitating Suharto's resignation in May 1998, and suggested directly to the New Order President that he step down. In explaining why he did this, Rais expressed his reasons in Islamic terms: 'I considered it as *wajib kifayah* (social obligation with religious implication) to speak up

---

[86] Cf. Barton 1997.
[87] *Tempo*, 11 January 1999.
[88] Rais 1995:281–2.

against what was clearly wrong. ABRI, Golkar, the other parties and the NGOs were silent. So, *Bismillah* (in the name of Allah) I braved myself to be the one to say it.'[89]

He was also outspoken in his calls for people to renounce violence in the 1998 chaos and sectarian conflict in Indonesia. In response to killings and rapes of Chinese around that time, he stressed in his statements that the Chinese are of Adam's flock too, and they should be protected, pointing out that there is no basis in the Qur'an or the Hadith for rioting or victimising the Chinese.[90]

Rais sees a firm link between the Muhammadiyah and the reformist Masyumi party that was banned by the Sukarno government in 1960. He has expressed opposition to the call by some for an Islamic State for post-New Order Indonesia,[91] given the diversity of the country. When pressed on this point in interview with an international Islamist periodical in July 1998, Rais commented as follows:[92]

Rais: I know the term Islamic State is very sensitive in my country. If I used the term Islamic State, there will be many groups in my country who will try to undermine my position.

Interviewer: In other words, it is your strategy?

Rais: Well, you are entitled to read between the lines in your own way. What matters is the substance.

Interviewer: There is nothing wrong in having the Qur'an as the constitution.

Rais: Yes, but to manage a modern state, you have to have a complete book of law. I think the Qur'an is not a book of law, it is a code of law – it is a source of law – so you cannot make a source of law as a book of law.

Amien Rais has written a vast number of articles in newspapers and journals. His writings have been collected into two volumes: *Cakrawala Islam: Antara Cita dan Fakta* (1987) and *Tauhid Sosial: Formula Menggempur Kesenjangan* (1998).

Cakrawala Islam: Antara Cita dan Fakta, his first book, comprises a selection of his essays which address a range of Islamic issues and

89 MSA News, 1 August 1998, [msanews.mynet.net/MSANEWS/] copied 30 July 1999.
90 *Republika Online*, 16 May 1998.
91 *Tempo*, 11 January 1999.
92 *Crescent International*, 1–15 September 1998, 6, 10.

challenges. These place a particular focus upon political issues and matters of state and the role of Islam in the modern world. His second volume, *Tauhid Sosial: Formula Menggempur Kesenjangan*, appeared after Rais had been occupying the position of Chairman of Muhammadiyah for some years, and it therefore gives an invaluable insight into the thinking at the upper echelons of that organisation. The very unique title of 'Social Tauhid (Monotheism)' is Rais's own creation and represents his attempt to fuse faith with society, a goal which modernist reformists had long set themselves.

Chandra Muzaffar (1947–)

Another important Muslim writer, thinker and political activist on the Malaysian stage is Chandra Muzaffar, an academic whose comments on contemporary events in Malaysia have been heavily critical of Government policies, the West and of Islamic revivalist groups.

With regard to the first of these, Chandra has particularly targeted authoritarian government as a focus of his criticism, and this caused dissatisfaction within Government ranks to the extent that he was detained for several months in 1987 under the Internal Security Act.

Following his release, he devoted himself to establishing and consolidating the Just World Trust (JUST). During the decade following his arrest Chandra built JUST into an influential international network, with branches in seventeen countries, including Australia, New Zealand, the United States, the United Kingdom, Sudan and Iran. Chandra succeeded in attracting to the JUST international advisory board a number of prominent leftist intellectuals including Professor Noam Chomsky, the late Erskine Childers, and Professor Richard Falk.[93]

During the 1990s Chandra found common ground with Prime Minister Mahatir in attacking the West for what the two deemed an inadequate and unbalanced view of human rights.[94]

His anti-western views come through clearly in his essay 'Japan, Islam & The West: Peaceful Coexistence Or Conflict? An Asian Muslim Viewpoint',[95] written as a response to Samuel

[93] Indikt 1997.
[94] *Far Eastern Economic Review*, 22 December 1994, 20.

Huntingdon's theory on the Clash of Civilisations. In this response, Chandra engages in powerful apologetics on behalf of Islam, refuting a series of challenges. These include the charge by Huntingdon that Islam is inherently undemocratic, to which Chandra responds as follows:

If we looked at Asian countries which have moved away from totalitarian or military rule to civilian and democratic forms of governance in the last 10 years, we would observe that two of the most significant instances are from the Muslim world. Pakistan with 120 million people and Bangladesh with 110 million people, today boast of active electoral politics, a multi-party system, a vibrant non-governmental organisation (NGO) community, a vocal media and an independent judiciary.

Chandra also takes the opportunity in this essay to refute claims that Islam is intolerant of other faiths and minorities.[96] In his response he demonstrates a familiarity with the broad sweep of Islamic history, saying:

Islam and Muslim empires, by and large, have an excellent record of treating non-Muslim minorities with respect and decorum. The seven hundred and fifty years of Muslim rule in Andalusia which witnessed the generous accommodation of Christians and Jews in almost every sphere of society was not the only outstanding example of Islamic tolerance. Many of the Uthmaniyya and Mughal rulers were also renowned for their accommodative attitude towards their non-Muslim subjects. Here in Malaysia, the Melaka Sultanate displayed a high degree of tolerance in its relations with the cosmopolitan population of the port of Melaka.

Chandra concludes his essay with a reference to the Qur'an providing the most appropriate framework for peaceful co-existence, saying:

the Holy Quran never tires of emphasising God's mercy and compassion for all human beings and indeed for all creation. It is this all-embracing, all-encompassing mercy and compassion that should be the essence of peaceful coexistence among all civilisations.

However, Chandra is no backward-looking neo-normative revivalist. Indeed, he has been as critical of Islamic revivalists as he has

---

95 [www2.jaring.my/just/Asia-jap.html] copied 31 July 1999.
96 Cf. Muzaffar (1995) for his views opposing communalism in Malaysia and arguing for universalism and pluralism being intrinsic to Islam.

of the West and of Malaysian Government policy. He has demon-strated neo-modernist leanings towards the concept of *ijtihad* in saying that 'even within the Qur'an and the Sunna there has to be a creative relationship'.[97] He rejects the approach of neo-norma-tive revivalists when he stresses that the message of the Qur'an has to be placed within changing contexts and not frozen in a particu-lar social paradigm:

Islamic resurgents ... are completely trapped in an exclusive concept of Islam dominated by laws and rituals and symbols.[98]

The targets of his criticism have not been merely *da'wa* groups such as *Darul Arzam*, but indeed PAS has aroused his ire because he con-siders that it has never championed the cause of the non-Muslim poor. Chandra ironically points out that PAS's sense of justice and compassion is confined to their co-religionists. He writes:

The Islamic Party of Malaysia (PAS) has all along demanded the 'restora-tion of Malay sovereignty' primarily because of the indigenous status of the community. What is important to us is that its demand has invariably been presented in the name of Islam.[99]

And further:

this negative attitude of various Muslim groups exposes the real nature of their political struggle. It is just another way of preserving Malayism.[100]

In an overall sense, Chandra is somewhat dismissive of the Islamic resurgence in Malaysia, saying that '... the impact of the present resurgence appears to be largely negative'.[101]

Chandra's influential place in Malaysian society was recog-nised when he was appointed as Director of the new Centre for Civilisational Dialogue at the Universiti Malaya in March 1997.[102] This Centre was responsible for co-ordinating the compulsory first-year course entitled 'Islamic and Asian Civilisations' that reaches almost 6,000 students throughout the Malaysian

---

[97] Muzaffar 1985:26.
[98] Muzaffar 1985:28.
[99] Muzaffar 1998:156.
[100] Muzaffar 1998:159.
[101] Muzaffar 1985:33.
[102] Though his roller coaster relationship with Malaysian authorities nose-dived when his appointment to this position was not renewed in 1999.

university system. More broadly, Chandra described the function of the Centre as 'the only centre of its kind in the world. It seeks to promote dialogue at the intellectual level among different civilisations.'[103]

Chandra has served for several decades as a type of public conscience, holding the leading actors on the Malaysian political and religious stage to account.

JAKIM Documents

Another source of influential writings on Islamic thought during the last years of the period we are examining was the Department of Islamic Development of Malaysia (JAKIM) in the Prime Minister's Department. As part of the official Islamisation programme, JAKIM set out to distinguish clearly between acceptable and unacceptable Islamic doctrine, speaking in terms of what it considered to be 'deviationist teaching'. JAKIM documentation defines deviationist teachings as follows:

any teachings or practices which are propagated by Muslims or non-Muslims who claim that their teachings and practices are Islamic or based on Islamic teachings, whereas in actual fact the teachings and practices which they propagate are contrary to Islam which is based on the Al-Qur'an and al-Sunna and against the teachings of Ahli Sunna Wal Jamaah.[104]

The document which provides the above definition proceeds to outline the history and sources of deviationist teachings in Malaysia. It identifies two primary sources: spiritual (*batiniyya*) teachings and theosophical (*wujudiyya*) teachings. Chief culprits for the first of these are identified as follows:

- *Kashf al-Asrar*, translated and compiled by Mohammad Salleh bin Abdullah Al-Mangkabowi in 1922
- *Hidayah Al-Anwar* by Syed Ghazali Jamalullail of Penang, written in 1933
- *Hakikat Insan* (1985) and *Ilmu Tajalli*, both written by Ahmad Laksamana bin Omar of Kelantan

---

103 [www.jaring.my/just/justmedia_mc.htm] copied 31 July 1999.

104 'Deviationist Teachings in Malaysia 1996', The Department of Islamic Development of Malaysia, Prime Minister's Department, [www.islam.gov.my/sesat/BI/deviatio.htm] copied 6 November 1999.

The deviationist *batiniyya* teachings are accused by JAKIM documents of attributing fictitious allegorical interpretations to Qur'anic words and phrases where more literal interpretations should be made. Furthermore, the *batiniyya* writers are accused of saint worship and advocating segregation from society.

With regard to the deviationist teachings derived from theosophy and the seven grades of God's emanation, the names of the early Malay mystics Hamzah Fansuri, Shams al-Din al-Sumatrani and 'Abd al-Ra'uf al-Singkili are identified as early proponents of these theosophical teachings by JAKIM documentation. It should be noted that Nur al-Din al-Raniri escapes such accusations, evidently earning a vote of orthodoxy from JAKIM theologians. A slightly later Malay theologian who is also considered as non-orthodox by JAKIM is Muhammad Nafis al-Banjari (d. 1778), on the basis of his work *Durr al-Nafis*.

The doctrines of the theosophical writers are attributed by JAKIM to Hindu and Neoplatonist sources. The JAKIM writers take particular umbrage with theosophical concepts that advocate direct communication between the student and God, as well as with the belief that religious teachers can attain the status of the Perfect Man.

The JAKIM documents on deviationist teaching identify victims of these teachings as being the ignorant, those lacking the dedication to study sacred scripture, those who have gone astray, liberals, rationalists and Islamic modernists. The documents then proceed with a comprehensive listing of those groups officially declared to be deviationist by JAKIM. Also provided is a historical overview of each movement and a specification of the precise doctrinal reasons why each is judged to be non-orthodox. The groups thus identified all fell victim to JAKIM accusations of heterodoxy during the 1990s, and include the following:

- The Anti-Hadith Movement, which spread throughout Malaysia after its founding in 1985, and which rejected the Hadith as a source of Islamic Law, as well as the basic Islamic doctrines concerning God's decree and predestination.
- The Darul Arqam movement, a neo-normative group which withdrew from society and established communes.
- The Martabat Tujuh/Sakaratul Maut group, founded in 1990 by Hamzah Embi of Selangor and accused of espousing

theosophical doctrines based on seven grades of God's emanation, including the Light of Muhammad.

- Tarekat Aurad Ismailiah, founded by Mahmud Haji Abdul Rahman in 1979 and accused of attributing Mahdi status to its founder as well as practising non-orthodox worship rituals including chanting 'praises to Allah loudly accompanied with intermittent beatings of the rattan to the tempo of the chantings while in the state of unconsciousness'.[105]

- The Yahya group of the Tarekat Naqshbandiyya, which was founded by Kadirun Yahya of Medan and entered Malaysia in the 1970s during the period of great expansion by *da'wa* groups. This group stands accused by JAKIM documentation of believing Kadirun Yahya to be the recipient of light (*Nur*) from God originally sent into the body of the prophet Muhammad and passed on through his descendants down to the modern day.

It can be seen from the above discussion that JAKIM's campaign against such groups is consistent with reformist attacks on various Sufi groups throughout the history of Islam, both in the Southeast Asian region and beyond. Such groups stand accused of undermining core doctrines and rituals of Islam and promoting beliefs in the supernatural powers of particular holy men. Other reformist movements which shared such concerns were the Wahhabis of the Arabian peninsula in the 18th century, the Padris in Sumatra in the 19th century, and a range of 20th-century Islamic reformists, both revivalist as well as modernist.

CONCLUSION

The Islamic thinkers discussed in the previous pages by no means represent an exhaustive list of modern Malay–Indonesian writers on key Islamic themes. Rather, they have been selected to provide a taste of the issues and inclinations of Southeast Asian Islamic writers in the 20th century.

The focus of this section has fallen upon themes and ideas, rather than the writers who have produced them. The following themes stand out as co-existing, and at times competing, in the Malay–Indonesian Islamic community of the late 20th century.

---

[105] [www.islam.gov.my/sesat/BI/aurad.htm] copied 12 November 1999.

Affirming the authority of the sources

Many of the writers surveyed manifested a primary determination to affirm the authority of the Islamic original sources: the Qur'an, Hadith collections and Islamic legal manuals.

Some of the Southeast Asian Islamic writers surveyed take a very scripturalist approach, prioritising the text over context, or engaging with issues of the modern world through a clearly scripturalist filter. The PAS thinkers surveyed fall very much into this category. The article by Nik Abdul Aziz Nik Mat discussed attempts to relate an event from the life of Muhammad to modern scientific explanations. Likewise, his PAS colleague Usman Hadi Awang is clearly scripturally driven, giving priority to the 7th-century Islamic texts in resolving detailed (and some would say irrelevant) modern day issues. Their inclination, like that of their party, is towards traditionalism rather than neo-normative revivalism.

Affirming modernist approaches

Another key theme to emerge from the works examined is a keen interest in, and affirmation of, a modernist approach. The essence of this approach is a willingness to engage with a re-evaluation of the primary Islamic sources to account for modern challenges, but a commitment to a holistic view of Islam as providing, through re-evaluation, answers to the demands of the modern world.

Thus we see in the writing of Hamka a commitment to rational argument, through reference to scripture, and a clear connection made with modern context. He addresses one of his primary concerns, namely a weakening of Islam among the Malay/Indonesians in the face of contemporary secular intellectual rationalism. He shows his modernist leanings also by roundly rejecting a separation between sacred and secular.

Likewise, Hadikusuma is committed to re-addressing the age-old debate on the subject of God's preordination of events. He shows concern that a viewpoint which exclusively focuses upon divine predestination can lead to indolent fatalism. He exhorts his readers to be energetic in their life's efforts and to take charge of their destinies inasmuch as Islamic orthodox belief allows.

Syed Muhammad Naguib Al-Attas eloquently argues that Islam is a rich storehouse of modern scientific knowledge and method. His efforts to link Islam with modern science are strongly reminiscent of modernist approaches seen elsewhere in the Islamic world.

Finally, Amien Rais' concept of 'Social Tauhid' represents his attempt to fuse faith with society, a goal entirely germane to the views of 20th-century modernists and central to the policies of the Muhammadiyah organisation which he came to lead in 1993.

Accommodating pluralism: the neo-modernists

A number of the writers surveyed engage with the challenging issue of how Islam should respond to pluralism in the modern world. They consider whether Islam should retreat to a purely scripturalist position, as would be the response of the leading PAS thinkers, or whether some accommodation should be made to changing times and circumstances.

Anwar Ibrahim stresses that Islam can and should adapt to multicultural and multi-religious social settings. He dismisses scripturalist approaches of Islamic traditionalists and radicals as hollow and irrelevant to the modern world. Similarly, Abdurrahman Wahid does not see the details of *fiqh* as being permanent. Rather, these legal codes based on the divine law need to be dynamic to reflect changing times and circumstances. In his view, Pancasila represents just such an outcome of adaptation of the divine law to contemporary circumstances, and provides a very effective framework for managing a pluralist society.

Anwar Ibrahim is inclined to separate religious issues and observance from the workings of the modern state, to prevent minorities feeling excluded from the structures of state. In this he is in harmony with Nurcholish Madjid, who affirms Islam as providing answers to modern challenges but rejects the combination of Islam and politics via Islamic political parties. Nurcholish's calls for reform in social and political affairs, with an emphasis on attaining 'a civil society', are again motivated in large part by a pluralist desire to ensure that all groups in society find fulfilment in the way the state is structured.

Harun Nasution's writing engages with the theme of pluralism from a different angle. His stout defence of the orthodox nature of Mu'tazilite thinking represents an attempt to achieve an inclusivist approach to a diverse faith, rather than adhering to a compartmentalised separation between orthodoxy and heterodoxy. Thus he is inclined to pluralism within Islam, making allowances for divergent viewpoints within a diverse faith. His writing provides us with a window into the ancient debate regarding the respective priorities of reason and revelation which has resurfaced on regular occasions throughout Islamic history.

Likewise, Nurcholish Madjid diverges from the modernists in affirming traditional Islamic thought as providing solutions to modern challenges such as pluralism, rather than requiring dramatic latter-day reinterpretations of the sources. Furthermore, he calls for the Islamic basis of modern solutions to be expressed within a national context – 'keIndonesiaan'.

It is on the basis of such differentiation from certain modernist approaches that the term 'neo-modernism' has been coined in recent scholarship. It could be usefully applied to this group of scholars.

Apologetics and polemics

The inclination towards accommodationist pluralism on the part of some Islamic writers does not mean that Islamic thought of a more adversarial type is no longer evident in Southeast Asia. Indeed, one still hears voices which loudly and clearly articulate ideological and religious oppositions.

A disdain for the West, and for a Christianity seen as a product of the West, is highly visible in the writings of some Malaysian and Indonesian Islamic scholars. Al-Attas speaks in a strongly stereotyping way in attacking western Christianity as a corruption of the original teachings of Christ. This is anti-Christian polemical writing at its most potent. In a similar vein, Hasbullah Bakry's writing is quite polemical, and sets out to undermine the fundamental tenets of Christian belief, and to portray established Christianity as a false, corrupt creed. Both Bakry and Al-Attas belong within a tradition of Muslim polemicists going back to the classical period.

Chandra Muzaffar's comments on contemporary international politics and society have been heavily critical of the West, though his focus is less theological than that of the two writers mentioned in the previous paragraph. However, Chandra's criticisms are directed towards other targets as well; both Islamic revivalist groups, and Malaysian Government policies have come under fire. To this extent the polemical edge of Chandra's writing is arguably more balanced, as he is prepared to subject all to a cutting scrutiny.

A clear polemical style characterises documentation about 'deviationist' Islamic sects produced by JAKIM in the Prime Minister's Department. This body, founded and funded by the UMNO-dominated Malaysian Government as part of its own Islamisation programme, has aggressively sought to identify non-orthodox Islamic groups in the 1990s which it deems to pose a threat to Islamic orthodoxy in Malaysia. The teachings of such groups are scrutinised by JAKIM, with banning orders issued by the Malaysian Government if their teachings are considered to fall outside the core doctrines found in the Qur'an and *Sunna*.

In this context, polemic and accusations of heterodoxy in all its forms is broadly associated with Islamic reformism, be it of the modernist variety or of a more revivalist variety harking back to a 'Golden Age'.

Rehabilitating Sufism

A further theme to occur in some of the writings examined is a concern to work towards a rehabilitation of Sufism. This was necessary as Sufi approaches had clearly experienced a process of marginalisation during the 20th century, in contrast with the Sufi dominance in the region during the 16th to 19th centuries. The onslaught of modernism and revivalism throughout the 20th century had taken its toll on Southeast Asian Sufism, and several scholars were determined to do their bit to bring about a resurgence.

A key agent in this process of rehabilitation was Hamka. However, his interest was not in affirming all Sufi practice uncritically. On the contrary, he was a vigorous critic of syncretism in Islamic worship, especially where there was clear evidence of un-Islamic spiritual influences upon Islamic practice. Rather, through a clear enunciation of what he saw as acceptable Sufi belief and practice, via his writings on Sufism, Hamka contributed to a process of rehabilitation for the mystical path in Indonesian Islam.

Further, we see this process developed in the life and writings of Muhammad Zuhri. Though this figure's influence is much more localised than that of Hamka, he nevertheless provides an insight into what is taking place increasingly at the regional level in Java. His original contribution is via a presentation of the Sufi path through late-20th-century social action approaches. This methodology is designed to make Sufism appear relevant to modern times, and also to deflect the powerful modernist critique of Sufism as being too 'other worldly' and thus irrelevant.

Postscript: what about the revivalists?

Note should be taken of the absence of clearly discernible neo-normative revivalist writings in the preceding discussion. This does not mean that they have not been produced by Southeast Asian writers this century. On the contrary, revivalist thinking can be clearly seen in a number of documents, such as the *jihad*-driven 1949 *Proklamasi Negara Islam Indonesia* (Proclamation of the Islamic State of Indonesia) by Kartosurwirjo, the leader of the abortive Darul Islam rebellion following the Indonesian achievement of independence from the Dutch:

> God willing, this Holy War or Revolution will continue until: the Islamic State of Indonesia emerges safe and secure, externally and internally, 100% de facto and de jure, in all of Indonesia; all forms of occupation and slavery disappear; all enemies of God, enemies of the faith and enemies of the State are driven from Indonesia; the Laws of Islam apply perfectly throughout the Islamic State of Indonesia.

However, such documents have never exerted anything other than marginal influence on the direction of events in Muslim Southeast Asia this century. Neo-normative revivalists have never looked like gaining power in any Southeast Asian Muslim society. And the revivalist calls for revolution, seen above and so prevalent in the Middle East in the latter half of the 20th century, have been absent from mainstream opposition groups such as the political party PAS in Malaysia and the social organisation Muhammadiyah in Indonesia.

For this reason we have not dwelt on the revivalist phenomenon in a Southeast Asian context. Significant conclusions can be drawn from the absence of discussion of this phenomenon.

12

EXEGESIS IN MODERN SOUTHEAST ASIA

After the compilation of 'Abd al-Ra'uf al-Singkili's *Tarjuman al-Mustafid* in the late 17th century, Qur'anic exegetical activity in the Malay language appears to have entered a very fallow period for almost 300 years. Individual writers rendered odd Qur'anic verses into Malay in order to inform their studies of the various Islamic sciences, but there is no evidence of a Malay scholar having attempted to author another full and comprehensive commentary upon the Qur'an in Malay until after the Second World War. Clearly *Tarjuman al-Mustafid* represented a major watershed in the study of Islam in Malay. This work came to represent the apogee of Malay-language exegetical activity, and it can be argued that this has remained the case up until the present day.

Federspiel[1] identifies three generations of exegetical activity in modern Indonesia as follows:

1. The period from 1900 to *c*. 1960, during which only partial translations and commentaries on the Qur'anic text were undertaken by Indonesian scholars.
2. The period from *c*. 1960, during which full translations and commentaries of modest volume were produced.
3. The period from the 1970s until the present day, when Indonesia has witnessed the production of increasing numbers of what Federspiel terms 'enriched commentaries'. By the mid-1990s there were ten full commentaries on the Qur'an available in Indonesian.[2]

---

[1] Federspiel 1994:130.
[2] Federspiel 1994:72.

The second-generation commentaries have proved to be enormously popular. Mahmud Yunus' *Tarjamah Quran Karim* has had twenty-three reprints, a testimony to its seminal role in the study of the Qur'an in modern Southeast Asia. However, its contribution has been very much in rendering the text meaning of the Qur'an rather than undertaking detailed exegesis by engaging with some of the more specialist areas of Qur'anic studies, such as philosophical argumentation or addressing the variant readings (*qira'at*). This was characteristic of this generation of commentaries, which include a number rendered into regional languages. An example is Mohammad Adnan's *Tafsir al-Qur'an Suci* which bases itself upon a verse-by-verse translation of the Qur'anic text into Javanese. Adnan, a faculty member of the IAIN Sunan Kalijaga in Yogyakarta from 1952 to 1969, completed this work in 1977 and it was published four years later.[3]

With regard to the third generation of commentaries, which includes the works by Hamka and Ash-Shiddieqy, another dimension of exegetical activity is reached, in terms of the breadth of source material referred to by the authors and the scope of the exegetical commentary accompanying the translations of the Qur'anic text. It is this generation of scholarship which makes an attempt to carry on the work of 'Abd al-Ra'uf in the late 17th century.

Federspiel makes the important point that, as with the first- and second-generation works of exegesis in Indonesia, the third-generation commentaries 'stress the meaning of scripture rather than its science'.[4] Nevertheless, the development of exegesis as a science should be seen as a process rather than an end product. We will now turn our attention to an examination of two of these third-generation commentaries, namely those by Hamka and Ash-Shiddieqy, to understand what stage exegesis has reached in modern Southeast Asia and to gain an insight into the interests and preoccupations of Malay–Indonesian exegetes.

HAMKA'S TAFSIR AL-AZHAR

Feener aptly describes this work as 'one of the most enterprising endeavors of modern Qur'anic exegesis, not just in Southeast

---

[3] Adnan 1981.
[4] Federspiel 1994:61.

Asia, but in the Muslim World in general'.[5] It is thus worthy of attention for this reason alone. Moreover, a consideration of Hamka's *Tafsir Al-Azhar* provides many insights into the educational formation and theological orientation of this leading Indonesian Islamic figure. The influence of his father as a leading reformist thinker in the Minang area, supplemented by the contact with reformist thought during his period in Java, makes itself abundantly clear in a number of ways in Hamka's commentary.

The target audience

Hamka states quite overtly in the introduction to his commentary that this work was intended to target a specific audience. This audience consisted of two groups. The first group is represented by young Indonesian Muslims for whom Hamka felt a responsibility to provide a clear sense of direction in their theological formation. Hamka believed that young Muslims in Indonesia and, indeed, in the broader Malay-speaking world, were thirsting during his time for a more comprehensive and rigorous study of the Qur'an than was available, but that they were held back by limited Arabic-language skills. Hamka described the need of this group metaphorically: 'they can see the house in the distance but not the path to get there.'[6] Hamka intended that his commentary should provide that path.

The second group which Hamka was targeting in writing his commentary involved those who were active in *da'wa* (mission): i.e. those who were teaching or preaching the Islamic faith. Again Hamka was concerned that members of this group most frequently did not have an adequate mastery of Arabic, and as a result the effectiveness of their work was compromised. Moreover, this group needed good resources to be able to carry out their task of *da'wa* in the face of the challenge from modern intellectuals, which represented a new challenge not faced in previous centuries by Indonesian teachers of Islam. Again Hamka intended that his commentary should provide this group with the tools necessary to carry out their task effectively.

Hamka's concern in defining his audience along the above lines clearly reflects the influence upon him of reformist ideology. He

[5] Feener 1998:62.
[6] Hamka 1967: vol. 1, 2.

was concerned with a weakening of Islam in the face of contemporary secular intellectual rationalism, and he was particularly troubled by the potential for young Muslims in the Malay-speaking areas to be deflected from the Islamic path by these influences. His goal was thus to provide these groups with the means to meet and overcome modern intellectual challenges and to reinforce the basic Islamic principles which were under threat in the area.

Ingredients for the exegetical task

In a sense, it could be said that Hamka demonstrated an exclusivist approach to Qur'anic interpretation, in that he called for a recognition of the importance of mastering a wide range of skills before attempting a task of Qur'anic exegesis. He set, as conditions for writing a commentary: a complete mastery of Arabic; a detailed understanding of previous works of exegesis; and a broad-ranging knowledge of associated works, such as the *Asbab al-nuzul*, and the prophetic Traditions, as well as works of jurisprudence. Thus his approach was not populist; he did not call for all Muslims with minimal exegetical tools to undertake this task.

However, he presented himself and his work as being well equipped to meet the needs of the Muslim populace. In drawing up his commentary, Hamka referred to a broad collection of works, and in doing so he met the criteria which he had enunciated, as listed above. He referred to various works of exegesis in Arabic, as well as exegetical works in Malay and Indonesian, and various products of mystical Sufi writers, as well as writings relating to the prophetic Traditions and works relating to jurisprudence. The list of Qur'anic commentaries on which he drew reads like a *Who's Who* of Qur'anic exegesis; he mentions the commentaries by al-Tabari, al-Razi, Ibn Kathir, al-Jalalayn, al-Khazin, al-Nasafi, al-Shawqani, al-Baghawi, al-Alusi, Rashid Rida, Tontowi Jawhari, and Sayyid Qutb. To supplement these works, he also draws on the renderings of the Qur'an into Malay and Indonesian by leading Indonesian scholars, such as Mahmud Yunus and Ash-Shiddieqy.[7]

---

7 Hamka 1967: vol. 1, ix–x.

The function of the commentary

Hamka's lengthy introduction to his multi-volume commentary is devoted to an explanation of basic knowledge about the Islamic sciences for the benefit of his readers. In this, he wishes to ensure that his readers have a solid grounding in basic elements of belief. Hamka points to the great diversity of knowledge in the Islamic sciences, while at the same time stressing that it is normal practice for specialists to be strong in some areas but weak in others. He speaks quite openly about his own areas of strength and weakness. He points out to his readers the different orientations of the chapters of the Qur'an which were revealed in Mecca and Medina, with the former being devoted to core belief and criticising idolatry and traditional worship practices, while the Medinan chapters focus on details relating to the establishment of a community, in terms of laws, punishments, interstate relations, and other appropriate matters of detail. Hamka develops his analysis of the Qur'an to a considerable degree of detail to ensure that those readers who lack the preliminary knowledge which he indicated was a prerequisite would gain this knowledge from *Tafsir al-Azhar*.

Hamka goes on to argue passionately that the text of the Qur'an is perfect in every respect, and has been protected from interpolations or imperfections over the centuries. In this Hamka demonstrates an interest in apologetics; he is aiming to provide his students with arguments to counter rational criticisms offered by intellectuals and the West. Indeed, he is very critical of Western powers which colonised the Islamic world for trying to disrupt the tradition of children studying and memorising the Qur'an.[8]

Hamka points to Muhammad's own debates with the doubters who attempted, through rational argument, to undermine his teachings; thus he encourages his own readers to find strength in the fact that the prophet himself faced such intellectual challenges. In this, the influence of modernist reformism is quite overt, in drawing on challenges faced by the prophet to equip modern Muslims to deal with contemporary realities and challenges.

In focusing upon the inimitability of the Qur'an, Hamka echoes the concerns of the early 20th-century modernists, such as 'Abduh, who sought to marry the traditional with the modern.

---

[8] Hamka 1967: vol. 1, 8.

Hamka underlines the standard Muslim belief that Muhammad was illiterate, and thus he uses this as the basis for his argument that differences between the Qur'an and certain parts of the Bible do not point to Muhammad's imperfect study with Jews and Christians, because the very fact that he was illiterate and unlearned clearly demonstrates that he never studied with these groups. Thus, the differences in the texts must point to imperfections in the Bible rather than in the Qur'an. Again, Hamka is providing his own readers with a battery of arguments on which they can draw in their own debates with modern rationalist challengers.

In addition to these arguments, other information with an apologetic function is provided by Hamka for his readers, to equip them to face the rationalist challengers. Such information relates to the prophetic sections of the Qur'an, as well as information in the Qur'an which supposedly refers to scientific knowledge far ahead of its time. On this latter point, he diverges somewhat from the approach of 'Abduh, who was interested in presenting the Qur'an as consistent with modern science but avoided suggesting that hidden clues to modern scientific discoveries were contained within the pages of the Qur'an.[9]

Turning his attention to the science of Qur'anic exegesis, Hamka urges his readers to adopt a critical attitude in their use of exegetical works. For example, he encourages young Indonesian Muslims to use his commentary merely as a key to unlocking and unpacking the content of the Qur'an, rather than as an end in itself. This strategy by Hamka is designed to encourage his readers to develop their own *ijtihad*, or ability to critically engage with the sources in addressing modern issues, rather than blindly following the dictates of scholarly publications.

On the Isra'iliyyat

Hamka relates his discussion of Qur'anic exegesis to what he presents as the three most essential source materials for this Islamic science: namely the *Sunna*, or details of the prophet's life; the accounts of the Companions of the Prophet; and the writings of the *Tabi'un* (the Followers), or the generation which succeeded the prophet and the Companions.

---

[9] McAuliffe 1991:84.

At this point, Hamka indicates in a most forthright manner strong criticism of unreliable sources which have been used in drawing up certain Qur'anic commentaries. Such sources, which he indicates are full of fairy tales, relate to the *Isra'iliyyat*. Hamka points out that these stories were brought into Islam by Jewish converts who then transmitted them to Companions of the Prophet and the Followers, and subsequently certain commentators included these stories without commenting upon them. Hamka urges his readers to beware of works which draw on these stories, in a way which is strongly reminiscent of other reformist writings which urged Muslims to be on the lookout for corruptions in Islamic texts and tendencies towards syncretism. Hamka also suggests that these stories from the *Isra'iliyyat* can be used for positive as well as negative purposes when he says:

Sometimes we also copy *Isra'iliyyat* stories in order to demonstrate that these stories are entirely inconsistent with the meaning of the Qur'an. The purpose is to combat the influence of exegetical works which are circulating within our society and which are used as instruments for capturing the attention of congregations by irresponsible religious teachers.[10]

Having identified certain potential pitfalls in the field of Qur'anic exegetical writing, it is to be expected that Hamka identifies some of the chief culprits who have fallen into the *Isra'iliyyat* trap. Indeed, he does not refrain from levelling criticism at the prime offender in this regard; namely al-Khazin, and his commentary which played such a significant role in the development of Qur'anic exegesis in the Malay-speaking states. Hamka is highly critical of al-Khazin for adding to the Qur'anic stories with details drawn from unreliable sources. Hamka adds that it is immaterial whether al-Khazin was conscious of what he was doing or not, as the effect is the same: it pollutes the text of the Qur'an. Hamka states emphatically that the primary goal of stories should be to elucidate the text of the Qur'an, not to entertain the reader:

God's intention is very clear in using stories for purposes of revelation, not for use in fabricating fairy stories; i.e. not for novels or legendary accounts such as the Ramayana and Mahabharata epics. When an exegete

---

[10] Hamka 1967: vol. 1, 26.

examines some commentaries, such as al-Khazin's commentary, he will encounter a significant body of added material which diverts the intention of Qur'anic stories away from their didactic or guiding purpose, creating fairy stories which, consciously or not, have polluted the Qur'an.[11]

Hamka's preoccupation with criticising the *Isra'iliyyat* is unusual for Southeast Asian scholars of Islam. As seen in chapter 9 of this present study, Muslim scholars from Southeast Asia more typically avoided engaging in the debate relating to the Judaism/Islam divide, and this avoidance on their part had allowed the commentaries by al-Khazin and al-Baghawi to play a prominent role in the history of the development of Southeast Asian Islam, especially in the field of Qur'anic studies. Hamka's targeting of the *Isra'iliyyat*, though somewhat belated in terms of the region, nevertheless again points to the influence of reformist ideology as it is one of the clearest examples of a modern Islamic scholar from the region seeking to eradicate pollutions from local Islamic practice. Hamka does not mince his words in damning the *Isra'iliyyat*:

… the *Isra'iliyyat* are like an obstacle which blocks believers from accessing the truth of the Qur'an.[12]

Indeed, so preoccupied is Hamka with undermining the previous influence of commentaries which he considered were tainted by the *Isra'iliyyat,* that he devotes detailed attention to clarifying what the *Isra'iliyyat* are, for the benefit of his readers, to enable them to identify these stories where they occur. In this context, Hamka was treading a fine line, given the difficulty of separating the so-called *Isra'iliyyat* from other stories which he regarded as authoritative. For example, in describing the fall of the Children of Israel in his commentary, Hamka provides a level of detail about the exodus of the Israelites from Egypt which could only have come originally from Jewish sources, such as:

Their family numbers when they moved to Egypt, according to one account related by Ibn Mas'ud, was 93 people – men and women, and when they emerged from there under Moses' leadership 400 years later their numbers had grown to 670,000 people.

The identification of Ibn Mas'ud as the source of these details provides the account with a measure of authority in Islamic terms.

---

[11] Hamka 1967: vol. 1, 27.
[12] Hamka 1967: vol. 1, 31.

However, if Ibn Mas'ud was indeed the source, and that should not be taken as given, then the same questions should surround how he came by these details. The most likely source for him would have been Jewish communities, which were quite numerous in Arabia during the life of Muhammad and his companions. This would then cast these details within the realm of the *Isra'iliyyat* also.

In taking up the banner of reformism, and seeking to cleanse certain areas of Islamic practice in Southeast Asia, Hamka may well have been playing a role somewhat similar to that of 'Abd al-Ra'uf in the 17th century, whose mission as we have seen had been to stabilise a society which had previously been torn apart by theological polemics. Both were similar in that they sought to give a clear sense of direction to their readers, who had supposedly hitherto been subject to various un-Islamic accretions in practising their faith. Both used the medium of Qur'anic exegesis as a device for spreading their message; indeed, Hamka pays 'Abd al-Ra'uf a compliment by referring to his commentary in very favourable terms.[13] To this extent it would seem that Hamka should be more appropriately seen as the modern 'Abd al-Ra'uf rather than the modern Hamzah Fansuri referred to previously.

Models for commentary-writing

Thus having criticised the commentary by al-Khazin and by extension, al-Baghawi, and having rejected them as reliable sources for exegesis,[14] Hamka's next task was to identify which exegetical styles he saw as providing a reliable model for compiling his own work and for the benefit of his readers. He then distinguished between the two different approaches to exegesis of Ibn Taymiyya and al-Zamakhshari, and, in so doing, reopened the ancient debate concerning the place of revelation versus reason for his Indonesian audience. Hamka described the very structured approach of Ibn Taymiyya, who was opposed to the use of *ray'*, or individual interpretation or opinion. Hamka proceeded to contrast this approach by Ibn Taymiyya with that of al-Zamakhshari, whose exegetical methodology was very much based on *ray'*, in the belief that constant musing over Qur'anic verses would

---

13 Hamka 1967:21.
14 The very role which both had always enjoyed in the Malay–Indonesian world!

inevitably lead to new ideas and fresh perspectives which allowed for the dynamic element of exegesis to be kept paramount. This approach was also adopted by al-Ghazali, the great medieval scholar of Islamic mysticism.[15] Al-Ghazali had taught that exegesis of the Qur'an should carry the stamp of the individual commentator, who should nevertheless also foreground the works of previous commentators, and pay special attention to the *Sunna*, the writings of the Companions and those of the Followers.

Hamka supported this latter approach to exegesis. He felt that it was not enough merely to cite from previous exegetical work but that it was also important to draw on one's own views and experiences in order to address the specific requirements of the time in which the commentator found himself. Hamka identified specific needs faced by Muslims in his Indonesian community, which he described as 'a country where Muslims outnumber other religious groups, but where [Muslims] thirst for religious guidance, and thirst from a desire to know the secrets of the Qur'an'.[16] Thus by adopting the Zamakhshari/Ghazali approach to commentary writing, Hamka considered that he was able to fulfil his own personal goal; i.e. speak to the particular needs of his own people whose requirements in terms of Islamic guidance were not being met by previous scholars or their writings.

It is not surprising therefore that Hamka identified the *Tafsir al-Manar* by Rashid Rida as his admired model of exegesis. His choice was not only based on the fact that it addressed wide-ranging issues in the Islamic sciences, encompassing theology, the Traditions, jurisprudence and history, but also because Rida's commentary was attuned to contemporary political and social developments.

Finally, the inclination of 20th-century Islamic modernists to re-evaluate certain aspects of Mu'tazilite doctrine, such as the debate about free will versus predestination, had an impact on Hamka, though he does not overtly engage with the Mu'tazilite debate as a major aspect of his writings, as does for example Harun Nasution. But at various points of his commentary, there are suggestions that Hamka is inclined towards human responsibility and freedom of action within the framework of Ash'arite orthodoxy, rather than

---

15 Cf. Heer 1998:48–54.
16 Hamka 1967: vol. 1, 37.

being concerned to stress a more predestinarian view. In his commentary on Q18:29, in explaining the phrase 'And whoever so wishes, then he will abandon faith', Hamka comments:

Because you are each given intellectual capacity ... If you are strong in faith, you will save yourself, because you have followed the voice of your own intellect. And if you wish to abandon faith, then the one who will bear the consequences of this apostasy is none other than you.[17]

Yet this reference to humans being able to save themselves is not expressed within a vacuum, as earlier in Hamka's comment on this verse he stresses that the framework of truth which enables people to make correct choices comes from God – 'Truth is above us all.' Thus his brief engagement with the free will versus predestination debate at this point of his commentary is consistent with an Ash'arite orthodox viewpoint. But it is expressed in a way which gives full weighting (within an Ash'arite framework) to human freedom of action, and in this Hamka shows his leanings towards 20th-century modernist thinking which was seeking to re-evaluate debates dating from the time of the Mu'tazila.

ASH-SHIDDIEQY'S TAFSIR AL-NUR

Another significant name in the field of commentating upon the Qur'an in modern Indonesia is that of T. M. Hashbi Ash-Shiddieqy.

His principal work in the field of Qur'anic exegesis, entitled *Tafsir al-Nur*, first appeared in 1956, some ten years before Hamka's *Tafsir al-Azhar*. A second edition appeared in the mid-1960s.[18] Ash-Shiddieqy's contribution to Qur'anic exegesis in Indonesian is much more matter-of-fact than that of Hamka. While the latter was concerned with providing a substantial introduction to his commentary upon the Qur'an, explaining the rationale for the approach which he took, Ash-Shiddieqy was more concerned with getting on with the job, as it were.

His multi-volume commentary – one volume is devoted to each *juz'* of the Qur'an – is focused and is rigorously structured according to a set format. Ash-Shiddieqy does not generally enter

---

17 Hamka 1992: vol. 15, 199.
18 Ash-Shiddieqy 1964.

too deeply into exegetical polemics, unlike the case of Hamka, who railed against the influence of the *Isra'iliyyat* in his introduction, as we have seen. Where Ash-Shiddieqy does encounter differences of opinion among his sources, he cautiously either presents varying viewpoints or identifies briefly his reasons for selecting one viewpoint over another, without being seen to challenge the very authenticity of these alternative viewpoints.

An examination of Ash-Shiddieqy's exegetical style would be beneficial. For our purposes we will look at one verse: the very significant first verse of Chapter 17 of the Qur'an, which refers to the prophet Muhammad's Night Journey. The text of the verse is as follows:

Glory to (God) who did take His Servant for a journey by night from the Sacred Mosque to the Farthest Mosque, whose precincts We did bless, – in order that We might show him some of Our Signs: for He is the One Who heareth and seeth (all things).

After presenting the text, Ash-Shiddieqy provides a summary of the meaning; namely that Muhammad was transported from Mecca to Jerusalem and back in one night. So that his readership is not deflected from the primary goal, Ash-Shiddieqy then promptly spells out the purposes of this verse, which he sees as being:

1. To demonstrate signs and wonders as evidence of the Unity and Omnipotence of God.
2. To provide open, not hidden, evidence of God's power.
3. To refute those who challenge Muhammad's authority; i.e. the Jews and the Quraysh.

Ash-Shiddieqy then refers to the difference of opinion between certain Islamic scholars as to the point from which Muhammad commenced this trip, but he does not resolve that particular issue for his readers. He similarly indicates some difference of opinion regarding the actual date of the journey; we encountered this earlier in examining Nik Abdul Aziz Nik Mat's discussion of the Night Journey. However, in referring to the debate about whether the journey was carried out only by the spirit of Muhammad or whether he was physically transported from Mecca to Jerusalem, Ash-Shiddieqy presents the varying viewpoints but aligns himself with one particular view in this case; namely the received opinion, expounded by al-Tabari, that the journey referred to the physical transportation of Muhammad, first to Jerusalem where he prayed with the prophets, and thence on to Heaven.

With regard to the detail of the latter part of this journey – the journey through the Heavens together with the Archangel Gabriel – Ash-Shiddieqy again presents briefly the difference of opinion regarding the issue of Muhammad's supposed negotiation with God about the number of daily prayers to be performed by the faithful. However, the author does not elaborate on this debate. He states in distinct terms that he supports Abu Bakr al-Baqillany, who rejects the account of the negotiation as being inauthentic. Ash-Shiddieqy rounds off his treatment of this verse by summarising the main purpose of the verse as being to refer to Muhammad's Night Journey from Mecca to Jerusalem, with the specific purpose of its serving as a sign of God's omnipotence.

This commentary is quite user-friendly. Its use of a standard format facilitates the task of the student in employing it for ready reference in reading particular Qur'anic verses, and Ash-Shidieqqy clearly aimed for his commentary to be accessible to as wide an audience as possible.[19] Ash-Shiddieqy's commentary draws on a range of classical sources, thus providing its readership with a broad mix of earlier expert opinion, though the core of his commentary is drawn from the 20th-century work of *tafsir* by the Egyptian al-Maraghi (d. 1945).[20] Where there is a difference of opinion between his various sources, Ash-Shiddieqy only provides his own opinion if he considers the issue to be crucial. Where controversies are of less importance, in his opinion, Ash-Shiddieqy either makes no mention of them or presents them for consideration by the reader without endorsing one particular point of view.

The modern commentaries on the Qur'an by Hamka and Ash-Shiddieqy represent the product of the resurgence of exegetical activity among Southeast Asian scholars of Islam, after many centuries of silence. The gap of several hundred years between the commentary by 'Abd al-Ra'uf of Singkel in the late 17th century

---

[19] Feener 1998:62.
[20] Feener 1998:62.

and the appearance of these two commentaries in the 1960s is puzzling for students of Indonesian Islam. Nevertheless, the fact that 'Abd al-Ra'uf's commentary continued to be widely circulated and used during the 18th, 19th and indeed the 20th centuries suggests that there is not as much of a hiatus as might first appear. However, the contributions to Qur'anic exegesis by Hamka and Ash-Shiddieqy signalled the commencement of a period of greater activity by Indonesian scholars of Islam in this particular field of Islamic Studies,[21] and their efforts are likely to act as significant signposts for Southeast Asian Qur'anic exegetes for some time to come.

STUDIES OF THE ASBAB AL-NUZUL

The *asbab al-nuzul* in particular, and the Hadith reports in general, played a significant role in the century and a half following the death of Muhammad in terms of their exegetical function, at a time when the production of discrete and specialised commentaries on the Qur'an was discouraged. Moreover, this important function of the *asbab al-nuzul* collections did not cease once the production of specialised Qur'anic commentaries commenced, but continued throughout the centuries in all corners of the Islamic world.

Some compilations of the *asbab al-nuzul* achieved a significant reputation over the years. One of the most reputable was that produced by the famous Jalal al-Din al-Suyuti (d. 1505), entitled *Lubab al-nuqul fi asbab al-nuzul.* We saw earlier how al-Suyuti's famous commentary, the *Tafsir al-Jalalayn,* produced in conjunction with his teacher Jalal al-Din al-Mahalli, had a significant impact in the Malay world through two routes: first, the distribution of the Arabic original, and second, as the primary source for 'Abd al-Ra'uf's Malay commentary *Tarjuman al-Mustafid.*

Al-Suyuti's compilation of the *asbab al-nuzul* has left a significant mark in the modern Malay–Indonesian world through its translation into Indonesian by Shaleh, Dahlan and Dahlan. In the preface to the Indonesian version,[22] the Indonesian translators clearly identify al-Suyuti's classic work as their principal source, and they also stress the importance of a study of the *asbab al-nuzul*

---

[21] Feener (1998:60) notes an 'unprecedented explosion in the production of exegetical works in a number of Southeast Asian languages' from this time onwards.

[22] Shaleh *et al.* 1984: 9–13.

to help Muslims better understand the contents of the Qur'an in a passive way, as well as to be better equipped to engage actively in Qur'anic exegesis. They state this as follows:

... the verses of the Qur'an were revealed within a variety of contexts ... In order to better understand the Qur'an, it is necessary to know the background to its revelation, commonly referred to as the *asbab al-nuzul* (circumstances of the revelation). In knowing the circumstances of the revelation of the verses of the Qur'an, we will better understand the meaning and intention of these verses, and will dispel confusion in interpreting them ...

However, the authors do not merely attribute this opinion to themselves. In support, they cite some of the greatest Islamic writers:

Imam al-Wahidi believes that a correct interpretation of a verse of the Qur'an cannot be done without knowing the context of the event and the revelation. Ibn Daqiq al-'Id believes that an explanation of the context of the verse's revelation represents a reliable path to understand the meaning of the Qur'an. Ibn Taymiyya believes that knowing the circumstances of the revelation of a verse assists us to understand the meaning of the verse, because knowing the context of the revelation provides the foundation of knowing its cause. There have been cases in history where reformist scholars experienced difficulty in interpreting some verses of the Qur'an. After they consulted the *asbab al-nuzul*, their confusion disappeared.

The Indonesian authors' skills in source criticism have thus opened a door into classical Islamic literature for their readership.

They are not content to just cite the various *asbab al-nuzul* accounts. Rather they advocate that these accounts should be subjected to scrutiny to ensure that they are reliable. In this way, they are advocating a type of critical approach which is in harmony with modernist views, and which represents a challenge to more traditionalist approaches:

Imam al-Wahidi believes that a discussion of the *asbab al-nuzul al-Qur'an* cannot be valid without knowing the details of its transmission or hearing directly from the people who witnessed its revelation, as well as knowing its causes and engaging substantially with the knowledge surrounding it.

In *The History* it is recorded that Muhammad ibn Sirin addressed a question to 'Ubayda regarding the meaning of a verse in the Qur'an. 'Ubayda replied: 'Be faithful to God, and admit honestly that the people who know when these verses were revealed have already passed away.' Because of that, in order to grasp the above-mentioned event, it is necessary to examine closely the account of the revelation of the specific verse, based on the Hadith of the Prophet.

Just as 'Abd al-Ra'uf used the Jalalayn commentary as his core and supplemented it with secondary sources in producing his own commentary, Shaleh, Dahlan and Dahlan have chosen to supplement their rendering of al-Suyuti's study of the *asbab al-nuzul* with additional Hadith reports drawn from other sources, which they list in their bibliography. They also state that al-Suyuti's *Lubab al-nuqul fi asbab al-nuzul* shares much in terms of Hadith reports with the Jalalayn commentary. Al-Suyuti chose his Hadith reports from a range of sources, principally the writings of al-Wahidi (d. 1076), but also from the six canonical Hadith collections, as well as the *Sunan* of al-Baihaqi, the *Musnad* of Ibn Hanbal and the commentary of Ibn Jarir.

Thus the Indonesian rendering of al-Suyuti's *Lubab al-nuqul fi asbab al-nuzul* serves as an important instrument for the transmission of the thinking of a range of early Islamic scholars. It reinforces critical modernist approaches which advocate use of *ijtihad* even in assessing the reliability of Hadith accounts.

The popularity of this work – the first edition quickly sold out and the 1984 version represents the fourth printing – further confirms its importance as an instrument in the transference of Islamic thought to the Malay–Indonesian world.

STUDIES OF THE VARIANT READINGS

In chapter 2 we explored the place of the variant readings within the field of Qur'anic studies and we examined their significance during the formative stages of Islam in the Islamic heartlands. We also touched upon the interest in the variant readings in early Malay Islamic works, principally the commentary on the 18th chapter of the Qur'an contained within Cambridge MS Or. Ii.6.45 and in 'Abd al-Ra'uf's *Tarjuman al-Mustafid*. But what of the modern era? What place does study of the variant readings have in Islamic scholarship in modern Southeast Asia?

While Ash-Shiddieqy's commentary includes a six-page discussion of the *qira'at* in its introductory section, it does not attempt to systematically present these readings throughout its multi-volume exegetical discussion as occurs in 'Abd al-Ra'uf's *Tarjuman al-*

Mustafid. Likewise, Hamka's *Tafsir Al Azhar* has much to say in expansion of narrative detail and theological issues, but it avoids entering into the linguistic details characteristic of Arabic-language classics such as al-Baydawi's commentary or, indeed, *Tarjuman al-Mustafid.*

So how do Indonesian Muslims learn about the *qira'at* in the present era? In fact, the study of the *qira'at* has come to be viewed very clearly as an area for specialists, with the result that little information on this subject is available in popular publications. This fact becomes clear when we consider where information on the *qira'at* can be found.

Discussion of the variant readings can be found mainly in two types of published works. First, introductions to Qur'anic translations and commentaries often contain discussion of the variant readings. Examples are: Ash-Shiddieqy's *Tafsir al-Nur,* and *Al Quraan dan Terjemahnya,* a rendering of the Qur'anic text into Indonesian which was promoted and funded by the Government Department of Religion in the early 1970s – this work devotes two pages to this subject in its introduction of 132 pages.

Second, the variant readings form the focus of a small number of specialist studies, such as Shalihah's *Perkembangan Seni Baca Al Qur'an dan Qiraat Tujuh di Indonesia.*

Al Quraan dan Terjemahnya

The preparation of *Al Quraan dan Terjemahnya* resulted from an initiative of the Department of Religion of the Indonesian New Order Government; indeed it represented a key component of the Government's five-year plan.[23] In addressing the variant readings, this work provides a summary which accords with the key elements of an orthodox Muslim perspective on the readings. It outlines the process of canonisation of the Qur'anic text, focusing upon the preparation of the 'Uthmanic edition, which it presents as the watershed event of the canonisation process.

However, in discussing the presence of variant readings, the editors of *Al Quraan dan Terjemahnya* are willing to refer to textual variation as evidence of error, though in doing so they identify

---

[23] Federspiel 1994:64–5. This work was supplemented in 1975 by the Government funded *Al Quraan dan Tafsirnya* in eleven volumes.

their source as the great classical scholar Ibn Khaldun. The discussion includes the following statement:

> The Qur'anic script could produce differences in reading, because the 'Uthmanic edition was written by the Companions, whose writing skills could not be considered as among the best, as is explained in the work *Muqaddima Ibn Khaldun*.[24] In this work, Ibn Khaldun says: 'Notice the effects which were caused by the script of the 'Uthmanic edition, which was handwritten by the Companions themselves. Their writing was not so good, with the result that sometimes written errors occurred, if considered from the perspective of skilful writing.'

The editors of *Al Quraan dan Terjemahnya* give further guidelines as to relative reliability, by stating that the seven readers identified by Ibn Mujahid reported genuine readings, while the extra three readings from the system of ten are less reliable, and the extra four from the system of fourteen are weak.[25] They also provide evidence of what they consider as fringe *qira'at*, pointing to those that add words to the Qur'anic text, such as the reading of Sa'd b. Abi Waqqas which added the phrase *min umm* to the Qur'anic phrase *la-hu akh aw ukht*.[26]

Given the wide distribution of *Al Quraan dan Terjemahnya*, we are able to reach some useful conclusions from the above discussion. The editors were concerned to inform their modern Southeast Asian readers about the process of evolution of the Qur'anic text, and were not afraid to provide evidence of variation on textual record due to a range of factors, including errors by the Companions of Muhammad. They were also concerned to provide clear guidelines to assist their readers with reconciling this information with standard Muslim claims about infallibility of the Qur'anic text. These guidelines included a clear distinction between reliable and less reliable information, and examples of readings which were clearly not to be trusted.

Shalihah's The Seven Readings in Indonesia

This work was originally written as a postgraduate research dissertation. After completing his research, Shalihah published his

---

[24] Cf. Ibn Khaldun 1967.
[25] *Al Quraan dan Terjemahnya* 1974: 131.
[26] *Al Quraan dan Terjemahnya* 1974: 131.

study, with the published version now widely available in Islamic bookstores in Indonesia.

Shalihah's study is wide-ranging, addressing issues such as the miraculous nature of the Qur'an, intricate details relating to recitation tones and styles, the emergence of the variant readings of Qur'anic words and phrases, and Qur'anic institutes in Indonesian which serve as centres for mission.

In discussing the variant readings, Shalihah identifies pedigree sources. He draws on the great 14th-century scholar Ibn al-Jazari (d. 1350) to present information on categories of the readings, ranging from *mutawattir* (firm) to *mudraj* (interpolated). This reflects scholarly rigour on the part of Shalihah, as Ibn al-Jazari was one of the most prolific and reputable writers on the subject of the *qira'at*.[27] Shalihah is concerned to educate his readers to make choices, not merely reporting on variation in the Qur'anic textual record, but also giving clear mechanisms for separating the reliable from the unreliable.

At times, Shalihah's argumentation lacks clarity, such as when he draws on Ibrahim 'Uthwa 'Awd to explain why the Qur'an was revealed in seven readings. On the one hand he argues that the seven readings represent different dialects of Arabic, then shortly afterwards he argues that the seven readings represent one dialect – that of the Quraysh – which absorbed elements of other dialects.

The Wisdom of the Qur'an was revealed in Seven Readings. Ibrahim 'Uthwa 'Awd explains this as follows ... [First] to facilitate the entire community of Islam, especially the Arab people who had received the Qur'an directly, because the Arabs themselves comprised various ethnic sub-groups. Among these sub-groups were differences in dialect and intonation in communicating, ... When reading the Qur'an, if they had all been obliged to adhere to one script (one reading system), this would have represented a burden for them. [Second] to unify the modern Islamic community by a single language which could unify them, namely the language of the Quraysh, through which the Qur'an was revealed and which encompasses multiple pronunciations of the Arabs ... The Quraysh absorbed what was attractive and chose what was pleasing from the pronunciation of the various ethnic Arab delegations which visited them from all corners and upland plains. They then selected and refined them, and absorbed them into their own language which was moderate and considered appropriate by the Arabs as a standard

27 Ben Chereb 1979:48.

language. On account of these exact reasons, the Qur'an was revealed in seven readings.

Nevertheless, central to his approach is a concern to transmit the frequently-heard Muslim scholarly explanation that the seven readings were provided in the revelatory process to facilitate the pronunciation of the Qur'anic text by Muslims within different linguistic contexts.

Thus Shalihah's study serves as an effective instrument for drawing on reputable classical sources to transmit orthodox Muslim viewpoints about a key subject in Qur'anic studies, namely the variant readings of the Qur'anic text.

The writers surveyed in this chapter all share a common goal: a determination to affirm the authority of the Islamic primary sources – the Qur'an, Hadith collections and Islamic legal manuals. This is done in various ways.

First, the second half of the 20th century witnessed the re-emergence of substantial Qur'anic exegetical writing in the Malay–Indonesian language, after a lengthy hiatus. With the completion of 'Abd al-Ra'uf's Qur'anic commentary around 1675, the Malay world had to wait almost 300 years before the appearance of detailed commentaries in Malay/Indonesian on the whole Qur'an. The *Tafsir al-Azhar* by Hamka and the *Tafsir al-Nur* by Hashbi Ash-Shiddieqy represent the beginning of a veritable explosion in exegetical writing in the modern era by Malaysian and Indonesian scholars.

Common to reformist goals, the new commentary writing was conducted in such a way as to attract a mass audience. Exegetical styles chosen were accessible to non-specialists. Moreover, Qur'anic exegesis was included in mass periodicals, as we saw in the previous chapter in our discussion of Abdul Hadi Awang.

Second, recent decades have seen an intense effort being undertaken by Malaysian and Indonesian scholars into new translations of classical Arabic works dealing with the primary sources. An example is the Indonesian translation of al-Suyuti's classic study of the *asbab al-nuzul*, a work which assists Muslims to better engage actively in Qur'anic exegesis.

Furthermore, recent Southeast Asian Islamic scholarship has addressed the study of the variant readings of the Qur'anic text, or the *qira'at*, a subject which had attracted much interest from 17th century Malay scholars but which seemed to have fallen out of the Malay spotlight afterwards. However, in the modern era this subject has come to be viewed very clearly as an area for specialists, with the result that little information on this subject is available in popular publications. In this context, Shalihah's modern study of the *qira'at* presents a variety of information drawn from reputable classical sources, and thus plays an important role in the process of transmission of Islamic thinking.

Apologetic writing is also evident in the literary products of Southeast Asian Muslim thinkers in recent decades. Hamka demonstrates an interest in apologetics in preparing his commentary on the Qur'an, as he goes to considerable lengths to provide his students with arguments to counter rational criticisms offered by intellectuals and the West.

Thus we again find similar themes to those encountered in chapter 11. The unifying factor is the dominance of non-Sufi reformist thought, centred upon a commitment to use the primary Islamic sources to engage with the challenges of the modern world.

13

PERSPECTIVES ON POPULAR PREACHING (1983–98)

A perusal of holdings on the shelves of Islamic bookshops throughout Indonesia and Malaysia during the 1980s and 1990s very quickly demonstrated the considerable amount of activity which took place during the period in the publication of works relating to Islam. Many of these materials were priced at an accessible level for the general public, and did not assume a great degree of specialist training.

Nevertheless, much publication of Islamic materials in Southeast Asia was also conducted with an eye to reaching a more specialist audience. In this context, it is noticeable that Islamic bookshops contain a number of recent re-editions of more specialist works such as the following:

- A multi-volume translation into Indonesian of the classical commentary by the Jalalayn.
- A multi-volume new edition of *Tafsir al-Azhar* by Hamka.
- Several translations into Indonesian of works by the classical Arab thinker Ibn Taymiyya, who has come to be regarded as a great model for contemporary radical Muslim theologians around the world.
- Translations into Indonesian of the widely distributed commentaries by Yusuf Ali and Muhammad Ali.

Publication of works on Islamic Sufism also continued, though they do not preponderate, which points to the diminishing profile of Islamic mysticism in the public face of Southeast Asian Islam in the modern era.

This chapter focuses upon an examination of popular preaching and Islamic comment by contemporary Islamic scholars and leaders presented in printed and electronic forms. Works consulted for this study appeared between 1983 and 1998. Such an examination will assist our study in several ways. First, it will complement preceding chapters, which focused on Islamic writings by specialists for more specialised audiences, by placing a focus on Islamic thinking for the Muslim masses of Southeast Asia. Second, it will enable us to track issues and ideologies which are perceived as relevant by Islamic congregations. Third, it will enable us to assess how Islamic religious leaders proceed with the task of educating their congregations.

Moreover, such a study will provide an insight into the use made by the Indonesian and Malaysian Governments in the period up to 1998 of Government-controlled media outlets for their respective Islamisation programmes.

Attention is devoted to Islamic comment in various forums. The era of modern technology offers a wide range of vehicles for Islamic preachers to use in educating their audience and, indeed, for Governments to influence their constituency: published sermons; devotional columns; Islamic programmes on the electronic media; audio and video cassettes dealing with religious issues; and other instruments of mass communication.

THE PRINT MEDIA

Various tools are available to Islamic preachers wishing to access a substantial and non-specialist audience via the print media. First, there are written publications designed for a popular audience distributed in bookshops. These include published collections of sermons from Friday mosque services. Second, there are the devotional columns in the news media – newspapers, magazines and popular journals – used by Islamic scholars for the dissemination of Islamic teaching at a popular level. Both the collections of sermons and the columns in periodicals are typically pithy and are presented in bite-sized pieces so that the audience will be able to read and digest the particular lesson being presented without requiring a considerable commitment in their time, energy or attention.

In an attempt to grasp the flavour of such popular Islamic publications, an examination was carried out of several volumes of published sermons as well as columns in widely-available

Indonesian and Malaysian periodicals. Several general character-istics of these materials were striking:

- The language used in the sermons and columns was often laden with Arabic loanwords, which now form a part of stan-dard Islamic discourse in Indonesian/Malaysian.
- The sermons and columns examined were heavily impreg-nated with references to and excerpts from the Qur'an and Hadith. Again, this serves to increase the tone of authority of the particular piece of discourse by overtly linking it with revealed scripture.
- In certain instances, the preachers made reference to writings by non-Muslim western scholars, where such writings accorded with their particular perspective, to add authority to their particular pronouncements.

One of the principal newspapers examined was *Republika*, which featured prominently in the Indonesian New Order Govern-ment's programme to increase the profile of Islam in Indonesian society during the 1990s. *Republika* was established with the bless-ings of the New Order Government in 1991 as part of its con-trolled Islamisation drive, designed to capture a wave of increased Muslim religiosity among the population at large in response to domestic and international trends. This newspaper includes on a daily basis a devotional column entitled 'Hikmah', which is writ-ten by a range of authors, both male and female, and typically con-sists of two basic parts. First, a message or moral is introduced to the audience via a story or reference to Islamic scripture. The use of narrative as a tool for theological exposition in this context has been very popular throughout the history of Southeast Asian Islam. The second part of the column is then devoted to an inter-pretation of the story presented, or the scripture referred to, in the light of modern-day exigencies and contexts. In this way, readers are provided with practical guidance to help them address the day-to-day issues which they encounter in normal life.

Another newspaper examined was *Harakah*, the organ of the Parti Islam Se-Malaysia, which includes several devotional col-umns on a regular basis. This was supplemented by other local Malaysian publications, such as *Buletin Kelantan*, a publication of the state government of Kelantan, and *Buletin Al-Barakah*, the bul-letin of the mosque in Tikam Batu in the state of Kedah. As with

Republika, the columns in *Harakah*, *Buletin Kelantan* and *Buletin Al-Barakah* are written by Islamic authorities for a popular audience. Unlike the Indonesian newspaper in question, however, the Malaysian publications are not a product of national government policy. On the contrary, *Harakah* is the mouthpiece of the principal Islamic opposition party in Malaysia. As such, our study should provide certain interesting comparative perspectives on the Malaysian and Indonesian scene.

THE ELECTRONIC MEDIA

The television serves as an effective vehicle for the transmission of Islamic doctrine and for the holding of discussion forums on Islamic matters in both Malaysia and Indonesia. In both countries, a block of time is set aside for Islamic programmes at the beginning and end of the day on government-controlled television stations. An examination of a sample of these programmes on Malaysian and Indonesian television from the mid-1990s provides a series of interesting observations about issues in focus in both countries, as well as many points of convergence and a few points of divergence between their respective programming. This examination points to several themes as being popular among both programmers and viewers. It also clearly demonstrates the influence of modernist thinking on government-sponsored programmes of Islamisation in both countries. In this context, it is important to see television programming as demonstrating part of the Malaysian and Indonesian governments' efforts to Islamise their respective countries in a modernist way during the 1990s, rather than taking the more radical approach of Islamist governments in some other parts of the Muslim world.

KEY THEMES ADDRESSED

Islamic Scripture and its injunctions

The place of the Qur'an. The theme of the centrality of the Qur'an was the subject of entire sermons.[1] Readers were reminded that God had given a book as a guide to every inspired religion, with the Qur'an being the last and final revelation.

---

1 Chizbulloh 1983:76–81.

Readers were urged to read the Qur'an regularly, and both Qur'an and Hadith references were quoted in support of this. It was pointed out that if Muslims studied the Qur'an properly, then not only they but in fact the whole *umma* would prosper. Authors decried the fact that many Muslims only infrequently read the Qur'an, and stressed that it was the responsibility of parents to ensure that their children were provided with the skills necessary to engage in reading the Scripture.

Likewise the television programmes examined stressed the authority of the Qur'an. Viewers were reminded that the Qur'an could not be compared and was not comparable to any other work. Traditional images of fathers teaching their children the Qur'an were displayed as central to family life, and the relevance of the content of the Qur'an for practical issues in daily life was stressed throughout. Advice on a range of matters by the speakers on the particular programmes was based on Qur'anic quotations and excerpts from the prophetic Traditions.

Responsibilities of parents to children. The above-mentioned theme of parental responsibilities was developed more broadly in various sermons.[2] It was stressed that parents must not neglect their responsibilities to their children in this life as the reward in the hereafter for both parents and children depends on this. Parents were set four principal targets in educating their children: the provision of a detailed knowledge of the Qur'an which would serve as a blueprint for the life of the child; a broad knowledge of both general and religious matters; development of a child's character to manifest compassion and love, purity in mind and spirit, and respect and obedience towards parents; and pious and devout behaviour by the children concerned. A very clear statement was made as to the centrality of the Qur'an in this educational endeavour by parents, with the author saying 'the Qur'an should as far as possible be the principal basis and top priority in the educational formation [of children]'.[3]

Devotional columns in the newspapers also reinforced these themes. In a 'Hikmah' column in *Republika*, for example,

---

[2] Chizbulloh 1983:19–23.
[3] Chizbulloh 1983:21.

H. Tutty Alawiyah[4] quotes Q8:28 to demonstrate that children are given to parents to test their commitment to the holistic development (in body, mind and spirit) of their children. Thus the universal questions which surround the issue of parenting are addressed within an Islamic framework.

A number of television programmes chose to focus on a reinforcement of traditional roles according to age and position, both within the family and within society at large. Many of the programmes chose to select as authorities Islamic scholars who were elderly, presenting a traditional scene of young enquirers seeking advice from wise, elderly scholars.[5] Moreover, children were exhorted to show obedience and respect to their teachers at school.[6]

Considerable attention was devoted by a number of Malaysian television programmes to emphasising traditional roles for fathers and mothers in the family situation. It was suggested that negative effects on children could result when both parents worked, with children being left for a large part of the day with a nanny, with the result that the children often became more attached to the nanny than to their own parents.[7] Moreover, it was stressed that men were intended to work for an income, and women were intended to look after the home. Fathers were assigned an important role in providing religious education and guidance for the children, though this should be reinforced by religious instruction in the school, in order for children to achieve a balance between the material and the spiritual world. In summary, it was clearly stated that God had designated the father as the head of the family and the male as the leader over the female. Interviews were shown with ordinary citizens who were presented as being members of successful families and who reiterated these themes.[8]

Exemplifying correct behaviour. The theme of scriptural modelling of correct behaviour occurs regularly in sermons and devotional columns. The issue of *Republika* of 25 April 1996[9] provides an

---

4   H. Tutty Alawiyah, 'Alquran dan HAM Anak', *Republika*, 2 December 1996.

5   *Hikmah Fajar*, KCTI, 31 October 1995; *Nuansa Islam*, TVRI, 31 October 1995.

6   Malaysian TV, 20 October 1995.

7   Malaysian TV, 20 October 1995.

8   *Dari Pusat Islam*, Malaysian TV, 28 October 1995.

9   A. Yani Wahid, 'Shafa dan Marwah', *Republika*, 25 April 1996.

example. The first part of the 'Hikmah' column was devoted to the story of Hagar and Ishmael and the appearance of the Well of Zamzam. Various references to the Qur'an are made during the column to place the story within its scriptural context. The second part of the column is devoted to an interpretation of the story for today. A strong moral is enunciated explicitly, presenting the lesson that believers should not give up hope, no matter how adverse the circumstances in which they find themselves. God owns all and only God can give livelihood to his servants, and if the believer follows the guidance provided by the Qur'an, he will be rewarded as Hagar and Ishmael were.

In a 'Hikmah' column on a related issue,[10] the appropriate role and behaviour of women in the modern world is addressed. According to the writer, this should be based on four model women referred to in the Qur'an; namely Maryam, Aisha, Khadija and Fatima. Women are exhorted to follow the four model women identified as this will make them virtuous and will help them avoid being distracted by the glamour and ways of the modern world.

A topic addressed in the television programmes examined related to the pilgrimage to Mecca, and the responsibility of those who had undertaken the pilgrimage towards their fellow Muslims after their return.[11] Returning pilgrims were reminded that they were responsible to impart a recognition of the equality of all people, and to remain humble in their dealings with fellow Muslims after their return. At the same time, returning pilgrims were urged to assume positions of leadership because of their experience, and to become active in the Indonesian Association of Hajis.[12]

Encouraging ritual duties. On a related note, many sermons, devotional columns and television programmes seek to affirm core elements of Islamic doctrine and ritual which are enunciated in the Qur'an and Hadith.

Several 'Hikmah' columns were devoted to exhorting believing

---

[10] Almuzzammil Y., 'Wanita Teladan', *Republika*, 23 April 1996.

[11] *Hikmah Fajar*, KCTI, 31 October 1995.

[12] *Ikatan Persaudaraan Haji Indonesia* (IPHI).

Muslims to rise for the morning prayer; [13] these columns are discussed in more detail below. Likewise the importance of alms giving is addressed as an issue.[14] Moreover, one column decries the fact that in modern times often religious events are only carried out for ceremonial reasons.[15] The author cites the example of millions of Muslims who participate in the pilgrimage, one of the five pillars of Islam, merely for personal profile and a sense of personal pride. The author writes that it would be better for funds spent by such pilgrims to be devoted to welfare activities.

In another column, an author addresses the issue of the sacrifice of animals,[16] which is associated with the Feast of the Sacrifice during the month of pilgrimage, and its practical relevance for believers in today's world. Believers are exhorted to conduct an animal sacrifice when they have the means to do so, because it demonstrates their gratitude to God, their compassion for the underprivileged, and a sign that they will reject anything that distracts them from God's path, such as wealth, status and lusts.

Many of the television programmes examined, especially those produced in Malaysia, exhorted viewers to be devout in their practice of the faith, making their didactic goal quite overt. Prayer times during the day were specified and viewers were urged to be energetic in their prayers, as well as in their observation of the other Pillars of Islam.[17]

Doctrines and debates

Predestination versus free will.   At various points of this present study, the issue of free will versus predestination by God has arisen. This issue is regularly addressed in both popular literature and popular sermons in modern Southeast Asian Muslim societies.

In analysing contributions from Malaysian Muslims submitted between 1975 and 1983 to the Government-sponsored Islamic short-story-writing competition, Peraduan Cerpen Berunsur

---

13 Rachmad Saleh, 'Bila Fajar Menyingsing', *Republika*, 9 October 1996; D. Zawawi Imron, 'Bangun Pagi', *Republika*, 25 February 1998.

14 Muhammad Rozi, 'Mencuri Hak Si Miskin', *Republika*, 24 June 1996.

15 Fauzul Iman, 'Skala Prioritas Beramal', *Republika*, 30 April 1997.

16 A. Ilyas Ismail, 'Makna Kurban', *Republika*, 24 April 1996.

17 Malaysian TV, 20 October 1995.

Islam, Tahir found that a number addressed this very issue.[18] Contributors to these competitions are not usually established writers, but are typically individuals in the Malay community who are generally unknown in the literary world.

Moreover, popular sermons addressing this issue are readily available in published form to Indonesian and Malay Muslims and the language of such sermons is specifically chosen to maximise accessibility and comprehensibility among ordinary Muslims. A sermon on the question of predestination by Mustofa[19] provides an example of the types of sermons on this issue which regularly appear in Muslim Southeast Asia.

A striking feature of Mustofa's sermon is its reference beyond the limits of Islam to the points of view of the other monotheistic faiths in his preliminary discussion, to set the scene, as it were. Mustofa indicates that the debate about predestination versus free will has existed for centuries within all faiths, and he then refers to the two basic positions on this question within Judaism and Christianity. He expresses the competing positions among the People of the Book in Islamic terms, with the Islamic titles 'Jabariyya' and 'Qadariyya' used to identify different Christian and Jewish groups. The views of the former group are misunderstood by Mustofa. He indicates that this group considered that mankind was not responsible for sin; in fact, the proponents of what became Augustinian orthodoxy considered mankind directly responsible for sin and the resulting brokenness in the relationship with God.

The author then turns his attention to the history of the debate within Islam, and provides a simplified overview of divergent positions, focusing on the Mu'tazila who were champions of human free will, and their opponents who proposed that mankind was subject to divine predetermination of events since the beginning of time. Mustofa then urges his audience not to merely follow a particular school, but hints at the importance of compromise. He stresses the importance of returning to the Qur'an and *Sunna* for guidance on this point. He quotes *Sura al-Nisa'*, Q4:79:

Whatever good (O man!) happens to thee, is from Allah; but whatever

---

[18] Tahir 1989:293.
[19] Mustofa 1986:240–5.

evil happens to thee, is from thy (own) soul.[20]

In undertaking exegesis of this verse, Mustofa also draws on the *asbab al-nuzul*. His methodology is significant for two reasons. First, he does not clearly refute the Mu'tazila in their entirety, which is interesting given that their views have been regarded as heretical by orthodoxy for almost a thousand years. Second, he allocates a paramount role to scripture to serve as the key element in understanding God's will on this point, rather than a centuries-long accumulation of exegetical interpretation. In other words, he is responding to the calls of modernist Muslims not to be shackled by centuries of accumulated dogma but rather for the Muslim individual to exercise *ijtihad* by returning to scriptural sources directly in formulating one's opinions about particular matters of doctrine.

Mustofa uses a parable to illustrate his interpretation. He presents the analogy of an architect designing a house, where the blueprint which is drawn up before construction represents the preordained plan of action. If the house construction itself later diverges from this blueprint, then the builder has chosen to diverge and it is he, not the architect, who is responsible for this divergence and who must accept the consequences. Similarly, says Mustofa, God has provided guidance in the form of the Qur'an and *Sunna*, he has provided mankind with intuition, the five senses, reason, and the *shari'a*, and all of these show the way to happiness and Paradise. If an individual chooses of his own accord to leave this path, it represents his own choice and he must take responsibility for his own actions.

Thus, having provided a predeterminist framework inasmuch as God has provided clear signs for individuals to follow, humanity is nevertheless allowed a measure of freedom of action to diverge from this divine blueprint. In this, Mustofa's teaching falls within the boundaries of Ash'arite orthodoxy. Nevertheless, his approach to the issue makes clear allowances for a measure of human freedom of action when he says 'the actions of this evil person are the result of his own efforts, not making use of his powers of reason to do actions which are in accordance with God's predestined order.' Mustofa's approach is far less rigidly

---

[20] Ali 1989:209.

predeterminist than the approach taken in *Lubb al-kashf* over three hundred years earlier, when its author 'Abd al-Ra'uf al-Singkili writes 'Thereupon Allah inclines whoever He wishes towards faiths which have gone astray.'[21]

Likewise, many other modern works, such as *Kitab Tauhid* by the Muhammadiyah scholar Hadikusuma, take this same rather less predeterminist approach. In this context, Martin, Woodward and Atmaja point out that such an approach is now commonplace in sermons on the issue of predestination in Muhammadiyah mosques in Indonesia.[22]

The right of the individual to interpret. While much of the television programming examined, especially in Malaysia, stressed a more traditional approach to authority, many of the programmes, especially in Indonesia, allowed some room for the individual Muslim to interpret Qur'anic references along rationalist lines according to the modern world. This relates to the *ijtihad/taqlid* debate referred to in previous discussion.

For example, viewers were reminded that the Qur'an urges believers against doing something which they don't understand. This rejects the notion of *taqlid*, or unquestioning obedience to the injunctions of established dogma. In this context, in response to a question from one viewer about the role of experts, viewers were told that the Qur'an makes it clear that all people have access to it and are in a position to apply its teachings to their own individual context.[23]

A particular application of this principle highlighted in discussion on Indonesian television related to the interpretation of Q2:222, which specifies certain prohibitions in regard to menstruating women. Yusuf Ali renders this verse into English as follows:

They ask thee concerning women's courses. Say: They are a hurt and a pollution. So keep away from women in their courses, and do not approach them until they are clean. But when they have purified themselves, ye may approach them in any manner, time, or place ordained for

---

[21] Voorhoeve 1952:91–3.
[22] Martin *et al.* 1997:143.
[23] *Lazuardi Imani*, TVRI, 19 October 1995.

you by Allah. For Allah loves those who turn to Him constantly and He loves those who keep themselves pure and clean.[24]

The scholarly authorities on the programme examined were asked whether a woman in menstruation could touch and read the Qur'an. In response, the authorities indicated that several verses of the Qur'an specified that individual Muslims must be in a state of purity when touching and reading the Holy Scriptures, but that many scholars did not interpret this in a physical sense, but rather indicated that it related to the state of mind of the person concerned. Thus a person with evil thoughts or destructive emotions at a given time should not touch the Qur'an. Hence, a menstruating woman should look to her state of mind rather than her physical state to decide whether she was in an appropriate condition to touch and read the Qur'an.[25]

Affirmation of reformed Sufi approaches.   It would be unusual if an excursion into popular Islamic preaching in modern Southeast Asia did not reveal some traces of Sufi influence, which has been so crucial in the formation of the character of Malay–Indonesian Islam since the earliest period. Indeed, it was noticeable in the sermons, devotional columns and television programmes examined that far from Sufism being portrayed as passé or un-Islamic in any way, strong Sufi resonances were regularly present.

In the 'Hikmah' column of 17 May 1996[26] devoted to *istiqama* (integrity/uprightness in faith), the author begins by quoting a Hadith from *Sahih Muslim*, thus setting the necessary scriptural foundations for his theological exposition. The Hadith in question is as follows:

Qul amantu bi'llah thumma istaqim
(Say 'I believe in Allah', and then act with integrity)

The author then turns his attention to scholarly interpretation to clarify for his readers the significance of the Hadith in question. After making a passing reference to the strictly orthodox Maliki Qadi 'Iyad b. Musa (1088–1149),[27] who relates this Hadith to

---

24 Ali 1989:89–90.
25 Indonesian TV, 15 August 1995.
26 A. Ilyas Ismail, 'Istiqama', *Republika*, 17 May 1996.
27 Talbi 1978:290.

Q41:30 (thus affirming its authority), the author devotes his principal attention to statements of the anti-Hanafi Abu al-Qasim al-Qushayri (986–1072), author of the great mystical work of exegesis *Lata'if al-isharat*.[28] This Sufi master, who above all sought to reconcile mystical practice with the principles of the *shari'a*, is quoted as making a number of statements as follows:

- rewards await those possessing *istiqama*
- punishment awaits those who do not possess this quality
- for Sufis true holiness equals *istiqama*, rather than empty symbolism, which can lead astray
- *istiqama*, only possessed by the truly God-fearing, can lead to the realm of God (which has Sufi resonance of communion with God)

In order to provide his readers with practical guidelines for the implementation of scriptural injunctions in their daily lives, the author then sets out four conditions for attaining proper *istiqama*, and points to Q46:13–14 in support:

1. Adherence to monotheism
2. Adherence to Islamic Law
3. Sincerity in works/practice of the faith
4. Struggle for truth in both easy and difficult situations

In a similar vein, another 'Hikmah' column[29] affirms Sufism as a valid point of reference. The author quotes a simple Sufi poem at the outset, which depicts a Sufi musing on the complexity of seemingly simple human actions. The writer then develops this theme, showing that science proves that seemingly simple human physical processes in fact involve a very complex interworking of multiple human parts. Having established a scientific framework, the author adds that in observing this complexity, we can marvel at the greatness of God, who created humans in all their complexity and beauty. He then refers to Q95:4 and Q39:41 in support, and in his column he has thus interconnected Islamic scripture with modern science, and also affirmed the Sufi perspective which was presented at the outset of his column.

---

28   Halm 1986:526–7.
29   Syaefudin Simon, 'Puisi Sang Sufi', *Republika*, 19 February 1998.

Another 'Hikmah' column dating from February 1998[30] exhorts believing Muslims to find the energy to rise for the morning prayer. There are strong Sufi resonances in the writing style in this column; the author claims that the believer who rises for morning prayer will have a beautiful encounter with the Creator; he speaks of an 'inner voice' telling the believer what he must do; and he states that morning prayer serves to cleanse 'the mortal flesh through awareness of the spiritual, both exterior and interior, to become One'.

Television programmes which focus upon the methodology of the study of the Qur'an at times include Sufi themes. For example, in one programme examined, students of the Qur'an were encouraged in reading the text to repeat the names of God as they occurred in the text over and over again. This practice, associated with the well-established Sufi practice of *dhikr*, was urged upon students so that the attributes represented by the particular name being repeated – e.g. compassion, mercy – would enter the character of the student and would erase the worldly attributes of aggression, greed, and other negative qualities.[31]

Thus a reformed Sufism stands affirmed in such writings and television programmes. In giving voice to such views, the various organs of the media are attempting to woo a particular traditionalist segment of their constituency. But in the process, they are striving to lead to a rehabilitation of Sufism so that it will be seen as relevant to the modern world, in much the same way as was the case with the writings by Hamka and Muhammad Zuhri discussed previously.

Mimbar Ulama: the traditionalist contribution.   Another periodical which regularly includes a devotional segment is *Mimbar Ulama*, the monthly magazine of the Majelis Ulama Indonesia (MUI) (Council of Islamic Scholars of Indonesia). The MUI tends towards conservatism, and its imprimatur is placed upon a range of publications. The volume of sermons by Chizbulloh referred to in this present discussion, for example, carries a statement by the Central Java branch of the MUI endorsing the contents of the work.

Mimbar Ulama includes a devotional segment entitled 'Bekal

---

30 D. Zawawi Imron, 'Bangun Pagi', *Republika*, 25 February 1998.
31 TVRI, 15 August 1995.

Dakwah'.[32] The author regularly addresses similar themes to those discussed in preceding pages, such as the importance of correct behaviour based on Qur'anic injunctions. In one issue[33] the author states clearly that the most meritorious person is the one who can implement the Qur'anic injunction specified in Q3:104:

Let there arise out of you a band of people inviting to all that is good, enjoining what is right, and forbidding what is wrong ...[34]

The writer concerns himself very much with correct behaviour, and in another issue of *Mimbar Ulama,* Syureich asks the question 'Why must mankind repent?' He responds by stating that mankind has been punished because of continuing disobedience to God. People should remind themselves that they are not angels or prophets, but rather humans with flawed characters which are inclined to conflict and evil. Nevertheless, says Syureich, God always 'opens the door of repentance' out of His mercy and compassion, because if He didn't do so, everybody in the world would be destined for Hell.[35] Here again we find resonances of the fine balance between God's overall plan and a measure of human choice which was enunciated in the sermon by Mustofa discussed previously.

Subsequent devotional columns in *Mimbar Ulama* address pressing issues of the modern world: the role of women;[36] the problems of youth; materialism; and economic and theological poverty.[37] Again, the Qur'an and the *Sunna* are presented as the reference point for readers engaging with these issues. The writer stresses that problems such as these can be surmounted if Islam is followed in all aspects of life.

A flavour of anti-reformist traditionalism appears from time to time in devotional columns in *Mimbar Ulama.* A clear example occurs in the May 1997 issue, in which Syureich writes about the state of the spirit in the grave, in the intermediate stage between life and paradise. He draws on the Hadith reports of al-Tirmidhi and Ibn Majah, plus manuals of *fiqh,* to describe the process of

---

[32] Issues examined for this present study were written by H. M. Syureich.

[33] *Mimbar Ulama,* no. 222 (February 1997), 59.

[34] Ali 1989:154.

[35] *Mimbar Ulama,* no. 223 (March 1997), 56.

[36] *Mimbar Ulama,* no. 224 (April 1997).

[37] *Mimbar Ulama,* no. 225 (April 1997).

interrogation of the soul which takes place in the grave. At this juncture, Syureich speaks strongly in support of visitations to and prayers at tombs, arguing that such visits remind Muslims that they must prepare for the Hereafter. Syureich draws on *Tafsir al-Maraghi* to claim that the prophet Muhammad eventually came out in support of the notion of visits to tombs. In taking this approach, Syureich has set himself against received wisdom among reformist Muslims which has generally criticised an over-preoccupation with tomb visitations, seeing it as an example of Sufi syncretism.

Islam and the modern world

Affirmation of modernist views. In 'Hikmah' one finds frequent references to cases where the content of Islamic scripture is portrayed to be in harmony with scientific knowledge and the requirements of the modern world. This effort to affirm the link between modernity and Islam is germane to the ideas of the great fathers of 20th-century Islamic modernism, Muhammad 'Abduh and Rashid Rida, as well as to the doyen of pan-Islamic thinking in the late 19th century, Jamal al-Din al-Afghani.

An example of this was seen in 'Hikmah' of 19 February 1998[38] referred to previously. In another such case, Didin Hafidhuddin[39] focuses on the close link between Islam and knowledge, and provides copious quotes from the Qur'an relating to knowledge and those who possess knowledge (Q11:14, Q39:43). In doing so, Hafidhuddin is leading up to his main point that the Islamic doctrine of *Tauhid* (Oneness of God, monotheism) demonstrates the unity of Islam and knowledge.

In taking this approach, Hafidhuddin is providing an essentially orthodox portrayal of the separateness of God and his creation. There is no suggestion of the immanence of God in his creation which characterised Malay Sufi writing in the 16th to 18th centuries. This is to be expected, given that the modernist thinking typically focused upon a transcendent deity separate

---

38 Syaefudin Simon, 'Puisi Sang Sufi', *Republika*, 19 February 1998.

39 Didin Hafidhuddin, 'Prinsip Tauhid', *Republika*, 14 June 1996. Hafidhuddin is a graduate of the IAIN Syarif Hidayatullah in Jakarta and the Institut Pertanian Bogor (IPB). He has taught on the staff of both IPB and Ibn Khaldun University in Bogor, where he served for a time as Dean of the Faculty of Shari'a. He has published widely on Qur'anic exegesis. Cf. Hafiduddin 1987:38.

from his creation and a shunning of Sufi teachings focusing on the immanence of God.

The ultimate conclusion in Hafidhuddin's article is that the greater one's knowledge, the greater one's awareness of *Tauhid*. Here again are resonances of modernist thinking, which attaches a high priority to modern education of Muslims and which has led to the development of many networks of modernist Islamic schools teaching Islamic subjects alongside secular scientific fields of study.

On a different issue yet similar tack, the 'Hikmah' column of 9 October 1996[40] addresses the dawn prayer and the discipline it inculcates in Muslims. The author points out that at the time of the dawn prayer, people are in deep sleep; thus their natural inclination is to wish to continue sleeping. The call to prayer at this time thus forces people to struggle against their mortal natures. Moreover, according to the author, it provides each individual with a healthier body and spirit, as medical and psychological research shows that the body and mind are more active in the early morning, the most productive time for a wide range of activities. Thus heavily implicit in the author's message is the notion that Islam accords with human needs and scientific knowledge (as reflected in the research findings mentioned). Islam is again portrayed as being consistent with the modernist thought of people such as al-Afghani, 'Abduh, and Rida.

Also addressing the topic of the morning prayer, 'Hikmah' of 25 February 1998[41] similarly exhorts believing Muslims to find the energy to rise in the early morning. The author draws on the Hadith to cite Muhammad's call to morning prayer – thus providing the requisite scriptural authority for his sermon – and warns that 'laziness and indolence will result in great [individual] loss'. Thus Islam again is portrayed as relevant to modern life, because it provides a framework for hard work, diligence and commitment, from which each individual will benefit.

In the 'Hikmah' column of 2 December 1996, H. Tutty Alawiyah[42] concerns herself with the rights of the child. She claims that the United Nations declarations on the rights of the

---

[40] Rachmad Saleh, 'Bila Fajar Menyingsing', *Republika*, 9 October 1996.
[41] D. Zawawi Imron, 'Bangun Pagi', *Republika*, 25 February 1998.
[42] H. Tutty Alawiyah, 'Alquran dan HAM Anak', *Republika*, 2 December 1996.

child and the teaching of the Qur'an are entirely consistent. In making this claim she too is affirming the belief in the relevance of the Qur'an to today's world.

Modernist influences on images and themes were quite clearly evident in both Malaysian and Indonesian Islamic television programmes. Many of the programmes were run as call-in shows, where scholars would initially discuss a theme and then viewers would be invited to ring the television stations to make comments or pose questions. This interesting use of modern technology resulted in certain anachronistic images. An instance was provided by one programme which centred upon a mixed-gender panel of experts, who made reference to Qur'anic texts in answering questions posed by the viewers, but whose discussion was accompanied by announcements that viewers could compete for a prize of 250,000 Rupiah[43]-worth of goods, including hair spray, perfumes, face cream, other cosmetics, and bleaching lotion. The winner of this prize needed to provide the correct answer to the question 'At what age did Eve die?' and have their name drawn from all those who correctly answered the question.[44] It is interesting to speculate whether viewers who took part in this contest were more interested in learning about the content of the Qur'an or in winning the prizes on offer.

Another example of such programmes adapting themselves to the context of the modern world was found in the depiction of gender roles. Previous discussion pointed to a traditional depiction of these roles on Malaysian television, and yet the very same television programme included a portrayal of male roles as somewhat more modern than might first be thought. For example, there were images displayed of fathers assisting with the dressing of the children, fathers were also urged to look after the health of their children, and there were strong statements that both father and mother should be involved in the upbringing of children. And, on the other hand, it was interesting to observe that often the principal hosts of such call-in programmes on Indonesian television were women.[45]

While Malaysian Islamic programming was generally more inclined towards traditional images than its Indonesian

[43] Equal to approximately US$120 at the time the programme was broadcast.
[44] *Lazuardi Imani*, TVRI, 19 October 1995.
[45] *Nuansa Islam*, TVRI, 31 October 1995.

counterpart, this was by no means a clear-cut distinction. For example, the block of time allocated for Islamic programmes in the morning on Malaysian television not only included discussion sessions and Islamic songs, but also, of course, the sounding of the call to prayer. Curiously, the call to prayer was at times juxtaposed with advertisements which depicted very modern scenes; among these was an image of a very shapely pair of female legs advertising stockings.[46]

Addressing daily concerns. The 'Hikmah' column also sets as one of its goals the discussion of issues of daily concern which affect the masses. In this, it is casting its net widely in reaching out to its target audience. This reflects the ambition of the editors of *Republika* to reach as wide an audience as possible through its devotional column.

Some 'Hikmah' columnists demonstrate a concern for modesty in dress, especially as it relates to women. For example, the column of 31 May 1996[47] addresses the vexed question of Islam and beauty pageants. The author starts by quoting Q7:26, which states that God gave Adam clothes to cover his nakedness. Having thus set the scriptural framework, the author turns his attention to the Miss Indonesia pageant, part of the Miss Universe contest. The evils of beauty pageants in the mind of the author are outlined, and the author underlines this by pointing out that foreigners are appointed to judge Indonesian contestants. Turning back to the scriptural framework defined earlier, the author exhorts people to use clothes to demonstrate their devoutness. He presents a quote from the Hadith, and then moves from general injunctions to specific recommendations by calling for young women to wear headcovering, and for men and women to be separated in swimming pools.

Another issue of concern to vast numbers of people is the ageing process. A column from June 1996[48] addresses it and the fears it holds for many people. The columnist provides his scriptural stage at the outset, citing Q40:67 which states that God gives

---

[46] *Tamadun Islam*, Malaysian TV, 19 October 1995.
[47] Bachrawi Sanusi, 'Aurat, Ratu, dan Perenang', *Republika*, 31 May 1996.
[48] Farid Nasution, 'Tua itu Indah', *Republika*, June 1996.

each person a different length of life. He lists the effects of the ageing process: outward signs, physical, mental, and psychological effects. Up till this point, he has essentially painted a portrait of the very factors which many people fear. Thereafter comes the didactic element. The author concludes that if the ageing process is part of God's plan, why should people fear it? He quotes a Hadith in support of this line of argument, and then lends further support by presenting a positive view of the rewards of old age: grandchildren, time for hobbies, time for good deeds.

Elsewhere the burning issues of wealth and poverty are addressed, touching the felt needs of large numbers of Indonesians.[49] In one column the author commences by introducing his moral through narrative, drawn from the writings of the Middle Eastern author Mustafa Lutfi Al-Manfaluti. A beggar is depicted as complaining of stomach pains from undereating, while a rich man complains of stomach pains from overeating. The rich man is thus portrayed as being punished by God for his greed; he is not allowed to enjoy his abundance of wealth, and is made to suffer for neglecting his duty to show concern for the poor.

This story is related to the model of Muhammad's community, referring to the Companion Hakam b. 'Amr al-Ghifari, lauded by the author for his concern for the poor, and presented as the father of socialism. The author then draws links with broader Islamic doctrine, pointing to the importance of almsgiving in Islam to demonstrate that Islam is concerned for the poor. The column finishes with a quote from *Sura* 107 which states that those who claim to be faithful Muslims but who ignore the poor are not truly faithful. Thus Islamic doctrine is affirmed, and readers have been provided with guidance on the perennial issue of the presence of poverty among the masses.

The 'Hikmah' column of 14 July 1996 is also concerned with daily questions posed by the masses.[50] The author commences by pointing out that all people have a subconscious desire to be nearer to God. References are then made to real-life contexts: conversations at boxing matches; the work of journalists; and discussion of money matters. The author then points out that both small and powerful consult Sufi groups for advice regarding failures and

49 Muhammad Rozi, 'Mencuri Hak Si Miskin', *Republika*, 24 June 1996.
50 Emha Ainun Nadjib, 'Hujan Deras dan Soekarno Muda', *Republika*, 14 July 1996.

chances of success. The column concludes with the observation that God alone has the means to overcome the darkness that is enveloping the world.

One of the columns by D. Zawawi Imron[51] stresses the importance of pronouncing the words 'God is Great'. By doing so believers will be reminded of their own smallness compared to God, which will in turn discourage arrogance and pride among them.

The individual scholars presented in the Islamic television programmes similarly addressed a range of practical matters in exegeting the Qur'anic text. For example, a quote from the Qur'an was used as the starting point for an excursion into the issue of cleanliness from a holistic perspective. One scholar cited the great classical Islamic thinker al-Ghazali in saying there were three necessary criteria for proper living: a healthy body, an intelligent mind and a purified spirit.[52] The human body was referred to as a blessing from God, and viewers were reminded that Islam gives guidance with regard to eating and drinking in order to demonstrate how to keep the body clean, both within and without. Simultaneously, the Islamic scholar stressed the importance of a daily routine and an orderly lifestyle in order to provide a positive effect on the health of the body. To supplement the discussion of bodily cleanliness, viewers were encouraged to maintain cleanliness of the mind with a reminder that if the spirit of the human being was clean and pure then the body would be clean and pure.

Various television programmes used references from the Qur'an and the prophetic Traditions as a jumping-off point to stress other matters relating to practical issues and personal behaviour, such as the need for children to respect, honour, and obey their parents,[53] the importance of being polite to other people regardless of whether they were relatives, and the importance of individual Muslims marrying to prevent their engaging in immoral behaviour. Viewers were reminded that God favoured marriage of all people in order to preserve his creation, and that it was a necessary step in the formation of a proper family unit.

---

[51] D. Zawawi Imron, 'Meresapi Takbir', *Republika*, 12 February 1998.

[52] TVRI, 20 October 1995.

[53] Malaysian TV, 20 October 1995.

Da'wa: a call to mission.   The theme of *da'wa* (call to mission) often appears as the principal subject of sermons and devotional columns, and is also frequently addressed within sermons devoted to other subjects. Mission is not necessarily portrayed as exclusively oriented towards the conversion of non-Muslims, but it is also portrayed as a necessary path which nominal Muslims can take to re-dedicate themselves to the faith in order for the *umma* to prosper.

A common theme is of Muslim nations declining in power because of divergence from Islamic injunctions.[54] Technological advances are not portrayed as providing a guarantee of prosperity; on the contrary, great empires such as that of Rome and the 'Abbasid Caliphate represent examples of technologically-advanced nations which decayed and fell. Islam is portrayed as representing the way to proper values, and the Qur'an is seen as the 'storehouse and source of necessary guidance'.[55]

Some writers adopt a more optimistic tone in terms of actual progress made by Islam in its perceived resurgence in the 20th century.[56] Muslims are encouraged to be optimistic about the future, given the great strides in the Islamic revival, such as that taking place in Japan because of the *da'wa* activities of the Japan Islamic Congress. The 15th century of Islam is regularly portrayed as a period of hope and great expansion, and for this to be realised, every individual Muslim has to throw himself into *da'wa* activities. Every Muslim is seen as having certain gifts which can be harnessed for the goal of mission: the scholar can use his knowledge, the wealthy can use their wealth, those without wealth or knowledge can contribute their energies, and those without wealth, knowledge or energy can contribute by giving a good example. Mustofa cites both western and Arab scholars in support of his view of mission, and also adds references from the Hadith in support of his thesis.[57]

The Malay scholar Nik Abdul Aziz Nik Mat, discussed in chapter 11, picks up on this theme of *da'wa* in his popular writing. In one

---

[54] This is a theme which is often repeated by both Muslim modernist and revivalist groups.

[55] Chizbulloh 1983:27.

[56] Mustofa 1986:75–83.

[57] Mustofa 1986:79.

address,[58] he reassures non-Muslims in his audience that Islam does not distinguish between people on the basis of ethnicity, but rather evaluates people according to belief and fear of God. Non-Muslims face their greatest loss, according to Nik Abdul Aziz, not in this world but in the Hereafter, where only Islam provides the bridge to eternal happiness. Muslims are thus responsible for explaining this to non-Muslims. But they should take care, says Nik Abdul Aziz, not to confuse faith with ethnicity. Becoming Muslim does not mean becoming Malay, he insists, and thus Indian and Chinese Malaysians need not forgo their cultural identity in embracing Islam. Nik Abdul Aziz shows in this address that he is concerned for *da'wa* to non-Muslims, considers that warning of punishment in the Hereafter is an effective method of *da'wa*, and demonstrates a commitment to contextualisation of the message of *da'wa*.

The theme of religious exclusivism encountered earlier in the writings of S.M.N. Al-Attas appears regularly in popular theological discourse. This is especially so in localised publications, such as *Buletin Al-Barakah*. This bulletin tends to affirm an exclusivist line, portraying non-Muslims as followers of false creeds who are destined for Hell. In an article discussing disbelievers and apostates, *Buletin Al-Barakah* is heavily critical of Muslims who look to non-Muslims for leadership, and those who quote sayings of Christians, Jews and unbelievers to Muslims.[59] In this way, this bulletin is playing its part in *da'wa* in calling on Muslims to cleanse their ways of living and make their behaviour more consistent with scriptural injunctions.

World-wide umma versus ethnic identity. Another issue addressed is a proper perspective on personal identity.

Muhammad Rozi,[60] in his discussion of wealth and poverty referred to above, chooses to build his argumentation upon the writings of a Middle Eastern author. In doing so, he is affirming a sense of the world-wide Islamic *umma,* suggesting that a person's religious, rather than national, identity is where the answers to daily problems are to be found. Moreover, many writers elect to

---

58 Nik Abdul Aziz Nik Mat, 'Islam jamin keadilan kepada bukan Islam', *Buletin Kelantan*, May 1998.

59 *Buletin Al-Barakah*, 14 November 1997.

60 Muhammad Rozi, 'Mencuri Hak Si Miskin', *Republika*, 24 June 1996.

write in a language style which makes conscious and heavy use of Arabic/Islamic loan words. The writing of D. Zawawi Imron[61] is illustrative of this. Not only are widely-used Arab loan words drawn upon, but also other Arabic expressions which are less commonly found in everyday Indonesian parlance. Thus rather than Arabness being portrayed as foreign and irrelevant to the needs of Indonesian readers, it is presented as a vehicle for asserting the international nature of Islamic identity, which has predominance over local, national or ethnic points of identity.

A difference apparent between the samples of Malaysian and Indonesian Islamic television programmes viewed relates to the degree of Middle Eastern influence in the images and flavours of Islam portrayed. Those Malaysian television programmes examined tended to emphasise a greater degree of Middle Eastern flavour than was the case with the Indonesian programmes examined.[62]

Hence, during breaks between Islamic programmes on Malaysian television, often songs in Arabic were sung which incorporated verses from the Qur'an, with the text in Malay being presented as subtitles.[63] Malaysian television programmes more typically commenced and finished with a series of greetings and farewells between scholars and students in Arabic, and parents were encouraged to give their children what were regarded as pure names, principally Arabic names, which have an Islamic meaning, in order to fulfil Hadith statements that such children will be characterised by a heavenly flavour.[64] Moreover, Malaysian television programming included specific instruction in the Jawi alphabet, which is based on the Arabic alphabet, with statements in these instructional programmes urging Malays to learn and use this alphabet.[65]

Related to this concept of increased Middle Eastern influence were statements occurring in various programmes seeking to identify Southeast Asian viewers with the broader Muslim world.

---

[61] D. Zawawi Imron, 'Bangun Pagi', *Republika*, 25 February 1998.

[62] Kessler (1997:327), whose research primarily focuses on Malaysia, similarly comments on a perception among some Southeast Asian Muslims that a measure of one's Islamicness derives from an external Arabised lifestyle.

[63] *Tamadun Islam*, Malaysian TV, 19 October 1995; Malaysian TV, 20 October 1995.

[64] *Dari Pusat Islam*, Malaysian TV, 28 October 1995.

[65] *Jawi*, Malaysian TV, 29 October 1995.

Indonesian Islamic programmes were interspersed with advertisements focusing on a statement stressing the concept of the world-wide Islamic community (*umma*),[66] while other programmes harked back to past glories of the Islamic Caliphate, decrying the abolition of the Caliphate by the secular Turkish authorities in 1924.[67]

Malaysian television programming, more than Indonesian, sought to affirm the link between Islamic and ethnic identification. Viewers of the Malaysian programmes were reminded that Malay marriages represented valid contracts.[68] This stressing of the Malay marriage in the midst of discussion about Islam served to reinforce the definition of Malay as necessarily Muslim (as well as to highlight intra-Muslim ethnic distinctions in Malaysia *vis-à-vis* Indian and Chinese Muslims). In an effort to counterbalance the result of the latter observation, comments were also made about the disunity of Muslim groups in other locations as contrasting with the community of Muslims in Malaysia which were, supposedly, united and strong.[69]

Pro-government political comment. On occasions oblique or overt pro-Government statements occur within popular preaching and devotional columns. This became especially pronounced during the latter stages of the New Order Government in Indonesia.

For example, in the 'Hikmah' column of 2 December 1996,[70] the author made very respectful reference to President Suharto's announcing of a new initiative designed to affirm the rights of the child. It was pointed out that this is consistent with both United Nations and Qur'anic guidelines, and thus this column served to reinforce a view that President Suharto had increasingly concerned himself with Islamic religiosity during the 1990s.

In a similar vein, the 'Hikmah' column of 18 February 1998[71] referred to the social and economic crisis in Indonesia resulting from the currency turmoil in Asian markets from late 1997, and

---

66 *Lazuardi Imani*, TVRI, 19 October 1995.
67 *Tamadun Islam*, Malaysian TV, 19 October 1995.
68 *Dari Pusat Islam*, Malaysian TV, 28 October 1995.
69 *Dari Pusat Islam*, Malaysian TV, 28 October 1995.
70 H. Tutty Alawiyah, 'Alquran dan HAM Anak', *Republika*, 2 December 1996.
71 HA Yani Wahid, 'Akhlak Mulia', *Republika*, 18 February 1998.

lamented that Suharto had been deserted by so many. The columnist suggested that the President had been made a scapegoat for many problems which were caused by others and were beyond his control.

In the column dealing with Islam and beauty pageants discussed previously,[72] the author referred to President's Suharto's decision to suspend beauty pageants, and claimed that most Indonesians were happy with this decision. This writer thus sought to affirm New Order Government claims that the Suharto regime carried mass support. Events in mid-1998 were to clearly disprove this.

THEATRICAL PERFORMANCES AND FILMS

There are various other ways in which Islamic leaders in Southeast Asia can educate their masses through combining traditional images with modern technology. This can take the form of theatrical performances and films focusing upon Islamic themes. For our present purposes, two examples will suffice.

In late April 1996, the Rajawali Citra Televisi Indonesia (RCTI), one of the leading television stations, combined with the Janur Kuning Foundation and the Association of Indonesian Hajis to present a theatrical performance at a major theatre in Jakarta.[73] The theme of the performance was the Islamic pilgrimage, and it coincided with the period of the pilgrimage itself. A multi-media approach was used, thus demonstrating an inclination to adapt modern technology for traditional themes. Seventy performers took part, the performance lasted for one hour, and it was widely broadcast throughout Indonesia by RCTI. It was organised into six parts, which variously represented the departure of the pilgrims for the Arabian peninsula, various songs and other activities, and various themes relating to the application of the pilgrimage experience to everyday life. Thus one of the five pillars of Islam had received nationwide attention through using the latest technological devices and methodologies. This provides a good example of Islamic modernism, whereby traditional

---

[72] Bachrawi Sanusi, 'Aurat, Ratu, dan Perenang', *Republika*, 31 May 1996.
[73] *Republika*, 24 April 1996.

themes are disseminated through the use of modern techniques and strategies.

Feature films are also a popular means among those with an Islamic agenda for disseminating their particular message. The Indonesian film industry has produced many films based on Islamic motifs since its establishment, and a new venture initiated during the mid-1990s was the production of the film *Fatahillah*,[74] a massive production by Indonesian standards which was to be filmed at sixteen different locations, with a total cast of 1,000 people, and focusing upon the character of Fatahillah, an Islamic teacher who was inspired by the King of the Islamic Kingdom of Demak to attack and defeat the Portuguese and drive them from the Javanese coast in the early period of Javanese Islam. Again a traditional theme is presented through modern technology, though in this instance the theme is more specifically Southeast Asian.

Discussion in this chapter reveals that certain themes recurred in popular Islamic preaching of the 1980s and 1990s in Indonesia and Malaysia, whether on the television, in mosque sermons or in other forums. While the materials consulted for this study have by no means been exhaustive, they have nevertheless provided us with a series of useful insights as to issues of Islamic theology and popular belief considered important by both preachers and congregations alike.

In considering the preceding discussion, several points are worthy of note.

1. Islamic scripture, both Qur'an and Hadith, and its application in practical situations underpins all popular preaching whether on television, in the mosques or in periodicals.
2. Preachers place a heavy emphasis on correct behaviour and attitudes in selecting their topics of discussion. Clear guidelines are given, with congregations left in no doubt as to what they should believe and what they should do.
3. An Arabic flavour is achieved through the use of formulaic statements in Arabic, the singing of songs in Arabic, and various Middle Eastern motifs.

---

[74] *Republika*, 24 April 1996.

4. Television programmes make full use of a range of modern conventions to maximise the popular appeal of their message.
5. Sufi themes continue to recur, but they present a reformed face of Sufism, which maintains a distance between mankind and a transcendent creator. The theme of divine in-dwelling, so prominent in earlier centuries, is not a characteristic feature of popular preaching in the modern media.
6. The issue of ethnic identity as part of Islamicness is more of an issue in the case of Malaysian preaching than it is in Indonesian sermons, though this is somewhat paralleled by a focus on national identity in Indonesian programming.
7. The information available suggests that Indonesian preachers are somewhat less coy about drawing on and making overt reference to western scholarship than is the case with Malaysian preachers.
8. While there is no clear-cut distinction between Indonesian and Malaysian preaching attitudes towards the question of *ijtihad*, the Indonesian preachers examined tended more towards encouraging Muslim individuals to make their own assessments of scriptural injunctions, whereas the Malaysian preachers examined tended more towards calling for obedience to scholarly guidelines and established beliefs and roles.
9. The imprint of government and/or Islamic authorities looms large over these materials in various ways; prefaces to published volumes by Islamic authorities endorsing the works, exhortations for individual Muslims to join official bodies (e.g. returning pilgrims joining the *Indonesian Association of Hajis*), and general calls for obedience to authority as an Islamic value, which could have a positive spin-off for government.

The latter point, related to the influence of government upon preaching in the media, demonstrates the Malaysian and Indonesian Governments' concern to meet the felt needs of their respective Islamic constituencies. In the Indonesian context, William Liddle's observations about the aspirations of young Indonesians are pertinent. He writes that they 'are looking for a new understanding of their religion that gives them a more realistic set of guidelines, really a code of ethics, for private and family life and for dealing with the outside world. They want to know what are the rights and responsibilities of husbands and wives, how to raise their sons and daughters to be good Muslims and good

Indonesians, how to relate to a modern banking system, whether and how to revitalise the concept of *zakat* (religious tax), and even how to deal with such exotica as test-tube babies, organ transplants, and homosexuality.'[75] The preceding examination of print and electronic media shows that the New Order Government of Indonesia and the Federal Government in Malaysia clearly attempted to take account of such concerns in media comment which carried their endorsements.

---

[75] Cited in Schwarz 1994:174.

14

CONCLUSION

Our excursion through a selection of Malay Islamic writings from the last seven centuries has enabled us to draw out some key conclusions, and identify some important trends.

We began with an overview of significant theological themes, debates, and movements from elsewhere in the Muslim world. This initial overview was designed to act as a control for our primary study of Southeast Asia. The purpose was to enable us to see to what degree Southeast Asian thinking represented echoes of developments elsewhere in the Muslim world.

We saw in the contextual study in Part I that there was a series of key debates undergirding Islam's early history in the Arab world. The first related to the respective priority to be attached to revelation and reason, with the conservative traditionalists of the *ahl al-hadith* arguing that a literal application of revelation through the *shari'a* should underpin Islamic belief and practice, while Islamic rationalists promoted the use of reason as a central instrument for crystallising the nature of God and God's plan for His creation. Following this debate was another involving the *shari'a*-minded, who found themselves in opposition to many Muslims involved in the spiritual quest, especially those theosophically inclined Sufis who demoted the *shari'a* in favour of a monist quest for realising union with God. In both debates, the *shari'a* minded asserted themselves, though each debate was to resurface at various points of Middle Eastern Islamic history.

As we embarked upon our primary study of the Malay world, it was observed that there is a time gap, broadly covering the period from 1300 to 1550, from which few records of Malay Islamic thought remain. It is thus extremely difficult for scholars to confidently paint a detailed portrait of Malay theological thinking during this period. This gap is partly filled by a source-critical examination of later writings, which identifies Arabic-language works in probable circulation in Southeast Asia during the 14th and 15th centuries. Such an examination was carried out for our study with several works of Qur'anic exegesis produced by Malay scholars.

As we proceeded through the centuries, it was striking that Sufi thinking became normative in the 16th-, 17th- and 18th-century Malay world. In particular Sufi theosophical writings represented a theological default in the 16th and early 17th centuries. The latter century, however, was also characterised by severe polemics at times, with some Sufi scholars launching a drive for reform, seeking to reconcile Malay mystical practice with the *shari'a*. This tension was to be played out further during the 18th century, with a more *shari'a*-minded reformed brand of Sufism gradually extending its influence through the writings which we examined from the period.

It was also noticed that there was an absence of Sufi exegesis of the Qur'an in this early period. This seems curious, given the Sufi dominance in other fields of Islamic writing. This may be due to destruction of early exegetical works of a Sufi nature, though such speculation requires further research before it can be confirmed. Whatever the case, that Qur'anic exegesis which did take place provided an arena for more *shari'a*-minded voices to make themselves heard. Furthermore, the few morsels of early Malay exegesis which survive manifest a penchant for narrative approaches to this field of Islamic scholarship. This bears out Wansbrough's claim that narrative exegesis is most typically produced by societies in the early stages of Islamisation.

The early exegetical writings were notable for two other factors. First, exegetes seemed to disregard the *Isra'iliyyat* debate, which had long been a significant issue among Arab exegetes. Second, early Malay exegetes showed clear interest in the variant readings (*qira'at*) of the Qur'an.

The 19th century came to represent a watershed for Islam in the Malay world. The region changed dramatically during that century under the impact of European colonialism. Such was also the case elsewhere in the Muslim world. In this context, new

Table 14.1. PATHS OF TRANSMISSION EVIDENT IN THE WRITINGS EXAMINED

Field/Topic	Source	Transmitter	Result	Period
Law	Various	Various	Shafi'i law	From 13th century
Sufism	Ibn al-'Arabi's *Fusus al-Hikam*	Hamzah Fansuri	Wujudiyya doctrines	Late 16th century
Sufism	'Abd al-Karim al-Jili's *Sharh Mishkat Futuhat*	Hamzah Fansuri	Wujudiyya doctrines	Late 16th century
Sufism	al-Burhanpuri's *Tuhfa*	Shams al-Din al-Sumatrani	Wujudiyya doctrines	Early 17th century
Qur'anic exegesis	Commentaries by Baghawi & Khazin	Cambridge MS Or. Ii.6.45	Narrative-based exegesis	c. 1600
Qur'anic exegesis	Commentaries by Baghawi & Khazin	Cambridge MS Or. Ii.6.45	*Isra'iliyyat*	c. 1600
Qur'anic exegesis	Commentaries by Baghawi & Khazin	Cambridge MS Or. Ii.6.45	Contextualisation to local norms	c. 1600
Qur'anic exegesis	Various sources reporting canonical *qira'at*	Cambridge MS Or. Ii.6.45	Malay record of variant readings of the Qur'an	c. 1600
Sufism	'Abdu'l-Rahman Jami's *Lawa'ih fi bayan ma'ani 'urfaniya*	al-Raniri	Rejection of radical monist doctrines	Mid-17th century
Comparative religion	Abu Shakur al-Salimi's *Kitab al-tamhid fi bayan al-tawhid*	al-Raniri	*Tibyan fi ma'rifat al-adyan*	Mid-17th century

Topic	Source	Author	Description	Date
Qur'anic exegesis	*Tafsir al-Jalalayn*	'Abd al-Ra'uf	Malay commentary on Qur'an	c. 1675
Hadith	al-Nawawi (d. 1277) *Forty Hadith*	'Abd al-Ra'uf	Prophetic model of belief and practice	c. 1680
Qur'anic exegesis	Various sources reporting canonical *qira'at*	'Abd al-Ra'uf	Malay record of variant readings of the Qur'an	c. 1675
Issues of authority of rulers	al-Ghazali's *Ihya' 'ulum al-din*	'Abd al-Samad al-Palimbani	Translation into Malay	1789
Issues of authority of rulers	al-Ghazali's *Ihya' 'ulum al-din*	Daud ibn 'Abd Allah ibn Idris al-Patani	Translation into Malay	1824
Responsibilities of rulers	al-Ghazali's *Nasihat al-Muluk*	Raja Ali Haji	*Thamarat al-Muhimmah*	19th century
Ideology	Egyptian reformists	Muhammadiyah	Modernist thinking	1912
Qur'anic exegesis	'Abduh/Rida (d. 1905/1935)	Hamka	Group verses for exegesis	1960s
Qur'anic exegesis	'Abduh (d. 1905)	Hamka	Delete grammatical & philological discussion	1960s
Literature	Stories	Hamka	Use of narrative to present religious themes	1960s

continued on page 320

Table 14.1. (*continued*)

Field/Topic	Source	Transmitter	Result	Period
Reformist ideology	Islamist writers	Hamka	Call to *da'wa* (Islamic mission)	1960s
Qur'anic exegesis	al-Zamakhshari (d. 1210)	Hamka	Use of rationalist critique in exegesis	1960s
Qur'anic exegesis	Various sources reporting canonical *qira'at*	Shalihah	Indonesian record of variant readings of the Qur'an	1983
Hadith	al-Suyuti (d. 1505)	Shaleh, Dahlan & Dahlan	*Asbab al-nuzul*	1984
Popular preaching	Arab writers	Malaysian/Indonesian preachers	Various	1980s and 1990s

solutions were sought for new problems, and old paradigms gradually gave way to new approaches. A thirst for change displaced a preoccupation with continuity.

Thus the second half of the 19th century witnessed a gradual shift away from Sufi writing, whether theosophical or reformed, towards non-Sufi modernist reformism in Islamic writings. It is important to remember the significance of Malay scholarly voices based in Arabia in creating this mood for change. Furthermore, Arab voices in the Malay world also acted as a conduit for new ideas. In this cauldron of new thinking, Sufism was gradually pushed to the margins of Malay Islamic writing.

This process was consolidated in the 20th century, with increased Islamic identity representing a response to the vacuum created by the demise of old authorities – colonial powers and traditional rulers – and many groups vied to fill the gap. Orthodox traditionalist scholars responded with streamlined organisations and activist voices, as seen in the writings of Malaysian PAS leadership. However, the stage came to be dominated by modernists and neo-modernists, who sought to harness the wisdom of the primary sources in engaging with the challenges of the modern world. Disparate voices were heard, and multiple concerns were addressed, ranging from the place of religion *vis-à-vis* the state, to anti-Christian polemic by certain writers examined. Furthermore, Sufism itself responded with a modernist response, based on a reassertion of the transcendence of God, a maintenance of the importance of the mystical quest, and an engagement with issues of the contemporary world. This was seen in the writing of scholars such as Hamka, Muhammad Zuhri, and several authors of popular sermons.

A common thread found in all the above phases was the external sourcing of many ideas addressed by Malay Islamic writers over the centuries. But this did not merely take the form of borrowing and imitation. Rather, a process of adaptation and further creative development has characterised Malay Islamic writings during the last seven centuries. Writers have been impressed by a particular stream of thought originating elsewhere, and have then taken it and contextualised it to Malay circumstances, producing dynamic new results.

In this context, the ancient debates from the Middle East were played out in the Malay world – but in reverse. While the Middle

East had seen the revelation-versus-reason debate precede that between the proponents of revelation and the speculative Sufis, in the Malay world the reverse order was the case. The battle between speculative Sufis and the *shari'a*-minded needed first to be resolved in the early centuries, and only then did the reason-versus-revelation debate assume priority during the 20th century when modernists and traditionalists came face to face on centre stage.

Table 14.1, though not comprehensive, provides an overview of themes borrowed, source texts used, and Malay texts produced over the course of the last seven centuries as encountered in our study of selected Malay Islamic writers.

Unfortunately, it has not been possible to include selections of writings from all significant Malay–Indonesian Islamic thinkers, as this would be a massive task requiring several volumes. Notable absentees, for example, are Shaykh Yusuf al-Maqassari (d. 1697), Muhammad Arshad al-Banjari (d. *c.* 1808), Shaykh Mohammad Tahir b. Jalaluddin (d. 1957), and a considerable number of Islamic thinkers from modern Indonesia and Malaysia. A consideration of each of these writers, and others, could have greatly enriched our study. Nevertheless, those writers and works examined in the preceding pages have been sufficient to provide us with key insights into the overall direction that Malay–Indonesian Islamic thinking has followed during the period from 1300 to 1998. And we have seen that, although the Malay–Indonesian Islamic world owes much to other parts of the Muslim world, Southeast Asian Islam has itself made a substantial creative contribution to the mosaic of world Islam.

SELECT BIBLIOGRAPHY

For ease of reference, where 'van' or 'von' occurs in a surname these terms have been ignored in organising the names alphabetically. Similarly, Arab surnames beginning with al- have been listed according to the first letter of the proper name. However, non-Arab surnames beginning with Al- have been listed under the letter 'A'.

Certain journal titles have been abbreviated as follows:

BKI	*Bijdragen tot de Taal-, Land- en Volkenkunde*
ICMR	*Islam and Christian–Muslim Relations*
JMBRAS	*Journal of the Malaysian Branch, Royal Asiatic Society*
JRAS	*Journal of the Royal Asiatic Society*
JSBRAS	*Journal of the Straits Branch, Royal Asiatic Society*
JSEAS	*Journal of Southeast Asian Studies*
RIMA	*Review of Indonesian and Malayan Affairs*
TBG	*Tijdschrift voor Indische Taal-, Land- en Volkenkunde*

Abbott, N. (1967), *Studies in Arabic literary papyri*, vol. 2, University of Chicago Press.

'Abd al-Ra'uf b. Muhammad 'Ali Fansuri (n.d.), *Tafsir Anwar al- Baydawi*, Penang: Persamar Press.

'Abd al-Ra'uf (1951), *Tarjuman al-Mustafid*. Singapore: Sulayman Maraghi.

Abd Rahim, R.A. (1999), 'The Traditional Malay-Muslim Legal Education during the Colonial Period', *Hamdard Islamicus*, XXII (3), 81–9.

Abdillah, M. (1997), *Responses of Indonesian Muslim Intellectuals to the Concept of Democracy (1966–93)*, Hamburg: Abera Publishing House.

'Abduh, M. (1966), *The Theology of Unity*, New York: Humanities Press.

Abdul, M.O.A. (1976), 'The Historical Development of Tafsir', *Islamic Culture*, 50, 141–53.

Abdul Hadi, W.M. (1995), *Hamzah Fansuri: Risalah Tasawuf dan Puisi-puisinya*, Bandung: Mizan.

Abdul-Samad, M.A. (1991), 'Modernism in Islam in Indonesia with special reference to Muhammadiyah' in M.C. Ricklefs, *Islam in the Indonesian Social Context* (pp. 57–68), Melbourne: Centre of Southeast Asian Studies, Monash University.

Abdullah, P. and Siddique, S. (eds) (1986), *Islam and Society in Southeast Asia*, Singapore: Institute of Southeast Asian Studies.

Abdullah, T. (1993), 'The Formation of a Political Tradition in the Malay World' in A. Reid (ed.), *The Making of an Islamic Political Discourse in Southeast Asia*. (pp. 35–58), Melbourne: Monash University Press.

Abdurrauf, T.S. (1971), *Mir'at At-Tullab*, Banda Atjeh: Universitas Sjiah Kuala.

Aboebakar, H. (1957), *Sejarah hidup K.H.A. Wahid Hasjim dan karangan tersiar*, Djakarta: Panitya Buku Peringatan Alm. K.H.A. Wahid Hasjim.

Adang, C. (1996), *Muslim Writers on Judaism and the Hebrew Bible*, Leiden: E.J. Brill.

Adnan, M. (1981), *Tafsir al-Qur'an Suci (Basa Jawi)*, Bandung: P.T. Alma'arif.

Ahmad, A. (1967), *Islamic Modernism in India and Pakistan 1857–1964*, London: Oxford University Press.

Ahmad Jullandri, R. (1968), 'Qur'anic Exegesis and Classical Tafsir', *The Islamic Quarterly*, XII (1 & 2), 71–119.

'Ak, K.A. al- (1407/1987), 'Muqrimat hamah fi bayyan manahij al-tafsir wa al-mufassirin' in A.M. al-Husayn al-Farra' al- Baghawi, *Ma'alim al-Tanzil* (2nd edn), Beirut: Dar al-Ma'rifah.

Al Allusi, A.M. Din (1992), *Arab Islam di Indonesia dan India*, Jakarta: Gema Insani Press.

Al Quraan dan Terjemahnya (1974), Jakarta: Departemen Agama.

Al-Attas, S.M.Naguib (1963), *Some Aspects of Sufism As Understood and Practised Among the Malays*, Singapore: Malaysian Sociological Research Institute.

—— (1966), *Raniri and the Wujudiyyah of 17th-Century Acheh*, Singapore: Malaysian Branch, Royal Asiatic Society.

—— (1970), *The Mysticism of Hamzah Fansuri*, Kuala Lumpur: University of Malaya.

—— (1972), *Islam Dalam Sejarah Dan Kebudayaan Melayu*, Kuala Lumpur: Universiti Kebangsaan Malaysia.

—— (1986), *A Commentary on the Hujjat al-Siddiq of Nur al-Din al-Raniri*, Kuala Lumpur: Ministry of Culture.

—— (1988), *The Oldest Known Malay Manuscript: A 16th-Century Malay Translation of the 'Aqa'id of al-Nasafi*, Kuala Lumpur: University of Malaya.

—— (1990), 'Extracts from 'Secular-Secularization-Secularism'', in Paul J. Griffiths (ed.), *Christianity Through Non-Christian Eyes* (pp. 111–25), Maryknoll NY: Orbis Books.

Alatas, S.F. (1997), 'The tariqat al-'alawiyya and the emergence of the Shi'i school in Indonesia and Malaysia', paper presented at the conference *The Arabs in Southeast Asia (1870–c. 1990)*, 8–12 December, Royal Institute of Linguistics and Anthropology, Leiden.

Algadri, H. (1984), *C. Snouck Hurgronje: Politik Belanda terhadap Islam dan Keturunan Arab*, Jakarta: Sinar Harapan.

Ali, A.Y. (1989), *The Meaning of the Holy Qur'an* (new edn), Beltsville, MD: Amana Publications.

Ambary, H.M. (1985), 'De l'animisme à l'Islam: le témoignage de quelques monuments funéraires de la région de Bone', *Archipel*, (29), 165–74.

Amiq. (1998), 'Two Fatwas on Jihad Against the Dutch Colonization in Indonesia: A Prosopographical Approach to the Study of Fatwa', *Studia Islamika*, 5 (3), 77–124.

Andaya, B.W. and Matheson, V. (1979), 'Islamic Thought and Malay Tradition: The Writings of Raja Ali Haji of Riau', in A. Reid and D. Marr (eds), *Perceptions of the Past in South East Asia,* (pp. 108–28), Singapore: Heinemann.

—— and —— (1982), *The Precious Gift: Tuhfat al-nafis,* Kuala Lumpur and New York: Oxford University Press.

Anderson, J.N.D. (1990), *Islam in the Modern World,* Leicester: Apollos.

Any, A. (1979), *Rahasia Ramalan. Jayabaya Ranggawarsita and Sabda Palon,* Semarang: CV Aneka.

—— (1985), *R. Ng. Ronggowarsito. Apa Yang Terjadi,* Semarang: PT Aneka Ilmu.

Arberry, A. J. (n.d.), *Fifty Poems of Hafiz,* Tehran: Padideh Publishing.

—— (1956), 'A Hanbali Tract on the Eternity of the Qur'an', *The Islamic Quarterly,* III (1), 16–41.

—— (1964), *Aspects of Islamic Civilization as Depicted in the Original Texts.* London: Geo. Allen & Unwin.

Ash-Shiddieqy, T.M. Hasbi. (1964), *Tafsir Al Quranul Madjied 'AN NUR'.* vol. XV, Jakarta: Bulan Bintang.

—— (1971a), *Hukum Antar Golongan dalam Fiqih Islam,* Jakarta: Bulan Bintang.

—— (1971b), *Sedjarah Pertumbuhan dan Perkembangan Hukum Islam,* Jakarta: Bulan Bintang.

—— (1972), *Ilmu-ilmu al-Qur'an. Media – media pokok dalam menafsirkan al-Qur'an,* Jakarta: Bulan Bintang.

Awang, O. b. (1980), 'The Trengganu Inscription as the Earliest Known Evidence of the Finalisation of the Jawi Script', *Federation Museums Journal,* 25, 43–60.

Ayoub, M.M. (1992), *The Qur'an and Its Interpreters,* Albany: State University of New York Press.

Ayubi, N.N. (1991), *Political Islam: Religion and Politics in the Arab World,* London and New York: Routledge.

Azra, A. (1992), 'The Transmission of Islamic Reformism to Indonesia: Networks of Middle Eastern and Malay–Indonesian 'Ulama' in the Seventeenth and Eighteenth Centuries', unpublished doctoral dissertation, Columbia University.

—— (1995), 'Hadhrami Scholars in the Malay–Indonesian Diaspora: A Preliminary Study of Sayyid Uthman', *Studia Islamika,* 2 (2), 1–33.

—— (1997), 'A Hadhrami Religious Scholar in Indonesia: Sayyid 'Uthman', in U. Freitag and W.G. Clarence-Smith (eds), *Hadhrami Traders, Scholars and Statesmen in the Indian Ocean, 1750s to 1960s* (pp. 249–63), Leiden: E. J. Brill.

—— (1999), 'The Transmission of al-Manar's Reformism to the Malay–Indonesian World: the Cases of al-Imam and al-Munir', *Studia Islamika,* 6 (3), 75–100.

Baghawi, A.M. al-Husayn al-Farra' al- (1407/1987), *Ma'alim al-Tanzil* (2nd edn), Beirut: Dar al-Ma'rifah.

Bahasoan, A. (1985), 'The Islamic Reform Movement: An Interpretation and Criticism', *Prisma: The Indonesian Indicator,* (35), 131–60.

Bakar, O.B. (1991), 'Sufism in the Malay–Indonesian World', in S.H. Nasr (ed.), *Islamic Spirituality II: Manifestations* (pp. 259–89), London: SCM Press.

Bakry, H. (1966), *Al-Qur'an Sebagai Korektor terhadap Taurat dan Injil,* Surabaya.

—— (1968), *Nabi Isa dalam al-Qur'an dan Nabi Muhammad dalam Bijbel,* Solo: A.B. Sitti Sjamsijah.

—— (21 March 1982), 'Membantah terhadap Hamran Ambrie'. *Panji Masyarakat,* (354), 19–22.

—— (1984), *Pandangan Islam Tentang Kristen di Indonesia,* Jakarta: Firdaus.

—— (1990), *Jesus Christ in the Qur'an, Muhammad in the Bible,* Kuala Lumpur: S. Abdul Majeed.

Baljon, J. (1968), *Modern Muslim Interpretation,* Leiden: E.J. Brill.

Balogun, S.U. (1997), 'The Status of Shari'ah in Malaysia', *Hamdard Islamicus,* XX (2), 51–8.

Barton, G. (1991), 'The International Context of the Emergence of Islamic Neo-Modernism in Indonesia', in M. C. Ricklefs, *Islam in the Indonesian Social Context* (pp. 69–82), Melbourne: Centre of Southeast Asian Studies, Monash University.

—— (1997), 'Indonesia's Nurcholish Madjid and Abdurrahman Wahid as Intellectuals', *Studia Islamika,* 4 (1), 34–75.

Batumalai, S. (1989), 'Responses to Islamic Resurgence in Malaysia', *Asian Journal of Theology,* 3 (1), 1–14.

—— (1996), *Islamic Resurgence and Islamization in Malaysia,* Ipoh: Charles Grenier.

Baydawi, N.D. Abi Sa'id al- (1996), *Tafsir al-Baydawi al-musamma Anwar al-Tanzil wa Asrar al-Ta'wil,* 5 vols, Beirut: Dar al-Fikr.

Beatty, A. (1998), 'Quoting God: Islamic and Non-Islamic Prayer in Java', paper presented at the conference *Inside the Mosque, Outside the Mosque,* 21–22 March, Maison de France, Oxford.

Beeston, A.F.L. (1963), *Baidawi's Commentary on Surah 12 of the Qur'an,* Oxford: Clarendon Press.

Bell, R. (1937), *The Qur'an Translated, with a critical re-arrangement of the Surahs,* Edinburgh: T.T. Clark.

—— (1991), *A Commentary on the Qur'an,* Manchester: University of Manchester Press.

Ben Chereb, M. (1979), 'Ibn al-Djazari', in *The Encyclopaedia of Islam* (2nd edn) vol. III (p. 753), Leiden: E.J. Brill.

Benda, H. J. (1958), *The Crescent and the Rising Sun,* The Hague: W. Van Hoeve.

Berg, L.W.C. van den (1887), 'Het Mohammedaansche Godsdienst- onderwijs op Java en Madoera en de Daarbij Gebruikte Arabische Boeken', *TBG,* 31, 518–55.

—— (1989), *Hadramaut dan Koloni Arab di Nusantara,* trans. Rahayu Hidayat, Jakarta: INIS.

Blachère, R. (1977), *Introduction au Coran* (2nd edn), Paris: Maisonneuve.

Bluhm, J.E. (1983), 'A Preliminary Statement on the Dialogue Established Between the Reform Magazine 'Al-Manar' and the Malayo–Indonesian World', *Indonesia Circle,* (32), 35–42.

Bluhm-Warn, J. (1997), 'Al-Manar and Ahmad Soorkattie', in P.G. Riddell and T. Street (eds), *Islam: Essays on Scripture, Thought and Society* (pp. 295–308), Leiden: E.J. Brill.

Boland, B.J. (1971), *The Struggle of Islam in Modern Indonesia,* The Hague: Martinus Nijhoff.

Bousfield, J. (1985), 'Good, evil and spiritual power: Reflections on Sufi teachings', in D. Parkin (ed.), *The Anthropology of Evil* (pp. 194–208), Oxford: Basil Blackwell.

—— (1988 [1983]), 'Islamic Philosophy in South-East Asia', in M. B. Hooker (ed.), *Islam in Southeast Asia* (pp. 92–129), Leiden: E.J. Brill.

Brakel, C. (1995), *Islamic Syncretism in Indonesia: From Historical Written Sources to Contemporary Ritual Practice in Java*, Jerusalem: Truman Institute, Hebrew University.

Brakel, L.F. (1969), 'The Birth Place of Hamza Pansuri', *JMBRAS*, XLII (2), 206–12.

—— (1975), *The Hikayat Muhammad Hanafiyyah*, The Hague: Martinus Nijhoff.

—— (1977), *The Story of Muhammad Hanafiyyah*, The Hague: Martinus Nijhoff.

—— (1980), 'Qur'anic quotations in the poetry of Hamza Pansuri', *International Congress for the Study of the Qur'an*, 8–13 May, Australian National University.

Brockelmann, C. (1938a), *Geschichte der Arabischen Litteratur*, Leiden: E.J. Brill.

—— (1938b), 'al-Tha'labi' in *The Encyclopaedia of Islam* (1st edn), vol. IV (pp. 735–6), Leiden: E.J. Brill.

—— (1992), 'al-Nawawi' in *The Encyclopaedia of Islam* (2nd edn), vol. VII (pp. 1040–1), Leiden: E.J. Brill.

Brockett, A. (1988), 'The Value of the Hafs and Warsh Transmissions for the Textual History of the Qur'an', in A. Rippin (ed.), *Approaches to the History of the Interpretation of the Qur'an* (pp. 13–45), Oxford: Clarendon Press.

Bruce, A. (December 1996), 'Notes on Early Mosques of the Malaysian Peninsula', *JMBRAS*, LXIX (2), 71–81.

Bruinessen, M. van (1992), *Tarekat Naqsyabandiyah di Indonesia*, Bandung: Mizan.

—— (July 1998), 'Studies of Sufism and the Sufi Orders in Indonesia', *Die Welt des Islams*, 38 (2), 192–219.

Burton, J. (1977), *The Collection of the Qur'an*, Cambridge University Press.

—— (1994), *An Introduction to the Hadith*, Edinburgh: Edinburgh University Press.

Calder, N. (1993), *Studies in Early Muslim Jurisprudence*, Oxford: Clarendon Press.

Camb. MS Or. Ii.6.45: Tafsir Sura al-Kahf (c. 1600), Cambridge University Library.

Carey, P.B.R. (1981), *Babad Dipanegara: An Account of the Outbreak of the Java War 1825–30*, Kuala Lumpur: MBRAS.

Cederroth, S. (1991), *From Syncretism to Orthodoxy? The Struggle of Islamic Leaders in an East Javanese Village*, Copenhagen: Nordic Institute of Asian Studies.

Chizbulloh, M.K. (1983), *Khutbah-Khutbah Pilihan*, Jakarta: Penerbit Amani.

Clarke, L. (1995), 'Sainthood', in J.L. Esposito (ed.), *The Oxford Encyclopedia of the Modern Islamic World*, vol. 3 (pp. 460–2), New York and Oxford: Oxford University Press.

Commins, D. (1995), 'Syria', in J.L. Esposito (ed.), *The Oxford Encyclopedia of the Modern Islamic World*, vol. 4 (pp. 156–60), New York and Oxford: Oxford University Press.

Cooper, J. (trans.) (1987), *The Commentary on the Qur'an by Abu Ja'far Muhammad b. Jarir al-Tabari*, Oxford University Press.

Cribb, R. (1992), *Historical Dictionary of Indonesia*, London: Scarecrow Press.

Crone, P. (1994), 'Two legal problems bearing on the early history of the Qur'an', *Jerusalem Studies in Arabic and Islam*, (18), 1–37.

Daudy, A. (1978), *Syeikh Nuruddin Ar-Raniry*, Jakarta: Bulan Bintang.

—— (1983), *Allah dan Manusia dalam konsepsi Syeikh Nuruddin ar-Raniri*, Jakarta: C.V. Rajawali.

—— (1987), 'Tinjauan atas "Al-Fath Al-Mubin 'ala Al- Mulhidin" karya Syaikh Nuruddin ar-Raniri', in A.R. Hasan (ed.), *Warisan Intelektual Islam Indonesia* (pp. 21–38), Bandung: Mizan.

Dawudi, S. al- (n.d.), *Tabaqat al-Mufassirin*, Beirut: Dar al-Kutub al-'Ilmiyyah.

Day, A. (1988 [1983]), 'Islam and Literature in South-East Asia: Some premodern, mainly Javanese perspectives', in M.B. Hooker (ed.), *Islam in Southeast Asia* (pp. 130–59), Leiden: E.J. Brill.

De Beer, P. (1983–4) 'L'Islam en Malaysie', *L'Afrique et l'Asie Modernes*, (139), 43–55.

Denffer, A.V. (1994), *'Ulum al-Qur'an: an Introduction to the Sciences of the Qur'an*, Leicester: The Islamic Foundation.

Dhahabi, M.H. al- (1985), *Al-Tafsir wa al-Mufassirun* (3rd edn), Cairo: Wahba.

Dif, S. (ed.) (1988), *Kitab al-sab'a fi al-qira'at li Ibn Mujahid* (3rd edn), Cairo: Dar al-Ma'arif.

Dijk, C. Van (1997), 'The Netherlands Indies and the Malay Peninsula 1890–1918: Pan-Islamism and the Germano–Indian plot', paper presented at the conference *The Arabs in South-East Asia (1870–c. 1990)*, 8–12 December, Royal Institute of Linguistics and Anthropology, Leiden.

Djajadiningrat, H. (1911), 'Critisch Overzicht Van de in Maleische Werken vervatte gegevens over de Geschiedenis van het Soeltanaat Van Atjeh', *BKI*, (65), 135–265 (trans. by T. Hamid as *Kesultanan Aceh*, Banda Aceh: Museum Negeri Aceh, 1979).

Djajadiningrat, P.A. Hoesein (1958), 'Islam in Indonesia', in K.W. Morgan (ed.), *Islam – The Straight Path: Islam interpreted by Muslims* (pp. 375–402), New York: Ronald Press.

Djamal, M. (1998), 'The Origin of the Islamic Reform Movement in Minangkabau: Life and Thought of Abdul Karim Amrullah', *Studia Islamika*, 5 (3), 1–46.

Dobbin, C. (1997), 'Muslim Creative Commercial Minorities. Some examples *c.* 1800–1950', in P.G. Riddell and Tony Street (eds), *Islam: Essays on Scripture, Thought and Society* (pp. 277–94), Leiden: E.J. Brill.

Dodge, B. (1970), *The Fihrist of al-Nadim*, New York: Columbia University Press.

Drewes, G.W.J. (1955a), 'De Herkomst van Nuruddin ar-Raniri', *BKI*, 111, 137–51.

—— (1955b), 'Indonesia: Mysticism and activism', in G.E. von Grunebaum (ed.), *Unity and Variety in Muslim Civilisation*, University of Chicago Press.

—— (1968a), 'Javanese Poems dealing with or attributed to the saint of Bonang', *BKI*, (124), 209–41.

—— (1968b), 'New Light on the coming of Islam to Indonesia?' *BKI*, (124), 433–60.

—— (1977), *Directions for Travellers on the Mystic Path*, The Hague: Martinus Nijhoff.

—— (1978), *An early Javanese code of Muslim Ethics*, The Hague: Martinus Nijhoff.
—— and Brakel, L.F. (1986), *The Poems of Hamzah Fansuri*, Dordrecht: Foris Publications.
Dutton, Y. (1999), *The Origins of Islamic Law*, Richmond (Surrey, England): Curzon Press.
Eaton, H.G. (1986), 'Review of Islam, Secularism and the Philosophy of the Future by S.M.N. al-Attas', *The Islamic Quarterly*, XXX (1), 65–8.
Ensiklopedi Nasional Indonesia (1990), Jakarta: P.T. Cipta Adi Pustaka.
Entelis, J.P. (1995), 'Tunisia', in J.L. Esposito (ed.), *The Oxford Encyclopedia of the Modern Islamic World*, vol. 4 (pp. 235–40), New York and Oxford: Oxford University Press.
Esposito, J.L. (1991), *Islam: The Straight Path* (2nd edn), New York and Oxford: Oxford University Press.
Farisi, A.A. al-Hasan b. Ahmad al- (1402/1983), *al-Hujjah fi 'ilal al-Qira'at al-Sab'*, Cairo: Dar al-Kutub.
Fayruz Abadi, A.T. b. Ya'qub (n.d.), *Tanwir al-Miqbas min Tafsir Ibn 'Abbas*, Cairo: Dar al-Fikr.
Fealy, G. and Barton, G. (eds) (1996), *Nahdatul Ulama, traditional Islam and modernity in Indonesia*, Clayton, Vic.: Monash Asia Institute, Monash University.
Federspiel, H.M. (January 1991), 'An Introduction to Qur'anic Commentaries in Contemporary Southeast Asia', *The Muslim World*, 81 (2), 149–65.
—— (1993), *The Usage of Traditions of the Prophet in Contemporary Indonesia*, Tempe: Arizona State University Press.
—— (1994), *Popular Indonesian Literature of the Qur'an*, Ithaca, NY: Cornell University Press.
Feener, R.M. (1998), 'Notes Towards the History of Qur'anic Exegesis in Southeast Asia', *Studia Islamika*, 5 (3), 47–76.
Firestone, R. (1990), *Journeys in Holy Lands: The Evolution of the Abraham-Ishmael Legends in Islamic Exegesis*, New York: State University Press.
Fitzgerald, L.P. (1992), 'Creation in al-Tafsir al-Kabir of Fakhr al-Din al-Razi', unpublished doctoral dissertation, Australian National University.
Fox, J.J. (1991), 'Ziarah Visits to the Tombs of the Wali, the Founders of Islam on Java', in M.C. Ricklefs, *Islam in the Indonesian Social Context* (pp. 19–39), Melbourne: Centre of Southeast Asian Studies, Monash University.
Gardet, L. (1965), 'Dhikr' in *The Encyclopaedia of Islam* (2nd edn), vol. II (pp. 223–7), Leiden: E.J. Brill.
Gatje, H. (1996 [1976]), *The Qur'an and its Exegesis: Selected Texts with Classical and Modern Muslim Interpretations*, Oxford: Oneworld Publications.
Geertz, C. (1960), *The Religion of Java*, New York: Free Press.
Gibb, Sir Hamilton (1947), *Modern Trends in Islam*, University of Chicago Press.
Gilchrist, J. (1989), *Jam' al-Qur'an: The Codification of the Qur'an Text*, Benoni, RSA.
Goldfeld, Y. (1988), 'The development of theory on Qur'anic exegesis in Islamic scholarship', *Studia Islamica*, 67, 5–27.
Goldsack, W. (trans.) (1923), *Selections from Muhammadan Traditions (Mishkatu'l-Masabih)*, Bangalore and Madras: The Christian Literature Society for India.
Goldziher, I. and Jomier, J. (1965), 'Djamal al-Din al-Afghani', in *The Encyclopaedia of Islam* (2nd edn), vol. II (pp. 416–19), Leiden: E.J. Brill.

Grinter, A. (1979), *Book IV of the Bustanu's-Salatin: A Study from the Manuscripts of a 17th-Century Malay Work written in North Sumatra,* unpublished doctoral dissertation, SOAS, London.

Guillaume, A. (1956), *Islam* (2nd edn), London: Pelican.

Haanie, A.D. (1929), *Islam Menentang Kraemer,* Yogyakarta: Penyiaran Islam.

Hadi, A. (1985), 'The Contribution of Islam to Indonesian Culture and the Challenges of Modernism', *Prisma: The Indonesian Indicator,* (35), 120–30.

Hadikusuma, Djarnawi (1987), *Kitab Tauhid,* Yogyakarta: P.T. Percetakan Persatuan.

Hafiduddin, D. (1987), 'Tinjauan atas "Tafsir al-Munir" karya Imam Muhammad Nawawi Tanara', in A.R. Hasan (ed.), *Warisan Intelektual Islam Indonesia.* (pp. 39–58), Bandung: Mizan.

Haleem, M.A. (1989), 'The Hereafter and Here-And-Now in the Qur'an', *The Islamic Quarterly,* XXXIII (2), 118–31.

Hallaq, W.B. (1993), 'Was al-Shafi'i the master architect of Islamic jurisprudence?' *International Journal of Middle East Studies,* (25), 587–605.

—— (1997), *A History of Islamic Legal Theories: an introduction to Sunni usul al-fiqh,* Cambridge: Cambridge University Press.

Halm, H. (1986), 'al-Kushayri, Abu 'l-Kasim', In *The Encyclopaedia of Islam* (2nd edn), vol. V (pp. 526–7), Leiden: E.J. Brill.

Hamid, I. (1982), 'A Survey of Theories on the Introduction of Islam in the Malay Archipelago', *Islamic Studies,* 21, 89–100.

Hamidullah, M. (1979), *Introduction to Islam,* London: MWH.

Hamim, T. (1997), 'Moenawar Chalil: The Career and Thought of an Indonesian Muslim Reformist', *Studia Islamika,* 4 (2), 1–54.

Hamka (1952), *Sedjarah Umat Islam,* Bukittinggi and Jakarta: Nusantara.

—— (1956), *Pelajaran Agama Islam,* Jakarta: Bulan Bintang.

—— (1958), *Ajahku,* Jakarta: Widjaya.

—— (1961), *1001 Soal-Soal Hidup,* Jakarta: Bulan Bintang.

—— (1967), *Tafsir Al-Azhar,* Jakarta: Pembimbing Masa.

—— (1990), *Tasauf Moderen,* Jakarta: P.T. Pustaka Panjimas.

—— (1992), *Tafsir Al Azhar,* Jakarta: P.T. Pustaka Panjimas.

Harun, S. (1988), 'Hakekat Tafsir Tarjuman al-Mustafid Karya Syekh Abdurrauf Singkel', unpublished doctoral dissertation, Institut Agama Islam Negeri Syarif Hidayatullah, Jakarta.

Hasan, A.R. (1987), 'Warisan Intelektual Islam dan Pengembangan Wawasan Masa Depan: Sebuah Pengantar', in A.R. Hasan (ed.), *Warisan Intelektual Islam Indonesia* (pp. 11–20), Bandung: Mizan.

Hasjmy, A. (1976), *Ruba'i Hamzah Fansuri,* Kuala Lumpur: Dewan Bahasa dan Pustaka.

—— (1980), 'Syekh Abdurrauf Syiah Kuala Ulama Negarawan Yang Bijaksana', *Universitas Syiah Kuala Menjelang 20 Tahun* (pp. 367–81), Banda Aceh: Universitas Syiah Kuala.

Heath, P. (1989), 'Creative Hermeneutics: A Comparative Analysis of Three Islamic Approaches', *Arabica,* XXXVI, 173–210.

Heer, N. (1998), 'Al-Ghazali: The Canons of Ta'wil', in J. Renard (ed.), *Windows on the House of Islam: Muslim Sources on Spirituality and Religious Life* (pp. 48–54), Berkeley: University of California Press.

Heffening, W. and Schacht, J. (1979), 'Hanafiyya', in *The Encyclopaedia of Islam* (2nd edn), vol. III (pp. 162–4), Leiden: E.J. Brill.

Hefner, R.W. (1987), 'Islamizing Java? Religion and Politics in Rural East Java', *Journal of Asian Studies*, 46 (3).

Hering, B.B. (1986), 'Aliran Syndromes under Sukarno and under Suharto', in B.B. Hering (ed.), *Studies on Indonesian Islam* (pp. 1–13), Townsville: Centre for Southeast Asian Studies, James Cook University.

Hermansen, M.K. (1998), 'The Prophet Muhammed in Sufi Interpretations of the Light Verse (Aya Nur 24:35)', *The Islamic Quarterly*, XLII (2–3), 144–55, 218–27.

Hooker, M.B. (1984), *Islamic Law in South-East Asia*, Singapore: Oxford University Press.

—— (ed.) (1988 [1983]), *Islam in South-East Asia*, Leiden: E.J. Brill.

Hooker, V.M. (1994), 'Transmission Through Practical Example: Women and Islam in 1920s Malay Fiction', *JMBRAS*, LXVII (2), 93–118.

Ibn Khaldun. (1967), *The Muqaddimah: An Introduction to History*, trans. F. Rosenthal, London: Routledge and Kegan Paul.

Ibrahim, E. and Johnson-Davies, D. (trans.) (1977), *An-Nawawi's Forty Hadith* (2nd edn), Damascus: Holy Koran Publishing House.

Indikt, A. (24 April–10 May 1997), 'JUST, The Facts: Malaysia's Islamic brains trust', *Australia/Israel Review*, 22 (6).

Ishak, M.O. (1986), '"Urf and Customs as being practised among the Malay Community', *Arabica*, 33 (3), 352–68.

Iskandar, T. (1958), *De Hikayat Atjeh*, The Hague: M. Nijhoff.

Iskandar, T. (1964), 'Nuruddin ar-Raniri Pengarang Abad ke-17', *Dewan Bahasa*, VIII (10), 436–41.

—— (1966), *Nuru'd-din ar-Raniri Bustanu's-Salatin Bab II, Fasal 13*, Kuala Lumpur: Dewan Bahasa dan Pustaka.

—— (1967), 'Three Malay Historical Writings in the First Half of the 17th Century', *JMBRAS*, XL (2), 38–53.

Ito, T. (1978), 'Why did Nuruddin ar-Raniri leave Aceh in 1054 AH?' *BKI*, 134, 489–91.

—— (1984), 'The World of the Adat Aceh: A Historical Study of the Sultanate of Aceh', unpublished doctoral dissertation, Australian National University.

Jackson, P. (1988), 'The Mystical Dimension', in *The Muslims of India: Beliefs and Practices* (pp. 249–77), Gujerat: Anand Press.

Jafar, I. (1998), 'The Concept of Love in Modern Indonesian Qur'anic Exegesis: a Study of Tafsir al-Azhar', [www.indosat.net.id/alauddin/ oflove.html].

Jamal, M. (prod.) (1993), 'Anwar Ibrahim on Islam and Pluralism', *Islamic Conversations*, London: Epicflow (for Channel Four).

Jansen, J.J.G. (1997), 'Sayyid Qutb', in *The Encyclopaedia of Islam* (2nd edn), vol. IX (pp. 117–18), Leiden: E.J. Brill.

Janson, A., Tol, R. and Witkam, J.J. (eds) (1995), 'Mystical Illustrations from the Teachings of Syaikh Ahmad al-Qusyasyi: A facsimile edition of a manuscript from Aceh (Cod. Or. 2222) in the Library of Leiden University', *Manuscripta Indonesica*, vol. 5, Leiden: INIS and Leiden University Library.

Jassin, H.B. (1978), *Tafsir Quran Karim: Bacaan Mulia*, Jakarta: Djambatan.

Jeffery, A. (1937), *Materials for the History of the Text of the Quran*, Leiden: E.J. Brill.

—— (ed.) (1958), *Islam: Muhammad and His Religion*, Indianapolis and New York: Bobbs-Merrill.

—— (ed.) (1962), *A Reader on Islam: Passages from standard Arabic writings illustrative of the beliefs and practices of Muslims*, The Hague: Mouton & Co.

Johns, A.H. (1953), 'Nur al-Daqa'iq by Shams al-Din of Pasai', *JRAS*, 137–51.

—— (1955a) 'Aspects of Sufi Thought in India and Indonesia in the first half of the 17th century', *JMBRAS*, XXVIII (I), 70–7.

—— (1955b), 'Daqa'iq al-Huruf by 'Abd al-Ra'uf of Singkel', *JRAS*, 139–58.

—— (1957), 'Malay Sufism', *JMBRAS*, XXX (2).

—— (1965), *The Gift Addressed to the Spirit of the Prophet*, Canberra: Australian National University Press.

—— (1975), 'Islam in Southeast Asia: Reflections and New Directions', *Indonesia*, (19), 31–52.

—— (1978), Friends in Grace: Ibrahim al-Kurani and 'Abd al-Ra'uf al-Singkeli', in S. Udin (ed.), *Spectrum – Essays presented to sutan Takdir Alisyahbana on his seventieth birthday* (pp. 469–85), Jakarta: Dian Rakyat.

—— (1980), 'Ibrahim al-Kurani: Seventeenth-Century Defender of Sufism', lecture at the Ghalib Academy, Delhi.

—— (1981), 'From Coastal Settlement to Islamic School and City: Islamization in Sumatra, the Malay Peninsula and Java', *Hamdard Islamicus*, 4 (4), 3–28.

—— (1984), 'Islam in the Malay World: An Exploratory Survey with Some Reference to Quranic Exegesis', in R. Israeli and A.H. Johns (eds), *Islam in Asia, Vol. II: Southeast and East Asia* (pp. 115–61), Jerusalem: Magnes Press.

—— (1987a), 'An Islamic System or Islamic Values? Nucleus of a debate in contemporary Indonesia', in W.R. Roff (ed.), *Islam and Political Economy of Meaning* (pp. 254–80), London and Sydney: Croom Helm.

—— (1987b), 'Islam in Southeast Asia', in M. Eliade (ed.), *The Encyclopedia of Religion*, Vol. 7 (pp. 404–22), New York: Macmillan.

—— (1988), 'Qur'anic Exegesis in the Malay World: In Search of a Profile', in A. Rippin (ed.), *Approaches to the History of the Interpretation of the Qur'an* (pp. 257–87), Oxford: Clarendon Press.

—— (1995), 'Sufism in Southeast Asia: Reflections and Reconsiderations', *JSEAS*, 26 (1), 169–83.

—— (1997a), 'On Qur'anic Exegetes and Exegesis: A Case Study in the Transmission of Islamic Learning', in P.G. Riddell and T. Street (eds), *Islam: Essays and Scripture, Thought and Society* (pp. 4–49), Leiden: E.J. Brill.

—— (1997b), 'Shams al-Din al-Sumatrani', in *The Encyclopaedia of Islam* (2nd edn), vol. IX (pp. 296–7), Leiden: E.J. Brill.

——. (1998), 'From Arabic into Javanese: the Gift Addressed to the Spirit of the Prophet', in J. Renard (ed.), *Windows on the House of Islam: Muslim Sources on Spirituality and Religious Life* (pp. 283–6), Berkeley: University of California Press.

Jones, R. (1974), *Nuru'd-din ar-Raniri Bustanu's-Salatin*, Kuala Lumpur: Dewan Bahasa dan Pustaka.

Jonge, H. de (1997), 'Snouck Hurgronje on the Hadhramis in the Dutch East Indies (1889–1936)', paper presented at the conference *The Arabs in South-East Asia (1870–c. 1990)*, 8–12 December, Royal Institute of Linguistics and Anthropology, Leiden.

Junus, M. (1977), *Tarjamah Quran Karim* (3rd edn), Bandung: PT AlMa'arif.

Juynboll, T. and Voorhoeve, P. (1960), 'Atjeh', in *The Encyclopaedia of Islam* (2nd edn), vol. I (pp. 739–47).

Kahane, R. (1984), 'Notes on the Unique Patterns of Indonesian Islam', in R. Israeli and A.H. Johns, *Islam in Asia Volume II: Southeast and East Asia* (pp. 162–88), Jerusalem: Magnes Press.

—— (1993), 'Modern Interpretation of Animistic Metaphors: An Example from Indonesia', *Sojourn: Social Issues in Southeast Asia*, 8 (1), 11–34.

Kamajaya (1985), *Lima Karya Pujangga Ranggawarsita*, Jakarta: Balai Pustaka.

Kaptein, N. (1995), 'Meccan Fatwas from the End of the Nineteenth Century on Indonesian Affairs', *Studia Islamika*, 2 (4), 141–60.

—— (1997a), *A Bilingual Meccan Fatwa Collection for Indonesian Muslims from the End of the Nineteenth Century*, Jakarta: INIS.

—— (1997b), 'Sayyid Uthman on the Legal Validity of Documentary Evidence', *BKI*, 153 (1), 85–102.

Karim, M.R. (ed.) (1986), *Muhammadiyah: Dalam Kritik dan Komentar*, Jakarta: Rajawali.

Karim, M.F. (1982), *Imam Gazzali's Ihya Ulum-id-Din*, New Delhi: Kitab Bhavan.

Kathir, A. a. Isma'il Ibn (1412/1992), *Qasas al-anbiya'*, Damascus: Dar Ibn Kathir.

Kaye, B. (Spring 1997), 'Many Aspects of Pluralism', *St Mark's Review*, 171, 2–5.

Kessler, C.S. (1997), 'Fundamentalism Reconsidered: Towards the Reactualisation of Islam', in P.G. Riddell and T. Street (eds.), *Islam: Essays on Scripture, Thought and Society* (pp. 324–40), Leiden: E.J. Brill.

Khan, M.M. (ed.) (n.d.), *Sahih al-Bukhari*, 9 vols, Mecca: Dar Ahya us-Sunnah.

Khazin, A. a. 'Ali al- (n.d.), *Lubab al-Ta'wil fi Ma'ani al-Tanzil*, Beirut: Dar al-Thaqafah.

Khuluq, L. (1998), 'K.H. Hasyim Asy'ari's Contribution to Indonesian Independence', *Studia Islamika*, 5 (1), 41–68.

Knappert, J. (1985), *Islamic Legends: Histories of the Heroes, Saints and Prophets*, Leiden: E.J. Brill.

Knysh, A. (2000), *Islamic Mysticism: A Short History*, Leiden: E.J. Brill.

Kroef, J.M. van der (1953), 'The Arabs in Indonesia', *The Middle East Journal*, 7 (3), 300–23.

Kumar, A. (1985), *The diary of a Javanese Muslim: Religion, politics and the pesantren 1883–1886*, Canberra: Australian National University Press.

—— (1997), 'Pancasila Plus, Pancasila Minus', in P.G. Riddell and T. Street (ed.), *Islam: Essays on Scripture, Thought and Society* (pp. 253–76), Leiden: E.J. Brill.

Kurzman, C. (ed.) (1998), *Liberal Islam: A Sourcebook*, New York: Oxford University Press.

Laffan, M.F. (1996), 'Watan and Negeri: Mustafa Kamil's "Rising Sun" in the Malay World', *Indonesia Circle*, 69, 156–75.

Lambton, A.K.S. (1979), 'Islamic Political Thought', in J. Schacht and C.E. Bosworth (eds), *The Legacy of Islam* (2nd edn), (pp. 404–24), Oxford University Press.

Laoust, H. (1979), 'Ibn Qayyim al-Djawziyya', in *The Encyclopaedia of Islam* (2nd edn), vol. III (pp. 821–2), Leiden: E.J. Brill.

Lapidus, I.M. (1988), 'Islam in Indonesia and Malaysia', in *A History of Islamic Societies* (pp. 749–83), Cambridge University Press.

Lee, H.K. (1999), 'Sainthood and Modern Java: a Window into the World of Muhammad Zuhri', unpublished Master's dissertation, LBC, Brunel University.

Levtzion, N. (1997), 'Eighteenth-Century Sufi Brotherhoods', in P. G. Riddell and T. Street (eds.), *Islam: Essays on Scripture, Thought and Society* (pp. 147–60), Leiden: E.J. Brill.

Lizzini, O. (1996), 'Islamic Angelology', *Encounter: Documents for Muslim-Christian Understanding*, 227.

Lombard, D. (1967), *Le Sultanat d'Atjèh au temps d'Iskandar Muda 1607–1636*, Paris: Ecole Française d'Extrême Orient.

—— (1986), 'L'Empire Ottoman Vu d'Insulinde', in C. Lemercier-Quelquejay (ed.), *Turco-Tartar Past Soviet Present*, Paris: Peeters.

McAuliffe, J.D. (1991), *Qur'anic Christians: an Analysis of Classical and Modern Exegesis*, Cambridge University Press.

Madjid, N. (1985), 'An Islamic Appraisal of the Political Future of Indonesia', *Prisma: The Indonesian Indicator*, (35), 11–26.

—— (1995), 'Dar al-Islam dan Dar al-Harb: Damai dan Perang dalam Islam', *Ulumul Qur'an*, VI (2), 80–92.

—— (1996), *Islam, kerakyatan dan ke-Indonesiaan: pikiran-pikiran Nurcholish 'Muda'*, Bandung: Mizan.

—— (1997), *Islam, kemodernan dan keIndonesiaan*, Bandung: Mizan.

—— (1998a), *30 sajian ruhani: renungan di bulan Ramadlan*, Bandung: Mizan.

—— (1998b), 'The Necessity of Renewing Islamic Thought and Reinvigorating Religious Understanding', in C. Kurzman (ed.), *Liberal Islam: A Sourcebook* (pp. 284–94), New York: Oxford University Press.

—— (1998c), 'Worship as an institution of Faith', in J. Renard (ed.), *Windows on the House of Islam: Muslim Sources on Spirituality and Religious Life* (pp. 65–74), Berkeley: University of California Press.

Mahalli, J. al- and Suyuti, J. al- (1401/1981), *Tafsir al-Qur'an al-'Azim li'l-Imamayn al-Jalalayn*, Indonesia: Dar al- Fikr.

Mahmud, M.A. al-Halim (1987), *Manahij al-Mufassirin*, Cairo: Dar al-Kitab al-Misri.

Ma'mur, I. (1996), 'The Place of the Islamic court in the Judicial System of Modern Indonesia', *Hamdard Islamicus*, XIX (2), 75–87.

Margoliouth, D.S. (1894), *Chrestomathia Baidawiana: The Commentary of El-Baidawi on Sura III*, London: Luzac.

Marrison, G.E. (1951), 'The Coming of Islam to the East Indies', *JMBRAS*, XXIV (1), 28–37.

Martin, R.C., Woodward, M.R. and Atmaja, D.S. (1997), *Defenders of Reason in Islam: Mu'tazilism from Medieval School to Modern Symbol*, Oxford: Oneworld.

Matheson, V. (1971), 'The Tuhfat al-Nafis: Structure and Sources', *BKI*, 127 , 379–90.

—— and Hooker, M.B. (1988), 'Jawi Literature in Patani: The Maintenance of a Tradition', *JMBRAS*, LXI (1), 1–86.

Mawdudi, S.A.A'la (1988), *Towards Understanding the Qur'an*, Leicester: The Islamic Foundation.

Maxwell, W.E. (1890), 'Raja Haji', *JSBRAS*, 22, 173–224.

Mez, A. (1996), *The Renaissance of Islam*, Dhaka: Bangladesh Co-operative Book Society.

Milner, A.C. (1986), 'Rethinking Islamic Fundamentalism in Malaysia', *RIMA*, 20 (2), 48–75.

Milner, A. (1988 [1983]), 'Islam and the Muslim State', in M.B. Hooker (ed.), *Islam in South-East Asia* (pp. 23–49), Leiden: E.J. Brill.

—— (1993), 'Islamic Debate in the Public Sphere', in A. Reid (ed.), *The Making of an Islamic Political Discourse in Southeast Asia* (pp. 109–26), Melbourne: Monash University Press.

Mobini-Kesheh, N. (1996), 'The Arab Periodicals of the Netherlands East Indies, 1914–1942', *BKI*, 152 (2), 236–56.

Moris, Z. (1999), 'Mulla Sadra and Hamzah Fansuri: A Comparative Study of some Aspects of their Metaphysical Teachings', *The World Congress on Mulla Sadra*, Sadra Islamic Philosophy Research Institute, Tehran. ([www.mullasadra.org/papers/zailan moris.htm] copied 6 November 1999)

Mudzhar, M.A. (1990), 'Fatwas of the Council of Indonesian Ulama: A Study of Islamic Legal Thought in Indonesia 1975–1988', unpublished doctoral dissertation, University of California, Los Angeles.

Mujiburrahman. (October 1999), 'Islam and Politics in Indonesia: the political thought of Abdurrahman Wahid', *ICMR*, 10 (3), 339–52.

Mukherjee, W. (1997), 'Kaum Muda and Kaum Tua in West Java: the Literary Record', in P.G. Riddell and T. Street (eds), *Islam: Essays on Scripture, Thought and Society* (pp. 309–23), Leiden: E.J. Brill.

Mustofa, H.A. (1986), *Kumpulan Khutbah Jum'at Pilihan*, Surabaya: Al Ikhlas.

Muzaffar, C. (1985), 'Islam in Malaysia: Resurgence and Response', *Islamic Perspective*, 2 (1), 5–38.

—— (1998), 'Universalism in Islam', in C. Kurzman (ed.), *Liberal Islam: A Sourcebook* (pp. 155–60), New York: Oxford University Press.

Nagel, T. (1986), 'Kisas al-Anbiya', in *The Encyclopaedia of Islam* (2nd edn), vol. V (pp. 180–1), Leiden: E.J. Brill.

Nash, M. (1991), 'Islamic Resurgence in Malaysia and Indonesia', in M.E. Marty, *Fundamentalism Observed* (pp. 691–739), University of Chicago Press.

Nasr, S.H. (1981a), *Islamic Life and Thought*, London: Geo. Allen & Unwin.

—— (1981b), *Knowledge and the Sacred*, New York: Crossroad.

Nasution, H. (1977), *Teologi Islam: Aliran-aliran sejarah analisa perbandingan*, Jakarta: Universitas Indonesia.

—— (1995), *Islam Rasional: Gagasan dan Pemikiran*, Bandung: Mizan.

—— *et al.* (eds) (1992), *Ensiklopedi Islam Indonesia*, Jakarta: Djambatan.

Nawawi, M. al- (n.d.), *Marah Labid*, Indonesia: Dar Ihya' al-Kutub al-'Arabiyyah.

Nicholson, R.A. (1914), *The Mystics of Islam*, London (repr.) Routledge & Kegan Paul, 1963.

Nieuwenhuijze, C.A.O. Van (1920), 'Nur al-Din al-Raniri als Bestrijder der Wugudiya', *BKI*, 76, 162–71.

—— (1945), *Samsu'l-Din van Pasai*, Leiden: E.J. Brill.

Nik Mat, N.A. Aziz (1998), 'Mukjizat Israk dan Mikraj', *Harakah Online*, Tazkirah, 17 August.

Noer, D. (1973), *The Modernist Muslim Movement in Indonesia 1900–1942*, London: Oxford University Press.

Nor bin Ngah, M. (1983), *Kitab Jawi: Islamic Thought of the Malay Muslim Scholars*, Singapore: Institute of Southeast Asian Studies.

Osman, M.T. (1976), 'Raja Ali Haji of Riau: A figure of Transition or the last of the Classical Pujanggas?' in S.M.N. Al-Attas (eds), *Bahasa Kesustraan Dan Kebudayaan Melayu: Essei-essei penghormatan kepada Pendita Za'ba* (pp. 136–60), Kuala Lumpur: Kementerian Kebudayaan, Belia dan Sukan Malaysia.

Othman, M.R. (1997), 'Hadhramis in the Politics and Administration of the Malay States in the late Eighteenth and Nineteenth Centuries', in U. Freitag and W.G. Clarence-Smith (eds), *Hadhrami Traders, Scholars and Statesmen in the Indian Ocean, 1750s to 1960s* (pp. 82–93), Leiden: E.J. Brill.

Peacock, J.L. (1978), *Purifying the Faith: the Muhammadiyah Movement in Indonesian Islam*, Menlo Park, CA: Benjamin/Cummings Publishers.

Pelras, C. (1985), 'Religion, Tradition and the Dynamics of Islamization in South Sulawesi', *Archipel*, (29), 107–36.

Perret, D. (April 1995), 'La dissolution du mouvement Al-Arqam en Malaisie', *La Transmission du Savoir dans le Monde Musulman Périphérique* (CNRS, Paris), (15), 12–13.

—— (Septembre 1997), 'Récents développements concernants les mouvements islamistes "déviationnistes" en Malaisie', *La Transmission du Savoir dans le Monde Musulman Périphérique* (CNRS Paris), (17), 67–74.

—— (Mai 1996), 'Un mouvement "antihadith" sur le devant de la scène en Malaysie', *La Transmission du Savoir dans le Monde Musulman Périphérique* (CNRS Paris), (16), 1–3.

Peters, F.E. (1990), *Judaism, Christianity and Islam, the Classical Texts and their Interpretation*, Princeton University Press.

—— (1994), *A Reader on Classical Islam*, Princeton: Princeton University Press.

Philips, A.A. Bilal (1997), *The Exorcist Tradition in Islaam*, Sharjah: Dar Al Fatah.

Piscatori, J.P. (1986), 'The nature of the Islamic revival', in *Islam in a World of Nation-States*, Cambridge: Cambridge University Press.

Pruvost, L. (June–September 1997), 'Islamic Identity and Divine Law: Notes on the Concept of Shari'a', *Encounter: Documents for Muslim–Christian Understanding*, (236–7).

Qayrawani, 'Abd Allah b. Abi Zayd (copied January 2000), A.B.M. Daura (trans.), *The Risala: A Treatise on Maliki Fiqh*. ([iiu.edu.my/deed/lawbase/risala_maliki/index.html])

Qutb, S. (1979), *In the Shade of the Qur'an*, London: MWH.

Rais, M.A. (1985), 'International Islamic Movements and Their Influence Upon the Islamic Movement in Indonesia', *Prisma: The Indonesian Indicator*, (35), 27–48.

—— (1987), *Cakrawala Islam: antara cita dan fakta*, Bandung: Mizan.

—— (1995), 'ICMI Harus Menyentuh Akar Rumput Umat', in N. Ali-Fauzi (ed.), *ICMI: Antara Status Quo dan Demokratisasi* (pp. 281–6), Bandung: Mizan.

—— (1998), *Tauhid Sosial: formula menggempur kesenjangan*, Bandung: Mizan.

Rakhmat, J. (1985), 'Islamic Fundamentalism: Myth and Reality', *Prisma: The Indonesian Indicator*, (35), 97–109.

—— (1986), *Islam Alternatif: Ceramah-Ceramah di Kampus*, Bandung: Mizan.

Ranggawarsita, R.N. (1908), *Serat Wirid,* Surakarta: Jawi Kandha.

—— (1987), *Serat Cemporet,* Jakarta: Balai Pustaka.

—— (1988), *Serat Jayengbaya,* Jakarta: Balai Pustaka.

—— (copied December 1999), M.M.Medeiros (trans.), *Book of Mystical Teachings,* [www.xs4all.nl/~wichm/wirid.html].

Raniri, Nur al-Din al- (n.d.), 'al-Fawa'id al-bahiyya fi al-ahadith al-nabawiyya', in margin of Daud al-Fatani, *Jam' al-fawa'id,* Singapore.

Reid, A. (1984), 'The Islamization of Southeast Asia', in M.A. Baker, *Historia* (pp. 13–33), Kuala Lumpur: Malaysian Historical Society.

—— (1993), 'Kings, Kadis and Charisma in the Seventeenth-Century Archipelago', in A. Reid (ed.), *The Making of an Islamic Political Discourse in Southeast Asia* (pp. 83–108), Melbourne: Monash University Press.

Reijn, E. van (1983), 'Amir Hamzah and Hamzah Pansuri', *Indonesia Circle,* (32), 11–24.

Ricklefs, M.C. (1984), 'Islamization in Java: An Overview and Some Philosophical Considerations', in R. Israeli and A.H. Johns, *Islam in Asia* Vol. II: *Southeast and East Asia* (pp. 11–23), Jerusalem: Magnes Press.

—— (1993), *A History of Modern Indonesia since c. 1300* (2nd edn), Basingstoke: Macmillan.

—— (1997), 'Islam and the Reign of Pakubuwana II, 1726–1749', in P.G. Riddell and T. Street (eds.), *Islam: Essays on Scripture, Thought and Society* (pp. 237–52), Leiden: E.J. Brill.

—— (1998), *The seen and unseen worlds in Java, 1726–1749: history, literature, and Islam in the court of Pakubuwana II,* St. Leonards, NSW.

Riddell, P.G. (1984), 'The Sources of 'Abd al-Ra'uf's *Tarjuman al-Mustafid*', *JMBRAS,* LVII (2), 113–18.

—— (1986), 'Tafsir al-Qur'an: Une Ligne de Transmission?' *La Transmission du Savoir dans le Monde Musulman Périphérique* (CNRS Paris), (6), 12.

—— (1989), 'Earliest Qur'anic Exegetical Activity in the Malay-Speaking States', *Archipel,* (38), 107–24.

—— (1990a), *Transferring a Tradition: 'Abd al-Ra'uf al-Singkili's Rendering into Malay of the Jalalayn Commentary,* Berkeley, CA: Centers for South and Southeast Asian Studies, University of California.

—— (1990b), 'The Use of Arabic Commentaries on the Qur'an in the Early Islamic Period in South and Southeast Asia', *Indonesia Circle,* (51), 3–19.

—— (1993), 'Controversy in Qur'anic Exegesis and its Relevance to the Malayo–Indonesian World', in A. Reid (ed.), *The Making of an Islamic Political Discourse in Southeast Asia* (pp. 59–81), Melbourne: Monash University Press.

—— (1997a), 'The Transmission of Narrative Based Exegesis in Islam: al-Baghawi's Use of Stories in his Commentary on the Qur'an, and a Malay Descendent', in P.G. Riddell and T. Street (eds), *Islam: Essays on Scripture, Thought and Society* (pp. 57–80), Leiden: E.J. Brill.

—— (1997b), 'Religious Links between the Hadhramaut and the Malay–Indonesian World, c. 1850 to c. 1950', in U. Freitag and W.G. Clarence-Smith (eds), *Hadhrami Traders, Scholars and Statesmen in the Indian Ocean, 1750s to 1960s* (pp. 217–30), Leiden: E.J. Brill.

—— (1997c), 'Islamic Variations on a Biblical Theme as seen in the David and Bathsheba Saga', *Vox Evangelica,* XXVII, 57–74.

—— and T. Street (eds) (1997), *Islam: Essays on Scripture, Thought and Society*, Leiden: E.J. Brill.

Rinkes, D.A. (1909), *Abdoerraoef Van Singkel*, Heerenveen: Hepkema.

—— (1996), *Nine Saints of Java*, trans. G.W.J. Drewes, Kuala Lumpur: Malaysian Sociological Research Institute.

Rippin, A. (1988), *Approaches to the History of the Interpretation of the Qur'an*, Oxford: Clarendon Press.

—— (1990), *Muslims: Their Religious Beliefs and Practices*. Volume 1: *The Formative Period*, London: Routledge.

—— (1993), *Muslims: Their Religious Beliefs and Practices*. Volume 2: *The Contemporary Period*, London: Routledge.

—— (1994), 'Tafsir Ibn 'Abbas and criteria for dating early tafsir texts', *Jerusalem Studies in Arabic and Islam*, (18), 38–83.

—— and Knappert, J. (eds) (1986), *Textual Sources for the Study of Islam*. University of Chicago Press.

Robinson, F.C.R. (1991), 'Mawdudi, Sayyid Abu'l-A'la', in *The Encyclopaedia of Islam* (2nd edn), vol. VI (pp. 872–4).

Robinson, N. (1996), *Discovering the Qur'an: a Contemporary Approach to a Veiled Text*, London: SCM.

Robson, J. (1971), 'Ibn Mujahid', in *The Encyclopaedia of Islam* (2nd edn), vol. III (p. 880), Leiden: E.J. Brill.

—— (1979a), 'al-Baghawi', in *The Encyclopaedia of Islam* (2nd edn), vol. I (p. 919), Leiden: E.J. Brill.

—— (1979b), 'al-Baydawi', in *The Encyclopaedia of Islam* (2nd edn), vol. I (p. 1129), Leiden: E.J. Brill.

Roff, W. (April 1970), 'Indonesian and Malay Students in Cairo in the 1920s', *Indonesia*, (9), 73–87.

—— (1984), 'The Meccan Pilgrimage: Its Meaning for Southeast Asian Islam', in R. Israeli and A.H. Johns (eds), *Islam in Asia* vol. II: *Southeast and East Asia* (pp. 238–45), Jerusalem: Magnes Press.

—— (1994), *The Origins of Malay Nationalism* (2nd edn), Kuala Lumpur: Oxford University Press.

Ronkel, S. van (1896), 'Account of Six Malay Manuscripts of the Cambridge University Library', *BKI*, 46 (2), 1–53.

—— (1913), 'Commentaries Upon the Kur'an', in *Supplement to the Catalogue of the Arabic Manuscripts preserved in the Museum of the Batavia Society of Arts and Science*. (pp. 12–31), Batavia.

Ropi, I. (July 1998), 'Muslim–Christian Polemics in Indonesian Islamic Literature', *ICMR*, 9 (2), 217–30.

Rosenthal, F. (trans.) (1989), *The History of al-Tabari*, New York: State University of New York Press.

Saeed, A. (1999), 'Towards Religious Tolerance through Reform in Islamic Education: the Case of the State Institute of Islamic Studies of Indonesia', *Indonesia and the Malay World*, (27/79), 177–91.

Santrie, A.M. (1987), '"Martabat Alam Tujuh": Suatu Naskah Mistik Islam dari Desa Karang, Pamijahan', in A.R. Hasan (ed.), *Warisan Intelektual Islam Indonesia* (pp. 105–30), Bandung: Mizan.

Sastrawiria, T. and Wirasutisna, H. (1955), *Ensiklopedi Politik*, Djakarta: Perpustakaan Perguruan Kem. P.P. Dan K.

Schacht, J. (1964), *An Introduction to Islamic Law*, Oxford: Clarendon Press.

Schimmel, A. (1978), *The Triumphal Sun: A Study of the Works of Jalaloddin Rumi*, London: Fine Books.

Schrieke, B. and Horovitz, J. (1993), 'Mi'radj – 1. In Islamic exegesis and in the popular and mystical tradition of the Arab world', in *The Encyclopaedia of Islam* (2nd edn), vol. VII (pp. 97–100), Leiden: E.J. Brill.

Schwarz, A. (1994), *A Nation in Waiting: Indonesia in the 1990s*, Sydney: Allen & Unwin.

Seale, M.S. (1978), *Qur'an and Bible: Studies in Interpretation and Dialogue*, London: Croom Helm.

Seferta, Y.H.R. (1986), 'The Ideas of Muhammad Abduh and Rashid Ridha concerning Jesus', *Encounter: Documents for Muslim–Christian Understanding*, (124), Rome: Pontifical Institute for the Study of Arabic and Islam.

Serjeant, R.B. (1964), 'The Constitution of Medina', *The Islamic Quarterly*, VIII (1 & 2), 3–16.

Shadily, H. *et al.* (eds) (1980–84), *Ensiklopedi Indonesia*. Jakarta: Ichtiar Baru/Van Hoeve.

Shahin, E.E. (1995), 'Rashid Rida, Muhammad', in J.L. Esposito (ed.), *The Oxford Encyclopedia of the Modern Islamic World*, vol. 2 (pp. 410–12), New York and Oxford: Oxford University Press.

Shaleh, Q., Dahlan, A. and Dahlan M.D. (1984), *Asbabun Nuzul*, Bandung: Diponegoro.

Shalihah, K. (1983), *Perkembangan Seni Baca AlQur'an dan Qiraat Tujuh di Indonesia*, Jakarta: Pustaka AlHusna.

Sham, A.H. (1993), *Puisi-Puisi Raja Ali Haji*, Kuala Lumpur: Dewan Bahasa dan Pustaka.

Shellabear, W.G. (1898), 'An Account of some of the Oldest Malay MSS now extant', *JSBRAS*, (XXXI), 107–51.

Shepard, W.E. (1987), 'Islam and Ideology: Towards a Typology', *International Journal of Middle East Studies*, 19.

Sikand, Y. (July–December 1996), 'Modern Interpretation of the Concept of the Waly of God', *The Bulletin of the Henry Martyn Institute of Islamic Studies*, 15 (3–4), 16–24.

Simuh. (1987), 'Aspek Mistik Islam Kejawen dalam "Wirid Hidayat Jati"', in A.R. Hasan (ed.), *Warisan Intelektual Islam Indonesia* (pp. 59–78), Bandung: Mizan.

Sivan, E. (1983), 'Ibn Taymiyya: Father of the Islamic Revolution', *Encounter*, 60 (5), 41–50.

Snouck Hurgronje, C. (1906), *The Acehnese*, Leiden: E.J. Brill.

—— (1931), *Mekka in the Latter Part of the 19th Century*, Leiden: E.J. Brill and London:Luzac.

Soebardi, S. (1975), *The Book of Cabolek: A Critical Edition with Introduction, Translation and Notes; A Contribution to the Study of Javanese Mystical Tradition*, The Hague: M. Nijhoff.

Sonbol, A.E. (1995), 'Kamil, Mustafa', in J.L. Esposito (ed.), *The Oxford Encyclopedia of the Modern Islamic World*, vol. 2 (pp. 398), New York and Oxford: Oxford University Press.

Speight, R.M. (1988), 'The Function of Hadith as Commentary on the Qur'an, as Seen in the Six Authoritative Collections', in A. Rippin (ed.), *Approaches to the History of the Interpretation of the Qur'an* (pp. 63–81), Oxford: Clarendon Press.

Stark, F. (1936), *The Southern Gates of Arabia: A Journey in the Hadhramaut*, London: John Murray.

Steenbrink, K.A. (1984), *Beberapa Aspek Tentang Islam di Indonesia, Abad ke-19*, Jakarta: Bulan Bintang.

—— (1990), 'Jesus and the Holy Spirit in the writings of Nur al-Din al-Raniri', *ICMR*, 1 (2), 192–207.

—— (1995), 'Qur'an Interpretations of Hamzah Fansuri and Hamka', *Studia Islamika*, 2 (2), 73–96.

Stoddart, W. (1979), *Le Soufisme*, Lausanne: Trois Continents.

Street, T. (1988), 'Angels in Medieval Islamic Theology. A Study in Fakhr al-Din al-Razi', unpublished doctoral dissertation, Australian National University.

Sudewa, A. (1995), *Dari Kartasura ke Surakarta: studi kasus Serat Iskandar*, Yogyakarta: Lembaga Studi Asia.

Sundaram, J.K. and Cheek, A.S. (1988), 'The politics of Malaysia's Islamic resurgence', *Third World Quarterly*, 10 (2), 843–68.

Supomo, S. (1997), 'From Sakti to Shahada: The Quest for New Meanings in a Changing World Order', P.G. Riddell and T. Street (eds), *Islam: Essays on Scripture, Thought and Society* (pp. 219–36), Leiden: E.J. Brill.

Suyuti, J. al- (1976), *Tabaqat al-Mufassirin*, Cairo: Wahba.

Tahir, U.M. Mohammad (1989), 'The Notion of "Dakwah" and Its Perception in Malaysia's Islamic Literature of the 1970s and 1980s', *JSEAS*, 20 (2), 288–97.

Talbi, M. (1978), "Iyad b. Musa', in *The Encyclopaedia of Islam* (2nd edn), vol. IV (pp. 289–90), Leiden: E.J. Brill.

Talib, Y.A. (1990), 'Munshi Abdullah's Arab Teachers', *JMBRAS*, LXIII (2), 27–34.

Thackston, W.M. (1978), *The Tales of the Prophets of al-Kisa'i*, Boston: Twayne.

Tha'labi, A.I. al-Nisaburi al- (1985), *Qisas al-Anbiya' al-musamma 'Ara'is al-Majalis* (4th edn), Beirut: Dar al-Kutub al-'Ilmiyyah.

Thomas, D. (1992), *Anti-Christian Polemic in Early Islam*, Cambridge University Press.

Tibawi, A.L. (1965), 'Al-Ghazali's Tract on Dogmatic Theology: edited, translated, annotated and introduced', *The Islamic Quarterly*, IX (3 & 4), 65–122.

Trimingham, J.S. (1971), 'Role of the Orders in the Life of Islamic Society', in *The Sufi Orders in Islam* (pp. 218–44), Oxford University Press.

Tudjimah (1961), *Asrar al-insan fi ma'rifa al-ruh wa'l-rahman*, Djakarta: Penerbitan Universitas.

Vajda, G. (1978), 'Isra'iliyyat', in *The Encyclopaedia of Islam* (2nd edn), vol. IV (pp. 211–12), Leiden: E.J. Brill.

Vakily, A. (1997), 'Sufism, Power Politics and Reform: Al-Raniri's Opposition to Hamzah al-Fansuri's Teachings Reconsidered', *Studia Islamika*, 4 (1), 113–35.

Voorhoeve, P. (1951), 'Van en over Nuruddin ar-Raniri', *BKI*, 107, 353–68.

—— (1952), 'Bajan Tadjalli', *TBG*, 23 (1), 87–115.

—— (1955), 'Lijst der Geschriften van Raniri', *BKI*, 111, 152–61.

—— (1959), 'Short note: Nuruddin ar-Raniri', *BKI*, 115, 90–1.

—— (1960), "Abd al-Samad b. 'Abd Allah al-Palimbani', in *The Encyclopaedia of Islam* (2nd edn), vol. 1 (p. 92), Leiden: E.J. Brill.

—— (1979), "Abd al-Ra'uf al-Singkili', in *The Encyclopaedia of Islam* (2nd edn), vol. I (p.88), Leiden: E.J. Brill.

—— (1980), *Bayan Tajalli*, Banda Aceh: Pusat Dokumentasi dan Informasi Aceh.

Vredenbregt, J. (1962), 'The Haddj: Some of its Features and Functions in Indonesia', *BKI*, 118 (1), 91–154.

Waardenburg, J. (1984), 'Muslims and Other Believers: The Indonesian Case', in R. Israeli and A.H. Johns, *Islam in Asia* Vol. II: *Southeast and East Asia* (pp. 24–66), Jerusalem: Magnes Press.

—— (1988), 'Muslim enlightenment and revitalization: movements of modernization and reform in Tsarist Russia (*c*. 1850–1917) and the Dutch East Indies (*c*. 1900–1942)', *Die Welt des Islams*, 28, 569–84.

Wahid, A. (1985a), 'Islam, the State and Development in Indonesia', *Islamic Perspective*, 2 (1), 75–112.

—— (1985b), 'The Islamic Masses in the Life of State and Nation', *Prisma: The Indonesian Indicator*, (35), 3–10.

—— (1995), 'Intelektual di Tengah Eksklusivisme', in N. Ali-Fauzi (ed.), *ICMI: Antara Status Quo dan Demokratisasi* (pp. 70–5), Bandung: Mizan.

—— (1997), *Kiai nyentrik membela pemerintah*, Yogyakarta: LKIS.

Wansbrough, J. (1977), *Quranic Studies*, Oxford University Press.

Watt, W.M. (1948), *Free Will and Predestination in Early Islam*, London: Luzac.

—— (1974), *The Majesty that was Islam: the Islamic World 661–1100*, London: Sidgwick & Jackson.

—— (trans.) (1994), *Islamic Creeds: A Selection*, Edinburgh University Press.

Welch, A.T. (1986), 'Kur'an, al-', in *The Encyclopaedia of Islam* (2nd edn), vol. V (pp. 400–29), Leiden: E.J. Brill.

Wensinck, A.J. (1971), *A Handbook of Early Muhammadan Tradition*, Leiden: E.J. Brill.

Wieringa, E. (1998), 'The Mystical Figure of Haji Ahmad Mutamakin from the Village of Cabolek (Java)', *Studia Islamika*, 5 (1), 25–40.

Wild, S. (ed.) (1996), *The Qur'an as Text*, Leiden: E.J. Brill.

Williams, J.A. (1961), *Islam*, London and New York: Prentice-Hall.

Winstedt, R.O. (1923), 'Some Malay Mystics, Heretical and Orthodox', *JMBRAS*, I, 313–18.

—— (1969), *A History of Classical Malay Literature* (2nd edn), Kuala Lumpur: Oxford University Press.

Woodcroft-Lee, C.P. (1984), 'From Morocco to Merauke: Some observations on the shifting patterns of relationships between Indonesian Muslims and the World Islamic Community, as Revealed in the writings of Muslim intellectuals in Indonesia', in R. Israeli and A.H. Johns, *Islam in Asia* Vol. II: *Southeast and East Asia* (pp. 67–114), Jerusalem: Magnes Press.

Woodward, M.R. (1985), *The Shari'ah and the Secret Doctrine: Muslim Law and Mystical Doctrine in Central Java,* unpublished doctoral dissertation, University of Illinois, Urbana-Champaign.

—— (ed.) (1996), *Toward a New Paradigm: Recent Developments in Indonesian Islamic Thought,* Tempe: Arizona State University Press.

Yasadipura II, R.N. (1980), *Serat Sanasunu,* Jakarta: Departemen Pendidikan dan Kebudayaan.

Yusuf, B.L. (1994), 'Evolution and Development of Tafsir', *The Islamic Quarterly,* XXXVIII (1), 34–47.

Yusuf Ali, A. (1983), *The Holy Qur'an,* Brentwood: Amana Corp.

Zafar, A.R. (1989), 'Considerations on al-Masabih al-Sunnah', *The Islamic Quarterly,* XXXIII (3), 188–205.

—— (1991), 'Transmission of Hadith and Biography', *The Islamic Quarterly,* XXXV (2), 118–39.

Zamakhshari, A. a. al- (n.d.), *al- Kashshaf 'an haqa'iq al-tanzil wa 'uyun al-aqawil,* 4 vols, Beirut: Dar al-Fikr.

Zoetmulder, P.J. (1995), *Pantheism and Monism in Javanese Suluk Literature,* Leiden: KITLV Press.

INDEX